ALLE ZEIT WACH 1842

Eduard V. Popov

Talking with Computers in Natural Language

With 66 Figures

Springer-Verlag
Berlin Heidelberg New York Tokyo

Prof. Dr. Eduard V. Popov

Computing Center of the Academy of Sciences of the USSR,
ul. Vavilova 40, 117933 Moscow, USSR

Translator:

Dr. Tomasz R. Werner

Institute of Theoretical Physics
University of Warsaw
Hoża 69, 00-681 Warsaw, Poland

Title of the Russian original edition: Obščenie s EVM na estestvennom jazyke.
Publisher "Nauka", Moscow 1982

ISBN-13:978-3-642-71084-1 e-ISBN-13:978-3-642-71082-7
DOI: 10.1007/978-3-642-71082-7

Library of Congress Cataloging-in-Publication Data.

Popov, Ė. V. (Ėduard Viktorovich)
Talking with computers in natural language.
Translation of: Obshchenie s ĖVM na estestvennom iazyke.
Bibliography: p.
Includes index.
1. Interactive computer systems. 2. Question-answering systems. 3. Linguistics – Data processing.
I. Title. QA76.9.I58P6613 1986 006.3'5 86-11895
ISBN-13:978-3-642-71084-1 (U.S.)

2145/3140-543210

Contents

Preface VII
Introduction XI

1 Theories and Principles of Designing the Model of Conversation

1.1 Main Characteristics of the Process of Conversation 1
1.2 An Analysis of Existing Linguistic Models 14
1.3 Principles of the Model of Conversation 40

2 Principles of Construction and General Organization of the Model of a Participant in the Conversation

2.1 Initial Premises for Designing the Model of a Participant in the Conversation 53
2.2 Problems Connected with the Model of a Participant in the Conversation 57
2.3 Existing Systems of Conversation 76
2.4 Composition and Structure of the Model of a Participant in the Conversation 84
2.5 General Structure of the Model of a Participant in the Conversation 91

3 The Structure of Knowledge and Methods of Representing Reality: Knowledge About the Surrounding Environment

3.1 WHAT Is to Be Represented and HOW? 99
3.2 The Model of the Surrounding Environment – Preliminary Notions 100
3.3 Structure of Knowledge of the Surroundings 109
3.4 Classification of Methods of Representing Knowledge 121
3.5 Representing Knowledge About the Model of the Surrounding Environment 127

4 The System's Knowledge About the Language and the Participants in the Conversation

4.1 Connected Text and Linguistic Concordances 141
4.2 Knowledge About the Language of Conversation 143
4.3 Representation of Individual (Dictionary) Pieces of Knowledge About Language 154

4.4 Knowledge About the System Itself: Methods of Representing This Knowledge 176
4.5 Knowledge of the User 184

5 Input Sentence Analysis

5.1 General Outline 189
5.2 Morphological Analysis of Word Forms: Presyntax 190
5.3 Syntactic Sentence Analysis 196
5.4 Semantic Analysis of a Sentence (SEAS) 207

6 Connected-Text (Discourse) Processing

6.1 General Structure 221
6.2 Determining the Linguistically Expressible Interdependencies Between Sentences in a Discourse 221
6.3 Context and Its Role in Discourse Processing 229
6.4 Interpretation of an Input Text: Inferring 240

7 Synthesis of Statements in Natural Language

7.1 General Model of Synthesizing Texts 255
7.2 Semantic Synthesis of the Graph of an Answer 256
7.3 Syntactic Synthesis of an Output Sentence 264
7.4 Morphological Synthesis of the Word Forms of the Sentence Being Synthesized 272

8 Work to Date on Designing Systems of Conversation

8.1 General Outline of the POET System 275
8.2 Representation of Knowledge in the POET System 278
8.3 Practical Operations of the POET System 280
8.4 The POET System as a Means of Automatically Describing Inquiries and Documents 290

Epilogue 291

References 293

Subject Index 299

Preface

The growing efficiency and lower prices of computers make it possible to apply them more widely in the economy. However, the wide use of computers in everyday life is hindered by a number of factors which constitute what we shall call the "problem of contact" or of "talking". The difficulty is that languages used by computers differ substantially from users' languages and are not understood by specialists who are unfamiliar with programming. This is why those specialists who use computers need the help of programmers to communicate. Since this form of communication has many more or less obvious shortcomings, great efforts have been made to find a solution to the problem of contact. Two approaches can be distinguished here: (1) making the computer language similar to the natural language; (2) making the user's language resemble that of computers through formalizing the former.

This book deals with the first approach. We shall consider those systems which make it possible to "talk" with the user in limited natural language (LNL). The term "natural language" (NL) has been used in the title of this book instead of LNL. The reason for not using the term "limited natural language" is that this term has two meanings: (1) a dialect of a natural language; (2) a formal language whose operators are expressed by words taken from a natural language (e.g., a programming language whose operators can be written down as words from the Russian language). In this book we shall consider man's communication with the computer in LNL as a dialect of a natural language. The literature which has been published on this subject so far has – from the practical point of view – the following basic shortcomings:

1. The systems described reduce talking with the machine to the problem of a literal understanding of separate sentences, disregarding their connection with the aims and potential of those participating in the conversation. They are designed to work only with strictly limited subjects (Winograd, 1972). ["Talking" (conversation) will usually be taken here to mean "talking" (conversation) with the computer; trans. note.]
2. A purely linguistic model of the process of talking with the machine is considered, disregarding the model of the surrounding world and with no computer realization of that model (Mel'chuk, 1974a).

The following reasons induced the author to write this monograph on talking with computers in natural language:

1. The lack of books on ideas, methods, and algorithms for designing systems of real-life complexity which would allow contact between user and computer in a natural language (Russian).
2. A desire to examine the system of talking with computers, not in terms of a model of a language, but in terms of a model of participant in the conversation, including models of a language, of the surrounding world, of other interlocutors, and of the system itself.

The book is composed of eight chapters. The first analyzes the "connected text" and examines the existing linguistic models which are models of languages. The chapter ends with a description of the proposed model of conversation with the machine.

The second chapter describes the principles of constructing the model of a participant in the conversation (MPC), to be applied in real talking systems. It outlines the requirements which such systems should meet, and on this basis critically analyzes existing talking systems. It also describes the general organization, composition, and structure of the proposed MPC (which would meet all the requirements).

The third and fourth chapters describe the knowledge which is necessary for the MPC to be able to achieve the objectives defined for the conversation and the methods of representing this knowledge. Knowledge about surroundings, language, the user, and the MPC itself, along with means of representing this knowledge, are also considered in these chapters.

How the MPC functions is taken up in the fifth, sixth, and seventh chapters. The model has three stages: analysis, processing, and synthesis. The first stage, in accordance with linguistic tradition, is divided into three components: morphology, syntax, and semantics. The analysis consists in transforming a sentence in a natural language into an internal representation which expresses the meaning of the sentence. The stage of processing connects the sentence to the preceding text, interprets the sentence in the general context of the dialogue, and makes calculations and eductions which are necessary to formulate the reaction (i.e., answer) of the system to the input text. During the stage of synthesis this answer is translated from the machine representation into a sentence in the limited natural language. This is done by means of semantic, syntactic, and morphological synthesis.

The eighth chapter describes the POET system. This is one of the first working systems to conduct a conversation with the user in limited Russian. It is designed on the basis of principles presented in the foregoing chapters.

The book is intended for a wide circle of specialists in automated systems interacting with man in a natural language. Above all, however, it is intended for specialists in algorithms and programming who work on systems for communicating with machines. For this reason, special attention is paid not only to the question of "HOW TO REPRESENT" (usually considered in works on programming and artificial intelligence) but also of "WHAT TO REPRESENT" (usually not mentioned at all) to make the system understand and generate texts in NL. While investigating the problem of "WHAT TO REPRESENT", we focus our attention on a description of the model of dialogue, the model of the user, and the model of the system itself. In our opinion, it is oversimplification of precisely these components which makes many systems of talking with machines useless or, at best, unsuitable for further development.

Finally, it should be pointed out that the approaches described in this book, while being practical steps on the road to the construction of a talking system of real-life complexity, are still far from representing a final solution to the problem of talking with the machine in NL. Therefore, if the author seems at times to be too categorical, this is most probably due to the form in which he has presented his arguments and does not represent his real intentions. In fact, some of the author's statements (particularly in the first and second chapters) should be considered invitations to reflection rather than assertions of the truth.

Introduction

Specialists in both the pure and the applied sciences are extremely interested in constructing systems of conversation in a natural language. In its purely scientific aspect, this problem is being studied by linguists, psychologists, and specialists working on "artificial intelligence"; in its technical aspect, the subject is being taken up primarily by specialists in computer science and programming, who use realizable models of conversation to construct automated control systems, information retrieval systems, systems for automatic translation, etc. This problem is rapidly gaining importance because of the increasing application of computers in the economy. It can safely be said that there is currently no branch of industry where computer science is not being put to practical use. However, the wide use of computers in everyday life is hindered by the fact that, as yet, conversations with a machine can be carried out only by specially trained people – programmers. Therefore, the demand for people from this profession is constantly growing. In the USA, for instance, the demand for programmers increases by 20% each year. American experts claim that if the demand for programmers is to be met by the year 2000, all US citizens will have to be taught programming. This is obviously out of the question. To solve the problem of man conversing with machine, it will be necessary to make the language of the conversation resemble natural (human) language, instead of increasing the number of programmers. The existence of such a language will ensure more effective contact between man and machine and will enable people from all walks of life to talk with the machine without prior preparation. What we have said will be more convincing if we realize that in the 25 years that computers have been used in practice their speed of operation has increased about 10^5 times and the capacity of their operating store has risen approximately 10^3 times, yet the speed of the "conversation" with the machine (i.e., programming with debugging) has only increased 2–3 times. The factor just mentioned is also reflected in the breakdown of the price of computer systems. While in the early stages of development the price of software was negligible compared with the price of hardware, the cost of software now constitutes about 70% of the total price. All these things make it clear why the problem of talking with the machine is so important. One possible way of moving toward a solution to this problem would be to design systems of programming which would allow "natural" means of communication to be used in the conversation between user and computer. Most of the work on this subject is still at the laboratory stage. Research into "natural" means of communication is generally centered on one of the following three directions:

1. Conversation with the computer in LNL in the form of a text
2. Conversation with the computer in LNL in the form of speech
3. Conversation with the computer using images.

Work is most advanced on the first of these three. Important achievements have been made in this direction by both Soviet and foreign researchers. While not even attempting to list all those who have obtained important results in the theory and practice of conversation systems, we shall mention only those whose works have been used, directly or indirectly, by the author in his own research. As regards systems of conversation, these are T. Winograd, G.S. Pospelov, A.P. Yershov, L.T. Kuzin, and I. Wilks; as regards linguistics – R.C. Schank, V.A. Zvegintsev, Y.D. Apresyan, A.K. Zholkovsky, and C.T. Fillmore; and as regards the representing of information – M. Minsky, D. Bobrow, D.A. Pospelov, Y.I. Shemakin, V.A. Uspensky, and G.G. Hendrix. Moreover, separate parts of the system of conversation have been considered by such researchers as V.R. Lesser, G.G. Belonogov, O.S. Kulagina, V.M. Briabrin, R. Davis, and A.C. Scott, among others. However, in spite of the many successes attained here, only experimental systems of conversation in LNL exist so far, and these are still unsuitable for practical use. In our opinion, the main reason for the inability to mass-produce such systems is the attempt to reduce the problem of conversation to research into the model of a language or, in better cases, to investigate this model in connection with the model of the surrounding world. Such an approach is permissible only in specific, trivial cases. In general, when we consider systems of real-life complexity, the existence of a two-sided dialogue is assumed (i.e., of a dialogue with mixed initiative). Within this dialogue, the system, in the case of any difficulties or incomprehension – inevitable in conversation between man and man, and thus all the more so between man and machine – should be able in plain terms (a) to explain the reasons for the difficulty and outline the current state it finds itself in; (b) to make clear to the user the scope of its possibilities and stored information; (c) to indicate how the input text should be altered to ensure that it is fully understood by the system. Everything we have said leads us to the conclusion that we should take the MPC as our theoretical basis for constructing systems of dialogue (regardless of the form of the language used in the conversation). Such a model should contain the models of a language, of the surrounding world, of the user, and of the system itself.

To move from experimental systems of conversation to systems applicable in industry we have to solve a number of complicated theoretical and technical problems. These involve, above all:

1. Examining the process of talking and determining its most important characteristics
2. Studying the existing models of conversation and, if they do not take into account all aspects of the problem, designing a new one
3. Designing the MPC, which plays a key role in designing the base system of conversation to be applied in industry
4. Constructing this base system.

1 Theories and Principles of Designing the Model of Conversation

1.1 Main Characteristics of the Process of Conversation

The process of conversation is an extremely complex one and still requires further study; it is therefore still impossible to design a model of conversation which would take into account all its nuances. Without claiming to present a full picture, we shall define the term "conversation" ("talking") as follows: Conversation is a two-way process of imparting information about a certain – real or hypothetical – world involving two participants: the author of each piece of information and the recipient; the objectives of the conversation are specified, as is the nature of possible connections between the pieces of information concerned, which, in turn, should be expressed in the form of statements comprehensible to both the author and the recipient. It is assumed that conversation is carried on by means of interrelated sentences and not by means of independent pairs of sentences. This is because an isolated sentence is insufficient to describe a complex situation, since language (and perhaps also human thought) imposes rather strict limitations on the length of sentences. The interrelation of sentences in a text can be attained by linguistic means (by grammatical means, e.g., forms and tenses, by anaphoric or modal means, by stylistic concordance, by the concordance of presuppositions, etc., see also Sect. 4.1) or by extralinguistic means (i.e., by causal and time nexuses existing in the surrounding world).

In order to understand each other during the process of conversation, the two participants assume the roles of author and recipient alternately; i.e., the two take the initiative by turns. Only in trivial cases does each participant keep performing the same role; reading a book can serve as an example here – the writer permanently plays the role of author, and the reader that of recipient. A statement by one participant (*A*) expresses not only what he wants to say but also his assumption as to how the second participant (*B*) will respond. This is particularly manifest in the case of an interrogative sentence, but it is also true in other cases. If *B*'s answers conform exactly to *A*'s anticipations, participant *A* will have the initiative permanently. It seems obvious that this is a rather untypical kind of conversation, possible only if *A* has full information about *B*'s knowledge. When *B*'s answers fail to meet, or only approximate, the expectations of *A*, as expressed in his questions, these answers are what are often called indirect, or approximate ones. If we want a system to be able to "talk" with a human being, it should understand indirect answers and provide such answers itself. Let us note here that an answer may have the form of a question. Indirect answers seem to be a requisite form of conversation when:

1. A precise answer to the question is unnecessary or gives no valuable information.
2. The system wants to inform the user about a structure and the substance of its knowledge.
3. The meanings of certain words in the question are not precisely defined.

In order to understand the user's indirect answers the system should be equipped with particular skills enabling it to infer.

In defining the term "conversation", we said that the statements made by the two participants should be comprehensible to both. By this we mean that they have to be unambiguous in syntactic, semantic, and pragmatic terms; this, in turn, makes it necessary for the participants to have common knowledge about the surrounding world and a common language. Each of them should also have information about himself and his partner. The fact that the language (i.e., that which allows the conversation to be carried on) and the surrounding world (i.e., that which is talked about) should be at least partially common seems fairly obvious. Otherwise the participants would not be able to find points of contact in a reasonable period of time. Less obvious is the necessity for each of the participants to have information about the other's knowledge and about his own knowledge and method of functioning. This information is essential, both to determine common terminology and points of view on what is being discussed, and to make it possible for each of the participants to "understand" his current situation and that of his partner. Up to now, it has usually been assumed in devising a conversational system that the user has detailed information about the system (and, of course, about himself), enabling him to "understand" every situation which might arise during the process of talking, even unexpected ones, i.e., the burden of both initiative and responsibility for final success was laid on only one participant in the conversation – the user. However, mixed initiative is necessary to conduct the conversation if the user's information about the system is, for some reason, incomplete – i.e., initiative is passed from one participant to the other in turn. Hence, the system should be able to take over the initiative from the user. In order to do so, it must have certain knowledge about itself ("self-knowledge"), about its current situation ("self-recognition"), and about the user (see Sects. 4.4 and 4.5). To sum up: in general, a system participating in a conversation with the user should possess knowledge about a language (the model of a language), about the surrounding world (the model of the surrounding world), about its partner in the conversation (the model of the user), and about itself (the model of the system).

Before we go on to a detailed analysis of the process of conversation, let us consider a short dialogue between a user and a system, involving the booking of airplane seats (the conversation takes place in city *C*). This example will illustrate the types of problems likely to arise in the course of a conversation.

	SYSTEM:	Good day. I am here to help you plan your journey by air. Where would you like to go?
(1)	CLIENT:	I would like to fly to city *D*, on May 28th.
	SYSTEM:	At what time would you like to leave?

(2) CLIENT: I would like to arrive at *D* before 10.00 a.m.
SYSTEM: Would flight No. 102 suit you? Arrival time is 9.15 a.m.
(3) CLIENT: And what is the next flight?
SYSTEM: Flight No. 310. Departure at 8.30 a.m., arrival at 10.00 a.m.
(4) CLIENT: I'll take the first one.
SYSTEM: In whose name am I to book the ticket?
(5) CLIENT: Bobrov.
SYSTEM: I am now repeating the booking: flight No. 102 from city *C* to city *D* on Wednesday, May 28th; departure time 7.30 a.m., arrival time 9.15 a.m. When would you like to return?
(6) CLIENT: On Friday evening.
SYSTEM: Does departure at 7.45 p.m. suit you?
(7) CLIENT: Yes.
SYSTEM: I am now repeating the booking: flight No. 307 from city *D* to city *C* on Friday, May 30th; departure time 7.45 p.m., arrival time 9.30 p.m. Thank you. Good-bye.

This dialogue is, of course, absolutely clear to a human being; nevertheless, it presents considerable difficulties for a computer. In order to conduct this dialogue the system has to be able to take over the initiative, to understand indirect answers and anaphoric references, to understand incomplete sentences (ellipsis); in other words, it has to be able to interpret the dialogue. Let us take a look at some of the hidden complexities in the above dialogue.

In this example, in sentence 3 the client takes over the initiative from the system. Instead of replying to the system's question with "yes" or "no", he poses his own question. In sentence 2 the client uses an indirect answer. He does not give the time of departure, which is what the system has inquired about, but instead tells the system at what time he would like to arrive in city *D* – this information being more important for him. In sentences 3 and 4 the client uses anaphoric references. In order to unravel the meaning of sentence 3, the system must refer to the preceding sentence, while to understand 4 it must refer not to the preceding one, but to 2. Let us note here that "next flight" in sentence 3 should be interpreted as "the next scheduled flight", yet "the first one" in 4 does not mean "the first scheduled flight", but "the first of the flights mentioned in the dialogue". In sentence 6, the client's reference is also not totally obvious. He says, "on Friday". In order to understand this answer, the system has to interpret "Friday" as the first Friday after the date of departure, i.e., after May 28th, and must be able to associate this day of the week with the proper date (i.e., the system has to know that "Friday" in this case means Friday, May 30th).

Ellipsis is used by the client in sentences 5 and 6. For their meaning to be clear, these must be transformed into full sentences. This can be done with the help of the preceding sentences, using them as patterns into which the elliptic constructions can be inserted.

1.1.1 Language and Speech

In the above description of "conversation" ("talking"), we used the word "language". Generally speaking, this word is known to everyone, but its meaning is in fact not so clear as it may seem to be at first sight. The study of languages is what is involved in linguistics, but even linguistics has not formulated a definition of the word "language" which might be accepted by all specialists. Language is usually considered either from the point of view of its function as a means of communication, or from the point of view of its internal structure as a complex sign (semiotic) system.

Linguistics distinguishes the notions "language" and "speech" (according to F. de Saussure 1916) and "linguistic competence" and "linguistic usage" (according to Chomsky 1965). In contemporary linguistics, "*speech*" denotes not only speech in oral or written form, but also so-called internal speech, i.e., thinking by linguistic means (words, etc.) without speaking aloud (see, e.g., Maslov 1975).

The *act of speech* is usually a two-way process consisting of speaking/listening in its oral form or writing/reading in its written form. The act of speech is a manifestation of linguistic activity. During it, a text is created. A text – as linguists understand the word – need not be in written form: oral speech, expressed by a voice, also constitutes a text. Sometimes the term "internal text" is used by analogy with "internal speech", the term denoting an act of speech performed only in the mind.

Language is a system of elements, possessed by a certain group, which constitute units of different levels (words, significant parts of words, etc.) plus a set of rules governing the usage of these units. The system of units is called the *vocabulary of the language*, while the system of rules for creating and understanding intelligible statements is called the *grammar* (in the broad sense) of this language (see, e.g., Maslov 1975).

Language should be distinguished from speech, just as we distinguish, for instance, a word in a dictionary from countless uses of this word in different texts, with different shades of meaning. Speech is the form of existence taken by language. Language functions, and is "directly given", in speech. In contrast to speech, the character of language is abstract, i.e., "only what is general exists in language" (V.I. Lenin).

The following example will make the above clearer:

Voron k voronu letit,
Voron voronu krichit:
'Voron! gde b nam otobedat?'

[Raven flies to raven,
Raven croaks to raven:
'Raven! where are we to dine?']
(Pushkin)

How many words do we have in this fragment? As far as "words of speech" are concerned – there are 12 of them. But, if we pass on from speech to language, then there are only nine words – we then count *voron* (1st, 5th, and 8th word in the passage) as one word, and *voronu* (3rd and 6th word) as a second one [*voronu* – dative case of the noun *voron*: a raven; trans. note]. In this case we are counting only different so-called *word forms* as separate words. Were we then to take no account of the grammatical forms of a given word, we could say that there are only eight words in the passage. In this case, the two word forms *voron* und *voronu* would be counted as one word. A word thus understood (solely in terms of its lexical meaning) we call a *lexeme*.

F. de Saussure (1916) wrote: "Historically, speech always anticipates language". He maintained that speech has a primary relationship to language, as it is a directly observable phenomenon, while language is secondary, being obtained from speech by a process of abstracting. At first sight, this may seem to be rather paradoxical – one could say that it is impossible to perform any act of speech without a set of language units and without rules which tell us how to connect these units together – both these elements constitute the so-called language norm which speech should conform to. And, generally speaking, these arguments hold true: by making speech conform to the "norm" of the language, we make it easily comprehensible with a minimum of intellectual effort. However, this norm is not as obligatory as it might seem to be; speech is additionally "supported" by concrete situations. One can present numerous examples to show that the "norm" is not obligatory, from "truncated", elliptic constructions to such acts of speech as grunting, tongue-clicking, etc. The point here is that language, with its norm is not the most important element in speech – what is actually most important is rather the meaning of statements and the objectives of the participants in the given conversation. It is this fact which should be taken as our starting point in trying to construct systems with a capacity for understanding. Unfortunately, this concept is still insufficiently developed (and moreover, not always accepted, although in our opinion it is undoubtedly true). Hence, in order to construct a realizable system, we are forced to take a middle course and pay a great deal of attention to the norm of a language. This makes the system less flexible and highly sensitive to deviations from the language norms determined by linguists but commonly ignored by people in the process of conversation. Due to the cardinal role played by meaning, human speech is able to overcome practically all resistance offered by language by linking the act of speech to a given situation.

The predominant role of meaning does not mean that speech is boundlessly "free". It is limited by difficulties in linking speech to situations. In according such importance to meaning, we cannot neglect to observe the language norm. Indeed, using natural language, we very often encounter situations where a deviation from the norm would change the meaning completely. This is demonstrated by the following examples, in which two or three expressions have different meanings, although they differ from one another only morphologically and syntactically:

a) *desat' komand, komanda desat', komand desat'*
   [ten teams, team (number) ten, there are ten teams; trans. note]
b) *Skol'ko zavodov perevozily ugol'?*
   [How many firms transported coal?; trans. note]
   Skol'ko zavody perevezly ugla?
   [How much coal did (these) firms transport?; trans. note]

The above examples are typical of the Russian language and show that not only semantics but also morphology and syntax must be used to establish the meaning of a sentence.

1.1.2 Different Levels of Textual Analysis

The following levels of analyzing a text can be distinguished in linguistic analysis of the Russian language (Zvegintsev 1976):

1. Discourse (i.e., the connected text)
2. Sentences
3. Word phrases
4. Words
5. Morphemes
6. Syllables
7. Phonemes
8. Differentiating signs

The first five of these levels are used in analyzing a text given in oral or written form, while the last three are employed to analyze sounds. Since we are interested in analyzing written texts only, we shall confine ourselves to levels 1–5.

The units of each level (excepting the highest, under certain conditions) are involved in connections with units of the same level and also in connections (of a functional character) existing between units of higher and lower levels. These connections can be understood as a relationship of means and ends, as units of a lower level serve as a means to a certain end: creating the units of a higher level.

Since we are interested in the process of conversation in general, we shall limit our considerations here to the highest two levels – discourse and sentences. Many linguists, by tradition, do not study the level of discourse, as they maintain that it goes beyond the bounds of linguistics. However, a new school has recently developed, which has been variously termed "textual linguistics", "hypersyntax", "the study of the connected text", etc. Strictly speaking, whether we should deal with one level (discourse) or with several (item, paragraph, chapter, text, etc.) is still an open question. For our purposes, it will be sufficient if we assume that only one level exists above the sentence – the level of discourse (i.e., the connected text). We shall define *discourse* as two or more significatively connected sentences. This connection is due to at least the following types of linguistic concordance (i.e., concordance sufficiently observable on the linguistic "surface"; Zvegintsev 1976): grammatical concordance (e.g., forms, tenses), modal concordance, and stylistic concordance.

Significative connections between sentences manifest themselves in natural language as anaphores and presuppositions (see Sect. 1.5.5). It should be stressed here that anaphoric references (i.e., language units which can be understood only after references to the text) have a metalinguistic nature. It can be demonstrated that they are unavoidable, regardless of the way a text is organized.

We now come to another interesting problem: how are we to determine, both theoretically and in practice, which levels are connected with language and which with speech? It is commonly accepted that the level of the sentence should be regarded as the border line here (Zvegintsev 1976); discourse is speech (it is the product of speech), while levels lower than the sentence belong to language. There is, however, no such commonly accepted view on the role of the sentence. Some definitions allocate the sentence to the sphere of speech, others to that of language

(Zvegintsev 1976). Moreover, in almost all of these definitions, the sentence is considered in terms of its own level; its connections with the higher level are neglected. In our opinion, in searching for attributes which would allow us to define the units of any level (the sentence level included), we should direct our attention to the higher level, beyond which these units do not exist as classes of distinguishable units. This general principle means, in particular, that the sentence does not exist beyond the limits of discourse. Hence, the chief, distinguishing attributes of the sentence should be looked for at the level of discourse, not sought in the internal, structural, and formal characteristics of the sentence. We accept the definition given by Zvegintsev (1976, p. 172): "The sentence is the minimal and principal unit of conversational speech ..... The process of conversational speech involves interchanging thoughts and ideas, rather than morphemes, words or word phrases. But thought must of necessity always refer to an object (though this object may be extremely abstract, fantastic or conceptual in nature). Thus, in saying that the sentence is the basic unit of conversation, we are in fact saying that the sentence is capable of transmitting thoughts and ideas, i.e., that it has meaning, and that it refers to specified objects, i.e., it is situational."

1.1.3 Types of Speech Activity

The following acts may be distinguished in the process of conversation (Austin 1962): *locutionary acts*, *illocutionary acts*, and *perlocutionary acts*. A locutionary act consists in uttering (or writing) a sentence with a specified meaning (or sense). Sentences spoken by the participants in a dialogue can be classified as either direct or indirect (Searle 1975). In a *direct locutionary act*, a literal understanding causes a breakdown of the process of communication, as the essential meaning is not expressed explicitly. For instance, an indirect indicative sentence can be used to ask for information ("I need Petrov's telephone number."), while an indirect interrogative sentence can be used to communicate information ("Don't you know that Mikhail has bought a car?") or to express a wish ("Will you shut this window?").

In performing locutionary acts we can use speech in many different ways. We can advise, propose, order, promise, etc. The choice of which way we use speech penetrates into grammar, though perhaps in distorted form. We shall call the performing of this act an *illocutionary act*. In other words, we can say that if we use different methods to try to attain objectives which are not directly expressed in a locutionary act (though they always accompany it), our locutionary act embodies different illocutionary forces (Searle 1977). Hence, the ways in which locutionary acts function are just illocutionary forces.

The following example illustrates the difference between uttering a sentence with a specified meaning (a locutionary act), and a sentence with a specified force (an illocutionary act). The sentence: "John said: 'He will kill your husband' ", has one direct (literal) meaning (as a locutionary act). However, this utterance can have several different illocutionary forces: in one case it can have the force of a threat; in another, of a promise; in still another, of expectation.

Illocutionary forces, however, should not be confused with the results which can be obtained by a locutionary act. Indeed, a conversation usually has a certain influence on the activities, thoughts, and feelings of its participants. This influence may be planned by the speaker. This is what we call a *perlocutionary act*.

It is easy to see that all the acts just mentioned, which taken together go to make up the process of talking, cannot be defined in isolation from each other. Let us now illustrate each of the above definitions with the help of two examples (Austin 1962):

1. Locutionary act:
   a) He said to me: "Shoot her."
   b) He said to me: "You should not do it."
2. Illocutionary act:
   a) He advised me to shoot her.
   b) He protested against what I was going to do.
3. Perlocutionary act:
   a) He induced me to shoot her.
   b) He annoyed me.

We have shown that locutionary acts are accompanied by illocutionary acts. Let us now consider different methods of transmitting the meaning of a locutionary act: linguistic methods, i.e., those expressed in terms of a language, and extralinguistic ones, i.e., those expressed not by means of language but by situational reference.

1.1.4 The Expressible (Linguistic) Meaning of a Locutionary Act

Any natural language is in fact a system of signs; as such, it is therefore something to be studied by *semiotics*, the general theory of sign systems. The problems of semiotics are studied in three principal aspects, corresponding to the following three branches of semiotics: syntactics, semantics, and pragmatics.

Syntactics deals with the structural aspects of combinations of signs from a given system, and the rules for constructing and transforming such combinations and abstracting from their meaning and functions.

Semantics deals with sign systems as vehicles for expressing meaning; it analyzes the relation between the structure of sign combinations and their meaning and studies the interpretation of the signs, sign combinations, and sets of sign combinations which compose a text.

Pragmatics studies the relation between the recipient of a sign system, the interpreter, and the sign system itself. Pragmatics deals with the receipt of meaningful expressions from a sign system in the context of the recipient's potential and ability for understanding. Pragmatics can be said to explain how the receiving system, on the basis of information not comprised in the received expression, selects the proper interpretation from all the interpretations possible. In terms of Sect. 1.1.3, semantics is related to the locutionary act and pragmatics to the illocutionary act.

The syntax of natural language is one of the subjects studied by linguists. As regards the semantics and pragmatics of NL, however, linguists did not consider these to be within their sphere of interest until very recently, which is why these branches have virtually not been studied by them at all. All the principal propositions of semantics and pragmatics have been arrived at by means of semiotics. Most of the noteworthy concepts which have been developed as a result of this approach are applicable solely to semantics (and not to pragmatics).

The correspondence between the expression of signs and their interpretation is a central concept in semantics. Detailed analysis, however, shows this correspondence to be triplex rather than binary, because the notion of interpretation can be split into two levels: intensional and extensional. A sign may be characterized on the one hand by an object which corresponds to it (the *denotation*, or *referent*), and on the other hand by the properties of that denotation which are expressed by it (the *concept*, or *designation*), i.e., by ideas concerning the denotation conveyed by the sign. The concept is information which the sign conveys about possible denotations (i.e., this is not full information about the denotation but only that part of it which is expressed by this particular sign), and about their location in reality, their place in the universe. The choice of denotation depends on the particular sign situation, i.e., on context. The concept, on the other hand, does not depend on the context, but is constant and specific for the sign – or, to be more precise, is determined by the location of the sign within a certain sign system. It should be stressed that this independence of the concept from the context does not mean that it always describes the same denotations in different universes. The relation of the sign (*S*) to its denotation (*D*) and concept (*C*) can be visualized with the help of a Frege triangle, the three vertices of which correspond to *S*, *D* and *C*. Let us consider the example of the sign "table". The particular table referred to in the given sign situation is the denotation; the concept is a general idea about tables as a class of things with flat, horizontal surfaces, used, for instance, for eating or working at. The connection between the denotation and the concept exists objectively, independently of the sign. The sign is only a means of communication, used to convey information about this connection.

Not claiming to be strict in our usage, (see, e.g., Schreider 1971) we shall call the four signs *S*, *U*, *K*, and *I* a sign system, with *S* representing the set of signs, *U*, the universe (i.e., the set of denotations), *K*, the system of knowledge (i.e., the set of notions used to describe concepts and the relationships between them), and *I*, the interpretations relating a given denotation or concept to a sign.

The set of word forms of a language performs the role of *S* in a natural language. *U* – the set of denotations – corresponds to the set of entities existing in the world we want to present (for instance, the set of employees in a given workforce). *K* – the system of knowledge – would, in the case of this workforce, consist of the relevant notions (employee, salary, position, surname, first name, patronymic, age, sex, date of birth, etc.), relations (bigger, smaller, being male, being female, etc.) and functions (summing up, counting, etc.).

As regards interpretations, it must be said that this problem has as yet been insufficiently studied by semiotics. One of the propositions made so far states that an entity within the universe can be related with a sign in two different ways: extensionally and intensionally. The *extensional* method consists in a clear distinguishing of this entity within the universe. The *intensional* method consists in distinguishing the entity within the universe in terms of the system of knowledge, by specifying the features and attributes which single this entity out from the universe. The class of all permissible denotations of a sign is called the *extension* of this sign. The *intension* of a sign is a description of a concept, expressed in terms of the general features of the denotation of this sign and its relationship with other denotations.

It should be stressed that it is impossible to characterize a sign by its extension only (Schreider 1974). This is because in referring to the denotation we do not make clear which of its features are important to us. For instance, if in explaining the notion "red" we refer to "the poppy" (extensionally), our interlocutor may arrive at the conclusion that red is a kind of flower.

Two features are said to be *intensionally equivalent* if each of them is a consequence of the other independent of the universe (but not independent of the system of knowledge).

Let us note at this point that the choice of the denotation for a given sign in a given universe may depend on the context. The concept, meanwhile, in any universe, permanently corresponds to the sign in a given sign system, i.e., in a given system of knowlege. For instance, in a given universe, the sign "I" may correspond to different denotations, depending on the context. The concept related to this sign may be described in this particular universe as "the sign denoting the author of this information". Let us note that the concept depends on the universe, as it can be expressed only in terms appropriate to this particular universe. The identity of concepts from different universes does not mean that they describe identical denotations.

There are no one-to-one correspondences in binary relationships between sign, denotation, and concept; these relationships are not even unequivocal. It is therefore not possible to reduce them to one binary relationship. A sign is said to be a *homonym*, or a *homograph*, if it can denote different concepts. The word "fencing" may serve as an example here. This denotes (a) a barrier, (b) the receiving of stolen goods, and (c) the art of swordplay. Homonymy may also take the form of *polysemy* – a cluster of related concepts expressed with one word. "Key", for instance, denotes a key used to open a door, a list of words or phrases giving an explanation of symbols or abbreviations, the set of instructions used to decipher secret messages, etc. All these meanings have something in common – the idea of "opening" or "penetrating".

A word is said to be a syntactic homonym when it can occur (depending on context) in different grammatical categories. For instance: "they *work* hard", "a *work* horse", "a *work* of art"; "the *wind* blows", or "*wind* your watch". Syntactic homonyms occur not only at the level of words, but also at the level of phrases:

1. I'll teach you. (Metaphorically or literally?)
2. The writer's invitation. (He invited or was invited?)

Homonyms can also be found at the level of morphology. The Russian word *stol* [a table; trans. note] has the same form in both the nominative and accusative cases, while *teritoria* [territory; trans. note] has the same form (*teritorii*) in the nominative and accusative plural, and also in the genitive, dative, and locative singular.

Synonymy occurs when the same denotation corresponds to different signs. If different signs refer to the same concept we speak about perfect synonymy. The signs "H_2O" and "water" provide an example of synonymy. They have a common denotation, but the concepts corresponding to them are different, as "H_2O" denotes just a substance, while "water" may also denote a fluid with possible admixtures of chemical compounds other than H_2O. Strictly speaking, perfect synonyms do not exist, as different signs must have different meanings when used autonomously (see below). However, with certain limitations, we can point to examples of perfect synonyms – "motorcar" and "automobile", "to jump" and "to leap". Homonymy and synonymy should not be considered to be flaws in a natural language. Thanks to homonymy, it is possible to reduce the number of signs necessary to denote the whole great variety of real objects and notions. Synonymy enables us to characterize denotations in various ways and carry out substantial transformations of a sign.

In the sentences "*Synthesis* has nine letters", or "*Table* is a singular noun", the words in italics are used autonomously. Their meaning here differs from that to be found in a dictionary. In the above sentences these words represent themselves alone (i.e., they denote these words themselves, not their usual concepts or denotations).

Descriptors or alphanumeric symbols used to identify documents are examples of the autonomous usage of a word.

1.1.5 Extralinguistic Phenomena in the Locutionary Act

The meaning of a text is not just the sum of the meanings of the sentences it contains. Each sentence conveys a "hidden" (i.e., linguistically inexpressible), implied meaning. This implied meaning can be brought to light by means of presupposition. Generally speaking, we can define *presuppositions* as the illocutionary conditions of locutionary acts, as unspoken premises which ensure the proper understanding of locutionary acts.

The problem of presuppositions originated deep in the confines of philosophy, from whence it penetrated into linguistics. An unequivocal definition of presuppositions does not exist in either philosophy or linguistics. However, it is commonly accepted that presuppositions reflect some objectively existing phenomena. Let us mention two alternative definitions of this notion. The first is a philosophical one (Strawson 1952), while the second is linguistic (Zvegintsev 1976). According to Strawson, a statement S presupposes a statement S' if, and only if, the truth or falsity of S' is a precondition of the truth or falsity of S. Zvegintsev (1976, p. 220), summarizing the definitions given by several linguists, proposes the following definition: "A presupposition is the set of all the conditions which must be satisfied

(a) to make the given structure of an utterance pertinent;
(b) to ensure that the given objectives of communication (in philosophical language: illocutionary forces) are effectively embodied in this utterance;
(c) to make the direct meaning of the utterance understandable."

The following classic example will make the above definition clearer: "Shut the door, please". The presuppositions we can distinguish here are as follows:

1. The mutual relationship between the "speaker" and the "listener" is such that the speaker is able to make this request of the listener.
2. The listener is in a position to comply with this request.
3. The door is specified, and the listener knows which door the speaker is referring to.
4. This particular door is currently open.
5. The speaker wants this door to be closed.

Thus, it turns out that each sentence unavoidably conveys certain additional information, which can be of great importance, about the conditions which this sentence must comply with. It is precisely these conditions which constitute the "invisible", implied meaning of any "visible" text. We can therefore say that the primary task involved in the problem of presuppositions is to make this "invisible" meaning explicit.

Let us note here that it is only recently that linguistics has begun to study categories of this kind – ones not formally expressed in a text, yet somehow existing in it. In this connection, linguists seek answers to the following questions: Is there some connection, some consistency, between "visible" linguistic texts and their "invisible", implied meanings? Are the illocutionary conditions really not reflected in the linguistic structure? If they are, then how? Let us note, however, that the answer to the question of which information is relevant and which is irrelevant largely depends on the structure of the given language (see, e.g., Zvegintsev 1976, p. 270). As an example, let us consider the following sentence in Russian: *Vrach beglo govorila po-nemetski* [The physician spoke German fluently]. The presuppositions assumed here are as follows:

1. The physician is a woman.
2. German is not her mother tongue.
3. The statement concerns her general degree of proficiency in the German language, not one specific case of her speaking.
4. The personal merits of the physician are being assessed.
5. The proficiency in German refers to the past.
6. The statement refers to a specific physician.

The first presupposition is expressed by the form of the verb which is used [*govorila* – past tense, third person singular, feminine of the imperfective verb *govorit'*: to speak; trans. note]. The second presupposition is related to the use of the adverb "fluently"; this adverb would not have been used about her mother tongue. The third is related to transformation; this presupposition would not apply if the sentence read: "The physician spoke to him in German." The fourth is a consequence of extralinguistic knowledge: it is known that not all physicians speak foreign languages. The fifth follows from the grammatical form of the verb *govorit'* [to speak]. The sixth is not a simple consequence of any element of sentence structure – it follows from the context of the sentence as a whole. In the sentence we are examining the information about, the sex of the physician is given explicitly in the verb form (*govorila*), but the information that the sentence concerns a specific physician is not. However, in the English translation of this sentence – "The physician spoke German fluently" – the sex of the physician is in no way specified, but the fact that the sentence concerns a specific physician is, thanks to the use of the definite article "the". Generally speaking, it can be said that the principal difference between languages is not what *can or cannot* be expressed, but what information a speaker *has to or does not have to* include in what he says.

Some further conclusions can be drawn from the example given above. It turns out that presuppositions (excluding logical ones) are not universal (independent of particular languages). Their form changes from one language to another, largely depending on the structural features of the given language. The aforementioned difference between languages makes the problem of automatic translation very complex. For instance, in order to translate the sentence about the physician from English into Russian, one would have to infer the information about this physician's sex from a wider context. Disregarding this information might warp the meaning of the text.

As we can see from the above example, presuppositions can take various forms. The four main forms can be set out as follows (Zvegintsev 1976, p. 270):

1. An explicit, regular form (as in the 1st and 5th presuppositions above)
2. An explicit, irregular form (as in the 2nd and 3rd presuppositions above)
3. An implicit form implied in extralinguistic knowledge (as in the 4th presupposition above)
4. An implicit form implied in the context of the sentence as a whole (as in the 6th presupposition above)

These four forms of presupposition can be considered degrees to which empirical data and cognitive categories are "inserted" into the language. Many attempts to classify presuppositions have been made by linguists (for a review, see Zvegintsev 1976, p. 239). However, these have so far been based on various different conceptions and in consequence have tended to produce chaos rather than order.

1.1.6 The Concept of "Tacit Knowledge" in the Process of Conversation in NL

"Invisible", implied meanings are encountered in natural language (NL) not only at the level of discourse and need not be expressed by presuppositions. In fact, they constitute one of the essential features of any NL; they occur everywhere – at the level of discourse, of the sentence, of word phrases. What is very important here is the fact that "tacit knowledge" is contextually dependent, i.e., in different cases different elements remain "tacit".

At the level of discourse "tacit knowledge" can be found both globally and locally. In global terms, it involves participants' a priori knowledge of the structure of a discourse, not explicitly expressed by linguistic means (see Sect. 1.3.1). In local terms, it involves a lack of explicit connections between sentences. Linguists claim these connections are made by presuppositions. At the level of the sentence, tacit knowledge is seen in the practice of not specifying all aspects of the situation which a sentence refers to. For example: "In 1976 more than ten factories producing *A* were built." No indication is given here as to who built these factories.

At the level of word phrases (i.e., inside the sentence) there can also be no information specifying introduced notions. For instance: "What is the proportion between trucks with increased load-bearing capacity and all the trucks owned by the kolkhoz?" Here the word phrase "trucks with increased load-bearing capacity" contains certain implicit information. For a human being it is obvious that this means "trucks with increased load-bearing capacity owned by the kolkhoz", not just "trucks with increased load-bearing capacity" in general. Tacit knowledge of a much simpler form can frequently be found in word phrases. For instance, such word combinations as "gas fitter", "gas mask", "gasworks", or "coal gas" are understood, roughly speaking, as "a workman who installs or repairs gas pipes and appliances", "a mask used to protect the face and lungs against poison gases", "a plant for manufacturing gas", and "a kind of gas produced from coal".

In ending this section, we would like to call the reader's attention to what we consider the essential feature of conversation in a natural language. This is the fact that the recipient of a text receives more information than is explicitly contained in the text. The additional information is rooted in knowledge the recipient possessed previously. This phenomenon is characteristic for each process of intellectual perception; this process consists in associating the given information with all information possessed previously which is in any way connected with it and in unifying and adjusting the explicit and "hidden" information, i.e., the "visible" text and the "invisible", implied meanings. Linguistics explains this phenonenon of perceiving more information than the input text contains in terms of presuppositions. In our opinion, this explanation is insufficient. In fact, the connections between sentences are ensured not only by presuppositions but also by inference (implications), i.e., conclusions which can be drawn on the basis of a given sentence concerning events which may, or must, happen. The connections of a given sentence made by presuppositions and by inference are of a completely different nature – presuppositions precede the sentence, inference follows it. Inference is a subject rather seldom dealt with by linguists, who consider it to be more related to logic. Be that as it may, this does not diminish the role of inference in the process of establishing connections between the sentences of a text. Several authors explain this question using the concept of "scripts" ("frames"; Schank and Abelson 1977; Rieger 1976).

1.2 An Analysis of Existing Linguistic Models

In this section we shall describe some of the better known linguistic models used in practice. Existing conversational systems will be reviewed in Sect. 2.3.

1.2.1 The Parameters of Comparison

There are currently various approaches to the problem of modelling the process of conversation. The most important characteristics of the process of conversation in NL have already been outlined in the preceding section. In our opinion, the degree to which these characteristics are taken into account tells us a great deal about the quality of a given model of conversation. Let us now examine several of the most highly developed models in terms of the following parameters:

1. The degree to which the most important features of the process of conversation are taken into account
   a) "Speech" or language
   b) Discourse or sentence
   c) Sense or pseudosense
   d) Provision for "tacit knowledge" in NL
   e) Provision for the synonymy and homonymy which occur in NL
   f) The role of extralinguistic knowledge
2. The volume of the knowledge encompassed in the model, which defines the "depth" of understanding of a given text (the models of a language, of the surrounding world, of participants in the conversation)

The model of a language, rather than that of a conversation, is commonly used to analyze the process of conversation. As a result, the methods used are inadequate to solve the problem of conversation. During the work of a system, this is reflected in the following ways:

1. It is impossible to foretell whether a given input text in NL will, or will not, be accepted and processed by the system.
2. It is difficult, or even impossible, to explain to a user unfamiliar with linguistics and programming what limitations are imposed on the language of conversation.
3. The system is not able to explain the reasons for its failures in processing an input text; it cannot avail itself of the user's help.

It would seem to be impossible to construct the model of conversation without the help of linguistics. However, linguists are usually interested in the model of language, not of conversation – this fact may be explained by the very definition of linguistics, a branch of science which studies languages. Moreover, until quite recently, linguists maintained (and some of them still do) that the semantic problems of a language – solutions to which are necessary to understand the phenomenon of conversation – lie outside the framework of linguistics. No linguist considers it his or her business to deal with extralinguistic knowledge (the semantics of the surrounding world, pragmatics, etc.). Recently, however, some linguists have found it necessary to construct not only a model of language but also a model of "speech" (Zvegintsev 1976). The designing of such a model would be a great step forward in building the model of conversation. The author is also aware of one work devoted to an analysis of the principles of designing the model of human dialogue (Mann et al. 1977). However, while linguists may have had their own good reasons for failing to take up the model of conversation, there is no justification whatsoever for the same failing on the part of specialists in artificial intelligence.

Thus, since a model of conversation does not yet exist, we shall consider a few models of language – those which are the most appropriate for our purposes and which have been used in dialogue systems. Then we shall present our version of a model of conversation (Sect. 1.3). Of all the models of language, we shall be examining those which are based on semantics. These models are usually of the SENSE-TEXT type (Zholkovsky 1974). Let us note here that by no means all models of language are of this type; for instance, transformative creative grammars are not (see Popov and Firdman, 1976 p. 326). Models of the SENSE-TEXT type are not creative – they do not generate texts as creative grammars do, but translate texts into senses and vice versa. The SENSE-TEXT approach to the problem of describing a natural language was not widely accepted in theoretical linguistics for quite some time, despite the fact that this approach was obvious to those working on the construction of dialogue systems. The following remark, made by one of the authors of the SENSE-TEXT model, is worth quoting here: "There are many ideas and approaches in theoretical linguistics which have to be very carefully justified to be accepted, to overcome psychological barriers – the same ideas and approaches turn out to be not only optimal, but also quite obviously the only ones possible in the automatic processing of texts" (Mel'chuk 1974a, p. 17).

The idea may be simple, but this does not mean that it is easy to develop it in detail. Credit for solving this problem goes to linguists. Almost all models of the SENSE-TEXT type were developed for automatic translating (AT) and not for systems conducting conversations with the computer in NL. Though these two tasks have much in common, there are some differences of a rather basic nature which make it impossible to use the SENSE-TEXT model in conversational systems without certain modifications.

Now let us examine the differences between the tasks usually performed by a system perceiving NL (SNL) and AT systems (Popov 1978a).

1. The main purpose of AT of a text from one language into another is to transform the text into senses and vice versa. In contrast to SNL, neither the relation between the utterances constituting the text and the model of reality nor the veracity of these utterances is relevant. In other words, AT needs knowledge about language, while SNL also requires additional general and particular knowledge about reality and "speech".
2. Understanding the sense (meaning) of something is a task common to both SNL and AT. However, "deep" understanding of a phrase may not be demanded of AT systems, especially when technical or business texts are being translated. Yet SNL has to catch "invisible", implied meanings (characteristic for natural language – see Sect. 1.1) to understand the intentions of a participant in the conversation; these implied meanings pass automatically from one language to the other during the AT process (or so designers of AT systems expect, though in our opinion, they are not always justified in doing so). The following example will make this clearer: "Somewhere near the village of *N* something began dripping from the carburetor. Mikhail crawled under the car". We can expect an AT system to translate this correctly, though it does not understand *why* "Mikhail crawled under the car". However, if on the basis of this text, one asks "which part of the car did Mikhail repair?", the need to understand the implied meaning is evident.
3. SNL and AT systems deal with different input texts. For SNL, the natural language may be limited as regards subject, grammar, and – very importantly

– size, yet SNL remains useful. AT systems, on the other hand, should deal with natural languages without any limitations as regards their grammars. The length of (connected) texts should also be virtually unlimited. These conditions impose very strict speed and cost requirements on AT systems. Indeed, for it to be efficient, an AT system ought to translate texts more rapidly and cheaply than a human translator (AT systems, after all, can always be replaced by men). Another question arises here: what is the most convenient and reliable way of loading the text to be translated into the AT system? This problem turns out to be extremely difficult, given the great size of these texts. The requirements an SNL should meet are not so strict, however, because (a) the SNL cannot be replaced by a man if the system works in a "question-and-answer" regime and the size of the data base (DB) exceeds the potential of human memory (the size of practically all data bases does); and (b) the input texts are usually short (a few lines).

4. The natural regime for SNL is the dialogue between the user and the system. In this regime it is possible to clear up doubts connected with input material. An AT system cannot work in such a regime or, if it can, the dialogue that occurs is not between the system and the author of the text or the user for whom the text is being translated, but between the system and someone who is familiar with translating and who corrects the results of the machine's work. But if such a "someone" exists, then why is he himself not doing the translating instead of the machine?
5. The input and output languages of SNL are usually the same (or one is a subset of the other). Hence, in developing SNL, we are not forced to overcome all the complex and unresolved problems which AT systems encounter owing to the grammatical and semantic incompatibility of languages that result from the different approaches to subdividing reality employed by different languages (Mel'chuk 1974a, p. 190). This last factor means that AT systems have to divide the sense of words into atoms of sense. Such a division need not be obligatory in the case of SNL.

All these differences lead to the conclusion that the SENSE-TEXT (ST) model (suited to the tasks of AT) does not provide a satisfactory reflection of the characteristic features of the process of conversation. This is why we have developed the model of the process of conversation (see Sect. 1.3), geared towards a two-way conversation rather than translation.

Before considering the existing models of language, let us make one more thing clear. Our criticism of these models (see Sect. 1.2.7 and 2.3) does not mean that they are inadequate to the tasks for which they were designed (although this may sometimes be the case). It simply means that they are inadequate to the modeling of the process of conversation.

1.2.2 Component Analysis

Before examining the ST model, let us look at the component analysis method, which reflects the state of linguistic semantics before the SENSE-TEXT approach was developed. Component analysis (Katz and Fodor 1963; Katz 1966, 1967) originates from the traditional division of lexis – first into the general and conceptual, then into more detailed subdivisions. Many dictionaries (the excellent *Roget's Thesaurus*, for instance) have been constructed in this way.

Component analysis was based on the premise that the semantics of natural languages can be adequately expressed in terms of a finite, unstructuralized set of semantic components (i.e., atoms of sense). It was assumed that an infinite number of lexical units of an infinite number of languages could be described by a finite set of semantic components (also called semantic markers, semantic parameters, etc.). Hence, the universal set of semantic components was supposed to describe the conceptual system of human knowledge, which itself was supposed to possess universal features.

The technique of distinguishing semantic components consists in analyzing words and defining certain features which divide them into different semantic groups. Such features as being "animate", "grown-up", "inanimate", "male", and "female" may serve as examples here. These features are then arranged in pairs: "animate – inanimate", "human – nonhuman", etc. We may then distinguish more detailed features (e.g., "fish", "animal", etc.), before finally, at the end of this process, arriving at "atoms of sense". The meaning of a word is represented by a set of such semantic components. This method would seem to be quite natural; however, several serious shortcomings become evident when we try to put it into practice. It turns out to be much too cumbersome when applied to the ambiguous words so frequent in natural languages. In such cases one has to construct a two-tier system of components: first the proper meaning of a word has to be singled out, then the semantic parameters of this particular meaning are specified.

Extremely sensitive semantic differentials are necessary in order to use component analysis in studying the possibilities of arranging words in sensible combinations. Even then there are unresolved problems with metaphorical usage. Even more difficult problems (irresolvable ones, in our opinion) arise when we attempt to use the component analysis method to determine the meaning of a whole sentence, not saying a word about the text. However, all this criticism does not mean that the component analysis method should be completely abandoned. In some cases it may be useful, for example, as a semantic component of the model of government (see Sect. 4.3.3) or in solving problems such as selecting one meaning of a word from several possible ones (Apresyan 1974, p. 13). Nevertheless, this method certainly cannot solve all the problems of semantics.

1.2.3 Semantic Cases (Roles)

A great contribution to linguistic research in the field of expressing sense structures has been made by C.T. Fillmore (1968, 1969, 1970, 1971). He accepts the hypothesis about the component structure of meaning and the idea of subdividing the meaning of a word into simpler and simpler components, right down to the atoms of sense (Fillmore 1969). But then he goes further. Starting from the commonly accepted notion of the argument structure of a predicate, he comes to the conclusion that it is necessary to specify not only the number of arguments of a given predicate but also their roles (their semantic contents). Similar ideas were considered at the same time by Soviet linguists (cf. Apresyan 1968, 1969). Fillmore distinguishes the following roles (or cases): an agent – an animate initiator of an action; a contragent – a force the action is directed against; an object – a thing which is the object of an action; an addressee – the one the action is performed for (or against); a patient – a thing which is acted upon; a result – a thing created by the action; an instrument – a stimulant or direct physical cause of an action; a source – the initial state of an object before the action. This system of roles (modified many times in Fillmore's succeeding works) is not clear in all details (Apresyan 1974 p. 26). Nevertheless, this system is a great step forward in both theoretical research and practical application. Fillmore has also developed a more detailed conception of lexical meaning (i.e., sense). The generally accepted conception of meaning is based on its multilayered structure. Besides the fundamental and specific meaning of a word we distinguish shades of meaning – stylistic and emotionally expressive elements of this meaning. Fillmore goes further and splits the specific meaning into two components: the specific meaning and the presupposition (see Sect. 1.1.5). The difference between these two components can be seen in the different influence negation has on each of them. Negation affects the meaning, but does not change the presupposition. For instance, the sentence "Peter is not a bachelor" does not mean that Peter is not a man. Taking the meaning of the word "bachelor" to be roughly "an adult man who has never married", negation affects only the second part of this definition, the part determining the specific meaning. Fillmore's research leads him to the conclusion that presuppositions (contained in lexical meanings) include three fundamentally different classes of semantic elements:

1. Elements of extralinguistic (i.e. encyclopedic) knowledge about a particular event. This knowledge can be included neither in a definition of the lexical meanings of words nor in a description of their arrangements (e.g., in the sentence "Shut the door", this knowledge refers to which particular door is meant and the fact that this door is open).
2. Elements which can be directly included in a definition but cannot be included in a description of word arrangements
3. Elements which can be included in a description of the arrangement of words rather than in definitions of their meaning

We should stress here that linguists include encyclopedic knowledge in their understanding of meaning (sense). In our opinion, two direct conclusions can be drawn from this: (a) the meaning of a sentence is neither the simple sum nor even a function of the meanings of its constituent words (see Sect. 1.3.3); (b) in order to determine a meaning it is necessary to use encyclopedic knowledge, which cannot be included in a definition of words. We are calling attention to these fairly obvious facts because when the designing of functioning systems is involved, a great many researchers (primarily linguists) begin expressing sense solely by reference to the meaning of words.

One of the most important results of Fillmore's work was the reassessment of the normal structure of definitions in defining dictionaries. Fillmore considers the dictionary the essential means of determining semantic (role) structures and the rules governing their translation into surface structures. We shall not go into detail on the structure of definitions proposed by Fillmore, as it is very similar to a concept which is well known in Soviet literature, namely, the "model of government" (MG; cf. Apresyan 1974, p. 119). The MG describes the syntactic and semantic properties of words and is widely used in the compound lexicon (CL) of the model examined in Sect. 1.2.6. Let us now consider three models of the SENSE-TEXT type which are the most interesting for our purposes:

1. The preference semantics model (Wilks 1972)
2. The conceptual dependency model (Schank 1975a)
3. The SENSE-TEXT model (Zholkovsky 1974)

We would like to caution readers against the typical mistake of confusing the SENSE-TEXT approach (model) with the one particular model which bears the same name. We shall refer to the SENSE-TEXT approach by the abbreviation ST, while the particular SENSE-TEXT model shall be referred to as PST. These two notions (ST and PST) are not identical, since, despite its many advantages, the PST model does not include all possible approaches (nor, in fact, does it aim to). In contrast to those who have popularized the PST model, its authors themselves do not equate this model with all models of the ST type.

1.2.4 The Preference Semantics Model (PS)

The PS model was developed by Wilks at Stanford University. His work expands on certain conceptions of the Cambridge Linguistic Circle (Masterman et al. 1964). In presenting his model, Wilks took upon himself the following tasks (which – in our opinion – he did not fully accomplish):

1. Analyzing connected texts instead of individual sentences
2. Making provision for all sensible sentences, not only grammatically correct ones (in contrast to Chomsky)
3. Formalizing semantic analysis
4. Developing a machine-oriented analytical procedure
5. Investigating the sense of a sentence not just by listing word meanings together with the relevant syntactic structure (as Chomsky does), but by constructing a structuralized form of the message which expresses the sense of the sentence (see below)
6. Being able to process sentences containing unknown words

In order to characterize a text, Wilks defines the following entities: word senses, message forms, text fragments, and semantic compatibility. A message form is taken to be a theoretical construct which allows us to select the proper sense of a word contained in a given part of a text (i.e., which allows us to eliminate ambiguity of meaning). This particular sense is the one which forms the "message" consistent with the given fragment of the text. This sense, or meaning, may fit several message forms; in this case the message form consistent with the text is chosen. Message forms are considered to be consistent if they comply with the rules of semantic compatibility which are applied to the whole text. The PS model is based on the following assumptions (not definitively proven by the author in question):

1. The sum of all possible message forms is finite.
2. A formal method of expressing message forms exists.
3. A formal method of arranging message forms into a fragment of a text exists.

In order to express the entities distinguished in a text by the PS model, the following notions are introduced:

1. "Semantic formula" – representing the meaning of a word
2. "Template" – representing the message form
3. "Rules of sequence" – expressing the rules of semantic compatibility of message forms

The semantic formulae, templates, and rules of sequence may be expressed in terms of semantic elements, classifiers, and markers. The *semantic formula* is used to express the meanings occurring in a natural language. A formula consists of semantic elements enclosed in parentheses. Selected atoms of sense, called *classifiers*, play the role of semantic elements. In different versions of the model Wilks distinguishes 53–60 different classifiers. The classifiers have no concrete language form. Wilks lays down rules for constructing formulae from elements and then for interpreting these formulae. Let us take the verb "to shoot" as an example. The corresponding semantic formula expresses the meaning "Person-subject causes the movement of a thing (i.e., a bullet) with the aim of hitting an animate object" and can be written down as follows:

((PERSON-SUBJECT) (ANIMATE OBJECT)
((TO HIT TARGET) ((THING TO MOVE) CAUSATION)))

Let us note that the formula consists of elements (atoms of sense), not of words from a natural language.

Wilk's semantic formulae express the meanings of utterances without reference to the division of the utterance into words or to the counterposition "objects versus relations". This feature enables Wilk's semantic formulae to express meanings more precisely than several other representations do (e.g., semantic networks and Schank's quasigraphs, see Sect. 1.2.5). Moreover, a formula may also be considered an indirect procedure involved in constructing the proper template.

Templates are divided into simple templates and full templates (also called simply "templates" for short). A simple template consists of three semantic elements (described above). The following may serve as an example of a simple template: PERSON + TO BE + KIND. This means: "The person is a person of a specific kind". This template conveys generalized information about many concrete utterances – for instance, "Ivan is a policeman". The PS model lays down rules for generating templates from simple templates. As we have already noted, the model is based on the hypothesis that the number of templates is finite and not very great. Two templates taken from one sentence can be unified to form one with the help of the "rules of sequence" which express the semantic compatibility of these templates. Another notion used in the PS model is that of the semantic proximity of two full templates (*A* and *B*). This is shown by the identity of the classifiers of *A* and *B*. A text (or a fragment of a text) is considered to be "tied" if all the templates in this text are in proximate pairs.

An analysis of a fragment of a text proceeds approximately thus: First – with the help of certain special marker words (prepositions etc.) – the text is divided into fragments. Next, each word in the text is assigned all its dictionary meanings. Then simple patterns (templates) – which are known in the system – are superimposed, one by one, onto the fragment under consideration (morphology and syntax are not taken into account, which is a major deficiency of the model). The template is considered to have been superimposed when each of its elements is projected onto an element of any of the meanings of any word. Then certain rules of extension are applied; these transform the simple template into a full template by adding the words which were not included in the template. This procedure may prove very complicated, as more than one simple template may be found during the first stage. When the full template has been obtained, the next sentence (or part of a sentence) is processed in the same way, until templates for the whole text have been found. The semantic proximity of the templates is then examined (with the help of "super templates"). Finally, a representation of the whole text is obtained. If ambiguity occurs, the denser representation is chosen, i.e., the representation with the highest recurrence of semantic elements.

The weakness of the PS model is that it is analysis oriented (see also Sects. 1.2.7 and 2.3). In his more recent works, Wilks has developed his model further, introducing "scripts" and "frames". We shall not examine these works here, as they have not yet been applied to any functioning system, and they involve a representation of knowledge rather than models of a language or a conversation.

1.2.5 The Conceptual Dependency (CD) Model

This is a model which R.C. Schank and his group have been developing since 1968. Up until 1975 the group worked at Stanford, thereafter at Yale. Let us note that this group has favored the introduction of their own terminology and method of presentation to illustrate already existing concepts. The model they use sets itself the following objectives:

1. The processing of a text in a natural language should not only produce a conceptual (i.e. semantic) representation of the text, but should also ensure that it is "understood" by the listener. This means that the system should be able to draw logical conclusions from a text, recognize the aims and intentions of the speaker, etc. In other words, this is not just a model of a language, but is also a model of thinking (these are the authors' objectives, not their results).
2. The model should ensure the understanding and interpretation of anomalous phrases as well as of grammatically correct ones.
3. The model should be able to correct mistakes during the analysis of homonymous texts.
4. A meaning should be represented in terms of atoms of sense, at the same time revealing similarities and differences between words.
5. The semantic representations (SEMRs) of synonymous phrases should be identical, with similar SEMRs corresponding to similar phrases.

6. It is the text, and not separate phrases, which should be the object of analysis. (However, as yet, only isolated phrases can be considered to have been analyzed successfully.)
7. The model should be of practical use (capable of being used by a computer); it should also make it possible to process a machine translation.

The CD model is constantly evolving and developing. In this connection it should be noted that the review of the work of Schank's group given by Mel'chuk (1974b) has in many respects become obsolete. It therefore seems necessary to give a more detailed account of the CD model in the years 1975–1976. The Schank group has neglected syntax and morphology at the level of theory. In the beginning, this could have been explained by a desire to stress the essential difference between the CD model and Chomsky's standard theory (see Popov and Firdman 1976, p. 326). However, as far as the realization of the model is concerned (Schank 1975a), elements of syntactic analysis are taken into account (albeit "hidden" in semantics). We agree that the role of semantics is paramount, but there is no need to neglect syntax and morphology. In fact, they are particularly important as regards the Russian language where they are much more complex than in English. Moreover, even if a theoretical analysis of a phrase is possible without syntax, a synthesis cannot be carried out without syntax, even theoretically. We shall not examine the syntactic aspects of the CD model in detail. Let us merely note that (in synthesis) the CD model utilizes the method of extended transition networks (Woods 1970).

Semantic representation in the CD model is based on the notion of a CD network. This is something similar to a labeled, oriented graph, although it is not, strictly speaking, a graph. We shall call this construct a *quasigraph*. Roughly speaking, it differs from a graph in two ways:

1. Besides binary relations there are also threefold (e.g., "X passes from Y to Z") and fourfold ones (e.g., "parameter Y of state X has changed from Z_1 to Z_2").
2. The lines of a quasigraph connect not only vertices but also other lines.

In our opinion, there was no need to use quasigraphs instead of graphs (this illustrates the independent line followed by the Schank group). The vertices of a quasigraph are marked with the symbols of semantic units (SU) of four kinds: PP – the names of physical objects (picture producers); ACT – the names of actions; PA – the characterization of objects (picture aiders); AA – the characterization of actions (action aiders). Roughly speaking, PP correspond to nouns, ACT to verbs, PA to adjectives, and AA to adverbs.

In more recent works, the authors have added three more vertices: State – the value of a state, LOC – a location, and T – time. *State* describes the state of an object in terms of standardized units. The state "health", for instance, can be described using a scale ranging from +10 to −10, with −10 corresponding to death and +10 meaning "in perfect health". We shall consider states in more detail later on. *LOC* may be considered to represent spatial coordinates or may serve to characterize an event (conceptualization – see below). *T* – the time corresponding to an event – may be one point in time (an instant) or an interval.

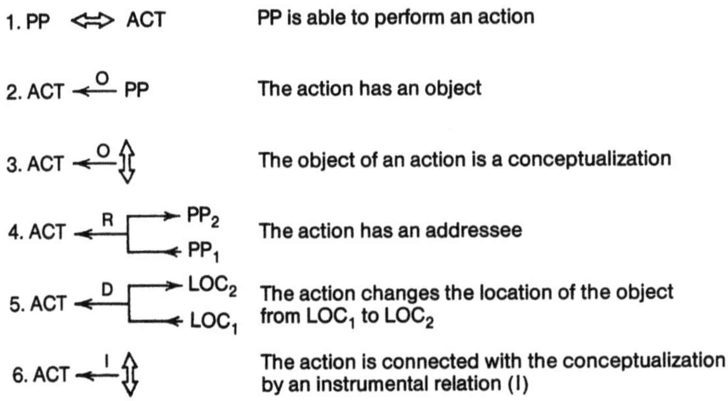

Fig. 1.1. Representation of semantic cases in the CD model

More than one label may be assigned to any one line of the quasigraph. Lines are usually binary, but two types of line are threefold and one is fourfold. The direction of the line is from dependent element to the main element. Two lines in opposite directions connecting two objects (vertices or lines) are replaced by one line with arrows at both ends (⇔).

Three kinds of line can be distinguished. The first specifies the role of participants in the action (ACT). These lines are called *conceptual* (i.e., semantic) *cases of action*, and are of the following types:

1. Lines connecting an action with an actor, i.e., with the person performing an action; a graphic representation of such a line is shown in Fig. 1.1, 1
2. Lines specifying the object (*O*) of an action (see Fig. 1.1, 2 and 3)
3. The line *R*, representing the link between an action, the person receiving (PP_2), and the person giving away (PP_1) the object (see Fig. 1.1, 4)
4. The line *D*, representing the link between an action (which produces a change of an object's location) and the object's initial and final locations (see Fig. 1.1, 5)
5. The line *I*, connecting an action with an instrument, expressed as the second conceptualization (see Fig. 1.1, 6)

A *conceptualization* is an essential unit at the conceptual (i.e., semantic) level; thoughts (utterances) are built of these units. A conceptualization includes an action, a variety of its conceptual cases, and the participants in the action (their states). For reasons of brevity, we shall sometimes call a conceptualization an event.

Lines which can be attached to conceptualization or actions are classified as lines of the second kind. These can be divided into two types: lines connecting an action (ACT) with the characterization of the action (AA; for a graphical representation of such a line, see Fig. 1.2) and lines characterizing the location (LOC) or time (T) of a conceptualization (see Fig. 1.2, 1 and 2).

Lines of the third kind represent cause-and-effect relationships between two actions or between an action and a state. The line *R* (see Fig. 1.2, 4) connects an

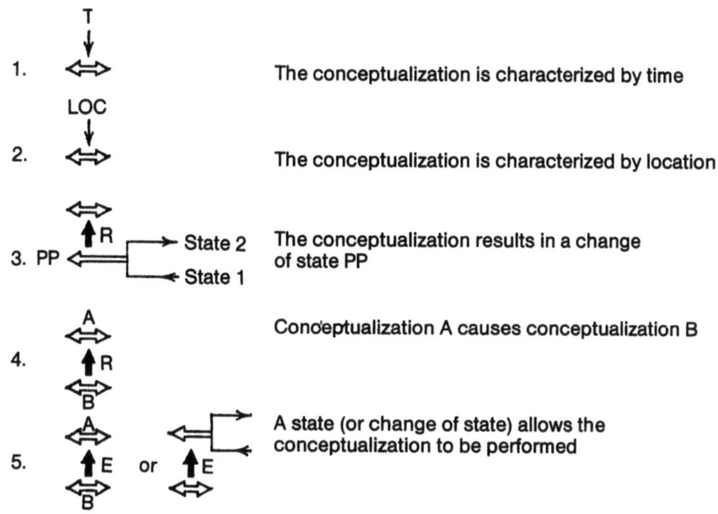

Fig. 1.2. Lines of the second and third kinds used in the CD model

event (action) *A* with another event (action) *B*, *B* being the cause of *A*. This type of relation is called a *reason causation*.

The line *r* (see Fig. 1.2, 3) is attached to a state *A*, *or change of state (from* A_1 to A_2), which is the result of an event (action) *B*. This type of relation is called a *result causation*.

A line of type *E* (see Fig. 1.2, 5) is attached to an event (action) *B* resulting in a new state which is the precondition for another event (action) *A* to be performed. This type of relation is called a *possibility causation*.

The ways in which vertices and lines may be connected are governed by conceptual syntactic rules. The number of these rules varies in different versions of the model, ranging from 15 to 20. Several modifiers are used in the CD model to characterize conceptualizations: *p* – past, *f* – future, *nil* – present / – negation, *ts* – start of a transition, *tf* – finish of a transition, *c* – conditional action, *k* – continuous action, *?* – interrogation, ∞ – timelessness.

All possible actions are expressed in terms of so-called *primitive actions*. Themselves finite in number, these primitive actions are capable of expressing the tremendous variety of actions in the surrounding world described in NL in a virtually infinite number of ways. Only 11 primitive actions are used in the CD model. A conceptual action is defined as something that can be done by an actor and an object. An animate being usually plays the role of actor. Two categories of action are distinguished here: physical actions (actions upon physical objects) and mental actions (manipulating ideas, etc.).

The theory of the CD model does not stipulate that there should be precisely 11 primitive actions – it merely states that there are approximately 20 of them, not several thousand or tens of thousands, as is the case with the number of actions in the surrounding world. Let us examine these primitive actions. Five of them describe physical actions performed by human beings:

PROPEL, MOVE, INGEST, EXPEL, GRASP

Certain limitations are imposed on the kind of object which can participate in a given action. These limitations constitute the so-called conceptual semantics of an action. The real meaning of each action is taken to be the set of inferences which may be true when a given action is performed.

The above-mentioned conceptual syntactic rules, together with the conceptual semantics of an action, are used to determine which PP or classes of PP can participate in given actions.

PROPEL means "to apply force to". Cases *O* and *D* (see Fig. 1.1) apply to this action. The object concerned should be a physical one. The CD model checks whether the force exerted on the object corresponds to its size and weight, i.e., whether the force involved is sufficient to move the object. Case *D* indicates the direction of the force. In contrast to the other actions, the actor of PROPEL may also be an inanimate object (e.g., a machine).

MOVE means "to move a part of the body". Case *O* connects this action with a part of the body. Case *D* indicates the direction of the movement of the part of the body concerned.

INGEST means "to introduce something into an animate object" (an actor). The object which is introduced should be smaller than the actor. If it is bigger, there is an automatic inference that before it was "ingested" it was divided into parts. Case *D* indicates the direction from the location of the object to the body of the actor.

EXPEL means "to discharge something from an animate object" (e.g., air). The object which is expelled should previously have been introduced (INGESTED). The direction of case *D* ist the opposite of its direction in INGEST.

GRASP means "to fix a part of the body on a physical object". The object should be of appropriate size. Case *D* indicates the part of the body used by the person "grasping".

The CD model is designed to describe a model of thinking. Hence, it is used to model the way in which reality is perceived by human beings rather than to arrive at absolute truth. In particular, Schank notes that people tend to focus their attention on the results of an action instead of the action itself. This is reflected in the introduction of two other primitive actions which reflect a change of state.

PTRANS means "to change the location of something". This action may be applied to any physical object. It governs cases *O*, *D*, and *I*. Case *D* indicates the initial and final locations of the object involved. Case *I* is very important to PTRANS, as it determines the actual action performed.

ATRANS means "to change an abstract relation". This action involves a combination of a physical object and the abstract relation between it and another object. Case *R* indicates the animate object who plays the role of recipient.

Two actions – SPEAK and ATTEND – function as instruments of some other action (usually MTRANS). *SPEAK* means "to utter a sound". Some type of sound is the object here. The direction of the sound is always indicated by case *D*, showing the direction from the source of the sound. *ATTEND* means "to direct one's attention or sensation to a stimulus". A sensory organ is the object here (the nose, eyes, ears, tactile organs). Case *D* indicates the stimulus. This action is never used autonomously and usually needs MTRANS as an instrument.

Two mental actions are used in the model: MTRANS and MBUILD. In order to describe these actions the following preliminary definitions are introduced. Human memory is taken to consist of three parts: a conceptual processor (CP), an auxiliary memory (AM), and a long-term memory (LM). The CP is used in any process of thinking. It is assumed that at any particular moment the CP is processing only one symbol. The AM stores all symbols used in the current thinking process. The LM stores all information known by the actor performing the thinking process. It is assumed that only true facts are stored in the LM. The model does not use the notion of short-term memory (used in psychology), as man is not conscious of this.

MTRANS means "to transmit information". The object of this action is a conceptualization. In case *R*, part of the head of a given person (*A*) – such as the LM – may function as the recipient, while a sensory organ or part of the head of person *A* or of some other person may function as the initiator of the action. This action is a constituent part of every language form which expresses mental acts.

MBUILD means "to create (build) or combine thoughts". A conceptualization is the object of this action, which creates a new conceptualization. Case *R* is always directed to the LM.

The CD model concentrates on representing actions (the procedure which we have just described) rather than representing states. The authors of the model are aware of this problem. States are represented by means of a relative scale of discrete integers. For instance, the following scale is used to describe a state of health: −10 (dead); −9 (seriously ill); −8 – −3 (ill); −2 (feeling bad); 0 (normal health); +7 (feeling very well); +10 (in perfect health). The model includes states of health, of fear, of irritation, of hunger, mental states, physical states, etc. Some states are measured with the help of an absolute – rather than a relative – gradation. These include, for example, length, color, intensity of light, mass, or velocity. Some states are not measured by numbers at all. They express relations between objects (proximity, inclusion, possession, etc.). The values assigned to states are used to compare the characterizations of objects. Figure 1.3 shows graphical representation of the following sentences:

1. John has killed Mary.
2. John has gone to New York.
3. John has strangled Mary.
4. John read about Nixon in an encyclopedia.

The CD model pays great attention to reasoning (inference). As we have already noted, the real meaning of an action is the set of all inferences which can be made in connection with it. Inference is one of the basic methods of eliminating inexplicitness. The authors of the CD model are aware that people usually extract much more meaning from a text than is explicitly contained in it. This is possible due to knowledge of the surrounding world and an ability to reproduce, by inference, what was missing in the input text. Inference is considered to be the logical processing of the semantic representation of a text – i.e., of the representation obtained at the stage of analysis. The authors of the CD model distinguish between inference and logical reasoning (in the strict, mathematical sense of the term). The chief differences between these two are as follows:

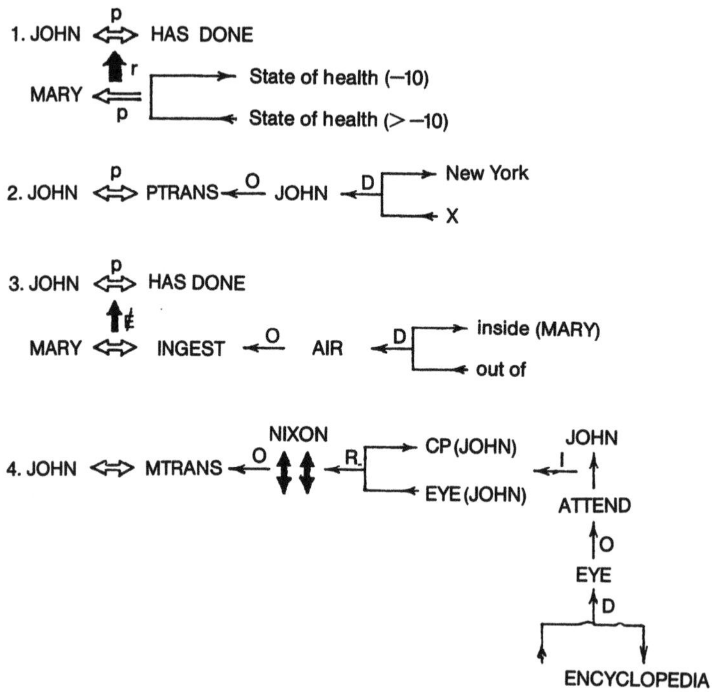

Fig. 1.3. The conceptualization network of four sentences (see text)

1. Inference is performed "spontaneously", independently of external factors, while reasoning usually depends on external factors.
2. Contrary to reasoning, inference need not always be logically correct (from the mathematical standpoint); i.e., an inference may be false even if the original premise was true.
3. Logical reasoning usually has precisely specified objectives, while inference is performed haphazardly.
4. The source of a particular true fact is not important in reasoning (as all facts may be derived from axioms). In inference, on the other hand, it is important to know how the given facts have been obtained, since this determines their credibility.

Inferences are primarily based on knowledge of the surrounding world. Rieger divides inferences into 16 different classes (Schank 1975a, Chap. 5). It is assumed that all 16 classes are applicable to every input sentence. Let us take a look at some of these classes.

1. Resultative inferences: determining (on the basis of knowledge of the world) the most probable consequence of an action or state mentioned in the input text
2. Motivational inferences: determining the reasons for an actor performing an action specified in the input text

3. Function inferences: determining the most probable use made of a given object, given its particular properties
4. Missing enablement inferences: determining which state has to be changed for an actor to be able to do what he wants to
5. Intervention inferences: determining what an actor can do to prevent an undesired state from occurring
6. Action-prediction inferences: determining the action which the actor will most probably undertake, given his needs and wishes
7. Normative inferences: determining entities which usually exist in the world, even if this fact has not been stated explicitly
8. State-duration inferences: determining the duration of an action or state mentioned in the input text
9. Enablement-prediction inferences: determining what can be said about an entity in advance, given the known set of facts concerning it
10. Situation inferences: determining information which may be characteristic for the situation mentioned in the text

Inferences are drawn on the basis of facts from the surrounding world and of a set of axioms concerning human behavior. Each fact is characterized by the following parameters: credibility, degree of truth/falsehood, source (the information used to obtain the fact), descendants (which facts can be derived from the given fact), the time the fact was received, and the time the system was brought to bear on the fact. In more recent works, the model's authors note that some attempts have been made to use scripts to establish cause-and-effect relationships between the sentences of an input text (Schank 1975b; Wilensky 1977).

Summarizing, we can say that the chief semantic methods utilized in the CD model are as follows:

1. Knowledge about the language (stored in a lexicon) and knowledge about the surrounding world (stored in a semantic memory) – expressed in terms of semantic atoms and scripts (Schank 1975b). To this author's knowledge, semantic memory is absent in practical applications of the CD model, the only exception being the SAM system (Schank 1975b), which contains certain rudimentary knowledge about the world.
2. A detailed classification of English words
3. A set of rules which make it possible to draw inferences concerning an input text (on the basis of knowledge possessed by the model)

The following factors seem to be the principal deficiencies of the CD model:

1. All phenomena are considered at one level of detail (the "primitive" level). This makes it impossible to describe complex events in terms of simpler "subevents" (which is necessary for concise representation and successful implementation of highly abstract tasks). It is also impossible to break down primitive actions (atoms) into smaller parts. Systems of real-life complexity should be able to vary the level of detail according to the particular task to be performed.
2. The CD model is a model of a language, not of conversation. Consequently, linguistic devices and devices for describing the surrounding environment are

imprecisely differentiated. It does not specify what information about the surrounding world is necessary, nor how this is related to the language (see Sect. 1.3.1).
3. The CD model, being a model of a language, does not make provision for a model of the user. This results in an excess of possibilities during the process of inference. A model of the user would make it possible to determine the user's aims and intentions in the dialogue and, consequently, give direction to the process of inference (see Sect. 1.3.4).
4. Sense is treated solely as a concept (see Sect. 1.2.7).

1.2.6 The PST Model (Zholkovsky 1974)

The PST model has been described in full detail in the Soviet literature. It is the most detailed model of the Russian language developed by Soviet linguists and is designed for use by computer (although this has not yet been accomplished). Its origins lie in the work of A.K. Zholkovsky, N.N. Leonteva, and Y.S. Martemyanow (Zholkovsky et al. 1961). The main ideas involved in this model are as follows: Synonymy of language expressions need not be a result of lexical synonyms – it may also stem from other properties of the language (syntactic variants of an expression, lexically dependent variants, the different "points of view" of different participants in a situation, etc.). The authors of the model developed a language (a "language of semantic factors", see Sect. 1.2.2) especially designed to describe the "essence" of words and the semantic similarities of lexically different words. The essential features of this language (as compared with other contemporary approaches) are the following: (a) a sense is built of "atoms"; (b) a meaning is highly structuralized rather than represented by a set of semantic factors; (c) there are certain rules of transformation (though these are rather elementary).

All this enables us to obtain the same representation of synonymic sentences in a natural language, even if these sentences look quite different. Moreover, this is the first work to deal with the problem of dictionaries and filters (for analysis and synthesis) as necessary components of the model which carries out the transformation TEXT ⇔ SENSE.

Continuing our presentation of the PST model, it should first be stressed that it has been designed to effect the transformation SENSE ⇔ TEXT in both directions. However, it is the direction of synthesis (SENSE → TEXT) that has been developed in most detail. Besides, certain limitations have been imposed on the model, of which the following are the most important for our purposes:

1. Only the linguistic part of the model has been developed in detail, i.e., that part which establishes the relations between senses and texts but does not "process" these relations. The authors describe a calculus, i.e., a set of permissions and prohibitions (what one is or is not allowed to do), not an algorithm, i.e., a set of procedures which would determine what to do and how to do it.
2. Language is modeled as a means of effecting the transformation SENSE → TEXT, disregarding other aspects such as "the model of reality – SENSE", a mechanism for inferring, etc. (see Sects. 1.2.7 and 2.3).

3. The model has been developed to process separate sentences only, not connected texts.

While describing the PST model, we would like to quote a remark made by one of its authors. The point he made was that, due to the tremendous complexity of the problem, a "full" PST model still does not exist. Large gaps remain even in the theory of the model, not to mention its practical application. Nevertheless, while many important questions are still to be answered, the PST model as it stands at present includes all the essential components and the necessary relations between them; i.e., "a consistent but far from complete picture is presented: the outlines of all the figures have been sketched out, but still very roughly as yet" (Mel'chuk 1974a, p. 6). We found it necessary to stress this fact, as those who attempt to apply the model in practice (using computers) are forced to fill in the theoretical gaps which exist at present. Doing so involves carefully choosing the limitations which are to be imposed (both on the input language and on the subject matter) and solving certain particular theoretical problems. Since synonymy and homonymy are extremely widespread in natural languages, the PST model effects the transformation from sense to text not in one step but in many. Utterances are considered at the levels of semantics, syntactics, morphology, phonology, and phonetics. The last two levels are mentioned but not described – consequently, we shall not consider them here.

Before describing the model, we have to define what the authors understand by the term "sense". "Sense" is understood as a synonym of "concept" and "intension", as opposed to "denotation" and "extension" (Mel'chuk 1974a, p. 10). The authors write: "Sense, by definition, is the invariant in all synonymous transformations, i.e., what is common to texts of identical meaning" (see Sects. 1.2.7 and 1.3.3).

The *level of semantics*, in the form of the so-called semantic representation (SEMR), describes the contents of an interrelated fragment of a text (i.e., utterance) without dividing it into phrases or words. This representation is understood to be the means whereby a sense is registered. The SEMR consists of two components: a semantic graph and information about the communicative organization of a sense. The *semantic graph* (SG) is a linked, oriented graph. The vertices of the SG are marked with symbols of semes (atoms of sense). Two types of semes are distinguished here: predicates (predicative variables) and the names of objects or classes of objects (object variables). Logical connections and quantifiers are treated as predicates. Lines of the SG express connections between semes-predicates and their arguments (a numbered arrow is directed from the predicate toward the argument).

The information about the communicative organization of the sense includes:

1. The division of the sense into a theme (what is being talked about) and a rheme (what is being said). Accordingly, the SG is divided into two parts, marked "theme" and "rheme" respectively.
2. The definition of what is "new" and what is "old" (known). This is used to establish the linear (one-dimensional) order of a text when a phrase is synthesized from a multidimensional SEMR.
3. The definition of which parts of the sense are more/less important

Let us note here that the problems of communicative organization have not been developed sufficiently by linguistics; consequently, they are not fully clarified in the PST model.

The authors of the model indicate that in moving from sense to text one has to know how to divide an initial SEMR into parts corresponding to the phrases of a language. These parts should then be divided into smaller parts, corresponding to the lexical units of a language. In other words, it is necessary to know how to "summarize" an SEMR in a sensible way, i.e., how to divide (during synthesis of an output text) and unite (during analysis of an input text) semantic representations. The authors themselves are forced to admit that they are not in possession of the technique required for "summarizing". In our opinion, the need for this technique is not quite as obvious as it seems to be for the authors of the PST model (see Sect. 1.2.3, regarding the sense of a sentence not being the "sum" of the senses of its constituent words).

The *level of syntactics* of the PST is split into two sublevels: deep syntax and surface syntax. A *deep syntactic representation* (DSR) consists of the following components:

1. The *deep syntactic structure of a phrase* (DSS). A DSS is a tree of dependences (i.e., a tree of syntactic subordination; cf. Popov and Firdman 1976, p. 319). The vertices of a DSS are the main word forms of a phrase given as abstract or generalized lexemes with certain morphological information (the number of nouns; the tense, aspect, and mood of verbs).
2. Information about the communicative organization of a phrase
3. Information about the prosodic characteristics of a phrase
4. Information about equivalences between objects which appear more than once in a DSS. This flows from the fact that a DSS is represented by a graph of a specific type – a tree graph.
5. Information about groups of words which cannot be expressed by a tree of dependences

The problem of syntactic connections between phrases has not been solved by the authors of the PST model. Hence, they consider internal syntactic connections only within the phrase.

A *surface syntactic representation* (SSR) consists of five components which are analogous to the components of a DSR but are as close to the text phrase as possible. The vertices of the SSR are all the word forms of a phrase (not just the main ones). Each vertex of the SSR is an "incomplete" deep morphological representation of a word form. The lines of the SSR correspond to the surface syntactic relations (SSREL) of a natural language. About fifty SSRELs have been distinguished in the Russian language.

The *level of morphology* has two sublevels: deep morphology and surface morphology. A *deep morphological representation* (DMR) of a phrase consists of:

1. The chain (i.e., the linearly ordered sequence) of the DMRs of all word forms of the phrase
2. Information about the prosodic characteristics of the phrase (intonation, pauses, stress, etc.)

Information about the communicative organization of a phrase and about groups of words is expressed here by the order of the DMRs of word forms, or by prosody; information about equivalences between objects is expressed chiefly by the choice of anaphoric pronouns (inserted in the chain of the DMRs instead of the corresponding word forms). A DMR word form is a lexeme with a set of morphological characteristics which specify this word form.

The *surface morphological representation* (SMR) of a phrase consists of two components which are analogous to the two components of the DMR. An SMR word form is a chain corresponding to the word form and consisting of morphemes, supramorphemes (families of morphologically meaningful prosodic phenomena), and morphological operations analogous to morphemes (ordering, conversion, etc.).

The transition from one level to another is accomplished by means of semantic, syntactic, and morphological components. *Semantic components* (SEC) are described in outline in the PST model. A detailed analysis of these components has still not been achieved. They are usually divided into three stages:

1. An SEMR is divided into parts corresponding to the phrases which are to be constructed with the order of these parts then being determined (this problem remains to be developed).
2. Base deep syntactic structures (base DSSs) are developed for every SEMR in a phrase. The base DSSs should express the synonymy in the DSS which cannot be conveyed by lexical functions (LF) (see Sect. 4.3 for a description of LF). This stage involves the use of rules of the type $X \rightarrow Y$, where X stands for a semantic subgraph of the SEMR of a sentence and Y for a "subtree" of the deep syntactic tree. The authors of the PST model indicate the importance of these rules and give qualitative examples of them. However, they go on to declare that no such rules have yet been established for any language. Moreover, no serious attempt to establish these rules has been undertaken (see critical remarks in Sects. 1.2.7 and 1.3.3).

   In addition to these rules, another mechanism is necessary to distinguish base DSSs – an as yet undiscovered mechanism which would yield information absent in terms of the output language and would marshal and reorganize "superfluous" sense information.
3. All the synonymous DSSs of every base DSS are constructed using the lexical and syntactic rules of paraphrasing. These rules are based on the LFs of words as set out in a phraseological dictionary. All pieces of information about a word in the natural language are important in the PST model. It is assumed that an "ideal" entry in a dictionary should contain all the syntactic, semantic, and stylistic characteristics of the given word; it should also contain all possible modifications of this word and derivations from it. In addition, the words (or combinations of words) which are related by meaning to the given word should be specified: lexical correlates, i.e., "replacing" words which may or should replace the given word in a particular context; "parameter" words, which express certain senses when put together with the given word in the form of idioms.

In the PST model the relations connecting words to their lexical correlates are expressed by LFs (Apresyan 1974). An extremely important point to note here is that work on the PST model has shown that almost all lexical correlations in many – perhaps all – languages can be described using less than one hundred LF parameters.

Thus, at this stage transformations of the phrase (paraphrases) are performed by means of lexical and syntactic rules. The lexical rules set semantic equivalence between formulations of a sense in terms of different LFs. The syntactic rules govern the syntactic transformation of one DSS into another – this transformation is necessary after the lexical rules have been applied (Apresyan 1974, Chap. 7).

In order to accomplish all the necessary transformations at this stage, information from a dictionary is widely used. The pattern for an entry in the dictionary is as follows: (a) headword; (b) information about morphology; (c) interpretation of the word in terms of semes; (d) the model of government (MG) and its necessary preconditions (see Sect. 4.3.3); (e) lexical functions; (f) phraseology, etc.

The syntactic component (SYC) is described in detail in the PST model. This involves translating the DSR of a phrase into its DMR. The translation is accomplished in two steps:

1. All the alternative surface syntactic structures (SSSs) which correspond to a given DSS are established. In order to accomplish this, the following operations have to be performed: The vertices of the DSS – generalized lexemes – are transformed into Russian lexemes with a preliminary morphological characterization. The symbols of the phrase are then replaced by corresponding lexemes (along with the SSRELs between them), while the symbols of LFs are replaced by their value, i.e., by concrete lexemes. The SSRELs between chosen lexemes are established on the basis of semantic relations and certain "deep" words.
2. All the alternative DMRs are determined for each SSS of a phase, as is the prosodic characterization of the phrase. This can be done by performing the following operations: The relationships of agreement and government (syntactic relationships) are established and used to achieve a full morphological characterization of every future word form (i.e., DMR word form). The sequence of words (more precisely – of DMR word forms) in the output phrase is then determined, i.e., a chain of DMR word forms is constructed. Next, certain operations specific to the given language are carried out to simplify this chain (replacement of certain word forms by pronouns, deletion of equivalent terms, etc.). Information about prosodic characterization of a phrase (contained in the DSR) is then added to the chain of DMR word forms.

Morphological components (MC) are used to transform the DMR of a word form into a phonetic transcription of this word form. SMR word forms (roughly speaking – a chain of morphemes) are assigned to each DMR, and then a phonetic transcription is assigned to each SMR.

1.2.7 Critical Remarks on Existing Models of Language

The above analysis of models of a language allows us to draw some instructive conclusions. The history of the work conducted on models of a language demonstrates the indefatigable optimism of researchers who have attempted to describe a language by the simplest means possible. All the models can be classified according to the degree to which semantic methods are utilized:

1. Models of a language without semantics
2. Models in which component analysis is used (the sense of a word is represented by an unstructuralized set of "atoms" of sense)
3. Models in which the above-mentioned sets of "atoms" are structuralized
4. Models evolved from those of item 3 by adding the calculus of semantically invariant transformations
5. Models of a language in which not only the semantics of a sentence but also the semantic structure of the connected text is taken into account (work on these models is still at an initial stage)

In spite of the optimism we have referred to, every attempt to construct a functioning system has failed because of the inadequate instruments applied. Probably the most alarming aspect of this is that even now there are numerous groups of programmers continuing the work of these hopeless optimists and engaging in unwarranted simplifications of an NL – some doing so with respect to semantics, others with respect to syntax. Although the highest "level" of analysis has already been reached (from the semantics of a word we have passed on to the semantics of a text) this does not mean the groundless optimism has been abandoned. It can be seen in small "alterations" of the methods used to clarify inexplicitness of sense and to represent a sense.

While specialists in artificial intelligence have made visible shifts in approach here (from semantic networks expressing relationships between words, to frames expressing the relationships in the surrounding world which are reflected in texts), the vast majority of linguists are still trapped in word semantics. They hope that the sense of a text can be expressed by the sense of its constituent words without any reference to various pieces of information about the surrounding world. They base this approach on the definition of linguistics as a branch of science dealing with language; however, linguistics understood in such a limited way cannot solve the problem of comprehension. Linguists not only refrain from using anything other than strictly linguistic instruments when working on problems of sense, but even criticize those who do use them. Schank, for instance, has been criticized by certain authors (Mel'chuk 1974b, p. 44) for his attempts to expose all the inexplicitness of the sense of utterances in his SEMR. The phrase "I like books" is often cited as an example here. In Schank's SEMR this is treated as "I like to read books" (correspondingly, "I like sweets" is treated as "I like to eat sweets"). Linguists are doubtful whether such a "deep" SEMR has a purely linguistic character. However, if they themselves tried to construct systems of "understanding" or "answering questions", Schank's approach would turn out to be the obvious one; moreover, they would probably criticize him for not going far enough in exposing inexplicitness of sense. In our opinion, sense inexplicitness is one of the chief characteristics of an NL, although linguists do not want to recognize this fact (they do not consider exposing inexplicitness of sense essential for performing the tasks of AT). It is true that this inexplicitness cannot be brought to light by linguistic means – but then this is not necessary. In order to expose the inexplicitness of an expression, linguists introduce different senses specific for one word. Hence, it is claimed that "gas" has a different meaning in such expressions as "gas mask", "gas stove", or "gas fitter" (Apresyan 1974, p. 13). In our opinion, the meaning of the word "gas" is in fact the same in each of these examples; the difference lies in what is not explicitly being said: "a mask used to protect the face and lungs against poison gas", "a stove using the energy of a burning gas", "a workman who installs or repairs pipes conveying gas". If one does not feel bound by the principle that linguistic means alone may be used to expose inexplicitness, this can be done on the basis of knowledge about the surrounding world (without artificial extension of the word sense). When this approach is adopted, the proper meaning is chosen automatically (if it is unique to the given situation) without referring to the rules of semantic compatibility suggested by linguists (Apresyan 1974, p. 14). According to these rules, all the meanings of the given word should be examined before selecting the one where the semantic elements are repeated most frequently. Let us note here that overt extralinguistic information about the subject of the text should be stored in the system as well, if not to understand phrases in an NL, then to direct the retrieval of information required by the user. The need for extralinguistic knowledge becomes evident when we analyze a sentence. Nothing but knowledge of the surrounding world can determine which word an adverbial phrase refers to; there are very few linguistic instruments which let us distinguish between adverbial phrases and noun qualifiers [particularly in Slavonic languages; trans. note]. Let us consider two sentences:

1. *O stroitelstve egipetskikh piramid v 3-m–2-m tisachiletii do n.e. napisana kniga.*
2. *O stroitelstve egipetskikh piramid v 1958 godu napisana kniga.*

["A book about the building of the Egyptian pyramids in the years 3000–2000 B.C. has been written" and "A book about the building of the Egyptian pyramids was written in 1958"; in Russian these two sentences may be written with identical syntax and verb forms – as in the quoted examples – the only difference being the precise date itself; trans. note].

We know from extralinguistic knowledge that the adverbial phrase "in the years 3000–2000 B.C." refers to "building" in the first example, while "in 1958" refers to "was written" in the second example. Even if this problem can remain unsolved during automatic translation – which we very much doubt – it certainly has to be solved for systems designed to "understand" or answer questions. Indeed, if in the first sentence the phrase "in the years 3000–2000 B.C." were taken to refer to "has been (was) written", the meaning of the sentence would be drastically garbled, giving us the sensational news that a book was written in 3000 B.C.

Let us take another example: "Which steelworks has ordered machinery for the assembly line in Belgium?" It is not clear here (without extralinguistic knowledge) what is meant by "in Belgium": is this (a) "has ordered in Belgium" (an adverbial phrase) or (b) "the assembly line in Belgium" (a qualifier)? It is obvious that answering the original question is contingent on the choice of variant *a* or *b*. In our opinion, such situations also have to be clarified in AT.

Let us now consider how the notion of "sense" is understood in the existing models of a language (see Sect. 1.3.3). We have already made some remarks on semiotics (see Sect. 1.1.4). In particular, we said that the relationship between an expression (or word, sentence, or text) and its interpretation has a triplex rather than binary character. This is because the very notion of interpretation involves two components: an extensional and an intensional one. In other words, a "sense" (as it is commonly understood) is expressed by a concept *and* (but not *or*) a denotation. In our opinion, neither of these two aspects should be considered more important as far as "question-and-answer" systems are concerned (most authors assign priority to one or the other). They should be treated as one inseparable whole. The reasons for favoring either one are purely subjective, e.g., "concept" is a linguistic notion, while "denotation" is not. The following conclusion is then drawn: since I am a linguist, I shall consider sense to be a concept, ignoring the idea of denotation completely. This approach is typical of all the models mentioned (the CD model is, to some extent, an exception here). The CD model takes one step along the path toward making proper provision for knowledge about the surrounding world. However, this knowledge is linked to words, and does not itself form a model of the surrounding world. In other words, the information needed to understand a sentence (or text) is conveyed by the words of this sentence. This approach is practicable only if our vocabulary and knowledge of the surrounding world are very small – suitable for games rather than serious applications. This is the case, for example, with the MARGE system (Schank 1975a), the vocabulary of which consists of approximately 200 words (stored in an operating memory). Moreover, the system's structure makes it impossible to enlarge this vocabulary without fundamental changes to the system. It seems that Schank's group has not (as yet) set itself the task of linking the vocabulary to a model of the subject matter (of real-life complexity). Hence, in order to construct an adequate model of the process of conversation, sense should be expressed by both linguistic means (concepts) and extralinguistic ones (denotations), together constituting a coherent model of the surrounding world.

Let us now consider the notion of sense in the PST model. As defined by the model's authors, sense is "the invariant in all synonymous transformations, i.e., what is common to texts of identical meaning". The authors note that the notion of identity is not precisely defined in their model; it is assumed to be something that is intuitively obvious. This, however, is precisely why their definition of sense is neither sufficient nor constructive. The authors themselves understand the problem, but maintain that this shortcoming is not of key importance. They write: "In practical terms some difficulties may arise.... texts T_1 und T_2 may seem identical to one speaker but different to another. For our purposes, however, *it is sufficient to restrict ourselves* to considering solely *unquestionably identical texts*, while bearing in mind that identity ought to be understood within some stipulated margin of accuracy. Hence, *we have the right* [my emphasis – E. Popov] to assume that shades of meaning which are too subtle for our purposes can be ignored" (Mel'chuk 1974a, p. 10). As we see, the authors notice the complexity of the notion of "identity", yet maintain that typically – in the vast majority of cases – identity of meaning can be established with no serious difficulties. The above-quoted passage suggests that they recognize only one possible difficulty in establishing identity of meaning, namely, one arising from the subjective peculiarities of particular speakers. However, they believe these peculiarities can be ignored, at least in typical cases. Nevertheless, certain objective difficulties do exist as well, although the authors forget them. We could give the example here of so-called insoluble algorithmic problems (see Plesnevich 1974). However, in case the authors deemed these or of no practical value, we can also mention simpler examples.

1. "Which steelworks has ordered machinery for the assembly line in Belgium?" Let us assume "in Belgium" refers to "has ordered". We can then modify the sentence to read: "Which steelworks has ordered in Belgium machinery for the assembly line?" The two sentences are synonymous. If, however, "in Belgium" were to refer to "the assembly line", the sentence as modified would not be synonymous with the first one. In other words, it is not possible to say which modifications of the given sentence retain an identical meaning and which do not. The identity involved can be established only when the sense of the sentence has been determined (in the PST model, identity of meaning is used to determine sense). Thus, the problem here involves no subjective peculiarities of the speaker or listener.
2. Other authors interpret the identity of two texts a little differently. For Schreider (Schreider 1971) this identity means "being intensionally equal". He writes: "Two values can be regarded as intensionally equal (having the same content) if, regardless of the universe, each of them entails the other". The word "entail" is the most interesting aspect of this definition. Soon after this statement, Schreider explains – or at least the example he gives does – that deciding whether something "entails" or "does not entail" depends on the system of knowledge. He writes: "The two expressions 'elephant' and 'the animal described by Brehm on such-and-such a page' are intensionally equal in the system of knowledge of someone with secondary education. The same expressions, however, are intensionally different in the system of knowledge of a boy who has not read Brehm's books". Thus we can conclude that identity of meaning can be established on the basis of either (a) the equality of the structures which express the meaning of texts, or (b) the equivalence (but not simple identity) of these structures. Let us note that the second case would seem the most interesting and typical, and in fact involves semantics, while the first may be considered rather more a question of syntactic equivalence. Readers should not be surprised by the use of the word "syntactic" here – it is the syntax of semantics which is meant. The following example should prove useful in clarifying what the equivalence of structures involves. Let us assume a knowledge system possesses the information that (a) "elephants have a trunk and tusks", and (b) "no other creatures have a trunk and tusks" (this information may be stored inexplicitly; i.e., in order to retrieve it one has to review the descriptions of all creatures). Let us now consider the following sentences: "There is an elephant outside the house" and "There is a creature with a trunk

and tusks outside the house". Since each of these sentences entails the other (in the assumed knowledge system) we can say that they are intensionally equivalent. In another knowledge system, however, these sentences need not be intensionally equivalent. A system which possesses information on mammoths, "creatures having a trunk and tusks", may serve as an example. However, if the system additionally "knows" that mammoths are actually extinct (with both original sentences being in the present tense), we again arrive at the conclusion that the two sentences are intensionally equivalent. Finally, if the system knows of creatures called mammoths but does not know of their trunk and tusks, the sentences will again be intensionally equal. Identity of the sense of text does not imply identity of the information conveyed by them. Admittedly, each of the above sentences does have its own peculiarities. In the second sentence, for instance, the author wants to stress the fact that the person speaking does not know the word "elephant", or that it is precisely the trunk and tusks which will play a crucial role in the subsequent development of the story. Consequently, we should pose the question of whether interpreting sense as the invariant in synonymous transformations is justified at all. The point here is that identity of sense (aside from everything said above) depends on the way in which we study sentences – individually or in context. Two sentences may be considered identical in meaning when investigated individually, yet may prove to be different in different contexts. There are many reasons for this – from syntactic to semantic ones (see Zvegintsev 1976). Even putting a sentence into the passive voice may be inadmissible in a discourse. From the point of view of semantics, the two sentences examined above may not be identical in meaning in a discourse, since in the second one the possession of a trunk and tusks is a feature clearly distinguished from all the other features proper to elephants. It is precisely this phenomenon that may sometimes link several separate sentences into one connected text. For example, let us take the following sentences: "There is a creature with a trunk and tusks at the window. Grass is hanging on them". If we replace "a creature with a trunk and tusks" by "an elephant" we arrive at something incoherent: "There is an elephant at the window. Grass is hanging on them".

The authors of the PST model examine intensional identity only, completely forgetting about extensional identity (i.e., identity which can be established on the basis of the identity of denotations). As a matter of fact, extensional identity cannot be studied within the framework of the PST model, as this model includes only concepts (not denotations) in its definition of "sense".

Hence, both extralinguistic knowlege and context may determine whether two sentences are or are not identical in meaning. The authors of the PST model suggest using linguistic methods only, but, as we have seen, these are insufficient in studying the problem of identity of meaning. Thus, the authors have replaced one difficult problem (the definition of sense) by an even more difficult one (the definition of identity of meaning).

To summarize, we would like to point out that, by virtue of the fact that they are models of a language, all the models we have presented in fact deal with "pseudosense" rather than "sense", which is what we should examine in analyzing the process of conversation (i.e., speech). We shall return to this problem in the next section.

1.3 Principles of the Model of Conversation

In the preceding section we considered models of a language used in systems of comprehension. We were in fact forced to concentrate our attention on models of a language, owing to the lack of models of conversation. We would now like to outline such a model of conversation. Of course, this model is still far from complete; nevertheless, it appears to be sufficient to function as an initial approximation and a focus for constructive criticism. The author is himself aware of certain weaknesses in the model, although this does not mean that he knows how to remedy them.

First, we should like to preface our description of the model of conversation with the following remarks. We had intended to develop a full model of the process of conversation; however, as we are well aware, the construction that has been obtained is not uniform, i.e., we have failed to describe all the problems involved with the same degree of detail (as we have already said, work on the model is not yet finished). As a result, the range of problems dealt with in the model of conversation is considerably broader than the range of problems considered in the model of a participant in the conversation which is based on it (see Chaps. 3–7). In turn, the model of a participant in the conversation is broader in scope than the concrete application of the system of conversation (see Chap. 8).

1.3.1 The Model of Conversation

We have already defined (in Sect. 1.1) the process of conversation as a process of mutually imparting information concerning the surrounding world, conducted by two participants (an author and an adressee). The objectives of the conversation should be specified; utterances should be comprehensible to both the participants, who play the role of author and of addressee (recipient) alternately. The process of conversation is performed with ease by most people. But it is still not known what processes occur in the human brain when a person is speaking or engaged in comprehension. In order to construct an electronic system capable of conversing with human beings in an NL we first have to develop a functional model of the process of conversation. Let us note that the functional model M of the process X constitutes an artificially constructed system (perhaps substantially different in nature from X – in our case, this is undoubtedly so) which behaves similarly to X in some respect which we consider important. In our opinion, a model of conversation – as opposed to a model of a language – is essential, since by concentrating on a model of a language we cut ourselves off from a model of the surrounding world, and it is in this world, and only in this world, that speech and comprehension are possible.

A diagram showing a model of conversation is depicted in Fig. 1.4. The model consists of a model of the participants in the conversation, of the surrounding

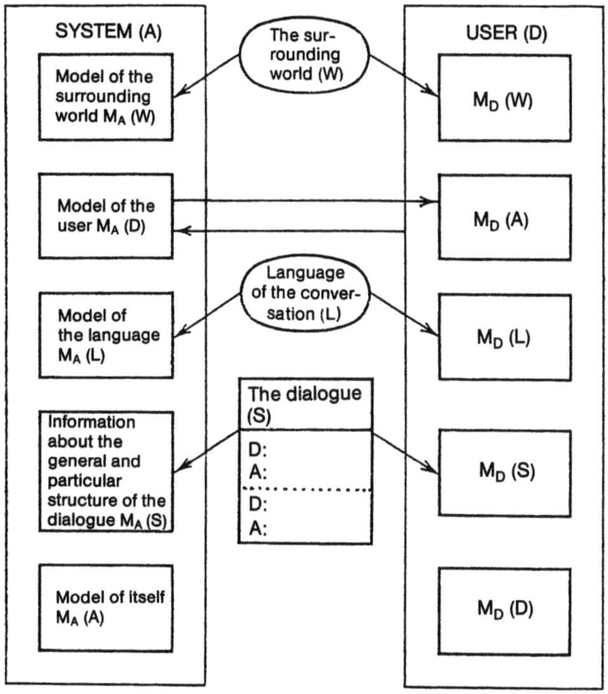

Fig. 1.4. General structure of a process of conversation

world, and of a text produced by the conversation. For the conversation to be possible, both participants should share a common language and knowledge of the surrounding world. In addition, each participant should have some information about his interlocutor. In the first place, this should be information about his partner's objectives (intentions), potential (abilities), system of notions, and structure of knowledge. Even if the knowledge possessed by one participant (*A*) includes all the knowledge possessed by the other (*B*), *A* should still have information about *B*. Indeed, if this were not the case, and *A* were to use concepts incomprehensible to *B*, the conversation would be impossible.

We shall confine our analysis of the process of conversation to dialogue, as this is the most important form of conversation between man and machine. Recent research has shown that the process of conversation between human beings consists not so much of transmitting meanings as of monitoring the other partner's objectives (Levin and Moore 1977; Schank and Abelson 1977). These objectives determine the general structure of the dialogue (its macrostructure) irrespective of the particular task being carried out by the participants in the conversation. On the other hand, it has been observed (Grosz 1976, 1977a, b) that the structure of this task substantially influences the way in which the dialogue is constructed.

This dependency between the structure of a dialogue and the task being carried out (i.e., its subject matter) will be called the *subject structure of a dialogue*. We shall not consider this in the present section, however, since it is determined by the structure of the task itself.

The general structure (macrostructure) of a dialogue depends on several factors: stylistic ones, emotional ones, semantic ones, etc. Many of these can be ignored in dealing with the conversation between man and machine. We shall assume here that the general structure of a dialogue is chiefly a function of the participants' objectives. Dialogue, as a process involving noncontradictory interaction between its participants, is made possible by the compatibility of its participants' objectives. This compatibility is expressed in the following:

1. The compatibility of the objectives is established at the outset, in the invitation to the dialogue and the acceptance of this invitation. Let us note, however, that "invitation" and "acceptance" need not be explicitly expressed in the dialogue.
2. Each participant is aware of the other's objectives and interprets his utterances according to this knowledge.
3. The objectives of the two participants are complementary. This is the case, for instance, in a purchasing dialogue (salesman/customer), a helping dialogue (helper/recipient of help), a supervising dialogue (superior/subordinate), etc.

The pair of objectives which determine the nature of the dialogue may be characterized by certain information common to both participants. This information specifies the following aspects of the conversation: (a) how the dialogue is initiated, conducted, and terminated; (b) what requirements the dialogue imposes on the participants; (c) what information can be conveyed indirectly in a given type of dialogue; (d) under what circumstances the dialogue can be accomplished successfully (i.e., under what circumstances the tasks for which the dialogue was initiated can be considered accomplished) and how this will be expressed in the participants' behavior.

This information about the dialogue allows us to cast light on several known linguistic phenomena:

1. The beginning and end of a subject under discussion are recognized by people engaged in conversation easily and unhesitatingly. Identification of these moments is hindered by the fact that people often do not give any explicit signal that they are changing or closing the subject. In the approach presented here the beginning and end of a subject under discussion are identified by the appearance of an objective and the achievement of that objective.
2. In the process of understanding connected texts people easily reconstruct information which was not explicitly given in the text. The traditional approach to this problem in SNL (see Schank 1975a) is to reproduce all possible inferences (deductions) which were not given explicitly in the text. This is done for each sentence of a text and its context. An important shortcoming of this approach is that there is no mechanism which makes it possible to guide the process of inferring and to limit the number and depth of the inferences made. In the approach presented here, the participants' objectives perform this limiting function. Comprehension of a text is considered to have been reached when each sentence can be assigned (perhaps with the help of inferring) to one of the objectives the participants aim to achieve.
3. The process of conversation is very concise; this is due not so much to the capacity of the constructions possible within an NL as to the prevalence of

indirect means of communication (i.e., reliance on tacit knowledge, see Sect. 1.1.6) including presuppositions, knowledge of preconditions, and indirect locutionary acts.

Many researchers working in the field of conversation systems do not appear to have understood that information about a dialogue is essential to accomplish a conversation successfully. This, in our opinion, is one of the main causes of the difficulties encountered in constructing a system of conversation between man and machine. We can distinguish three stages in any dialogue (although these are not always explicit): the setting of objectives, the attempt to attain these objectives, and the final stage of achieving (or abandoning) the objectives. The process of setting objectives can, in turn, be divided into the invitation to the dialogue and the acceptance (or refusal) of this invitation. An invitation to a dialogue involves identifying the nature of the dialogue, indicating the interests of the person issuing the invitation, specifying the participants, and defining the subject matter. An invitation to a conversation between human beings can be expressed in various ways – it may take a very short and inexplicit form. Accepting an invitation usually involves expressing thanks for the invitation, acknowledging the nature and subject matter of the dialogue, and agreeing to take part in the dialogue (i.e., to pursue the specified objectives). Acceptance may be expressed inexplicitly, for example, simply by starting to attempt to attain the given objectives. Instead of accepting an invitation, a person may refuse it, start to negotiate, or ignore it.

We shall distinguish here between several types of dialogue, according to the participants' objectives (e.g., a helping dialogue, a purchasing dialogue). The nature of a dialogue involves features characteristic not just of this one particular dialogue, but of a whole set of similar dialogues. A helping dialogue, for instance, characterizes all possible forms of this kind of dialogue, no matter who is participating and what his tasks in any particular case are. Three factors will be used here to characterize the nature of a dialogue: a set of parameters, a description of these parameters, and the structure of the dialogue. The set of parameters conveys information which specifies what aspects of a given type of dialogue may be varied. For the purpose of present applications, it seems sufficient to characterize any dialogue by three parameters: two of them (called "roles") correspond to the participants, while the third refers to the subject matter of the dialogue. The description of the parameters is an essential factor, in that it allows us to distinguish one kind of dialogue from all the other kinds. The description consists of a set of statements about the parameters. First of all, these statements express the participants' objectives and the states which should be observed during the process of conducting a dialogue of a given kind. These statements allow us to recognize an invitation to a dialogue, to determine the reaction to this invitation, to attain the objectives, and to terminate the dialogue of the given kind (all this is despite the fact that a considerable amount of information is not explicitly given in an NL). The descriptions of the parameters characterize those aspects of the dialogue which remain invariant during the whole dialogue of a given kind. Those aspects of the dialogue which systematically vary are represented in the structure of this dialogue. The structure of this dialogue takes the form of the set of the participants' subobjectives, which are partially ordered in time. Let us clarify what we have said about the factors of a dialogue with the help of a concrete example. The dialogue we shall consider is a helping dialogue (HD). (NB. The information in parentheses constitutes additional commentary for further clarification).

HELPING DIALOGUE

I. Parameters: RH (the recipient of help), GH (the giver of help), P (the problem to be overcome)

II. Description of the parameters
1. RH wants to overcome P.
2. RH wants to be able to overcome P.
3. RH is not able to overcome P.
4. RH is free to overcome P.
5. RH is a human being.

(This description both imposes certain limitations on the person who is to play the role of RH and determines what RH will be dealing with in the HD. The statements which make up the description make it possible to determine the participants' functions without any explicit reference to a particular dialogue.)

6. GH wants to help RH to overcome P.
7. GH is able to give help.
8. GH is a human being.

(The descriptions of the parameters are known to both the participants in the dialogue. RH, for instance, knows that – in order to take part in the HD – GH should want to give help. This information allows RH not to request help of someone who is known not to want to give help.)

III. The structure of the helping dialogue

(The structure consists of three components; two of them make up the stage of "diagnosis", and the third constitutes the stage of "solution". At the "diagnosis" stage, RH communicates: (a) what he has done and (b) what unusual event(s) have occurred. At the "solution" stage, GH wants to inform RH about what actions should be undertaken to solve the problem.)

1. RH wants GH to know about the actions RH has actually taken to overcome P.
2. RH wants GH to know about (a) all the unexpected events which have happened, or (b) all the expected events which have not in fact happened.
3. GH wants RH to know about which actions – relating to overcoming P – will make it possible to avoid undesired events and to induce the desired ones.

The information about a dialogue given above is geared toward the case of a dialogue between human beings. SNLs possess much less knowledge than a human being, and their ability to infer is incomparably smaller. Consequently,

SNLs need much more detailed information. Let us note here that fundamental difficulties arise if any inconsistency is encountered during the processing of an input question. Since the abilities of all existing systems are still very limited, it is not possible to teach a system to understand and answer all questions put to it by the user. Therefore, the problem to be tackled here is how – with the help of the system – to teach a user who is unfamiliar with programming what the system is able to do.

1.3.2 Knowledge Possessed by a Participant in the Conversation

The structure of the knowledge possessed by a participant in the conversation is depicted in Fig. 1.4 – this is the knowledge possessed by a participant A (denoted by M_A) concerning: the structure of the dialogue $M_A(S)$, the surrounding world $M_A(W)$, language $M_A(L)$, participant $D - M_A(D)$, and A himself $M_A(A)$. There is no doubt that $M_A(L)$ and $M_A(W)$ are absolutely necessary. However, it is by no means obvious what their contents should be. The knowledge of the presented model $M_A(L)$ resembles the knowledge about a language in the PST model (see Sect. 1.2.6) and will be described later on (Sects. 4.2, 4.3 – declarative knowledge; Sects. 5.2, 5.3, 7.3, 7.4 – procedural knowledge). There is, however, one difference here – we have included knowledge about the structure of a dialogue in the knowledge about a language (see Sects. 1.3.1 and 6.1). The structure, composition, and representation of knowledge $M_A(W)$ will be considered in Chaps. 3 and 6. A's knowledge about himself and about the other participants in the conversation – $M_A(A)$ and $M_A(D)$ – will be described in Chap. 2 (procedural knowledge) and in Sects. 4.4 and 4.5 (declarative knowledge). To all practical purposes these types of knowledge have been ignored both in existing models and in systems of conversation. We shall explain exactly why they are necessary in Sect. 2.4.1.

1.3.3 Sense and Pseudosense

In Sect. 1.1.2 we concluded that a sentence – the minimum and essential unit of a conversation – is characterized by completeness of sense and situational attachment (which establishes the relationship between the sentence and speech) and by grammatical form, i.e., conformance to the norms of the abstract language system adopted (which establishes the relationship between the sentence and language). Strictly speaking, not all language constructions normally regarded as sentences correspond to the above definition. Any sequence of unconnected sentences may serve as an example. Obviously, such a sequence of sentences does not meet the requirements we have imposed on any act of speech; it does not convey any thought – thought being always concrete and situational.

Alternatively, we can consider two categories of sentences: the sentence as a unit of speech (with situational attachment) and as a unit of language (without situational attachment). In line with Zvegintsev (1976), we shall call the first category "sentences", and the second "pseudosentences". Until fairly recently, linguistics was restricted to the study of pseudosentences. Let us note that both the sentence and pseudosentence convey a certain sense – in the case of the sentence, however, this sense is attached to a concrete situation; in the case of the pseudosentence it is not. We can therefore say that a pseudosentence has an abstract sense (pseudosense), i.e., a sense generated by language, while the sense of a sentence is concrete, generated by speech. Thus, in our opinion, the sense of a sentence constitutes an expression of the situation it refers to, while the senses (or meanings) of the words which make up the sentence are the product of a fragmentation of the sentence sense. The sense (or interpretation) assigned to a word in linguistics is in fact its pseudosense, determined on the basis of the most common usages of the given word in sentences. Remembering pseudosenses (this applies to both man and system) is in our opinion a matter of rather secondary importance – it simply contributes to economy of intellectual effort during the process of conversation, but does not perform any essential function in creating the sentence sense. We are aware that this opinion will be equivalent to high treason to most linguists (the sole exception known to us in this respect is Zvegintsev – see Zvegintsev 1976). This is because they see no difference between sense and pseudosense, assuming that the sense of a sentence is the sum of the senses of the words which make up that sentence. They view words as receptacles containing various meanings – the proper meaning is chosen according to the context. However, we have arrived at the conviction that the commonly accepted meaning of a word is nothing more than the meaning most frequently assigned to this word in the process of sentence sense fragmentation. As a matter of fact, the set of such meanings is infinite (and indescribable in advance); it is determined by the set of sentences (texts) in which the given word can be used.

At this point we would like to quote a passage from Zvegintsev (1976, p. 86) – a passage where the author criticizes the approach to word sense most widespread among linguists:

> ... words are quite groundlessly considered to have an independent relationship with the surrounding world, from which world they directly receive their meanings, which are then transposed from the words themselves – as if from the centers of the language – in all directions: down into morphemes and up into sentences. In this way, sentence sense is composed of word senses.... The level of words, like every transitional level, is on the one hand the result of the fragmentation of units of a higher level, while on the other hand itself consisting of divisible units. And just as morphemes get their meanings from above – from words, so words themselves get their meanings from above – from word phrases, and finally, from sentences. All this, of course – to digress for a moment – does not deprive a word of its "subject references" or negate the relationship involving referents and denotations.... The difference is that these relations are realized indirectly, via sentences.

We would just like to add here that the idea of building up from word senses to form the senses of lexical units of a higher level (e.g., word phrases, sentences, the discourse) is completely untenable, for the simple reason that it makes no provision for the tacit knowledge assumed in any NL (see Sect. 1.1.6), i.e., skipping words (or word phrases, or sentences) which convey part of the essential sense of a text in an NL. The following discourse, consisting of two sentences, will make this clearer. Let us consider one sentence B in two contexts, determined by the sentences A_1 and A_2.

1. Context A_1: Something was dripping from the carburetor.
   B: Mikhail crawled under the truck.
2. Context A_2: Because of the sun, the heat in the cab was unbearable.
   B: Mikhail crawled under the truck.

It is not clear how a single sentence *B* can convey different information in two different discourses, given that the words of the sentence do not change, if we assume that the sense of a discourse is constructed from sentence senses. We believe the only solution here is to consider a model of the world and the objectives of the conversation. We are convinced that one has to accept the idea that the sense of a discourse and of a sentence can be obtained on the basis of semantic and pragmatic interpretation, and that word senses are a product of the fragmentation of sentence sense.

The fallacy of the common approach to the problem of sense seems so obvious that it is hardly believable that this approach remains so popular. It is totally unclear what rules can be applied in order to build up a sentence sense out of word senses. One might expect that the lack of any progress in this direction would lead researchers to the conclusion that this particular approach is false and should be abandoned. Most linguists, however, still maintain that such rules are necessary and important (Mel'chuk 1974a, p. 70). However, even if such rules were found (and their number would certainly not be in single figures) there would still be a problem as to which particular rule should be chosen in a given case, and it is impossible to answer this question on the basis of word sense only. One has to realize here that the whole (i.e., the sentence or discourse) is not simply the sum of its constituent parts (words).

The following line of reasoning indirectly proves that it is impossible to obtain the sense of a sentence (far less that of a discourse) from its constituent words. It is a well-known fact that translators are incapable of producing a good-quality translation if the text in question concerns a branch of science they are not familiar with. This holds true even if they know the language very well and have been taught all the relevant terminology, i.e., the pseudosenses of words characteristic of the particular branch of science involved. The translation will be a poor one because of the translator's lack of extralinguistic knowledge. If a translator is not able to translate a text correctly (i.e., to assign the appropriate meanings to sentences), although he knows the pseudosenses of all the words, then a computer will not be able to either – such an assumption seems to be quite reasonable. Let us note here that the reverse situation can also occur: people knowing a language poorly can translate texts correctly if these texts concern subjects they are familiar with (i.e., subjects whose models are known to them).

Everything we have said about word sense leads us to the conclusion that the sense of a word (but not its definition) is assigned to this word dynamically in the process of interpreting a sentence; it is not something static, i.e., known in advance. It should be stressed that the above statements do not contradict the notion of defining a word's sense. We are simply claiming that the full definition of a given word should not be included in the sense of the given text in which this happens to occur. To use the language of semiotics, the same can be said in the following way: If we consider the sense of a sign as that which corresponds to this sign in this or that context, we are forced to interpret this sign dynamically (according to the context) not only in terms of its denotation, which is commonly accepted, but also in terms of our concept of it. In other words, a concept is not inherent in a given sign; it depends on the context in which the sign is used. The concept corresponding to the sign *ab* is not a simple combination of the concepts *a* and *b*.

Most linguists treat senses statically (i.e., as pseudosenses). It is this approach that leads them to believe in the existence of a unique level of concretization of sense. The notion of "atoms" of sense has its origins in this belief (Mel'chuk 1974a; Schank 1975b). Every sense is supposed to be expressible in terms of these indivisible "atoms" of sense. In our opinion, however, it is not possible to distinguish one unique level of detail in expressing senses. This level of detail is determined by the objectives and tasks of a man or of a system. Only after referring to these concrete objectives and tasks can we say whether a given level of detail is or is not sufficient. For instance: Is it necessary to include the full SEMR of the word "table" into the SEMR of the sentence "Nikolai barred the door with the table"? In this context it seems to be sufficient to represent the word "table" in the SEMR by something like "a hard, physical object (made of wood)". As we see, therefore, the full meaning of a word should not be included in the sentence SEMR – this is what we call dependence of a sign's concept upon context.

This approach which involves representing a sense by atoms of sense is very attractive and does not seem open to question. It does, however, have its shortcomings. True, in representing a sense by sense "atoms" one aims at expressing sense in the most explicit way possible, which, in turn, makes it possible to compare utterances and look for synonymy (or the lack of it). It is presumed to be beyond all doubt that the resultant semantic representation will be more convenient for performing transformations into different equivalent forms (at least incomparably more convenient than a natural language). Can we say, however, that this objective is in fact achieved? Some opponents of this approach claim – with good reason, in our opinion – that the representation thus obtained is actually far from convenient. Bobrow, for instance, not without a certain irony, gives the following description of the internal representation in the CD model of the sentence "John killed her for some reason": "John thought about something which caused him to do something which caused the woman to change her state into a state of the extreme deterioration of her health". It would certainly be difficult to expect that this representation could help the system to solve the initial problem. What, then, is the solution to this problem? One should look for the sense of utterances in a purposeful way. In other words, this process cannot be reduced, as it is at present, to inserting word meanings (expressed by sense atoms) into the sentence meaning. It cannot be formalized. The whole point is, once again, that the meanings of the words which constitute an utterance should not be drawn from a dictionary (their language sense), but ought to be formed in the process of uncovering the sense of the whole utterance (the locutionary sense); i.e. the meaning of a constituent word can be obtained by dissecting the sense of the utterance.

1.3.4 Pragmatics and Objective

Pragmatics is defined as the branch of semiotics that deals with the relation between a sign system and its user (the interpreter or addressee). We pointed out in Sect. 1.1.4 that no perceptible progress has been achieved in this field. Nevertheless, we believe elements of pragmatics are very important in the process of conversation and must be taken into account. There is as yet no unanimity on the tasks of pragmatics and the relation between these and those of semantics. Both fields deal with the problem of sense; pragmatics, however, includes the notion of the user (or addressee). Let us examine one of the most oft-quoted definitions of pragmatics, one that establishes the relation between semantics and pragmatics (Ingerman 1966, p. 9): "*Pragmatics* is the relation between a symbol and its user. (An object must have at least one meaning attributed to it before it becomes pragmatically significant.) A *rule of pragmatics* is one which selects from among the set of meanings *attributed to a symbol* [my emphasis; E. Popov] that particular meaning which is significant to a particular user at a particular time." Ingerman then goes on to define the notion of pragmatic ambiguity of the first and second kind.

A *pragmatic ambiguity of the first kind* exists when at the time the single meaning of a symbol or an accretion is required, there is no way of determining that single meaning. A *pragmatic ambiguity of the second kind* arises when in the course of determining the single meaning of a symbol or an accretion (at some specific time), the criteria by which the single meaning is being selected from among the set of possible meanings are such that there are no meanings which satisfy the criteria.

In speaking about the process of conversation we have already indicated that utterances should be intelligible to their addressee. From the standpoint of pragmatics we can say that the utterances of both partners should be pragmatically unambiguous.

One might ask here why semantics cannot perform the tasks assigned to pragmatics. The only answer that can be given to this question is simply that pragmatics takes into account the particular addressee, while semantics does not. In other words, semantics is objective, while pragmatics is subjective. There is nothing wrong with this. We shall only add that in order to use semantics in the process of interpretation we would have to have an objective model of the surrounding world (i.e., an objective universe and an objective knowledge system). In theoretical terms, this objective model is difficult to construct, but in practical terms we can content ourselves with the argument that human beings, when talking among themselves, obviously use some form of generalized representation of the world which is common to most of them and in this strictly practical sense – objective. One more point from the quoted definition of pragmatics remains rather obscure: "A *rule of pragmatics* is one which selects from among the set of meanings attributed to a symbol that particular meaning which is significant...." First, as we have already noted (see Sect. 1.3.3), meanings cannot be assigned to a symbol in advance (not to mention a sentence, i.e., an accretion); they are assigned to it at the stage of semantic analysis. Secondly, is it necessary (or even possible) to assign a given symbol (e.g., a sentence) all its possible meanings, and then go on to choose only one of them? Let us consider the following imperative sentence: "Go to Wierzbicki's for dinner." Readers might try to mention all possible interpretations of this sentence permissible from the standpoint of semantics. It is doubtful, however, whether any reader would arrive at the same interpretation as the one given to this sentence by the Polish general staff in 1939. During the retreat of the Polish army, a certain formation received the uncoded instructions: "Go to Wierzbicki's for dinner." The authors of this message had not used these words in their usual meaning. They presumed, however, that the addressee would understand the text correctly.Thus, in sending this message they had consciously taken into account the question of pragmatics. To the German general staff, the information conveyed no more meaning than it does to readers now; to Polish officers, however, it had a precise secret meaning. Wierzbicki was the owner of a well-known restaurant in a certain Polish town. Thus, the message indicated the place where the formation was to re-group.

We have used this example to show that it is in practice impossible to list all the possible meanings which can be assigned to a text (or sentence or word) by different addressees. Consequently, it would be reasonable to assume that the task of pragmatics should not be to select the one meaning which interests the addressee from all the possible meanings which can be found by means of semantics. The task of pragmatics is to direct – with the help of pragmatic knowledge – the process of interpretation so as to obtain the appropriate semantic meaning. One of the most important elements of pragmatic knowledge is the objectives (communicative tasks) of the participants in the conversation. Thanks to these objectives it is not necessary to deduce all the possible presuppositions which fit the given context. Let us consider the following example: "We are going to the concert tonight." Leaving aside the communicative tasks, we could list a tremendous number of presuppositions which correspond to this sentence: the listener knows what concert is meant, the speaker is able to move, he possesses the money and time, the weather is good enough, the speaker will be busy tonight, etc. Both participants in the conversation would soon get bogged down in this plethora of presuppositions if they did not take their communicative tasks into account. If it is known, however, that the above sentence has come in reply to the question "Are you busy this evening?" all the presuppositions except the final one turn out to be irrelevant to the communicative task (which in this case is to learn if the speaker is busy tonight). The communicative task also influences the structure of the utterance; i.e., the utterance conveys only that information which is needed to answer the question. Thus, in this example, the speaker does not mention the irrelevant details of his plans; he does not say, for instance: "This evening we shall take the no. 17 trolley bus to the stop beside the House of Culture, and then we continue on foot to the Bolshoi Theater; thus, we shall be busy this evening".

It should be observed here in passing that it is precisely the absence of the concept of objectives in the CD model that leads Rieger to suggest using "spontaneous" deductions – i.e., all the conclusions drawn from each sentence – to establish the sense interrelation between sentences (Schank 1975a). On the basis of the example quoted above it becomes evident that this would lead to an enormous number of deductions, confusing the system totally.

In closing this chapter let us say a few words about terminology. The term "understanding" is commonly taken to mean understanding by somebody, whereas "sense" is considered to be something which is objective. Therefore, it is pointless to say that a certain language construction, say *B*, does not represent the sense of the utterance *A* correctly; one can merely say that the information about *A* conveyed by *B* is incomprehensible to the participant in the conversation, *C*. Furthermore, the more intelligent *C* is, the more concise his thoughts are, in both their external and internal representations. He will seldom need more detailed explanations – except, perhaps, in the case of some evident misunderstanding. The limits of conciseness may perhaps be determined by objectives, not by senses. Indeed, the objective of the conversation may be expressed with the use of a different number of sentences and different semantic constructions, with remote and even dubious arguments being used, as often happens during a conversation between human beings. We can therefore introduce the following definitions:

1. A machine *has found the sense of a text* if it has accomplished a semantic interpretation of it (at the intensional level). If no concept at all has been found, we can speak of *an absence of sense in the utterance.*
2. A machine *has understood the sense of an utterance* if it has established its relation to the objective of the conversation. If this is not the case, we can speak of the *noncomprehension of the utterance.*
3. A machine *has found a piece of information* if it has assigned a denotation (or a set of denotations) to a concept (with the use of pragmatic knowledge). If no denotation has been found, the machine informs us of the *absence of information concerning the requested parameter*. Let us note that information may not be found although it is stored in the machine. This may happen for at least two reasons:
   a) The pragmatic knowledge necessary to direct the search for the information is lacking (or insufficient), and there is not enough time to review all of the information stored (this is equivalent to the phenomenon whereby a human being "forgets").
   b) The information has been requested in a form different from the one in which it is stored, and the machine has not managed to establish an equivalence between these two forms (this situation is also characteristic for human beings as well as computers).

Finally, we should note that the term "understanding" is a manysided one, and it is advisable to consider the depth of understanding achieved by a conversation system (see Sect. 2.2).

2 Principles of Construction and General Organization of the Model of a Participant in the Conversation

2.1 Initial Premises for Designing the Model of a Participant in the Conversation

The exceptional complexity of the problem of talking in a natural language means that it is not currently possible to construct a programmable system which would ensure full partnership in the dialogue with man. Indeed, the process of talking in an NL is very complicated and many-sided. At the very least it includes the following tasks: "understanding" and synthesis of texts, the automatic search for a solution, the recognition and synthesis of speech, and the representation and accumulation of information. From the nature of things, most problems of artificial intelligence (AI) have their counterparts in problems involving talking in NL. This fact has led many specialists in AI to maintain that AI is equivalent to talking in an NL with the machine (Schank et al. 1977).

In the preceding section we considered the model which takes into account such components of the process of conversation as participants, surroundings, language, and the structure of the dialogue. In this section, on the basis of the model of conversation already presented, we shall determine the composition and structure of a functioning model of a participant in the conversation (MPC), which will later be taken as a foundation for constructing the system of conversation. The knowledge necessary for the MPC to function properly will be presented in Chaps. 3 and 4 and algorithms of the functioning of the MPC in Chaps. 5, 6, and 7. Since the MPC is treated as a functioning model, we sometimes identify it with the computer realization of this model in the form of a base system which perceives a natural language (SNL). The term SNL denotes not a specific system but a base system designed to generate different specific systems of conversation from its modules.

2.1.1 Principles of Designing the Model of a Participant in the Conversation

Owing to the complexity of the question, the preparation of the model of a participant in the conversation should, in our opinion, be based on principles of versatility, "ability to accumulate", an interdisciplinary character, and experimental modeling (Popov 1979). Versatility is understood to be the following:

1. Versatility in choosing the way of representing the model's knowledege (information software). This obviates the need to change the model's mathematical

software during the development of the model when the class of phenomena represented in the model's knowledge is expanded.
2. Versatility of algorithms and programs (mathematical software). This makes it possible to expand the model's functions not by redesigning, but by setting the program.
3. Independence of mathematical software (MS) and information software (IS), which can be achieved by representing IS in the form of data (not programs). This makes it possible to enlarge and modify the description of the model of the surrounding world without changing the MS.

The principle of the "ability to accumulate" allows the process of construction of the SNL to be divided into several stages. The system should be designed in the form of modules; such a form ensures the possibility of changing the sequence of calls of different blocks of the system, the number of blocks, and their functions, without changing the whole SNL. The essence of the "ability to accumulate" is to construct more and more complicated versions of the SNL (keeping the former abilities) by successively removing the limitations imposed upon the process of conversation.

The principle of an "interdisciplinary character" means the necessity of close and permanent contact between specialists in various fields (especially linguists, programmers, philosophers, psychologists, and specialists in those fields the SNL is constructed for). The collective effort of philosophers, linguists, and psychologists is necessary to encompass all aspects of talking with the machine. The cooperation of programmers, linguists, and specialists in specific fields is necessary to examine what abilities the SNL needs (this is dictated by practice), to determine the permissible limitations of methods of conversation, and to specify stages of work. At present, instead of this close cooperation, there is a widespread tendency to divide the problem of conversation into two parts, one studied by linguists and the other studied by programmers. Unfortunately, this tendency has been generally, though tacitly, accepted. The reason for this is purely subjective: a reluctance "to interfere in somebody else's job". Those adhering to this tendency often do not justify their statements, merely citing other authors who have supposedly already done so. This tendency often manifests itself in attempts to prove that linguists should deal with calculations made on the basis of a set of permissions and prohibitions (what one may/must not do) and not (together with programmers) with algorithms, i.e., sets of prescriptions (what one should do). In other words, it is claimed that the aim of linguistics is to collect information about the language, not describe the mechanisms which apply this information in practice (Mel'chuk 1974a, p. 20). Our disagreement with this point of view is based on the fact that making calculations (in the above sense), not algorithms, is of very little help, if any, in constructing algorithms and programs. In fact, only algorithms can be carried out by computers, and the transformation of calculations into algorithms without the help of linguists is either impossible or, if it is possible, results in algorithms which in practical terms cannot be carried out in a reasonable period of time. In other words, this makes the problem of constructing the working MPC unsolvable.

The principle of experimental modeling requires us to study (with the help of modeling) the user's demands on the SNL. In the initial stage, experimental modeling can be performed without an SNL, or with an SNL of very limited abilities. In the extreme case (without an SNL) one performs the experimental modeling as follows: potential users, sitting at the console of a computer, ask the hypothetical SNL questions. These questions are answered by a consultant familiar with the field under consideration. Strictly speaking, it is better if the users posing questions do not know how the answer is obtained. Otherwise they may lose interest in the experiment. If any version of an SNL exists, the consultant answers the questions only if the SNL is unable to do so. Such modeling makes it possible to collect information on vocabulary, data of interest to the users, and functions that the users would like to have at their disposal, as well as to make a statistical assessment of the number of the SNL's failures and the reasons for them. It should be noted that during such an experiment one can also model the permissibility of different limitations on the process of conversation with the machine. For example, in this way it is possible to demonstrate the false character of any hopes that a user will know the structure of data or that a system will understand questions expressed by isolated sentences. Unfortunately, there are at present virtually no works which thoroughly study the user's demands on an SNL. There is nothing to refer to except Malthotra (1975). Yet such studies could help to determine the succession of operations aimed at constructing an SNL (at the stage of accumulation of its abilities); they would also make effective conversation possible even at the initial stages, despite the many limitations. It is due to the lack of such research that imposed limitations turn out to be incorrect only after the SNL has been constructed, i.e., when it is too late to make any major corrections. Unfortunately, it is quite usual for no efforts at all to be made to solve this problem; limitations chosen at random are taken. For example, the author knows of several groups (working without linguists) which are trying to construct an SNL on the basis of semantics only, paying no attention to the syntax and morphology of the Russian language. It thus turns out that the absurdity of such attempts, which is obvious to linguists, is just not grasped by programmers.

2.1.2 An Analysis of the Requirements to Be Met by the Model of a Participant in the Conversation

The requirements to be met by the MPC (=SNL) are determined on the one hand by the user's demands on the process of conversation and his or her specific limitations as a human being, and on the other by the current state of development of science and technology. As far as the SNL is concerned, science and technology are still not sufficiently developed to make it possible to construct a system which would realize the process of conversation in all its diversity. In our opinion, it is still impossible to ensure the following:

1. Conversation with a computer in an NL without any limitations on the permitted style of the language (see Maslov 1975, p. 20). One may distinguish many styles in, for example, the Russian language (colloquial, formal, journalistic, scientific, poetical, ceremonial). Of these diverse styles, the formal and

the scientific are the most suitable for an SNL as they are the most exact and formalized; making computers understand colloquial or poetical styles is not, in our opinion, a matter for the near future. It should also be made clear that the above styles refer to so-called literary language only, not to dialects, idiom, or slang (Maslov 1975, p. 10).
2. Constructing an SNL with complete knowledge in even one specific field, not to speak of many, i.e., knowledge greater in all aspects than that of any given user
3. Building an SNL capable of processing all input texts (i.e., 100% of cases) – even granted the limitations of points 1 and 2 above. The SNL's shortcomings in this regard can be the result of many factors, e.g., user's errors, ambiguity of input, the SNL's limited abilities concerning the complexity of inferring, its capacity to perceive the "connected texts", etc.
4. Constructing an SNL whose ability to infer would be comparable with that of human beings
5. Automatic insertion of IS into the SNL (information about the language, surroundings, participants, and their capabilities – all this in a form acceptable for SNL programs)

The following remarks should be made about the specific limitations of users:

1. It is impossible for the user's work to be free of error.
2. It is impossible to remember the vocabulary and structure of information stored in the system. For example, if the SNL stores information about tens or hundreds of thousands of parameters (this number would be typical for any real problem) the user cannot remember the names of all parameters, their retention periods (3 months, 1 month, 10 days, 1 day), the units of measurement (tons, kilograms, cans). Our experience in working on an SNL shows that not only the user but also the designer begins to feel lost when the number of parameters exceeds 200 (to say nothing of tens or hundreds of thousands).
3. The user does not know all the details of the SNL's functioning and its ability to infer; therefore, he or she cannot understand and analyze the reasons for the SNL's failures. For example, if an SNL answers that "the input question cannot be processed because of its unprojectableness", this will not be understood by the majority of users; they will not be able to change the question in such a way as would enable the SNL to process it.

These limitations, specific to the user and the present state of science and technology, lead to the conclusion that an SNL should be required to meet the following demands:

1. The system should carry out the process of conversation not in the form of separate, independent sentences, but in the form of a connected dialogue; only if this is the case can the aim of the conversation be attained despite the user's errors and the limited possibilities of the system (see also Sect. 2.2.5).
2. The SNL's knowledge is not complete and the user cannot remember what information is or is not in the system; therefore, it is necessary for the SNL to be able to inform the user about its knowledge, i.e., it should have a metaknowledge (see Sect. 2.2.2). At the same time, it ought to be able to work

either by automatically referring to its own knowledge or in accordance with the user's questions (the user's aim is to discover how the question should be changed).

3. The user does not know the knowledge of the system, in particular its "points of discontinuity" (see Sect. 2.4.1); therefore, the SNL ought to be able to warn the user, without waiting for any request on his part, that his question is getting close to the "point of discontinuity" (knowledge about the user is necessary for the SNL to recognize such points). Since the user may not know the moment when the system's knowledge is changed (changes may have been made by someone other than the person asking the questions) it is also necessary for the SNL to give information, without prior request, about critical deviations of those parameters most important for the user.
4. Information about a given object (event) has to be stored in different forms, with different degrees of detail to meet the different requirements of different users; for this reason, the SNL has to take the model of the user into account.
5. Since it is impossible to construct an SNL capable of giving a satisfactory answer to every question it is necessary that the SNL (a) inform the user about the reasons for its failures in a language which is understood by the user; (b) give hints to the user on how to change his input sentence so as to remove the causes of the failures; (c) be able to adopt the point of view imposed upon it by the user even if it cannot understand this point of view.
6. Since the SNL's abilities to infer are limited and are not known in detail to the user, the SNL has to be able to explain (on request) the logic of its inferences.

2.2 Problems Connected with the Model of a Participant in the Conversation

This section will be devoted to considering the essential problems which arise when one attempts to design a system which can understand a natural language. It must be stressed that no generally accepted view on the basic problems of an SNL exists. The list of these problems is not something subjective, but depends substantially on the requirements imposed on the SNL by the user (see Sect. 2.1). We believe that prior to designing the MPC (or conversation system) the following questions have to be answered:

1. *Knowledge Representation*. What internal representation of knowledge is used? (a) *Range of knowledge*. What knowledge (information) can or cannot be represented? (b) *Completeness of properties*. Are the properties of objects represented explicitly or inexplicitly? (c) *Basic notions*. Are there any basic notions (atoms)? If so, what are they? (d) *Variety of representations*. Is it possible to represent a fact by different methods and in different forms?
2. *Feasibility*. Is the system designed to work under real conditions? (a) *Knowledge input*. Is the system capable of receiving a large amount of initial knowledge (as is required in practice) and making operational modifications to this knowledge during exploitation? (b) *Metaknowledge*. Can the system work with a user who does not know all the details of the structure and contents of its

knowledge (as is always the case with large systems)? Can the system inform the user about its own knowledge? (c) *Errors*. How does the system behave when input information is processed incorrectly (owing to the user's mistake or limitations on knowledge and/or capabilities)?

3. *Actions*. How does the system modify its knowledge and actions? What actions are permissible? How are these represented in the system? (a) *Modifications and concordance*. How does the knowledge change when an action is performed? How can the concordance of changes in the surrounding world with changes in the system's knowledge be ensured? (b) *The problem of limits (the frame problem)*. How does the system determine the future consequences of an action currently being performed? (c) *Planning and realization*. How are the hypothetical (planned) and actual (realizable or currently realized) sequences of actions represented by the system?
4. *Projection*. How is an input task projected onto the system's knowledge? (a) *Assimilation*. How does the system transform an input task into part of the existing internal structure of its knowledge? (b) *Accommodation*. How can the system's internal structure be accommodated to an input task?
5. *Control*. How does the system organize itself to carry out an input task? (a) *Auto-control*. How does the system organize its modules and resources to carry out an input task? (b) *Self-knowledge*. What does the system know about its current state and about its own knowledge? How does it obtain this information? (c) *Accumulation of successes*. What does the system do when it does not know how to carry out an input task?
6. *Organization of Knowledge and Access to It*. How can the system determine which information is relevant at a given moment? (a) *Interrelation*. How are the elements of knowledge interrelated? (b) *Mechanism of access*. What is the mechanism for selecting the proper information? (c) *Matching*. How can different data structures be matched in order to establish their similarity or equivalence?
7. *Reasoning*. How can the system obtain facts without the use of information from the surrounding world?
8. *Depth of Understanding*. How does the information used (chosen) by the system depend on the class of tasks to be performed?
9. *Effectiveness*. What safeguards ensure the effective representation of knowledge and the effective solution of problems?

Let us now examine the above problems.

2.2.1 Problems of Knowledge Representation

Several problems concerning representation arise in designing a conversation system.

Representation of the Range of Knowledge. The essence of this problem consists in expressing a given range of knowledge in the chosen representation and determining those aspects of the range of knowledge which cannot be represented. Here one has to establish how objects and relationships from the real world are represented in the system in terms of units of representation and of relationship.

Let us note that the particular choice of how a given world is represented produces a division of relationships into those which are "remembered" explicitly and those which are not. If, for instance, the representation takes the form of black and white spots, then relationships such as "to be to the right/left of" can be expressed only inexplicitly, i.e., obtained by means of a process of inferring. If, however, the representation takes the form of a semantic network, these relationships can be expressed explicitly.

The Basic Notions. It has virtually been accepted by everyone that knowledge should be expressed in terms of indivisible units of sense (also called "atoms" or "primitives") (Apresyan 1974; Schank 1972; Wilks 1972). There is, however, no general agreement on what can actually play the role of an atom and what the number of these atoms is. Some authors believe these atoms can be "canonical words" (Fillmore 1968), while others claim that one should use the atoms of sense from which words are built (Schank 1972). It should be stressed that this approach does not correspond to reality. In actual fact, scientific progress involves the introduction of new basic notions; these are often produced by breaking down notions which were considered indivisible before. Thus, the system should not use any fixed basic notions – these should vary during the system's work; what was an atom yesterday may today have an internal structure. It is evident that a description of complex objects and events cannot be given in terms of a single set of atoms. In other words, complex notions may be described, but only if they are considered from several different points of view. In order to describe the engine of a car, for instance, one usually considers its mechanical and electrical arrangements separately (see Sect. 1.3.3).

Knowledge, as we know, can be represented in the form of atoms, which are more elementary than words; such a form makes inference easier. It should be borne in mind, however, that the smaller the atoms are, the longer the representation of a piece of information will be, and the more difficult it will then be to find a correspondence between this information and internal knowledge. Thus, the division into atoms makes it easier to infer but complicates the process of projecting input information onto an internal representation.

The Completeness of Properties. A representation is complete with respect to property A, if the fact that any object possesses property A is represented explicitly in the system. The completeness of properties simplifies processing substantially, since the lack of an explicit representation of a property guarantees that this property is absent altogether. In a dynamic world, however, it is extremely difficult to ensure the completeness of properties (see Sect. 2.2.3 on the frame problem). In addition, this would require great numerical effort from the system.

Variety. It is a well-known fact that the method and form in which a task is represented largely determine how difficult it is to perform the task (see Amarel 1968). A variety of forms and methods of representations allows the system to combine the advantages of each particular form. By the *method of representation* of a fact A we mean that internal language of the system which fact A is expressed in. By the *form of representation* of a fact A we mean the statement (expressed in any internal language) which corresponds to that fact. Thus, for instance, the fact "object *X* is in place *Y*" may be represented by different methods (e.g., with the use of predicate calculus or in the language PLANNER) and in different forms (in the form of coordinates of the place *Y* or by indicating the position of *X* with respect to a known object). Three problems, at least, must be considered if one wants to use different representations: the choice of representations, the compatibility of representations, and the transformation of one representation into another.

The Choice of Representations. As we have already said, a system may use various representations. Given this, any particular fact may be represented using different methods and forms. Consequently, the system should be provided with a mechanism which enables it to choose the proper form of representation for any particular fact. Let us take the following example: object *A* is in place *B*. This fact may be expressed by giving the absolute coordinates of *B* and *A*, by identifying the location of *A* with the location of another known object *C*, by specifying the relative coordinates of *A* with respect to *D*, etc. Moreover, this fact may be represented using various methods. Usually the choice of form is the key problem, as the method of representation is most often either fixed for the whole system or determined by the type of input information; e.g., there is one method of representing the system's vocabulary and another of representing information about the surrounding world. The method(s) by which the system's knowledge is represented must be considered very carefully.

The Compatibility of Representations. A diversity of representations means that a piece of information can be remembered by the machine in different forms. Let one of these forms change, and one has to check whether the others remain compatible with it. Let us assume, for instance, that the system knows that the relation between two objects (*A* and *B*) is "*A* is to the left of *B*". Fresh information about the movement of *A* is constantly being received by the system (in terms of coordinates). It is obvious here that the relation previously indicated has to be checked constantly during *A*'s movements. This problem may also be solved in another way. A basic form of representation can be chosen as the only one to change when new information is received. The compatibility between the basic and derivative forms can be restored when the latter forms are called. The use of diverse forms of representation within the one system complicates the problems of modification, of planning, and of concordance (see Sect. 2.2.3).

The Transformation of Representations. As we have observed, the choice of representation (of its form and method) determines the degree of complexity of processing the input information and of the process of modifying knowledge. Thus, there has to be a mechanism which enables one representation to be transformed into another. It may be the case, however, that information included in one representation cannot be translated into another. The coordinates of *A*, for instance, cannot be derived merely from the information that "*A* is to the left of *B*", even if the coordinates of *B* are known. The designer who employs a variety of representations within one system has to consider the problem of the relationship between remembering and calculating, as this problem may prove extremely important for the system's effectiveness.

2.2.2 Feasibility

This aspect characterizes the usefulness of a system in practical applications (i.e., industrial, not experimental ones) when problems of real-life complexity are to be solved. The chief distinguishing features of industrial systems – as opposed to experimental ones – are, in our opinion, the following: the large volume of information software (IS), the fact that the user does not have detailed knowledge of the structure and contents of the IS (because of this large volume), and the inadmissibility of situations where the system fails to process a piece of input information, yet does not explain the reasons for this failure.

The Knowledge Input. The problem of inserting the initial knowledge and of modifying this knowledge is extremely complex and laborious because of the large volume of the IS. We are convinced that no commercial systems can be produced until some effective method of inserting and modifying this knowledge is found. Indeed, developing IS for one particular application is more time consuming than designing the whole system's MS. Moreover, the MS is universal and not dependent to any great degree on the applications intended for the system. Let us note here that the IS (like programs) has to be debugged – this makes the problem of designing and modifying it even more complex. At the same time, this makes it necessary to work in an interpretative regime and introduce an archive facility. This facility remembers which IS has been used in which input texts and how modifications to the IS have influenced the processing of indentical (or similar) texts. Work with the SNL would become a slowly convergent process of modifications if this facility did not exist. For example, let us suppose that an error has been found in the (N + 1)th piece of information. The error must be corrected, and then – assuming there is no archive facility – all N pieces of information have to be checked once more as there is no other way to guarantee their correctness. As the number N increases, so the time necessary to eliminate one error becomes longer and longer. There are also other tasks to be performed by the archive facility. Generally speaking, the number of these tasks should increase as growing experience is accumulated in working with a large-volume IS. The problem of automatic – or at least partly automatic – correction of the IS should be carefully considered.

The Metaknowledge. Work on systems capable of conversing with human beings in a natural language is still at the initial stage, and it is as yet impossible to construct a system possessing full knowledge even in one field. Therefore, the system should be able to inform the user about the extent of its knowledge in the particular field the user is interested in. In order to do this, the system must be provided with metaknowledge; otherwise it would recite all stored information each time the user inquired about its knowledge.

It is the metaknowledge which enables the system to answer questions concerning its own knowledge. This is possible if access to the metaknowledge is direct, i.e., expressed explicitly. The system's metaknowledge should cover three areas: knowledge about the surrounding world, knowledge about the language the conversation is conducted in, and knowledge about the participants in the conversation. Metaknowledge about the language should comprise information about the input/output languages, together with a description of the limitations imposed on these languages and the structure of data. Metaknowledge about the surrounding world has to describe the structure of the subject matter about which information is stored by the system. In order to facilitate mutual understanding between the system and the user, the metaknowledge should also be provided with information concerning subjects related to the one which is known to the system. The following example should make this clear. Let us assume a system stores information about books, and that this information is arranged according to the subjects which the books deal with – the system should know that other arrangements are also possible (e.g., in alphabetical order according to author's names) although these arrangements are not used by this system. If a user were then to inquire about a book by referring to its author, the system would be able to reply that it stored information about books only on the basis of their subjects; the principles of this subject classification should then also be explained to the user. The metaknowledge of the structure of its knowledge can also be helpful to the system while inferring (see Sect. 2.2.7).

Metaknowledge about the participants in the conversation should comprise information about the importance and credibility of this or that fact for each participant. Knowing the importance and credibility of facts, it is easier for the system to discover contradictions within its own knowledge. Of course, more important and more credible facts take priority over those of minor importance and credibility. The importance of facts is also used to guide the system during the process of inferring.

Metaknowledge concerning the system itself is especially important. This comprises, in particular, knowledge about the system's whole potential; this is necessary if the system is to be able to answer user's questions concerning its capabilities and possibilities. The knowledge of the structure of the system is also part of the metaknowledge of this kind. This knowledge includes information about the number and application of its structural parts (modules) and about the interrelation between them. This information may be needed for the user to understand the current state of the system and the reasons for any failures. We shall consider this question in more detail when examining the problem of self-knowledge (Sect. 2.2.5). The metaknowledge the system has about itself is not necessary just for it to be able to answer user's questions concerning the system's knowledge. Knowledge of its potential, for instance, enables the system to make plans. Similarly, if two or more strategies are possible, the metaknowledge has to be used to select the one most suitable for a given task. The system may be provided with several alternative procedures; information about the resources needed by a given procedure and about the methods of assessing the results of this procedure (aprioric or dynamic) also has to be stored by the system.

Errors. The SNLs which currently exist or are being designed are unable to answer all possible input questions. There are several reasons for failures to answer a question: the user has made a syntactic mistake in the NL, the user's question is ambiguous or unprecise, the input information cannot be processed because of the system's limited capabilities, etc. A system intended for practical use should be able to inform the user about the reasons for its failures. It should also help users to modify input texts, using terms they understand. Alternatively, it can ask for information that is lacking. If a system is not able to do all this, the hopeless user will be forced to break off the conversation. It should be noted here that everything we have said assumes the SNL is functioning in a dialogue regime. Of course, there is also one other important source of error: contradictions in the information stored by the system. Referring to metaknowledge, we have already mentioned knowledge about the credibility of facts stored by the system. Such knowledge may be of help in eliminating certain contradictions, although in our opinion it is not sufficient to eliminate all of them.

2.2.3 Actions

This aspect characterizes the way in which the relationship is established between actions in the real world and static structures of knowledge. We should point out that both data and programs belong to static knowledge – carrying out the program (processing), on the other hand, is dynamic.

Modifications and Concordance. The main problem which arises when one tries to represent actions in a system is the following: How should the objective of the changes caused by the action be modeled? Here we shall use the term "operation" for a model of action. An action may be modeled in several ways. We shall present the essence of two basic approaches to this problem with the help of the following example. Let us assume a book is lying on a table at moment T_1. At moment T_2 we start to push the book toward the edge of the table. At moment T_3 the book goes beyond the limits of the table and falls. It is easy to represent the states of the world at moments T_1 and T_2. Indeed, at moment T_1 the world is static. From T_2 to T_i (where $T_i < T_3$), changes of the state of the world can be expressed by changes of two of three coordinates of the book and by the direction of movement (the standard representation of an action involving movement). At moment T_3, however, the standard representation of movement does not provide an adequate reflection of reality. The problem that therefore arises is the following: Should we connect the model of action with all its theoretically possible consequences (checking them during the process of movement)? Or would it be more useful to connect the objects and relationships of the world which is modeled (not actions) to procedures which check the conditions of these objects and relationships? In the above example the object ("a book") would be connected with the standard procedure to check if the object is still supported; if it is not, the fall of the object is then modeled.

The simplest way of representing an action A in the model is to express the differences between the initial and final points of the action. Sometimes, however, intermediate states which appear during the process of an action have to be modeled. This is the case, for example, in situations where an object is moving in an uneven (pitted or bumpy) world, or where there are more than one object.

The essence of the *problem of concordance* is the following: provision has to be made for the fact that a given representation does not adequately reflect actions from the real world in the model world. It may happen that actions which are impossible in reality are quite permissible in terms of a given representation.

If, for instance, the dimensions of objects are disregarded in the representation, then certain movements of these objects will be admissible in the model world but impossible in the real world for geometrical reasons.

The Problem of Limits (the Frame Problem). The essence of this problem is the following (Raphael 1971; Popov and Firdman 1976): How can a system determine which facts should change and which of them should remain unchanged after a certain action has been performed? Reviewing all the stored facts is, of course, unacceptable. The frame problem is not a consequence of selecting this or that particular way of representing knowledge. The problem involves more fundamental questions – it involves the relationships and interdependences existing in a world which is only modeled. It is sometimes falsely held that the frame problem applies to declarative representations only, not to procedural ones. True, this problem can easily be solved as regards what is explicitly indicated in a procedure. There are, however, certain "side effects" specific for the procedural representation, which means that it is impossible for the procedure to contain explicitly full information about its consequences. And if an action is not explicitly indicated in the procedure, the frame problem remains valid. Let us illustrate this with an example. Let the action "a movement of object *X*" be modeled in such a way that the old coordinates of *X* are erased and new coordinates are assigned to it. Such a procedure would not be suitable for modeling the event "The man crossed the river" if the man was holding a suitcase in his hands. Indeed, in such a situation it is necessary to change not only the coordinates of the man but also of the suitcase, and of each object inside it as well. In fact, a general solution to the frame problem cannot exist, as a solution to this problem would entail discovering and adequately representing all the interrelationships which exist within the scope of a particular subject area.

Planning and Realization. In the simplest model of the world, where only its current state is taken into account, time may be represented inexplicitly, in terms of changes in our knowledge about the world. In more complex models several different states of the world may be represented simultaneously (differing as regards the moment of time they correspond to). Such a representation allows a system to remember sequences of events – both actual and hypothetical (i.e., planned). When such sequences of events are represented, it is necessary that proper periods of time be assigned to each event. However, sometimes the moments when an event begins and ends remain unknown. Sandwall (1971) has proposed an alternative approach: recording only the time when changes are encountered. A fact is assumed to be true at a moment T_2 if it was true at an earlier moment T_1, and the system is unable to prove that since then it has become false. This approach obviates the need to repeat fact; however, it involves the effort of checking whether a fact is true.

Planning may be represented in the same way as actual sequences of actions. By the term "planning" we mean the search carried out by the system to find the sequence of actions which would lead to the desired state of the world. During planning changes are not actual, but hypothetical (i.e., they result from a process of modeling).

In a situation where several states of the world are simultaneously represented in a system, it is very advisable to distinguish the knowledge which is common to several states (which may be represented only once) from the knowledge which is specific to each particular state.

2.2.4 Projection

Input information is projected onto the internal representation using the system's knowledge. This knowledge guides and limits the set of all possible interpretations of the input information. Projection will be discussed in detail in Chaps. 5 and 6. The process of projecting may be divided into assimilation and accommodation.

Assimilation. The problem involved here is the following: The diversity (in both number and form) of the structures in the world surrounding us is obvious. This fact is expressed in a natural language. On the other hand, it is commonly accepted (owing to the lack of other constructive approaches) that the number of structures which exist in intellectual systems should be substantially smaller than the number of structures in the surrounding world. Assimilation consists in determining the way in which the diversity of input information should be projected onto the finite number of internal structures. The term "assimilation" is borrowed from psychology and was introduced into the problems of artificial intelligence by Moore and Newell (1973). The meaning conveyed by this term is rather broad. Indeed, analysis of a text, voice, or picture – all this can be considered an example of assimilation. However, the mechanisms of assimilation which have been developed are still rather primitive. Practically speaking, the existing systems do not deal with complex forms of assimilation such as metaphors, analogies, and methods of formalizing an input task (e.g., reducing a task to a known mathematical method).

Accommodation. The notion of assimilation leads in a natural way to the notion of accommodation. Accommodation (Moore and Newell 1973) consists in modifying an internal representation so as to broaden the class of problems which can be solved by the system. Accommodation can be said to involve creating new possibilities during the process of assimilation (which is how it differs from assimilation). However, these two notions are closely related, and there is no sharp dividing line between them.

2.2.5 Control

This aspect concerns the following: how can the system organize itself to be able to solve an input task? Several mechanisms are possible here. The simplest is to call subprograms in a fixed order. However, it is now clear on the basis of earlier systems for understanding dialogue that this approach is far from sufficient. Subsequently, another method of control was introduced. This is based on the existence of a set of procedures called by a selecting procedure, which analyzes the input (the "upward" method). Objectives are then used to structure control over the system – this method may be called the "downward" method.

Auto-Control. Both methods ("upward" and "downward") should be used together to control the system (Popov and Firdman 1976; Sects. 7.4 and 8.1). In Western literature, the "downward" method is sometimes referred to as "goal directed" (Bobrow and Winograd 1977a) or "concept driven" (Bobrow and Norman 1975). The "upward" method is called "data directed" or "data driven". The *integrated method*, combining both, can be applied effectively by means of multiprocessor processing.

Self-Knowledge. In order to talk to a user, the system should be able to formulate its own utterances and those of the user in terms comprehensible to the user. This is particularly important as we know that it is impossible to avoid a certain amount of misunderstanding during conversation. This is often caused by the user's mistakes, but can also be the result of the system's limited capabilities. Our experience with work on the POET system (Popov 1978a, b) leads us to conclude that it is impossible to foresee all possible mistakes and their consequences; therefore, one cannot prepare the system to react properly to these mistakes in advance. The only solution here is for the system itself to be aware of its current state and to be able to express this in terms comprehensible to the user. The difference between self-knowledge and knowledge of the world is an essential one. Knowledge of the world is equivalent to understanding input information expressed in an NL. The processes occurring in the surrounding world are understood due to input information expressed in a fairly explicit form. Self-knowledge has a different nature; information about internal processes within the system is expressed at the lowest level, by sequences of machine instructions. One possible solution to the problem of self-knowledge is for the system to interpret its own work at a level of abstraction determined by the terminology understandable to the user. It should be stressed, however, that the problem of determining the relevant level of abstraction is a very complex one and has yet to be resolved. We, ourselves, are convinced that to solve this problem the user's current objectives have to be known. The following example will help to clarify the problem. What can we say about someone who is sitting and writing something? We can say that: (1) he is moving his fingers; (2a) he is writing; (2b) he is sitting; (2c) he is lost in thought and is doodling; (3) he is preparing an article (a lecture, etc.); (4) he is performing his duties; (5) he exists (is living). By choosing one of these answers we determine the level of abstraction.

It is possible that a solution to the problem of levels of self-knowledge means interpreting the system's work at several levels of abstraction simultaneously. If the system were then to give an answer from an inappropriate level of abstraction, the user could demand an answer from a higher level (by asking "why?") or from a lower level (by asking "how?"). To return to our example, let us assume that the system gave answer no. 3 to the user's question (i.e., "the man is preparing an article"). If the user were now to ask "why?" the system would give answer no. 4. A more complex situation will arise if the user asks "how?". Three answers are now possible, and only one of them can be chosen (let us note here that several interpretations are possible at one and the same level – this all depends on the user's objectives).

As the notions of *self-knowledge* and *metaknowledge* are often confused, let us define them clearly. *Metaknowledge* is the system's knowledge of the knowledge it itself possesses, i.e., knowledge of facts and processes alike. Metaknowledge is static. *Self-knowledge* is the process whereby the system becomes aware of its own current state. Self-knowledge is a process; it is dynamic.

The Accumulation of Successes. In order to make the process of conversation between the user and the system converge, the system should be able to accumulate even partial successes; otherwise, the conversation may never be terminated. The above requirement has several consequences, one of which is the need to retain the context of a dialogue. Since contemporary systems are still inferior in abilities to humans, one cannot expect the system itself to be able to remove all the causes of its failures in processing information. The following approach, therefore, seems to be more realistic. A system need not remove the causes of a failure – it should rather provide guidance to the user to enable him to modify his utterance and thereby avoid failure. In addition, in order to achieve success one has to make provision for a proper regime of the system's work – a regime which would force the system to adhere to the viewpoint imposed by the user. It would probably be advisable to communicate what is to be imposed by the user in a language more limited than an NL. In order to be able to adhere to the user's viewpoint, the system should know at what stages of its work the framework imposed by the user is formed.

2.2.6 The Organization of Knowledge and Access to It

This problem could have been considered as an aspect of assimilation. Owing to its importance, however, we have decided to discuss it separately. Using a piece of information at the proper time can be considered one of the factors which determines the "intelligence" of a system. Systems which are not provided with mechanisms enabling them to determine what is the proper piece of information will of necessity encounter the problem of "combinatorial (exponential) explosion". Indeed, if the data base is large, the number of ways in which the desired information can be sought increases exponentially. The problem of access to knowledge has three main aspects: the interrelatedness of data, the mechanism of access to data, and the way in which data that have been located can be compared. Access can be regarded as the inverse of the process of memorizing data. These two operations specify contradictory requirements of the organization of knowledge. In order to find an object (to gain access to it) one has to know where it is. However, if this object is in a particular place (i.e., is memorized there) a certain amount of effort, or time, must have previously been expended on it. Using a dictionary is a typical example of this. To find words in a dictionary quickly they should be arranged correctly (e.g., in alphabetical order). Any arrangement of words, however, means increasing the time needed to insert (memorize) a new word. On the other hand, if words are not arranged in a definite order, access time increases substantially, while the time needed to insert new words decreases (a new word can then be memorized in any unoccupied memory cell). We shall now examine access only, as this operation is more common – particularly in contemporary conversation systems, where the volume of information received by the system during its work is small.

Interrelatedness. Most researchers reach the conclusion that the system's knowledge should be organized in larger units – larger than the vertices and lines of semantic networks or the formulae of logical calculus. This makes it easier to find the information required. These units have diverse names, such as "units", "chunks", or "clusters". We shall be using the term "units". Two kinds of links connecting elements of data structures can be distinguished: internal ones and external ones. *Internal links* connect the elements in one unit and are used to express the structure of a unit – this structure is important in inferring. *External links* express the diverse connections between the units (knowledge structures) of the model world. Most researchers classify external links only. For our part, we agree with the authors of KRL (Bobrow and Winograd 1977a, b), who claim that retrieval of information is more effective if we introduce a special form of external link – *associative links*, as distinct from *logical links*, which occur in semantic networks and express semantic relationships between elements of knowledge. We, ourselves, are convinced that logical links alone cannot provide an effective solution to both logical problems (inferring) and problems of retrieval.

Structures less refined than formulae (in logics) or vertices and lines (in semantic networks) may be obtained, for instance, by means of analyzing the contexts in which these formulae, vertices, lines, etc. occur. The structures called "frames" (Minsky 1975) and "scripts" (Schank and Abelson 1975) are also widespread (see Sects. 3.3 and 3.5).

The Mechanism of Access. This is one of the essential problems connected with the use of memory. What is involved here is retrieving, in a large data base, units of knowledge suitable for the task on hand. If unit B is stored in a memory area which begins with address A and this address is known to a procedure, we can say that the information contained in unit B is directly accessible without retrieval. If address A is stored in an element of unit B, we can say that A is indicated in B. This is the way in which the links of semantic networks are represented. Generally speaking, explicit representation of the links between units is a characteristic feature of networks. The method of explicit links, however, proves inconvenient in projecting input information onto the internal representation of knowledge. What is needed is a more general mechanism of access than the method of direct access. The task set for this mechanism would be the following: possessing a description of the unit required, it should be able to find all units in the memory which fit this description. Obviously, it is much more convenient to have the memory arranged and structuralized in some way – this speeds up the process of retrieval substantially. The search for the required object can be divided into two stages. In the first stage, preliminary retrieval is carried out on the basis of the above-mentioned associative links. Several units which fulfill the requirements imposed on the required object are chosen as possible candidates. In the second stage, the final choice is made by comparing (*matching* – see Popov and Firdman 1976) the description of the candidates with the description of the required object (or objects). Another important point here is that one usually uses only part of the description at the stage of retrieval – this part is known as the *key*, and only later are the descriptions of the candidates compared with the full description of the required object.

The description of the unit which is to be found is created on the basis of current input information and the context of the dialogue; the context substantially limits the set of possible candidates. Moreover, the role of context may be the primary one, selecting the particular set of objects (A), with the task of the current input sentence being only to distinguish, using laconic descriptions, between elements of the set A. Anaphoric references in natural languages may serve as a typical example of phenomena of this kind. Bobrow and Norma (1975) seem to have been the first to point out that context-dependent descriptions form the basis of the mechanism of access in systems of artificial intelligence. We would stress once again that effective retrieval is possible only if a separate, independent mechanism exists – a mechanism which creates associative (not logical) links between any combinations of units and which retrieves these units by means of associations. In order to design such a mechanism it is necessary to study the strategies which would make it possible to analyze the usefulness of associative links and of retrieval based on them. In attempting to design such a mechanism of access, we encounter several difficulties: What criteria should be chosen to assess the suitability of a given candidate? What should the system do when faced with contradictions? As far as we know, a general solution to these problems has yet to be found. Partial solutions, involving the problem of call by patterns, have been proposed in the CONNIVER system (Sussman and McDermott 1972) and in a paper by Bobrow and Raphael (1974). Let us mention one more example of a partial solution to the above-cited problem – this is the *mechanism of the search for intersection*, often used in semantic networks (Popov and Firdman 1976, Sect. 3.9). In this method, a symbol is defined in terms of the keys of two elements, A and B, (the vertices of a network) which are connected with the required symbol by explicit links. The search is conducted from both vertices simultaneously, and from each of them in all directions. The search ends when two paths intersect each other in a vertex X – one path going from A and of length l_A, and the second path going from B and of length l_B. In general, several intersections may be found in this way. Usually, one chooses the vertex X for which the sum of l_A and l_B is smallest.

Matching. The operation of matching is used not only to select the desired unit from all candidates, but also in classification, confirmation, decomposition, and correction. To understand an unknown input sentence we can compare it with several known patterns. This procedure enables us to *classify* the unknown sentence as that known expression (pattern) which gives the best result in matching. In the process of retrieval, matching plays the role of *confirmation* – it confirms that a particular candidate is the correct one, as against all others. If an unknown structure is compared with a known substructure and the result is positive, then we can say that a partial *decomposition* of the unknown structure has been carried out. Let us note here that the program of syntactic analysis constitutes one example of a program capable of distinguishing the substructures of sentences in grammar. The operation of matching may also be used to make *corrections*. This can be done on the basis of the form of the failure which took place during the operation of matching. There are various forms of matching operations. These include syntactic matching, parametric matching, semantic matching, and compulsory matching.

Syntactic Matching. Here it is the forms (not the contents) of units which are matched. The term "form" is used here in its classic meaning (Church 1956). In order to simplify the process of matching, all forms are stored in the same (canonical) representation (see Popov and Firdman 1976, Sect. 3.8). The matching is considered successful if the forms (also called "patterns") turn out to be identical. Usually, one assumes that a variable of one form may be identical to any constant (or expression) of another form. Sometimes some requirements are imposed on the variables of a form – these determine the type of constants which they can be matched with.

Parametric Matching. The result of syntactic matching has a binary character – either the patterns match each other or they do not. In parametric matching, a parameter is introduced which measures the degree of matching.

Semantic Matching. Here it is the functions of elements, not their forms, which are matched.

Compulsory Matching. In the MERLIN system, Moore and Newell (1973) introduced the notion of *mapping*, which can be regarded as compulsory matching. The essence of this kind of matching is that one structure is considered from the point of view of another. In this case, unlike normal matching, a positive result can, in principle, always be obtained. The question here is how strong the compulsion has to be. The compulsion may be exerted by special procedures connected with the structures. If no matching can be obtained by these procedures, the system reports that success would be possible if such-and-such parts of the structures concerned were to be regarded as matchable.

2.2.7 Reasoning

A system cannot store all facts in an explicit form. This would be not only ineffectual (taking into account storage capacity) but also impossible. The number of possible connections between elements of even an elementary world is infinite. Let us consider, for instance, a world which consists of one equilateral triangle with the sides being 1 cm in length. The number of all possible facts is infinite, even in this primitive world; indeed, the facts could, for instance, include the following: the length of the perimeter of the triangle, the doubled length of the perimeter of the triangle, the tripled length of the perimeter of the triangle, etc.

The term *reasoning (inferring)* will be used here to denote the process of obtaining new facts using rules of reasoning and the facts already stored explicitly in the system (without interaction between the system and the outer world). We shall sometimes use the term "inferring" to emphasize the less formal character of the reasoning. It is possible to distinguish various kinds of reasoning; we shall concentrate our attention on the following three: formal reasoning, specialized reasoning, and metareasoning.

Formal Reasoning. This type of reasoning is used if facts from the modeled world are recorded in a formal language. The portion of the statements which correspond to the input data are considered to be a set of axioms. The object of the exercise is to prove the truth (or falseness) of a theorem on the basis of the axioms and rules of reasoning. There are several logical formalisms designed – in principle – to express statements concerning a broad class of problems. The most widely used is predicate calculus of the first order, with or without equality (Mendelson 1964). For this particular calculus, universal proving procedures have been developed (Chang and Lee 1973; Popov and Firdman 1976). These procedures have the property of completeness; i.e., they always establish the existence of a fact if it can be derived from the axioms. The completeness of the technique of proving theorems and independence from the particular subject (which results from the universality of the rules of reasoning) are the most important advantages of formal reasoning. Yet the very strength of this approach conceals an inner weakness. The universality of the technique of proving theorems does not make it possible to use special knowledge (or does, but only with great effort). For instance, it makes it impossible to classify facts according to the type of reasoning used. The property of completeness is in fact very often useless, as it cannot ensure that the time and memory to be spent on the process of proving will be realistic in terms of contemporary systems. There is one more, very important shortcoming of systems which use the method of formal reasoning, i.e., the fact that such systems can operate only if there are no contradictions between facts (if such contradictions exist, any fact at all can be derived). Human beings, however, are forced to use knowledge (information) which contains contradictions (because of their incomplete information about the world, because of the diversity of points of view on the surrounding world, or to simplify conversation).

Specialized Reasoning. Several systems, in order to obtain specific facts, use specialized rules (or procedures). For instance, let us imagine a world consisting of objects whose location is explicitly given in terms of their coordinates. In this case, a special procedure may use reasoning to arrive at such conclusions as: "*X* is to the left of *Y*". The characteristic features of specialized reasoning, as opposed to formal reasoning, are the following:

1. It is explicitly indicated *which* facts are used and *how* (this is achieved by incorporating these facts in procedures or rules). Consequently, the process of retrieval is practically unnecessary.
2. Effectiveness (lack of retrieval) results in a sort of stiffness, as applicability of the rule is limited. On the other hand, precisely because it is limited, checking the applicability of this rule in various ways is simplified (or even eliminated).
3. Using specialized reasoning in the form of a procedure makes it impossible to obtain any intermediate results or justification for the final result. The final result is taken to be true, without proof. The only guarantee of its truth is the correctness of the procedure. In our opinion, in order to remedy this shortcoming the description of the procedure must be formulated in declarative form at a level of abstraction comprehensible to the system's user (not the designer). Then, if the procedure is carried out in an interpretative regime in the user's terms (i.e., self-knowledge) both the desired information on intermediate re-

sults and a justification of the final result may be obtained. An analogous approach was adopted at MIT (Minsky 1975, p. 273). Yet some problems remain unsolved, such as how one can guarantee the self-knowledge of a system at different levels of abstraction, or how one can switch from one level to another.

Metareasoning. This class of reasoning is particularly important, as such reasoning is widely used by man in his own intellectual activities. The following types of reasoning are usually referred to as metareasoning: inductive reasoning, reasoning by analogy, and reasoning based on the system's knowledge of itself.

Inductive Reasoning. Inductive reasoning uses a set of facts (A) to form the basis for a general rule. This general rule should be consistent with A, but need not be true. It may be rejected after the system has received new information. Using these general rules, information can be represented in a system more compactly. Despite the importance of inductive reasoning, attempts to apply it in systems have so far produced very modest results indeed.

Reasoning by Analogy. The essence of this type of reasoning is as follows: If, according to a certain criterion, two situations are similar, a result concerning the first situation is superimposed on the second. An incomplete form of reasoning by analogy – functional reasoning – has been used in the SCHOLAR system (Collins et al. 1975).

Reasoning Based on the System's Knowledge of Itself. Some questions can be answered without retrieval of a particular fact. Sometimes it is sufficient to know what the system knows (or does not know) in general. The SCHOLAR system uses reasoning of this kind (called "negative" by its authors), which functions as follows: Let us assume that some objects of a given class have the property X. Let us then choose one object from this class. If there is no indication that this particular object does or does not have property X, we say that it most probably does not. Let us use an example to clarify this further. The SCHOLAR system stores information on all the most important economic indices of a number of countries. Let us assume the following question is set: "Is petroleum one of the most important raw materials produced in Chile?" This question will be processed by SCHOLAR in the following way: failing to find information on petroleum production in Chile, and knowing that it knows all this country's important economic indices, it will not give the answer most other systems would, i.e., "I do not know", but will say something like this: "No, most probably petroleum is not one of the most important raw materials produced in Chile".

2.2.8 Depth of Understanding

A strict definition of understanding does not, and probably cannot exist nowadays. Moore and Newell (1973) propose the following definition: *System S understands the knowledge K if S uses K whenever it is relevant*. In this definition, the terms "uses" and "relevant" are not precisely defined; nevertheless, two essential facts are emphasized: understanding refers to knowledge, not to real objects, and understanding is characterized by the use of knowledge. Our definition of understanding (see Sect. 1.3.4) gives a precise meaning for the term relevant used in the above definition. We consider a piece of knowledge, e.g., an input sentence, to be relevant if the system can establish its connection with the objective of the conversation.

Simon (1977) indicates that understanding is substantially dependent on the tasks which are to be carried out by the system: *System S understands the task T if S possesses the knowledge and procedures K which are necessary to perform T.* This definition shows that understanding is a triple relation, connecting *S*, *T*, and *K*, and that both knowledge and tasks may be considered to be the objects of understanding. Moreover, the knowledge needed by a system depends on the abilities of the system. Depth of understanding may be measured by the tasks the system is able to perform. Table 2.1 is a list of tasks and corresponding knowledge. The list is arranged in order of increasing depth of understanding. We do not claim that this list is complete, nor that it is the only one possible (cf. Simon 1977), we only want to emphasize here that the term "understanding" is many sided, a fact that is often forgotten, or not noticed, even by specialists in conversation systems.

Let us now explain the contents of Table 2.1. In the early stages of work on designing conversation systems, only systems of the first type were constructed. Their knowledge concerned chiefly syntax, rarely the semantics of the language of conversation. The task of such systems involved projecting (mapping) input data onto the fixed format of internal knowledge. Systems of the second type use various types of information to obtain an answer. They are based on explicit knowledge and the rules of reasoning. Systems of the third type use intensional (not verbal) understanding. Let us use an example to illustrate the difference. A verbal system, confronted with the expression "its own unit", does not understand anything apart from the fact that "unit" has been labeled as "its own". An

Table 2.1

Knowledge used for understanding	Abilities of the system
1. Syntax and semantics of the particular NL	Retrieval, on request, of a piece of information stored in the system
2. Procedures of reasoning and semantics of the range of subject matter	Answering questions when reasoning or calculations are needed
3. Intensional characteristics of the objects and relationships of the modeled world	Performing actions in the real or modeled world
4. Metaknowledge of the subject matter and of the system	The system is able to explain its abilities and its knowledge of fragments of the subject matter and of the language.
5. A mechanism of "consciousness" based on knowledge of the objectives of actions and of their causes	The system is able to determine the causes and objectives of actions in the surrounding world.
6. Algorithms for solving problems with the use of self-knowledge	The system is able to solve problems, explaining the results and causes of its actions.
7. Generation of new forms of representation of knowledge (accommodation) and use of the new abilities in the process of assimilation	The system is able to understand and to represent new tasks involving various subjects.

intensional system understands the term "one's own" much more deeply. It knows what this term means (knows its definition) and is able to use this information to answer questions like "Has Mikhail a car?" In order to answer this question, the intensional system will check whether it has any information about Mikhail buying a car, being given one, inheriting one, etc. Let us take another example. An intensional system not only knows that a triangle is a geometric figure – it is also able to state whether a figure presented to it is or is not a triangle. We can say that a system of the third type knows the intensional definitions of objects and relationships and uses these definitions both to answer questions concerning the real or modeled surroundings and to manipulate these objects in those surroundings.

Systems of the fourth type have a metaknowledge of the subject matter and of their own abilities. This enables the user to learn from the system what it knows about the particular fragment of knowledge the user is interested in, and in what form (in terms of semantics, not syntax) a particular question concerning a fact taken from this fragment of knowledge should be posed. This ability is absolutely necessary for systems of real-life complexity, which contain hundreds of thousands of facts. Users of such a system are not able to (nor do they need to) know the structure and format of all facts which are stored in the system.

Systems of the fifth type, of a higher level of understanding, use knowledge about the actors' objectives and about the causes and consequences of actions. Such systems are able to give an answer to the question of *why* a certain action has been performed in the surrounding world and *how* a certain objective can be achieved. The LUIGI system (Scragg 1975) is one example of a system of this type.

Systems of the sixth type are capable not only of analyzing actions performed in the surrounding world, but also of observing their own work. Such systems can carry out tasks and then explain how a particular result has been obtained and why the system operated in the particular way it did. In case of a failure, the system indicates the reasons for it and helps the user to modify the input utterance. The MYCIN (Scott et al. 1977) and POET-2 systems (Popov 1978b) can serve as examples of systems provided with abilities corresponding to the fourth, fifth, and sixth types.

Systems of the seventh type are those which are able to create, or to modify, representations and operations to perform new tasks; they can also acquire new abilities to assimilate. These properties enable such systems to work with rich (various) ranges of subject matter. Systems of types one to six are able to acquire new knowledge if, in a given internal representation, understanding of this knowledge is possible. Systems of the seventh type, however, can receive new knowledge even if it requires a change of internal representation. As far as we know, no systems of this type exist so far; even the principles whereby such a system would function have not yet been developed.

2.2.9 Effectiveness

This is a very wide-ranging problem indeed. We shall focus on effectiveness of representation and effectiveness of performance. These questions are connected with many aspects already discussed (range of subject matter, method of access, reasoning, etc.).

At the risk of repeating ourselves, let us enumerate the problems connected with designing a system of AI, which also touch on the problem of effectiveness (in the broad sense of the word). *Effectiveness of representation* may be characterized by the following factors (at least): economy (compactness), ease of modifying knowledge, ease of access to the relevant knowledge, and explicitness, i.e., accommodation, by the AI system itself, of the knowledge representation to be analyzed. Economy of representation is characterized not only by a high level of the internal language and the diversity of its operators, but also by such aspects of this language as its "generative power" and hierarchy. *Generative power* involves the fact that a language is given in the form of a semantic system consisting of the simplest (basic) signs and rules which make it possible to create complex signs from a set of simple ones. This principle flows from the genetic character of the structure of intellectual systems, in which more complex elements are expressed in terms of a set of simple ones. *Hierarchy* denotes the "multi-level" structure of a language, each level of which is characterized by a specific completeness and precision in expressing the sense of signs. This principle flows from the hierarchical structure of intellectual systems. Such a structure is also natural, as different degrees of completeness and precision are needed at different levels of work (in different regimes).

The problems of ease of modifying knowledge and ease of access have already been considered (see Sects. 2.2.2 and 2.2.6). We would just like to supplement what has been said with one remark. To possess ease of modifying knowledge, the system should be expandable; i.e., it should be able to accumulate and change the structure of a language during the process of learning.

Explicitness of Knowledge is one of the most important features of the method of representation adopted. Indeed, this feature enables the system to analyze its knowledge of both the surrounding world (its consciousness) and of the system itself (its self-knowledge, consciousness of self). The fact that a system is "conscious" and "conscious of self" substantially increases the effectiveness of a dialogue between this system and the user; this is because the system is able to inform the user as to the causes of its failures and to help modify input utterances. In our opinion, a dialogue between an AI system and someone who is not a specialist is absolutely impossible if the system has no consciousness and no consciousness of self.

Effectiveness of Performance is the effectiveness of the procedures used by an AI system to perform its tasks (in particular, the time taken to perform these tasks – run time). It should be emphasized that this aspect of effectiveness depends on the use to be made of the AI system; what is considered effective for one purpose may be ineffective for another. The purpose that interests us here is conversing in an NL. The response time of the system should be comparable to the time of the input process in this case. This time is about 30 s, if we disregard first-class typists and take into account only the most common methods of the input process. To close this section, we would like to say a few words about effectiveness of formal and nonformal methods. The formalization of methods leads to the unification of the algorithms used in processing. This, in turn, makes it more difficult to provide for all the specific features of a particular task. Hence, it diminishes the effectiveness of performing this task.

2.3 Existing Systems of Conversation

Everything that has already been said about models of conversation and models of language indicates that there is no single formal apparatus which might guarantee the truth of all propounded ideas, theories, principles, and methods (either this does not exist at all or there are several such apparatuses). This fact, together with the complexity of the problem of conversing in an NL, leads us to the conclusion that only one criterion can be taken: a functioning model of a participant in the conversation, i.e., a construction or a system of programs which would ensure the correctness of the propounded assumptions. In other words, practical application is not the sole purpose of research on systems able to talk with the user; it is also necessary to check the correctness of the chosen methods and the adequacy of the means used in terms of the tasks to be performed. At the experimental stage, the latter purpose is actually more important. For the sake of brevity, systems of this kind (or models) will be called "systems with a natural language" (SNL). We do not intend to present a full review of all existing SNLs here, for two reasons. First, this would not be feasible, given the huge number of such systems. Second, such a review would not be very useful, as most systems differ from one another only with respect to technical details, not the models they are based on. From the multitude of systems which exist, we shall select one representative (is some cases two) of each class of system based on one model. This choice is based on the criterion of the completeness of the system ("completeness" meaning that the system has been developed to the stage of functioning programs, and that all the chief aspects of conversation in an NL have been taken into account). In particular, this means that systems for automatic translation are omitted (Kulagina 1973).

It should be emphasized that our choices and our criticism are not necessarily objective; they are determined largely by our likes and dislikes as well as by our knowledge. This does not mean that we are not ready to defend our point of view. On the contrary, we are convinced we are correct, but we adhere to the good tradition in science which tells us to treat all ideas (our own in particular) with a considerable dose of healthy skepticism. What we need is reasonable discussion, and it was precisely in order to elicit such a discussion that we decided to write this book.

Let us now recall the four models we have mentioned: the preference semantics model (PS; Wilks 1972, 1973), the conceptual dependency model (CD; Schank 1975a, b, c; Schank and Abelson 1975), the SENSE-TEXT model (Zholkovsky 1974), which we have abbreviated as PST, and the concept of semantic roles (SR; Fillmore 1968, 1969, 1970, 1971).

2.3.1 Systems Based on the PS Model

Systems of this class have been developed chiefly by the author of the PS model himself. They include Computable Semantic Derivation (CSD) and Preference Semantic System (PSS; Wilks 1972, 1973). These two systems deal mainly with semantic analysis of English texts. They were developed in the Artificial Intelligence Laboratory of Stanford University. Both are written in LISP 1.5 (McCarthy et al. 1962). They do not presuppose preliminary morphological or syntactic analysis. Semantic analysis is based directly on the input text. Prior to this, the text is fragmented – each fragment corresponds to an elementary utterance. The fragmentation is carried out on the basis of certain dividers (these are usually conjunctions, prepositions, and punctuation marks). In one of his works (1972) Wilks describes the results of a semantic analysis by machine of ten short texts (newspaper texts and texts concerning philosophy). It is particularly noteworthy that Wilks' system can process texts not just individual sentences, like many other systems.

The shortcomings of the CSD system, and of PSS, designed on the basis of the PS model, are as follows:

1. The system is an experimental one. As far as we know it has been used in analyzing only ten texts.
2. The words used in the experiment did not have all the meanings assigned to them in the natural English language. The meanings chosen were selected to suit the given texts. This is a very important aspect of Wilks' approach. A word could match with more patterns if all its senses were taken into account. This could lead to a situation where the given sentence has several different interpretations (including ones that a human being would not consider sensible).
3. Information is represented in the system in such a way that the vocabulary is stored in the operating store. This fact, which is aggravated by the slowness of operations resulting from the use of the language LISP 1.5, makes it impossible to extend the vocabulary to ensure that the system is capable of performing practical tasks.

In terms of problems of conversation, both CSD and PSS can be considered systems capable of understanding only pseudosenses, not senses (see Sect. 1.3.3). This stems from the fact that knowledge of the surrounding world is reduced to knowledge of the language (of the words of this language, in fact), and does not contain information about events taking place in the surrounding world. Not all problems of conversation are taken into account by these systems – the following questions are not dealt with, for example: conducting a connected dialogue (necessary in the event of misunderstandings or mistakes on the part of the system or the user), drawing inferences, reasoning and calculating, or inserting and modifying information software. The above-mentioned features of the CSD and PSS systems can be regarded as shortcomings if we consider these systems representatives of systems designed to converse in an NL. There are no indications in the relevant literature that work on the CSD and PSS systems is being continued by Wilks. Neither is there any information that he is working on a new system. The number of his published works, however, would indicate that the PS model is still being developed (Wilks 1976, 1977a, b). Given the small number of Wilks' collaborators, it is difficult to assume that this group is working on a practical system (as opposed to an experimental one), i.e., a system provided with a large amount of information software (thousands of words, tens and hundreds of thousands of facts) which can work within reasonable limitations of time and space.

2.3.2 Systems Based on the CD Model

Work on systems of this class has a long history. Under Schank's supervision, several systems have been designed: SPINOZA-I, SPINOZA-II (Schank et al. 1970), MARGE (Schank 1975a), SAM (Schank 1975b), and PAM (Wilensky 1977; Lehnert 1977). We shall now consider the MARGE system (Schank 1975a), as this is the most thoroughly documented. MARGE can work in two regimes: a "paraphrasing" regime and an "inferring" regime. In the first regime the systems's task is to construct the conceptual representation (CR) of the input sentence (in English), and then to generate various paraphrases of this sentence (based on the CR and using different words and different combinations of concepts). In the "inferring" regime, the system draws various inferences from the input sentence and then formulates them in English. The program needs approximately 70 000 words in its operating store; it is written in MLISP (Smith 1970) and is used with a PDP-10 computer. MARGE has three main components:

1. Analysis, whereby the conceptual representation of the input sentence (in English) is constructed (Schank 1975a, Chap. 4)
2. Memorization of the CR and drawing inferences on the basis of this CR (Schank 1975a, Chap. 5)
3. Synthesis, whereby the conceptual representation is translated into an English sentence (Schank 1975b, Chap. 6)

The analysis program was designed by C.K. Riesbeck, the memorization and inferring program by C. Rieger, and the synthesis program by N.M. Goldman and C.K. Riesbeck. The synthesis program was designed as an autonomous block (called BABEL; Goldman 1974; Goldman and Riesbeck 1973), which enables it to be used as a constituent part of other systems. The analyzer of the system does not presuppose a separate stage of syntactic analysis. This does not mean, however, that MARGE does not use syntactic information during the process of analysis. The analyzer is built of standard operators of three types:

1. Operators which can process conceptual representations; they construct the CR of a word and insert it into the CR of the phrase
2. Operators which expose syntactic relationships; in particular, they find strong prepositions and the limits of nominal word groups
3. Operators which can refer to the semantic memory (which stores knowledge of the surrounding world); the main function of these is to check if a given object has a given property

The main program scans all meanings of a given word and carries out an analysis based on : (a) "expectations" determined by previous context and (b) the information contained in the dictionary entry on the word. Thus, for instance, the dictionary assigns the following information to the verb "to advise":

1. The conceptual representation of the word
2. An indication to look for the word group "to + infinitive" in the input phrase and then to insert the CR of this group in the proper place of the CR of the word "to advise"
3. An indication that the nearest word on the right which denotes a human being also has to be inserted in the proper place of the CR of the phrase

Hence, all information needed during the process of analysis is given in the dictionary (in the form of instructions accompanying a word).

The component of memorization and drawing inferences works chiefly in the "inferring" regime. In recent versions of the system (Schank 1975c), this block is also used to reveal the connections between the neighboring sentences of an input text. This is carried out by generating inferences which are omitted in the text. The authors are convinced (as are we) that the main task facing the process of "understanding" is to draw information from the system – on the basis of information contained explicitly in an input text – which would make it possible to assign to the sentence in question as much sense as is necessary to link it with the preceding and following sentences. This task is extremely difficult, since people speaking in a natural language express explicitly much less than they understand.

Statements which are not explicitly mentioned in an input text are called "inferences". Using this terminology, we can say that the task facing "understanding" is to draw inferences. The process of "understanding" is based on the system's knowledge only, as this knowledge is the only "source" of inferences. Let us consider an example (given by Schank): "John looked out of the window and saw a huge boulder coming towards him. He grabbed his favorite dog and ran out into the street". In order to understand these sentences, which presents no problem for most people, a system should have approximately the following information: when a big object collides with a small one this usually entails the destruction of the latter; the boulder is an example of the first object and the house an example of the second; objects which are inside an object which is destroyed may also be destroyed; people usually take action to prevent undesirable consequences; damage or loss of their physical substance is considered to be undesirable by people; removing an object from a place which is being destroyed means preventing its destruction. The above-mentioned example demonstrates the crucial role that a block drawing inferences plays in the process of understanding.

The main characteristic of the synthesis program is the fact that it begins its work at the level of conceptual representation, which contains neither English words nor connections between vertices similar to those between English words. Thus, BABEL is one of the "most semantic" of all contemporary systems of synthesis. The most essential component of the system of synthesis is a set of D-rules. These rules take the form of discriminative networks (Feigenbaum 1963). The left-hand part of each D-rule represents a specific condition, while the right-hand part represents the name of an English lexeme. The left-hand part examines whether (a) a conceptual representation contains specific subgraphs (i.e., descriptions of specific actions, objects, etc.); (b) the actions and objects (of item a) possess specific properties which are stored in the system's encyclopedic memory; and (c) the memory of the system includes specific information (obtained, e.g., from context) concerning the actions and objects under consideration.

The left-hand part of a D-rule is an explanation of an English lexeme together with presuppositions, while the right-hand part is the heading of a dictionary entry corresponding to the base of the lexeme, with information about its morphology and its syntactic relationships. Using these rules, the synthesis program builds a syntactic structure from the CR; this structure is then transformed into an English phrase. The latter task is carried out by means of a program designed by Simmons and Slocum (1972). It should be stressed that Schank considers this program insufficiently "semantic", which in his opinion reduces the potential of MARGE. The following examples demonstrate how the MARGE system functions.

The "inferring" regime

Input 1:	John told Mary that Bill wanted a book.
Inference 1.1:	A book on what?
Inference 1.2:	Mary knows that Bill wants a book.
Inference 1.3:	Bill wants to read a book.
Inference 1.4:	Bill wants someone to stop having a book.
Input 2:	John gave Mary an aspirin.
Inference 2.1:	John assumes that Mary wants to have an aspirin.
Inference 2.2:	Mary is sick.
Inference 2.3:	Mary wants to feel better.
Inference 2.4:	Mary wants to take (swallow) an aspirin.

The "paraphrasing" regime

Input 3:	John advised Mary to drink wine.
Paraphrase 3.1:	John told Mary that drinking wine was good for her.
Input 4:	John killed Mary by throttling her.
Paraphrase 4.1:	John strangled Mary.
Paraphrase 4.2:	John throttled Mary and she died because she could not breathe.

The MARGE system was intended to be an experimental tool for examining the CD model. This fact influenced its structure. Algorithms are written in MLISP, which is convenient for such tasks: as a consequence, the vocabulary has to be stored in the operating store only, in order to reduce run time. This, however, limits the maximum capacity of the vocabulary to about 200 words. For the same reason, the model of the surrounding world, although included, is represented by a set of statements which are not interrelated and which do not form a complete model of any subject matter. All the above-mentioned deficiencies lead us to conclude that MARGE cannot serve any practical purposes without drastic changes in its structure (as a matter of fact, it was not intended to serve any practical purpose). The reader should not be misled by MARGE's ability to infer or paraphrase; this does not go beyond what is included in the definitions of words and description of the model of the world.

The SAM and PAM systems can analyze not only individual sentences but also connected texts by means of scripts (Schank and Abelson 1975). They are also based on the CD model. SAM, like MARGE, is an experimental system (Schank 1975b). In the work cited above, a description of SAM with only three scripts can be found. This author has not managed to find any detailed description of PAM.

In terms of problems of conversation, we can raise the following objections to the systems which are based on the CD model: their lack of connected dialogue (to determine the reasons for failures and help the user to modify his utterances) and their inability to work with large information software (which is necessary for carrying out practical tasks).

To end this description of systems based on the CD model, we would like to emphasize that Schank's group is one of the leading groups dealing with experimental SNLs; it is engaged in both theoretical and experimental research.

2.3.3 Systems Based on the PST Model

No system designed to correspond fully with the ideas of the PST model has yet been produced. The most interesting system of this kind, which is currently being designed, is the one from the "Informelektro" Institute (Apresyan et al. 1978). We shall not be examining this, however, as it is intended primarily for AT. Let us just remark here that this is undoubtedly the most advanced project as regards Russian syntax and morphology.

We shall also include the POET system as one of those based on the PST model. Strictly speaking, this system lies somewhere between the SENSE-TEXT models and models of the TEXT-SENSE-OBJECTIVE type. This also applies to other systems which will be described in the following chapter. All these systems, in contrast to those based on the SENSE-TEXT model alone, involve mainly a model of the surrounding world, not a dictionary. The model contains information about abstract and concrete notions and events in the real world. The reason we have included POET among the systems based on the PST model is that we would like to emphasize the great influence the PST model exerted on the POET system – particularly on the linguistic aspects, such as the structure of the dictionary, morphological analysis, and syntactic synthesis. A description of the POET system is given in Chap. 8.

2.3.4 Systems Designed on the Basis of the Concept of Semantic Roles

All these systems have one feature in common: they all use semantic roles (cases) to represent actions. The concept of semantic roles can constitute part of various models of language. In the PST model, for instance, the similar notion of the model of government is used. Under certain conditions, one could also include the systems TORUS (Mylopoulos et al. 1975a, b) and GUS (Bobrow et al. 1977) among systems of this type. Finally, one might consider here (again under certain conditions), systems which are designed to carry on a conversation using voice (not a written text), such as HEARSAY (Lesser and Erman 1977), HWIM (Woods et al. 1976), and SUS (Walker et al. 1976). However, we shall not discuss these systems here, since we are interested in semantic problems rather than in the problems of representing phrases by means of sounds.

TORUS is an intermediate system, in between a user and a data-base control system (Mylopoulos et al 1975b). Conversations take the form of separate sentences in English. Knowledge representation in TORUS is based on a semantic network with adjoining procedures (Mylopoulos et al. 1975b). The system is an experimental one; in 1975 it was working on the basis of a fragment of the English language consisting of approximately 200 words. The subsequent fate of TORUS is unknown to this author; in all probability, work on this system is not being continued.

The GUS system (Genial Understander System) is the first of a series of systems which are being developed in the framework of a research project on problems of understanding natural languages. The work is being carried on by the Xerox Palo Alto Research Center (D. Bobrow, R. Kaplan, M. Kay) with contributions from several well-known specialists from various universities (D.A. Norman, T. Winograd, G. Thomson). We find this group's work particularly interesting for three reasons. First, the scientists working on the project are among the best specialists in their field; in addition, the size of the group is large enough to carry on serious work. Second, apart from their work on systems of the GUS series, the same scientists (plus D. King, D. Levy, P. Martin, W.G. Lehnert, and B. Smith) are developing a series of languages for representing knowledge – Knowledge Representation Languages (KRL; Bobrow and Winograd 1977a). Given that the problem of representing knowledge is currently the central problem in understanding natural languages and in artificial intelligence in general, the KRL constitutes a reliable foundation for further research that may lead to major new achievements. Third, the research conducted within the above-mentioned project is being financed by a private corporation, although in the United States research of this kind is usually carried out by universities. The implications of this may not be apparent to the Soviet reader – this fact indicates that the corporation in question believes strongly that ultimate success is possible, i.e., that in a few years' time systems will be designed for practical purposes, not just experimental ones, conducting conversation between man and machine in an NL. GUS is particularly interesting, not so much because of the results which have been achieved as because of the design principles applied and the general approach to the problem of dialogue. So far the system's capacity is confined to one very narrow subject: air travel to and from one airport in California. We gave one example of a dialogue between a user and GUS in Sect. 1.1. We noted there that in order to conduct such a dialogue the system had to be able to take the initiative, understand indirect answers, unravel anaphoric references, understand elliptical sentences, and interpret input sentences. The authors of GUS emphasize that the dialogues GUS is able to conduct resemble real dialogues, but in fact are still not real dialogues. Studies of real dialogues have shown that there are situations where the system in its current state would be completely helpless. Some of these situations can be rather unexpected. It sometimes happens, for instance, that a client is excessively polite and wants to explain in detail why he cannot take this or that flight. Such details lie beyond the system's knowledge. The system cannot (as yet) manage phrases which contain imprecisely defined expressions. For example – GUS: "Does departure at 4 p.m. suit you?" Client: "Well, isn't there any flight closer to 9 p.m.?" It is clear to a human being that the client wants to leave at approximately 9 p.m.; the system, however, will propose any flight leaving after 4 p.m. Elliptical constructions can also create certain difficulties for the system, if the ellipsis cannot be unraveled on the basis of the context given by the preceding sentence. As regards the design principles of the system, we would like to stress the importance of the principle of independence. The system comprises several separate blocks (a morphological analyzer, syntactic analyzer, frame processor, and language generator) joined by interfaces. These blocks were assembled separately and then joined together by a control mechanism. The general organization of the system is based on the assumption that systems of understanding texts in a natural language should work in a multiprocessor mode (Kaplan 1975). The mechanism of procedural joining is widely used in GUS – it is useful for representing knowledge and debugging programs. This mechanism originated in the SMALLTALK system (Goldberg and Kay 1976). As regards the degree to which essential problems of conversation have been taken into account, GUS is the most advanced of all systems. Its deficiencies result from its experimental character. It is not provided, for instance, with a capacity to insert and modify the IS. It has no metaknowledge (no knowledge of its own knowledge), and it is unable to understand the cause of its failures; i.e., it has no self-knowledge (consciousness of self).

To end this section we would like to list the main difficulties which hamper the progress of work on designing an SNL for practical purposes:

1. The small number and isolation of groups working on designing an SNL, both in our country and abroad
2. The underestimation of the difficulties involved in work that is "not one's own field". Many linguists believe that the only really important problems are those that they are dealing with; on the other hand, programmers not infrequently imagine that they can manage with no help at all from linguists. And both forget about psychologists, philosophers, and specialists in many other fields, without whom the problem of conversation cannot be solved. The scale of this delusion is really colossal. When, for instance, this author, in one of his lectures, told his audience about the time-consuming nature of work on the mathematical software for the POET system (which took tens of man-years), many linguists expressed the opinion that this was not the result of the task's complexity, but rather testified to the poor qualifications of the programmers who took part in developing the system. The programmers' point of view is not much better. Most of them do not remember that such a task as developing the IS exists. They do not understand (or do not remember) that developing the IS for any system of real-life complexity must necessarily take tens of man-years.
3. The poor progress in basic research into models of conversation, knowledge representation, and understanding the semantics and structure of a connected text

4. The lack of serious investigations and study of the requirements imposed on the SNL by practice (with the sole exception of Malhotra 1975)

2.4 Composition and Structure of the Model of a Participant in the Conversation

2.4.1 Composition of Knowledge About a Participant in the Conversation

The composition of knowledge about a participant in the conversation has already been presented in Fig. 1.4. The need for the participant to possess knowledge about the language and the surrounding world does not seem open to question, although the composition of this knowledge is not obvious (see Sects. 4.2, 4.3, 5.2, 5.3, 7.3, 7.4, and Chaps. 3 and 6). However, the need for a participant (A) to possess knowledge about himself and the other participants (D) is not so evident; thus, before giving a detailed description of this knowledge (see Sects. 4.4 and 4.5), we shall explain why it is necessary.

Usually, A's knowledge about D, i.e., $m_A(D)$, does not contain all the knowledge possessed by D, i.e., $m_A(D) \subset m_D$. This holds true not only in conversations between human beings but also in the case of a conversation between man and machine. The fact that $m_A(D) \subset m_D$ is precisely the reason the dialogue has to be connected (i.e., it cannot take the form of separate sentences); this enables the participants to establish a single understanding of the subject of the conversation. It should be emphasized that the initiative cannot be held by one of the participants during the whole dialogue – in principle, the process of conversation is two-way. The situation where the initiative is held all the time by one of the participants (A) is possible only in rather unrealistic cases, where A has full knowledge of the other participant (D), i.e., $m_A(D) = m_D$. If this is the case, it is not necessary for D to take the initiative even once. Indeed, since $m_A(D) = m_D$, A always knows what D wants to say, so he is able to answer all D's questions without even being asked. Such a situation would correspond to telepathy.

We find it necessary to distinguish at least the following components of A's knowledge of the other participants in the conversation $m_A(D_j)$: knowledge of D's objectives, his interests and his abilities (possibilities), general information about D's knowledge of the surrounding world and of the language, and knowledge of the possible states of D in the course of processing the text. A's knowledge of himself (self-knowledge) should include at least A's knowledge of his own objectives, interests, and abilities, and knowledge of his own knowledge of the surrounding world, of the language, and of his own possible states in the course of processing the text.

Knowledge of the other participants' possible objectives is essential, since one can only understand texts if one understands the other participants' objectives. Thus, in order to determine the actual objective of the other participant, it is necessary to know the set of all his possible objectives, together with the motives for them. Knowledge of the other participants' objectives, intentions, and interests is also necessary to predict their wishes. Let us take an example: "Subject A often meets subject D. One day A meets D with a baby. A asks D: 'Who is this?'

D replies that this is his son. *A* expresses his astonishment that *D* did not tell him about the birth of his son. *D* replies that he did not tell *A* about his son as *A* did not ask about it". This example demonstrates that people's utterances are not always answers to some question. Indeed, *A*'s behavior would be considered rather strange if he asked all of his acquaintances every day if a baby had not been born in their families. This example concerned a dialogue between human beings, but all the conclusions from it remain valid in the case of a conversation between man and machine. It is reasonable to demand that a machine give the user, with no prior request, information which may be of interest to him. Obviously, this is particularly important if the information stored in the machine is liable to be changed or modified by other users.

A's knowledge of *D*'s abilities is necessary for *A* to know if *D* is able to solve problems which arise in the course of processing a text from *A*. For instance, will *D* be able to understand why "Mikhail crawled under the truck" in the following context: "The sun made the cab Mikhail was sitting in scorching hot. Mikhail crawled under the truck."? If *D* cannot cope with these sentences, one has to talk to him in greater detail. For example, "The sun shone. It was a very hot day. The roof of the cab was burning hot and it was stifling hot inside. Mikhail thought to himself that he would be cooler under the truck. Mikhail crawled under the truck".

A's knowledge of *D*'s knowledge of the language is necessary for *A* to avoid, in the course of his conversation with *D*, words and linguistic constructions which would be incomprehensible to *D*. For instance, the following sentence is in itself totally sensible: "A linear inference with resolution and with paramodulation of null disjunct is called a linear refutation with resolution and paramodulation". However, this sentence is most probably incomprehensible, not only to computers but also to most readers.

A's knowledge of *D*'s knowledge of the surrounding world is necessary for *A* to refer to facts which are known to *D*. For example, let *A* have information about a room in which there are tables with books on them. Let *A* identify the tables by their location and (or) inventory number. If the participant *D* has information which enables him to identify the tables by their location only, a conversation between *A* and *D* (without *A*'s knowledge of *D*'s knowledge of the surrounding world) may prove to be impossible or very difficult. Indeed, *D* may ask, "On which table does the book *C* lie?", and receive the answer, "on table number *N*".

A's knowledge of the possible states of *D* may be necessary for *A* to determine the reasons for *D*'s failures to understand *A*'s utterances. If *A* is able to predict which element of his utterance *M* may prove incomprehensible to *D*, he can modify *M* in advance, to ensure full understanding of *M* by *D*. *D* may fail to understand *M* for many reasons, such as usage of an unknown word, improper understanding of some language construction, or inability to establish a connection between a given sentence and the preceding one.

A's knowledge of his own objectives is necessary for *A* to be able to achieve them. Indeed, without this knowledge *A* could answer questions, but he could not take the initiative during the conversation.

A's knowledge of his own interests is necessary for *A* to be able to choose one decision from among all those possible. If, for instance, he books a ticket on a train from *L* to *N*, he ought to know whether he wants to go there by night or by day, first or second class, with or without changing trains, etc.

A's knowledge of his own possibilities is necessary for *A* to determine whether he is able to perform a particular task facing him. Let us assume, for instance, that *A* possesses information about the monthly production of a factory *N* in 1978. He is then asked: "What was factory *N*'s production in the first quarter of 1978?" *A* does not possess this information in explicit form; thus, the question and *A*'s knowledge are inconsistent. In order to avoid laborious and fruitless calculations, *A* should have some idea of his own possibilities.

A's knowledge of his own knowledge of the language is necessary for *A* to be aware of the limits of his abilities. For instance: *A* knows that, according to his knowledge of the language, the words "production" and "output" are synonyms. Or another example: suppose *D* wants to explain to *A* the meaning of word *P*, which is unknown to *A*. In order to use *P*, *A* should possess all the required information about this word. However, *D* can hardly be expected to know what this information should be, as it varies from man to man and – even more so – from system to system.

A's knowledge of his own knowledge of the surrounding world is necessary for several reasons – for instance, in order to explain to his interlocutor *D* what the scope of his (*A*'s) knowledge is, thus enabling the conversation to be carried on. There is another, less obvious, purpose of this knowledge. Let us use an example. *N* wants to book a ticket for a plane. He calls a travel agency, *A*, and the following dialogue takes place:

N: I would like to book one plane ticket to Kirovsk for the 16th of April.
A: Your name, address, and telephone number, please.
N: Nikoltsev, Vladimir Alexandrovich, 20 Lomonosov St., flat number 27, telephone number 2126974.
A: What flight would suit you?
N: I would like to leave before noon.
A: I have booked one ticket for Vladimir Alexandrovich Nikoltsev; flight number 25, to Kirovsk, on the 16th of April. Departure at 11:50. The number of your reservation is 315.

After arriving in Kirovsk, comrade Nikoltsev meets his colleague *A*, who arrived the day before. *N* learns from *A* the following: *A* paid only half as much for his ticket as *N* did; moreover, although he left Moscow at 12:50, he was in Kirovsk 2 hours earlier than *N*. Once back in Moscow, *N* calls the travel agency and complains: Why did they not tell him that up until the 15th of April tickets were being sold at a 50% discount? Why did they not tell him that if he had left at 12:10 p.m. he would had arrived in Kirovsk 2 hours earlier? He receives the same answer to both questions: "You did not ask about this". True, *N* did not ask, as he did not realize that such questions would be relevant. *N* did not know about the "point of discontinuity" (Siklossy 1977) which occurs in the surrounding world, or perhaps did know about it but was unaware of where exactly this point was. The example quoted above allows us to draw the following conclusion: If information contained in *N*'s utterance to *A* is close to a "point of discontinuity" known to A, then A, despite the lack of a request from N, should inform N about this fact.

In the above dialogue, N's utterances were close to two "points of discontinuity". The first involved the transition from the 15th to the 16th of April. As a matter of fact, it is quite possible for a small change in departure date to cause the price of a ticket to be twice as high. The second discontinuity consists in the fact that having left later, one can arrive at a destination earlier. The notion of "point of discontinuity" may be defined more formally. Let us consider a function F, depending on n variables: $F(v_1, v_2, \ldots, v_n)$. We shall say that the function F has a point of discontinuity in the neighborhood of point $V = (V_1, V_2, \ldots, V_n)$, where V_i denotes a value of the variable v_i, if the values of F in the neighborhood of point V can be very different from the value of F at point V. Let us note that we have used the expression "can be different", not "are different". By doing this, we want to stress the fact that the given singularity does not occur at all the points in the neighborhood of V. Obviously, the terms "neighborhood" and "very different" are not absolute – they depend on the subject matter, and on the user.

A's knowledge of his possible states in the course of processing a connected text may seem to be a rather superfluous luxury. However, this is not the case in systems with a degree of complexity above a certain level. This knowledge enables the system to explain to the user the reasons for its failure to understand his questions. This knowledge is also necessary for the system to be able to organize its resources effectively in the course of searching for an answer to the user's question (see Sects. 2.2 and 2.5). Knowledge of the user's (or the system's) own states should comprise: a list of the stages of processing a text (e.g., morphological, syntactic, and semantic analysis, etc.); a list of the goals achieved at each stage; the cause-and-effect relationships between stages in the course of achieving the final result; and the resources (time, memory, etc.) required for each stage of processing.

If participant A is a computer, there is another reason why knowledge about possible states is necessary – participant D (a human being) can "impose" on participant A a given method of understanding a text, one which seems to be correct to D. In order to be able to accept an "imposed" viewpoint, the system should know at which stage it forms what D wants to modify, and how this modification can be inserted at this stage. Personally, we are convinced that the system's ability to "accept what is imposed" is a necessary precondition for the objectives of the conversation to be achieved.

2.4.2 General Description of a Model of a Participant in the Conversation

This subject was already touched on in Sect. 1.3, where the general approach to the problem was outlined. We shall call the model which corresponds to this approach the TEXT-SENSE-OBJECTIVE (TSO) model. Let us now explain this name and clarify the connection between this model and the similarly named SENSE-TEXT model (Zholkovsky 1974), which we call the PST model. The PST model is a model of a language, whereas the TSO model is a model of a participant in the conversation, comprising models of the language, of the surrounding reality, of itself, and of its partner in the conversation. Roughly speaking, the word TEXT has the same meaning in both models (although in the TSO model it usually denotes a two-sided dialogue, while in the PST model this is one-sided). The word SENSE in the PST model refers to the concept of a sign (or signs) which occurs in an input text; in the TSO model, it refers to both concept and denotation (or denotations). In other words, a SENSE is expressed not only in abstract terms (language) but also in concrete terms (speech); the connection between the TEXT and the "knowledge" (the model of the surrounding reality and of the participants in the conversation) is established. The essential task to be performed by the PST model is to unravel a SENSE, whereas the TSO model seeks to determine the objectives of the participants in the conversation. In the TSO model – in contrast to the PST model – the transition from TEXT to SENSE and back again is carried out by means of both linguistic and extralinguistic knowledge (obviously, the same applies to the transition from SENSE to OBJECTIVE).

The PST model, being a model of a language, differs from the TSO model in not paying any attention to analysis of the connected text. For the same reasons, the PST model (again in contrast to the TSO model) ignores both the pragmatic aspect of processing a text when information about an interlocutor is required, and the aspect of "being conscious" of a text and of the participant's own state.

The resemblance between the PST and TSO models is based on the common linguistic principles of designing the morphological and syntactic components of the system. For this reason, in describing the TSO model we shall not consider these two components in detail. However, we shall take them into account when describing the principles of designing computer programs which realize the model of a participant in the conversation. This is because the PST model is a calculus, rather than the algorithm necessary to design a programmable system. In contrast to the PST model, the TSO model is a functioning model, i.e., it is an algorithm describing how a participant in the conversation functions. Consequently, in describing the TSO model, we shall pay special attention to the problem of interaction between different components, not confining ourselves simply to a description of each component separately.

We have already mentioned the requirements that a model of a participant in the conversation should meet (see Sect. 2.1). These requirements lead us to the conclusion that in order to be able to understand a natural language the model should be able to (Popov 1981):

1. Analyze an input text
2. Process an input text
3. Synthesize an output text
4. Interpret the system's actions at the metalevel ("consciousness of self")

The general structure of the TSO model is depicted in Fig. 2.1 which shows its scheme of functioning, its components (stages), and the most important connections between them. It should be stressed that this structure does not reflect all the features of real interrelations between the components (see below, Sect. 2.5). An analysis of an input text involves determining the senses of sentences constituting the text and "understanding" this text. The analysis is carried out by means of programs of morphological, syntactic, and semantic analysis. This has to be done in several stages owing to the complexity of a natural language, and

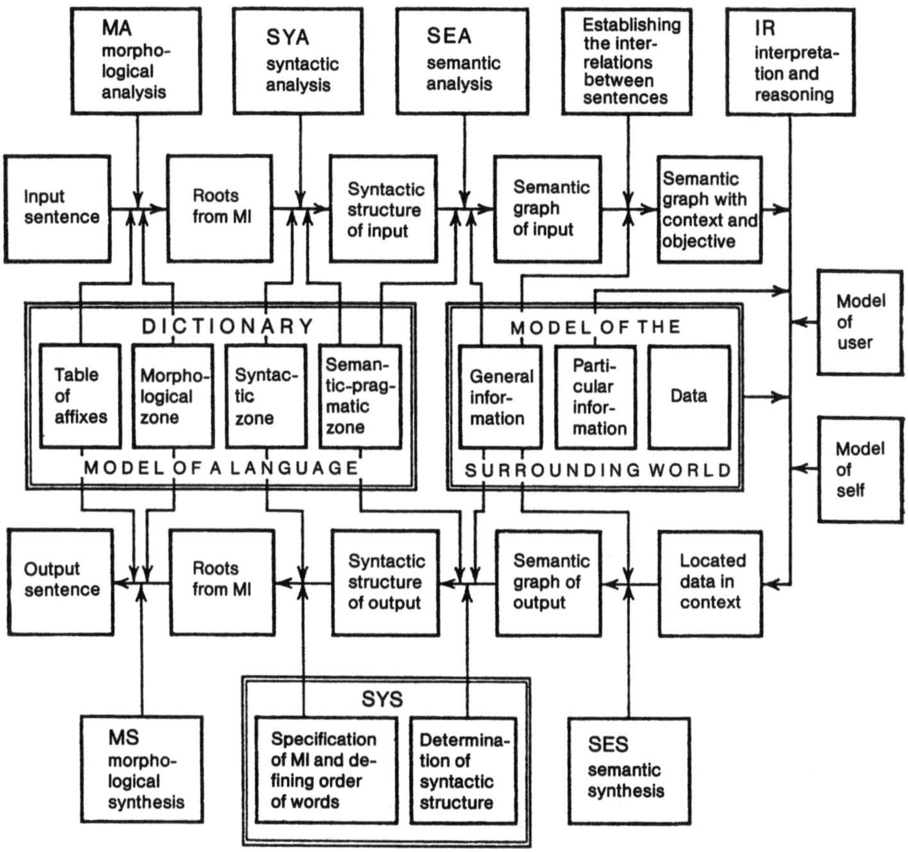

Fig. 2.1. The composition and structure of a model of a participant in the conversation

in particular to such features as: (a) "tacit knowledge" at various levels (see Sect. 1.1.6); (b) the synonymy and homonymy contained in all natural languages; (c) the context dependency of utterances and words in a natural language. In the course of morphological and syntactic analysis (MA and SYA), use is made of information about the language of the conversation stored in the model's dictionary. The dictionary contains information – inexpressible grammatically – about particular morphological, syntactic, and semantic features of Russian words (see Sects. 4.2, 4.3). The task of MA (see Sect. 5.2) is to determine the roots of words, find their definition in the dictionary, and then assign the proper morphological information (MI) to them, i.e., to specify the part of speech, gender, number, case, tense, etc. The SYA determines the generalized syntactic structure of each input sentence. This structure reflects the interrelations between the words in the sentence (see Sect. 5.3). At the stage of semantic analysis (SEA), a semantic graph of the text is developed. The graph represents (in explicit form) the sense relationships between the words and sentences of the input text. The TSO model uses two kinds of information about the subject matter: general and particular. This information is represented in the TSO model in the form of semantic networks (see Sect. 5.4 and Chap. 3). The term "understanding" will be used here to mean the following: determining objectives (intentions) which guided the user in uttering a given input text. The explicit determination of objectives allows us to establish the use to which different individual sentences are put and to link these sentences into a meaningful text. Knowledge of the user's objectives (see Sect. 4.5) is necessary in order to distinguish those aspects of the input text which are the most important and should be concentrated on in the course of processing the text.

The stage of processing involves establishing the connection between the sentence currently being considered and the rest of the text, projecting a text graph onto the knowledge base of the TSO, removing any incompatibilities that arise, and processing proper. Establishing the above-mentioned connections is performed by determining the referents of references and interpreting ellipses (see Sects. 6.2, 6.3). The projection is performed at the stage of interpretation (see Sect. 6.4). This involves a search for the fragments of the TSO's knowledge which correspond to the graph of the text. It should be stressed that an exact correspondence cannot always be established. There are many reasons for this kind of incompatibility: the situation in the input text has been described insufficiently (in terms of the knowledge processed by the system), an incorrect choice has been made as to how to interpret the input sentence, etc. Incompatibilities can be removed if the format of the text graph can be reduced to that of the system's knowledge. Let us give an example of a removable incompatibility. Let us assume the TSO possesses information about the monthly output of a certain factory in the year 1978. In processing a question concerning total production in the first quarter of that year, the system encounters an incompatibility. This incompatibility is, of course, removable; however, if the question were to concern production in January, while the TSO system had information only about quarterly production, this would correspond to an incompatibility which is not removable. Let us note that, generally speaking, the problem of whether an incompatibility is or is not removable is insoluble. In order to find a unique answer to this question the system would have to be provided with full knowledge of all possible cause-and-effect relationships existing within the given subject matter and would have to be able to carry out reasoning of unlimited complexity. We believe it would be advisable to store in the TSO a list of incompatibilities and of methods of removing them (replaced, where necessary, by the information that these cannot be removed). This information can be represented by production (see Sect. 4.4). Incompatibilities may be removed in various ways, from calculations to questions to the user. In the latter case, the removal of the incompatibility requires a change in the order of stages depicted in Fig. 2.1.

The substage of processing proper depends on the input text. If it is a question, the task performed at this substage is to search for an answer among the stored data, calculate it, or infer it. If it is not a question, the task performed is different: joining the information contained in an input text to the knowledge possessed by the TSO. This is an extremely difficult operation. Indeed, the information received may contradict, either explicitly or inexplicitly, the knowledge possessed by the TSO. Moreover, even if a contradiction is uncovered, it is often not clear what the primary reason for it is. We, ourselves, are convinced that this problem will not be solved in a general way in the near future. In terms of practice, it seems that the best we can do here is to ensure that input information given in an NL (perhaps a limited NL) is inserted into the system in the same format as that of the TSO's knowledge. A user who modifies or changes the system's knowledge (e.g., by means of an input text during a conversation) has to take full responsibility for ensuring a lack of contradictions.

This method of conversation between a user and the TSO seems to offer the most promise for making modifications to the information software of the model of the participant.

Synthesizing an output text involves determining – on the basis of the input text – the sense to be expressed in the answer and in translating this into Russian. The stage of synthesis is performed by the programs of semantic, syntactic, and morphological synthesis (SES, SYS, MS). At the substage of semantic synthesis, the sense to be expressed in an answer is determined according to the system's objectives. Let us note that at this stage (SES), the model of the user must be taken into account. It is the model of the user that determines which aspects of the answer are the most important for the user – these should be expressed explicitly – and which aspects the user is not so interested in – these aspects may be expressed inexplicitly, or "tacitly". The tasks performed by the stages of SYS and MS are analogous to the tasks of SYA and MA; they will be considered in detail later (see Chap. 7).

The last function of the TSO (see Sect. 2.5) – "being conscious" of its own actions – is necessary for the system to be able to explain its actions to the user. This is important when success is achieved – thanks to these explanations the user knows what the potential of the TSO is. Moreover, the system's reliability is enhanced in the user's eyes. But this is also important in the case of failure – the system is then able to help the user to understand and to remove the reasons for this failure. We would like to stress here that in "being conscious" of its actions the TSO may be debugged much more easily. This same feature allows the TSO to expand and modify its knowledge more effectively and more safely.

2.5 General Structure of the Model of a Participant in the Conversation

The general structure of the TSO model should ensure effective performance of all the model's functions and their interpretation in "metaterms" comprehensible to the user. However, there are several major problems here. First, the result obtained cannot be guaranteed to be the only possible and correct one at any stage. Several possible solutions may be found at virtually every stage. In principle, the information available at any one stage does not make it possible to choose the single correct solution. Since several solutions may be found at one stage, it is obvious that it may sometimes happen that at a subsequent stage some of these will have to be rejected. If this is the case, the TSO should be able to decide to which of the preceding stages it should return, and which of the remaining, alternative solutions should be chosen for further processing. Second, solving the problems encountered in processing texts written in a natural language requires a tremendous volume of knowledge and – to use Newell's terminology (1969) – the use of specialized ("strong") and not general ("weak") methods. The above-mentioned facts have important consequences – there are many various sources of the system's knowledge, and information coming from one source may contradict information from another. Such situations could be avoided if the system were organized in such a way as would enable it to apply various strategies for solving a problem (not just a linear strategy). Third, work on designing knowledge sources (KS) is not complete, and it is quite possible that they will prove incapable of yielding the proper solution. Such failures may be linked to the following factors:

1. The theory on which the work of the KS is based may be incomplete or even false. For instance, contemporary syntactic theories do not provide for the development of methods other than that of scanning for constructing the syntactic structure of a sentence in the case of all Russian phrases considered to be meaningful by most users of the Russian language.
2. The program realizing a theory may be incorrect because of an incorrect translation of the theory into the program (since there are no formal, general methods of checking whether the debugging is complete) or because of intentional heuristic simplifications of a theory when it is applied in practice.
3. A KS may function incorrectly because the data that this KS has received from a preceding KS is incorrect or incomplete. This situation occurs particularly frequently when errors in the functioning of a KS are caused by errors in the information software (the dictionary, networks, data).

Our experience with the SNL POET (Popov 1978a, b) leads us to conclude that such errors are inevitable and frequent in systems of real-life complexity. Consequently, hopes that such systems will be able to function can be fulfilled only if the structure of the SNL allows it to operate despite errors or incomplete information.

2.5.1 General Structure of the TSO Model

As we know, the system should be conscious of its actions (and express this consciousness in metaterms) and be able to operate despite errors or incomplete information. These factors impose several requirements on the structure of the TSO (SNL). First, if one KS yields incorrect or incomplete information, another should be able to correct this information or supply the missing information. Second, the TSO should be provided with a facility to discover incompatibilities (errors or incompleteness of information) and to determine the reasons for these incompatibilities. Third, when incompatibilities have been discovered, the system should be able to specify how these can be removed (by activation of some KSs, by asking the user about the missing information, etc.). Fourth, the system should interpret its actions in metaterms comprehensible to the user. Fifth, since processing an NL is extremely complex, requiring tremendously long calculations, it would seem advisable – at least at the experimental stage – to consider KSs independent. This allows us to add new KSs or to replace one with another; it also

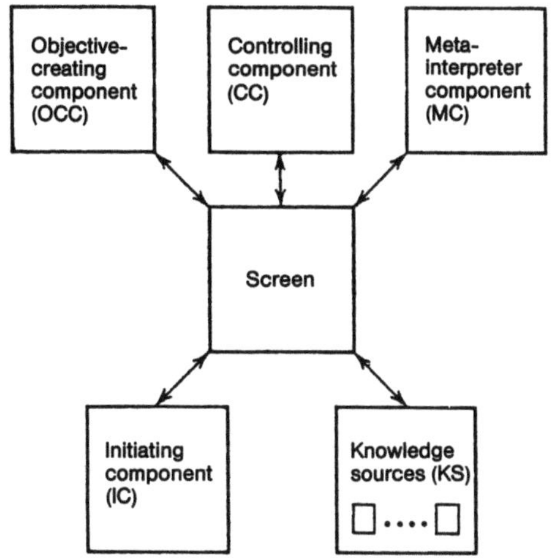

Fig. 2.2. General structure of the model of a participant in the conversation

makes it possible to use various controlling strategies in order to find the most effective variants of the structure of the TSO.

The general structure of the components of the TSO is depicted in Fig. 2.2. This structure makes it possible to meet all the above-mentioned requirements. The method of hypotheses and checks has been chosen as a method which ensures interaction between KSs despite errors and incompleteness of information. In this method, the search for a solution is considered to be an interactive process, each step of which includes (a) propounding a hypothesis which is a well-founded assumption concerning some aspect of the task under consideration, and (b) checking the likelihood of the propounded hypothesis.

In each of these steps use is made both of hypotheses propounded previously and a priori knowledge of the task. The iterative process is concluded when a sequence of hypotheses which meet all the requirements imposed on the full solution is constructed (a full solution being equivalent to the synthesis of the output text). The requirement that knowledge sources should be independent implies that the existence or functioning of one KS is not a necessary condition for the functioning of another KS. However, all KSs deal with the same, common problem – consequently, they have to interact in the course of constructing hypotheses. In order to resolve this contradiction, we introduce certain interactions between the KSs, but of a rather limited character. In the structure of the TSO which we propose (Fig. 2.2), interactions between knowledge sources are realized only by means of a "screen", which stores information about that part of the knowledge possessed by the TSO which has been excited (activated) in the course of a dialogue. On this screen we shall distinguish between knowledge of the TSO's sequence of states in the process of dialogue on the one hand (in particular, all propounded hypotheses), and on the other, knowledge of the surrounding world and of the user's language which has been excited in the course of processing a text. At any moment in time the screen contains all the propounded hypotheses which are partial solutions to the problem. Let us note that these propounded hypotheses may include competing ones. Each KS has access to all pieces of information on the screen. Each KS can transmit information to another KS in only one way: by changing the information on the screen by means of the creation (or annihilation) of a hypothesis, the modification of a hypothesis, or the modification of a connection between hypotheses. This form of interaction between the KSs enables each of them to operate independently and separately from the others; a KS can disregard both another KS which utilizes the results obtained by the given KS and the KS which provided it with the initial data. The following programs, marked in Fig. 2.1, can serve as examples of KSs: MA, SYA, SEA, MS, SYS, and SES. In addition to these programs there are programs that carry out the access to knowledge (see Chap. 3), which are also knowledge sources. We shall refer to all the above-mentioned programs as the processing component (PC) of the TSO.

Three KSs play a special role. These are the ones that realize "consciousness of self" and, in the course of their work, deal with metaknowledge. The first of them shall be called the "objective-creating component" (OCC). Three essential tasks lie before the OCC: assessing the current state of the system, explaining why this particular state has occurred, and proposing further actions which should be undertaken. In order to be able to perform these tasks, the OCC should, in metaterms:

1. Express its objective (X) (i.e., determine the state the system is aiming at), the user's objective (Z), and the objectives of the other active actors existing in the given subject matter
2. Specify the current state of the system (Y)
3. Explain the degree of compatibility/incompatibility between current state Y and final objective X
4. Explain how the system has reached state Y in its pursuit of X
5. Suggest further actions to be taken by the system (if there is a contradiction between X and Y)

As regards the function of "explaining", the following two tasks can be distinguished here: determining the current state of the system (DSS), and explaining the reasons (ER) which led the system to process an input text T in the particular way it has (after the processing of T has been accomplished). The task of DSS is to answer questions concerning the state of the system in the course of processing an input text. This task can be performed by means of a small set of fixed operators. The task of ER is more complicated. In the course of performing it, various problems may arise – these concern the current state of the knowledge base, or various aspects of the knowledge. Consequently, it is difficult to propose any small set of commands (operators) which would express all information that might be of interest to the user. Thus, it is advisable for the system to give all its explanations concerning the reasons which have led it to operate in a given way by means of a natural language.

It should be noted here that the recommendations (propositions) of the OCC are formulated at an extremely abstract level. The task that the OCC performs is to work out propositions about WHAT should be done. Answering the question of HOW this should be done is a function of the controlling component (CC). One could say that the CC is an interface between the "consciousness component," i.e., the objective-creating component, and the processing component, i.e., the component which performs the transformation of the OCC's abstract recommendations into specified changes of rules for calling up knowledge sources. The task which is to be performed by the CC is to prepare, according to an objective, a plan for achieving this objective; to choose, according to the plan, the appropriate KSs; and to establish an order of priorities among these KSs.

The metainterpreter component (the metacomponent – MC) performs the modeling of the actions which are to be undertaken by the system in order to carry out a task. It operates at the metalevel (see Sect. 2.5.2). The functions of the MC are as follows: (a) to check the conditions of the activation (X_i) of a KS (for the relevant KSs); (b) to perform, at the metalevel, operations (Y_i) for activated KSs of the highest priority; (c) to load the program which realizes the i-th knowledge source (Z_i).

The initiating component (IC) is perhaps not compulsory. Strictly speaking, its functions can be performed by the user. The IC is used to activate the system and generate a sequence of input texts. The usefulness of incorporating the IC in the SNL is based on the following: in the course of using an SNL (particularly an industrial SNL – i.e., a system of real-life complexity) its information software is constantly changed. These changes are initiated by human beings. Thus, there is a tempting possibility to have the system itself check – at least partially – whether these changes contain any contradictions. Such checks could involve the system generating, by itself, control input texts. For example, when changes concern the morphological zone of a word, the system could automatically, with the use of morphological synthesis, generate all the word forms corresponding to the given word and then subject them to morphological analysis. It is also possible to store in the SNL information about the texts in which this or that piece of information was used; when this piece of information undergoes any change, the system can then automatically find and check all the corresponding texts.

2.5.2 Activation of Knowledge Sources

The i-th knowledge source, which is contained in the processing component, may be taken to comprise three parts: X_i, Y_i, and Z_i. The symbol X_i stands for a precondition (antecedent), i.e., the set of conditions which have to be fulfilled for the i-th knowledge source to be activated; Y_i is the set of actions (changes) which can be performed by the i-th source – these are expressed in terms of metaknowledge; Z_i consists of the texts of programs which carry out the changes performed by the i-th KS. Let us note that Y_i is a description of the actions of Z_i in terms of metaknowledge. Thus, Y_i is a declarative abstraction of the procedural representation of Z_i. Y_i is used to assess the results of actions of the i-th knowledge source without the need of actually activating it. Naturally, Y_i expresses the types of changes rather than the changes themselves. If the state of the screen is such that it corresponds to the precondition X_i, the i-th knowledge source becomes activated; i.e., it is ready to operate, and in fact begins to operate, provided the processor is not busy. The activated KS performs the actions of Z_i which are expressed on the screen by the changes Y_i. Y_i propounds hypotheses and assesses or modifies hypotheses propounded by other KSs. The KS performs its actions while taking into account the current state of the screen, i.e., while considering the set of all hypotheses propounded previously. The changes Y_i, carried out by the i-th knowledge source, create certain new conditions on the screen, which in turn cause the activation of some other, let us say the j-th, knowledge source. It should be stressed here that such a model of activating the KSs ensures a very high degree of asynchrony and contains a potential for branching (Fennell and Lesser 1977). This fact is, in our opinion, extremely important for problems of artificial intelligence in the near future.

The model of activating the KSs which we have just described can be considered an asynchronously operating production system (PrS) (Newell 1973; Davis and King 1977; see also Sect. 4.4). A production system has three essential components: (a) a set of rules of production, stored in the production memory; (b) the interpreter of the rules; (c) the data base (data memory), which is used and modified by production. The set of rules of production is a set of pairs – "situation (i.e., conditions) – action" – of the form $T_j \rightarrow D_j$, where T_j stands for a set of conditions describing a given situation j, and D_j for the list of actions which are performed when the situation j arises in the data base. The interpreter of the rules establishes the order in which rules are to be tried and the number of appropriate rules which are to be carried out (the first rule only, all appropriate rules, or only those of the appropriate rules which meet certain criteria set by the interpreter). In some production systems rules are always tried in a predetermined order; in others the order may vary. In the latter case, only those rules are tried which have been found useful by the interpreter. Two methods of determining the usefulness of a rule may be distinguished (see Sect. 2.2.5): the *data-directed* (DD) and *objective-directed* (OD) methods. In the former a rule is recognized to be useful if its left part matches the data base. Thus, if the DD method is used, the left parts of useful rules are checked, then calculated (see Sect. 4.4 on the ambiguity of preconditions) and if they prove to hold good, the right part of the rule is carried out. In the latter method rules are regarded as useful if their right parts match the current objective of the system. The left parts of the useful rules are then calculated, and if the result is correct, the objective is considered to have been achieved (taking into consideration the value of the coefficient of specificity – see Sect. 4.4). If the information is not sufficient to determine whether the left part of a rule is or is not true, this missing information is considered to be a subobjective and the search for a solution is continued. This takes the form of a search in the tree of objectives AND/OR (Nilsson 1971). The two methos (DD and OD) are often combined.

Thus, there is an evident similarity between the proposed model of activating the KS and production systems. Indeed, the precondition X_i of a knowledge source may be compared with conditions T_j, and action Y_i of a knowledge source – with D_j. The control cycle of a production system involves choosing (on the basis of certain criteria) one of the productions for which the conditions T_j are fulfilled and then in performing its actions D_j. After these actions have been performed, the cycle is repeated until the current state of the data memory meets the conditions of any production.

2.5.3 Information Levels of the Screen

It is useful to divide the state of the screen into information levels which are determined by the structure of the task being performed. In our case the following levels should be taken into consideration: morphology, syntax, semantics, interpretation, and processing proper. There are several basic elements connected with each such level. Their function is to represent the task on hand at the given level. For example, the level of morphology contains words as its elements, the level of syntax has syntactic groups of words connected by syntactic relations, and the level of interpretation has utterances. Every hypothesis is characterized by the level from which it has been propounded. Such a hypothesis contains information about certain elements from the basic set of elements of the corresponding level. Most knowledge sources use information contained at one level only, or at a few adjacent levels; there is then no need to take the remaining ones into consideration. The interaction between a given KS and the whole system is performed in terms of the basic elements of the corresponding level. The sequence of levels forms a hierarchical structure in which an element of a given level can be described in terms of basic elements from lower levels. For instance: utterances at the level of interpretation are built of nominal groups of words from the level of semantics, which in turn are built of syntactic groups from the level of syntax containing words from the level of morphology. The essential relationships connecting hypotheses link hypotheses of the same level, or of adjacent levels. The creation or modification of a hypothesis which is based on hypotheses of lower levels can be taken to be an operation of abstraction, or synthesis. Modifications of hypotheses of lower levels based on those of higher levels can be taken to be concretization, or analysis. It should be stressed that movement between levels need not necessarily be corroborated (either fully or partially) by all intermediate levels; this is due to the incompleteness of knowledge, or to errors of the knowledge sources.

Let us note that the levels of the state of the screen which have just been introduced can be considered the preliminary base of a plan for fulfilling a task. Each level corresponds to a stage in the plan. The aim of each level is to construct and check a hypothesis appropriate to this level. The aim of the whole system, meanwhile, is to construct a general network of hypotheses, one which would sufficiently and with considerable probability (in terms of the KSs) cover all levels. At any moment in time, the screen may contain several incomplete networks, some of these comprising subnetworks. Each of these may be probable in its own sphere of application. By means of the above-mentioned operations of synthesis and analysis of hypotheses, these incomplete networks can be expanded or restricted, united from subnetworks, or divided into networks. The state of the screen is usually such that it meets the preconditions for activating several KSs. The task of the controlling component is to determine which KSs are potentially relevant to a task being performed and to establish priorities among the activated KSs. The problem of whether some KS (assuming it is potentially relevant) can contribute to a given situation is solved by the KS itself. However, the choice of potentially relevant KSs and the subsequent choice of one of the several activated (i.e., ready to operate) KSs is carried out in accordance with the current objectives of the system. The role of the strategy adopted here is decisive. Indeed, our aim is to design a system capable of functioning properly despite possible errors; it is this that leads us to the conclusion that the various KSs should be activated independently (not successively); this method, however, entails tremendous computational effort on the part of the system, on a scale too large to be acceptable. In order to make this effort more realistic, a strategy of directing attention has to be developed. This strategy would determine the potentially relevant KSs and establish a hierarchy of activated KSs. It should ensure a high reliability of the results yielded by the system.

Thus, the proposed structure combines a data-directed strategy (the method of activating KSs) with an objective-directed strategy (the method of establishing priorities among activated KSs).

3 The Structure of Knowledge and Methods of Representing Reality: Knowledge About the Surrounding Environment

3.1 WHAT Is to Be Represented and HOW?

We shall take *reality* to mean everything that takes part in, influences, or is reflected in the process of understanding. We shall consider this to include the surroundings in which the participants in the conversation operate, the participants in the conversation themselves, and the language in which the conversation is held. This author is convinced that developing a model of reality and methods of representing it (e.g., by computer) is in fact the central problem of artificial intelligence (AI). This problem, as we understand it, is a rather broader one than the problem of representing knowledge (PRK) – at least this applies to the PRK as it is treated by most specialists (i.e., some sort of knowledge exists; the problem involves finding the proper method of representing it). In our opinion, the chief part of the problem is omitted in this approach. What we are referring to here is the problem of where the knowledge which is to be represented is to be taken from, i.e., in our terminology, WHAT is to be represented. There then remains only the second part of the problem – HOW it is to be represented (by what method; for "form" and "method" see Sect. 2.2.1).

Looking at the history of research on this subject, we come to the conclusion that AI (perhaps for want of anything better, or rather because of an inability to do anything better) deals almost exclusively with the problem of HOW: declaratively or procedurally (semantic networks, predicate calculus, procedural representation). Then we have the widespread enthusiasm for the ideas of frames and scripts. All these questions are of great importance, yet they concern only the means by which WHAT can be expressed; they do not say a word about what this WHAT really is. The main reason for this approach is that it is easier to deal with HOW than with WHAT (particularly when we do not know "what is to be done"). It seems relevant to note here that, in this author's opinion, linguists dealing with the problem of "WHAT should be known about a language" have made a greater contribution to the problem of AI than have specialists in AI. This situation creates the impression that, with a few exceptions which are therefore particularly valuable ones (McCarthy and Hayes 1969; Moore and Newell 1973; Charniak 1975), specialists in AI do not seem to notice the problem of WHAT at all. Of course, this problem has been discussed by philosophers, in characteristic philosophical terms, but it has not been examined at the level of concretization necessary for AI. Moreover, the knowledge of surroundings used by SNLs again focuses on linguistic concepts, e.g., semantic cases (or the model of government). So far, no one has specialized in the problem of "WHAT should be known about the surrounding environment and about the participants in the conversation". For our part, we are convinced that the help of philosophers and psychologists will be essential here. This author, who is neither a philosopher nor a psychologist, has nevertheless attempted to summarize what he knows about these questions. Obviously, given what has been said above, it is clear that what this author knows about these questions is not all that much.

It should be emphasized that the problems of WHAT and HOW are interdependent. Indeed, a particular WHAT may be inexpressible (either in principle or in practice) by a particular specified method; i.e., the representation may be epistemologically incomplete or epistemologically inadequate (McCarthy and Hayes 1969). Before outlining the problem of "WHAT is to be represented and HOW", let us note that knowledge may be represented either in declarative form (in the information software – IS) or in procedural form, i.e., by means of programs (in the mathematical software – MS). Only information software will be discussed in this chapter. There is no definitive answer to the question of what falls into the category of MS as opposed to IS. As a matter of fact, the borderline between MS and IS depends on the knowledge possessed by the designer, or even on his own personal preferences. Nevertheless, in every particular system this borderline is fairly well defined. It is possible, for instance, to express both the grammar of a language and the process of sentence analysis in this language in terms of a program (MS). But it is also possible to design a universal program of sentence analysis (for languages of a specific type), and to express grammar in terms of IS, i.e., data. Intermediate variants are also possible. However, we always have two components: who performs the processing (MS), and what he uses in the course of this processing (IS).

It should be stressed that the problem of HOW can be investigated at various levels of abstraction – at the logical level, for instance, or at the physical level. Other levels can also be distinguished. Due to limitations of space, we shall study the problem of HOW at the logical level only.

The model of a participant in the conversation that we are proposing consists of the following models: of a language, of the surroundings, of the user, and of the model itself. Consequently, we shall analyze WHAT should be represented about the surrounding environment, the participants in the conversation, and the language (Sects. 3.2 and 3.3; Chap. 4), and HOW this knowledge should be represented (Sects. 3.4, 3.5, and 4.4). In order to avoid the traditional confusion over WHAT is to be represented and HOW it is to be represented, WHAT will be outlined in a formalized manner to stress that it is largely independent of HOW.

3.2 The Model of the Surrounding Environment – Preliminary Notions

In this section we shall be dealing solely with the general (not concrete) knowledge relevant to one or many areas of subject matter. There are two reasons for this: on the one hand, objective limitations of space and of our own knowledge, and on the other, the fact that there is a great variety of knowledge characteristic for different particular areas of subject matter.

3.2.1 Basic Notions

We shall begin our examination of the basic notions here with the notion of an "entity". By entity we shall understand objects, relations, sets, situations, events, moments in time, etc. In other words, *nothing* that is not an entity exists. From the whole set of entities, we shall distinguish those which are of greatest interest to us.

The Universal Set. It is convenient to regard all entities as elements of the universal set U. In order to avoid paradoxes, the set U itself will not be considered an entity.

The Time Set. The set of all moments in time, which is a subset and element of the set U, will be called the "time set" T. The importance of this set is obvious, as all entities existing in the surrounding world are considered through this set. Each entity from U is usually regarded as existing – in the real world or in a hypothetical one – in a certain relationship with a continuous subset of T. We shall use U_t to denote the set of all entities existing at the moment in time t. The set $U' = \bigcap_t U_t$ is the set of all entities which exist always. The set $\bar{U} = \bigcup_t U_t$ is the set of all entities which occur at any time whatsoever, in the past, present, or future. If $x \in U'$, then this tells us that *x exists constantly*. If $x \in U_t$, then this tells us that x exists *simultaneously* with the moment in time t. If $x \in \bar{U}$, this tells us that *x exists historically*.

The set U^* is a subset of the Cartesian product of the sets T and U, such that the pair $(t, x) \in U^*$ if, and only if, $x \in U_t$.

We shall assume that a set is invariable and exists constantly. By the *invariability* of a set we mean the invariability of the elements of this set. By phrases such as "to add an element l to the set $\{a, b\}$" we shall mean "to define the set $\{a, b, l\}$ that includes the element l and all elements of the set $\{a, b\}$". What we have said above does not prevent us from connecting a variable S with first one set $\{a, b\}$, and then another $\{a, b, l\}$. The assumption concerning the constant existence of a set has been made in order to obtain a constant independent of time while modeling, by means of which history can be described. An assumption concerning the existence of a set in a finite period of time would constitute an alternative approach here. For instance, we can assume that a set exists if all its elements exist. Such an approach would be inconvenient in the case of many sets. Indeed, in the set of all days of the year, at each moment there is only one element which exists – the one corresponding to the given day. On the other hand, the null set does not contain any element at all – nevertheless, there is strong evidence of its existence.

3.2.2 Formal and Informal Relations

The notion of a relation is understood quite differently in mathematics and in everyday life. In mathematics, a relation (a formal relation) is introduced in terms of a Cartesian product of sets. If $A_1, A_2, \ldots, A_n$ are sets, we define their Cartesian product $(A_1 \times A_2 \times \ldots \times A_n)$ as the set

$$C = \{(a_1, a_2, \ldots, a_n) \mid a_1 \in A_1, a_2 \in A_2, \ldots, a_n \in A_n\}$$

of all ordered sequences $(a_1, a_2, \ldots, a_n)$. A subset R of the Cartesian product $A_1 \times A_2 \times \ldots \times A_n$ of the sets $A_1, A_2, \ldots, A_n$ is called a "relation" (a formal relation) defined on sets $A_1, A_2, \ldots, A_n$. In other words, a relation R is a set of sequences of the type $(a_1, a_2, \ldots, a_n)$, which is a subset of the Cartesian product $A_1 \times A_2 \times \ldots \times A_n$. If $(a_1, a_2, \ldots, a_n) \in R$ (where $a_1 \in A_1, a_2 \in A_2, \ldots, a_n \in A_n$) we can say that elements $a_1, a_2, \ldots, a_n$ are *in the relation* R, or that the relation R for $a_1, a_2, \ldots, a_n$ *is true*. In the particular case when sets $A_1, A_2, \ldots, A_n$ are all identical, we can talk about the n-th Cartesian power A^n of the set A. This, obviously, is the set of all ordered sequences $(a_1, a_2, \ldots, a_i, \ldots, a_n)$, where $a_i \in A_i$ (n-tuples). Any subset $R \subseteq A^2$ of the Cartesian square A^2 is called a "binary relation" on A. Let us note that a formal relation, being a set, exists constantly (invariably). The mathematical formulation of the notion of relation has a purely extensional character (see Sect. 1.1.4). Indeed, a relation is defined on a particular set as the subset of n-tuples for which the relation is true.

In everyday life, people usually use an informal (intensional) notion of relation. A relation expresses the properties of a sequence of elements with no reference to any concrete set. For example, the relation "greater than" or the relation "redness" are normally understood by people without specifying the set of objects to which these relations refer. In this case it is presumed that people know the operation F, which enables us, given a particular sequence N, to determine whether the relation R is or is not true for this sequence N. Suppose that the relation is "greater than", and the sequence of elements N consists of integers a_i. The operation F may then be specified as follows: if $a_i > a_j$ then $(a_i, a_j) \in R$, where R is the relation "greater than". Let us note that it would be very inconvenient to define the relation "greater than" in an extensional way (i.e., by mentioning explicitly all pairs for which this relation is true) – in particular when the number of elements is very large.

It could be maintained that both extensional (formal) and intensional relations should be represented in the model of the surrounding environment. The fact of representing a relation in two different ways poses the problem of transforming one representation into the other (see Sect. 2.2.1). The chief difficulty connected with such transformations involves the transformation of a formal relation (F-relation) into an intensional one (I-relation). This is because such a transformation is equivalent to inductive reasoning (see Sect. 2.2.7). We have already observed that a formal relation (F-relation) is invariable. It may happen that this feature is inconsistent with the feature of variability of intensional relations (I-relations), which renders it very difficult to transform intensional relations into extensional ones. The variability of I-relations is especially obvious for relations of the type "is located at", i.e., relations expressing changes in the surrounding world. For example, an object A may be "located at" a place D, but at a different moment the object A may be "located at" a place B. It is quite easy to see that I-relations are variable because they do not define the situation they are intended to express completely. For instance: in order to formalize the relation "is located at", it is necessary to take into account the moment in time involved. If the information lacking is added to an I-relation it can be transformed into an F-relation. Let us illustrate the essence of the operation of formalizing an I-relation by using the example of the relation "is located at". Let a microworld consist of two objects, X and Y, three locations, A, B, and C, and one event, D. Let us assume that at the moment T_1 the relation "is located at" is true for pairs (X, A) and (Y, B). At moment T_2, after event D has taken place, the relation "is located at" is true for (X, B) and (Y, C). The state of the microworld at moment T_1 (in context 1) can be described by the formal relation $R_1 = \{(X, A), (Y, B)\}$, and at moment T_2 (in context 2) it can be described by another formal relation: $R_2 = \{(X, B), (Y, C)\}$. Thus, each context v corresponds to a formal relation R_v which has the same "value" as the informal relation "is located at". All these different R_v can be unified – the result we obtain is a new relation R, which conveys the information contained in all R_v in the following way: Let $(v, u, w) \in R$ if, and only if, $(u, w) \in R_v$:

$$R = \{(T_1, X, A), (T_1, Y, B), (T_2, X, B), (T_2, Y, C)\}.$$

In general, an informal relation may depend on m attributes. We can choose such attributes $b_1, b_2, \ldots, b_n$ $(n \leq m)$ such that, in specifying the values of $b_1, \ldots, b_n$ (context c), we are able to determine the values of $a_1, a_2, \ldots, a_m$ uniquely (in the above example $m = 3$, $n = 1$). Any I-relation can be determined in terms of a formal relation R_c, where the context c specifies the values of the attributes b_i. Thus, any variable I-relation can be connected with an invariable formal relation R and $(V_1, V_2, \ldots, V_n, X_1, \ldots, X_j) \in R$ if, and only if, $(X_1, X_2, \ldots, X_j) \in R_c$, where c is a context in which the attributes $b_1, \ldots, b_n$ have the values $V_1, \ldots, V_n$. Let us note that since the choice of $b_1, \ldots, b_n$ from among $a_1, \ldots, a_m$ is, in general, not the only choice possible, an I-relation can therefore correspond to several formal relations. We previously defined, for a formal relation, the notion of *being in a relation R* for a sequence $a_1, \ldots, a_n$. It is convenient to formalize this notion for I-relations and in fact for any relation (formal or informal). The fact that the entities (elements) $X_1, X_2, \ldots, X_n$ *are in an I-relation* in a given context c can be expressed by the formal relation H_c. For each context c and for each I-relation r

$$((X_1, X_2, \ldots, X_n), r) \in H'_c$$

if, and only if, $(X_1, \ldots, X_n) \in R_c$ and $(c, r, R_c) \in J$, where J is a formal relation between the I-relation r and the formal relation R_c which codes r in different contexts c. In a context c entities $X_1, X_2, \ldots, X_n$ are in the I-relation r if, and only if,

$$((X_1, X_2, \ldots, X_n), r) \in H'_c.$$

The entities $X_1, X_2, \ldots, X_n$ are in a formal relation R (independent of context) if, and only if, $(X_1, X_2, \ldots, X_n) \in R$. Let us use R' to denote a relation which may be either an I-relation or an F-relation. The entities $X_1, X_2, \ldots, X_n$ are in the relation R' if, and only if,

$$((X_1, X_2, \ldots, X_n), R') \in H_c$$

where H_c is defined in the following way:

$$((X_1, X_2, \ldots, X_n), R') \in H_c$$

if, and only if:

1. R' is the formal relation R and
   $(X_1, X_2, \ldots, X_n) \in R$, or
2. R' is an I-relation r and
   $((X_1, X_2, \ldots, X_n), r) \in H'_c$.

We shall use the term "statement" to denote an $(n+1)$-tuple of the form $(R', X_1, X_2, \ldots, X_n)$ where R' is a relation (formal or informal) and $X_1, \ldots, X_n$ are entities. A statement $(R', X_1, X_2, \ldots, X_n)$ is true in a context c if, and only if,

$((X_1, X_2, \ldots, X_n), R') \in H_c$.

For instance, in context 1 (see example above), characterized by the time T_1, the statements (*is located at*, *X*, *A*) and (*is greater than*, *5*, *4*) are both true. However, in context 2, the first of these two statements is false while the second is true (it is true in any context, as it contains a formal relation).

3.2.3 The Nature of Time

Here we shall be considering time (semantic time, as distinct from morphological time, or tense – see Sect. 4.2.7) not from the viewpoint of modern physics, but in terms of using this notion in the process of conversation in an NL. Within this frame of reference we shall distinguish several aspects characterizing time. First, time is ordered continuously and has no bounds. It can be defined in absolute or in relative terms. We say that "time is defined in absolute terms" (absolute time orientation) if there is a correspondence between an event and a "point" or "interval" on the time axis. The difference between a "point" and an "interval" is to a great extent relative, as, depending on the degree of detail in modeling, such notions as "an hour", "a day", "a year", etc., can be interpreted as either a point or an interval of time. However, in each particular system this difference is fairly clear cut and very often important. Thus, in dealing with a semantic representation it is very advisable to have the time characteristics of an event; these characteristics will be called "duration", and may assume the values of a "point" and of an "interval" (see Sect. 4.2.8). In principle, any event has a certain objective duration – thus, if a system (or human being) considers some event to be a point in time, then this is a conceptual fact rather than an empirical one. Time may be defined with varying degrees of concretization (detail), whether this is done in absolute or in relative terms. For instance, let us take the sentence *Ivan visited me on the 17th of May*. We can also say *Ivan visited me in May* – the definition of time is absolute, but less concrete than in the first sentence. One of the abstract ways of determining an absolute time orientation of an event is to define time relative to the current moment. It is usual to distinguish here between *real*, *current*, and *potential* events, i.e., events which have occurred up to the given moment (the past), events which are occurring at the given moment (the present), and events which may occur in the future. We believe it advisable for an internal representation to contain information about the time orientation of an event, in particular the past (*Pa*), the present (*Pr*), or the future (*Fu*), at several levels of concretization simultaneously. Obviously, the characteristics *Pa*, *Pr*, or *Fu* of an event may be derived from the values of the "point" or "interval", provided the model of reality allows us to specify the "current moment in time".

Defining the absolute time orientation of an event is not always possible, if only due to lack of information concerning the exact time when an event came to an end. A *relative time orientation* involves establishing a time correlation between a given event (A) and another event (B). We can distinguish various kinds of time correlations between events: one event may precede or follow another, it may occur simultaneously, be included in another, or intersect it, etc. All this can be formalized in the following way. The *time system* is an ordered pair $(T, \leq)$, where T stands for the set whose elements are called "points", and $\leq$ is the relation of partial order on the set T. A binary relation R on a set A is called a "partial order" if it is reflexive (xRx), transitive (xRy and yRz implies xRz), and antisymmetric (xRy and yRx implies $x = y$) for all elements x, y, and z of the set A (Maltsev 1970, p. 30).

A partial order in a given set T is called a "linear order" if, for all elements x and y of the set T, either $x \leq y$ or $y \leq x$ is true. The set T in which a partial (linear) order is defined is called a "partially (linearly) ordered set". A linearly ordered set is also called a "chain" (see Maltsev 1970, p. 31). If a set is partially ordered but is not a chain, we call it a "branch". Let us observe that the linear order of time corresponds to an absolute time orientation, while the partial order of time corresponds to a relative time orientation. In addition to the partial order of time (T), we can also distinguish other properties. These can be formally expressed in the following way: The set T is an *unbounded set*, i.e., it is infinite and has neither a largest nor a smallest element. The set T is also a *dense set*, i.e., for any two elements x and y, $x < y$, one can find an element z which lies between them: $x < z < y$ ($x < y$ denotes a partial order such that $x \leq y$ implies $x \neq y$). We should bear in mind that the above-mentioned properties cannot usually be fully reflected in the process of computer modeling. We are forced to treat time as finite and not dense. The future (f) and the past (p) will be determined with the use of the following two functions:

$$f(x) = \{z \mid z > x\}, p(x) = \{z \mid z < x\}.$$

In general, a subset of the set T has neither lower nor upper bounds. Nevertheless, in many particular cases it is convenient to introduce the notions of the beginning and end of a subset t of the set T. The *beginning* of the subset t of the set T is the greatest of the lower bounds of t (if such a bound exists), while the *end* of the subset t is the lowest of the upper bounds of t (again, if it exists). This definition flows from the fact that time (generally speaking) is a branch.

It is advisable to distinguish a special type of subset t – a time interval (or segment). A *time interval* $S \subseteq T$ is a chain such that for any $x \in T$, if there exist $y \in S$ and $z \in S$ such that $y \leq x$ and $x \leq z$, and if $\{x\} \cup S$ is a chain, then element $x \in S$.

There is one more important aspect which characterizes time. This is the interdependence between time and the notion of existence. In particular, all entities are considered to exist in the course of a certain time interval.

Let us mention the essential relations of order between time intervals – these relations must be taken into account in the course of the process of conversation in a natural language. Let A and B be time intervals which are included in a linearly ordered subset t of the set T. We may now distinguish the following relations of order between the time segments:

1. $Until_t(A, B)$ if, and only if, (iff) $(\forall x)(\forall y)(x \in A \wedge y \in B \supset x < y)$
2. $During_t(A, B)$ iff $A \subseteq B \wedge A \neq B$
3. $Simultaneously_t(A, B)$ iff $A = B$
4. $Exceeds_t(A, B)$ iff $A \cap B \neq \emptyset \wedge (\exists x)(\forall y)(x \in A \wedge y \in B \supset x < y) \wedge$
   $\wedge (\exists y)(\forall x)(y \in B \wedge x \in A \supset y > x)$
5. $After_t(A, B)$ iff $until_t(B, A)$
6. $Includes_t(A, B)$ iff $during_t(B, A)$
7. $Is\ exceeded_t(A, B)$ iff $exceeds_t(B, A)$

For the sake of simplicity, if it causes no confusion we shall omit the subscript t. It is also possible to reformulate these relations so as to express them in terms of the beginnings and ends of time intervals. This can be done in the following way: Let A and B be time intervals with beginnings and ends at points (a_1, a_2) and (b_1, b_2) respectively. Let A and B be included in a linearly ordered subset t of the set T. The above-mentioned relations can now be expressed in the following way:

1. *Until* (A, B) iff $a_2 < b_1$
2. *During* (A, B) iff $b_1 \leq a_1 \wedge a_2 \leq b_2 \wedge \sim (a_1 = b_1 \wedge a_2 = b_2)$
3. *Simultaneously* (A, B) iff $a_1 = b_1 \wedge a_2 = b_2$
4. *Exceeds* (A, B) iff $a_1 < b_1 \wedge b_1 < a_2 \wedge a_2 < b_2$
5. *After* (A, B) iff *until* (B, A)
6. *Includes* (A, B) iff *during* (B, A)
7. *Is exceeded* (A, B) iff *exceeds* (B, A)

It can be demonstrated that any binary relation between time intervals with points of beginning and end which can be determined in terms of $<$ and $=$ can also be derived from the above-mentioned relations. A relation of order between more than two time intervals can be expressed in terms of binary relations. For instance: *between* (A, B, C) iff *until* $(B, A) \wedge$ *until* (A, C).

3.2.4 Variations of Informal Relations in Time

The most important informal relations depend only on time. We shall call these relations "time relations" (TR). We can distinguish two essential forms of variation of a TR in time: discrete and continuous variations. The relation "to have" (in the sense of "to possess") may serve as an example of a relation of the first kind, while the relation "to be located at" (when an object is moving in space) is an example of the second kind of relation. Generally speaking, every informal (depending on time) time relation r can be placed in correspondence with a constant formal relation R^*. If r at time t corresponds to a formal relation R_t, R^* is the smallest set which includes all $(n+1)$-tuples $(t, a_1, a_2, \ldots, a_n)$ such that $(a_1, a_2, \ldots, a_n) \in R_t$. The relation R^* will be called an "asterisk" relation. In considering the notion of time "within" a relation itself, we make this time relation invariable (constant). The similarity of R^* and the set U^* (see Sect. 3.2.1) is established by the following relationships:

$(t, x) \in U^*$ iff $x \in U_t$,
$(t, a_1, a_2, \ldots, a_n) \in R^*$ iff $(a_1, a_2, \ldots, a_n) \in R_t$.

The relation R^* can conveniently be used to memorize the history of events. For example the fact that a robot (ROB) at time T_1 is at a point described by the coordinates (X_1, Y_1) can be expressed with the help of the triple $(T_1, ROB, (X_1, Y_1))$, which is an element of the set AT^*. At a moment T_2 the robot changes its location and the coordinates (X_2, Y_2) are now assigned to it. The change of the robot's state can be represented by the following true and constant statements:

1: $(AT^*, T_1, ROB, (X_1, Y_1))$ and 2: $(AT^*, T_2, ROB, (X_2, Y_2))$.

The statement $(AT, ROB, (X_1, Y_1))$ would be true only in the context T_1.

In order to represent information about the invariability of an informal relation in the course of a time interval, we introduce the sets R^{**} and U^{**}. A triple (t_1, t_2, x) is an element of U^{**} if, and only if, $I = [t_1, t_2)$ is a one-sidedly open continuous time interval, such that

1. For any $t \in I$, $x \in U_t$.
2. If I' is a continuous time interval such that:
   (a) for any $t \in I'$, $x \in U_t$ and (b) $I \subseteq I'$, then $I = I'$.

By analogy, $(t_1, t_2, a_1, \ldots, a_n) \in R^{**}$ iff

1. For any $t \in I = [t_1, t_2)$, $(a_1, a_2, \ldots, a_n) \in R_t$,
2. If I' is a continuous time interval such that:
   (a) for any $t \in I'$, $(a_1, a_2, \ldots, a_n) \in R_t$ and (b) $I \subseteq I'$, then $I = I'$.

The relation R^{**} expresses discrete changes. The problem of representing continuous variations is more complex. We shall examine this later (see Sect. 3.3).

Changes which take place in the surrounding world can be approximately defined in terms of a transition from one set of circumstances and situations to another. Consequently, we can consider these changes in the surrounding world variations of informal relations. Thus, the informal relation r may correspond to the formal relation R_{c_1} in a context c_1 and to the relation R_{c_2} in a context c_2. The relation r is invariable in the context c_1 or c_2, but when the transition from context c_1 to c_2 takes place, one associates different formal relations with the relation r. In other words, a change can be regarded as a replacement of one formal relation R_{c_1} by another, R_{c_2}, if the focus of attention moves from one context, c_1, to another, c_2. Alternatively, we can approach the problem of expressing changes which occur in the surrounding world from another angle, namely, by investigating such formal relations as R^*.

Of all the diverse changes occurring in the surrounding world, the most important are those changes of time relations which are connected with a transition from one context, A, to another, B, where A and B differ from one another only as regards current time. Changes of this kind will be called "time changes". In order to define a time change more formally, we introduce the class of all contexts which are characterized by the same moment in time t. This class will be denoted by $I(t)$. Contexts belonging to one class will be called "isochronic contexts" (I-contexts). The notion of an I-context is closely related to that of a macrostate. A *macrostate* is the set of all conditions and situations corresponding to an I-context. A macrostate M_c connected with an I-context c may be characterized by the set S_c of all statements which are true in the context c (see Sect. 3.2.2). The set S_c is called the set of macrostates of M_c. Let us note that statements derived on the basis of a formal relation are true in all M_c and consequently in all S_c, whereas statements derived from time relations (informal ones) are only elements of certain S_c. Thus, a *time change* is a change of informal relations which arises owing to the transition from one I-context to another (i.e., it is the difference between the sets of macrostates corresponding to two I-contexts). Utilizing the set J (see Sect. 3.2.2), we can write:

$$(I(t_1), r, R_1) \in J, (I(t_2), r, R_2) \in J, R_1 \neq R_2,$$

where r is an informal relation expressed (a) in terms of a formal relation R_1 in an isochronic context $I(t_1)$, and (b) in terms of a relation R_2 in a context $I(t_2)$. Consequently, the change of r resulting from the transition from $I(t_1)$ to $I(t_2)$ may be derived from the set J. The sequence of time changes in the course of a certain time interval will be called a "chain" (or "sequence") of changes.

3.2.5 Indirect References

The notion of indirect references which we are about to introduce plays an important role in problems connected with representing continuous sequences of changes and with expressing quantificational statements. Both in mathematics and in natural languages we commonly use a relationship between two entities, one of which is interpreted as a symbol representing the other. If a symbol (an entity) s represents an entity v, we say that v is the *value* of s. The informal relation existing between s and v will be called a *value*. Obviously, the value of s may vary, depending on a context q. We shall denote the value of a symbol X in a context q in the following way: $\mathrm{val}_q(X)$. If the context is evident, we shall omit the subscript q and write val(X). In order to differentiate a symbol from its value we shall denote the symbol of a variable in the form of this variable enclosed in quotation marks (for instance, 'A' denotes the first letter of the alphabet) and denote a value in the form of a variable (for instance: A stands for a value corresponding to a variable A). References to any n-tuple or statement (special case of an n-tuple) can be made in a similar way. However, where such references are made, the structure of the n-tuple which is referred to is not reflected. In order to overcome this difficulty, we shall introduce the notion of a template. This is analogous to the notion of an S-expression in the language LISP (McCarthy et al. 1962). Thus, for instance, the template corresponding to the statement [*AT*t ROB* ⟨*times*⟩ 5 *t*] is equivalent to the S-expression

[*LIST* [*QUOTE AT**) *t* (*QUOTE ROB*) (*TIMES* 5*t*)).

If we perform the calculation of this S-expression in LISP with $t = 7$, we obtain (*AT** 7 *ROB* 35). This result of the S-expression in LISP is equivalent to the *n*-tuple (*AT**, 7, *ROB*, 35) and may be interpreted as an indication that the location of a robot *ROB* in time 7 is at the point 35.

3.3 Structure of Knowledge of the Surroundings

The structure of knowledge should be designed to allow the system to solve problems (first of all, this means answering questions). In addition, knowledge should be organized in units convenient for interaction with man. In this section we shall consider how to express sets of similar facts in the form of units which compactly (with the help of quantificational statements) represent information and may be regarded as forming a whole. The proposed formalisms may be utilized to represent continuous changes characterizing specific events occurring in the surrounding world. In order to make the representation of information more consistent and compact, we shall introduce a certain hierarchy and classification of knowledge. The proposed structure of knowledge enables us to represent entities at various levels of abstraction and makes it possible to reconstruct the lacking ("concealed") input information.

3.3.1 Patterns and Quantificational Statements

The statements introduced above are convenient for representing concrete facts. In practice, however, we often need to represent compactly a set of similar facts that may be considered to form a single whole. Here we shall describe a method of grouping facts in units (which we shall call "patterns") and of representing these patterns in terms of quantificational statements. The need for presenting such quantificational statements stems from the fact that, in practice, it is often inadvisable (or even impossible) to represent information in terms of a set of concrete statements. This is because the number of such statements is usually very large (infinite) and/or some of them may be indefinite.

There are two quantifiers commonly used in mathematics – these are the universal quantifier (∀) and the existential quantifier (∃). However, expressions using these quantifiers are not particularly useful in a semantic network, which is one of the most common methods of representation. In the following we introduce the relations $\overline{\forall}$ and $\overline{\exists}$, which can be used to code any quantification. This can be done by indicating whether or not a certain entity (*n*-tuple) is included in a certain set ($\overline{\forall}$, $\overline{\exists}$). Such a form of representation means we have no difficulty in expressing any quantification in a semantic network, as will be demonstrated later (see Sect. 3.5).

Before investigating quantificational statements, it is necessary to define the notion of "context" more precisely. We have already used this notion to mean a set of initial premises concerning the surroundings. Consequently, any context q corresponds to a set A_q of restricting conditions. These conditions usually take the following form: "the value v is assigned to the symbol s". The set G of all pairs (s, v) will be called a "connecting set". A context $C(G)$ assigns the values of the right-hand components of the pairs to the left-hand components. For instance, if $G = \{(factory, \text{ZARYA}), (products, \text{BOLTS})\}$ then:

1. $\text{val}_{C(G)}$ ([TO MAKE *factory products*]) = (TO MAKE ZARYA BOLTS)
2. $\text{val}_{C(G)}$ (['TO CONNECT' $*$]) = (TO CONNECT {(*factory*, ZARYA), (*products*, BOLTS)})

Let us note that $*$ denotes a reference to the set G. In order to formalize the notions of a pattern and of a quantificational statement it is convenient to define the notion of the $\bar{\in}_q$ relation first. This may be done as follows:

$$s \,\bar{\in}_q\, R \text{ iff } \text{val}_q(s) \in R.$$

Let us now consider how the $\bar{\in}_q$ relation can simplify the problem of representing a set of similar facts. Any fact can be represented by a statement which has the form $n \in R$, where n is an n-tuple and R is a relation. A set of similar facts (i.e., of facts which may be expressed in terms of one relation) can be represented by a set of relationships like $n_1 \in R$, $n_2 \in R$, ..., $n_m \in R$. If an n-tuple n is indirectly referred to, using a template d in various contexts, then the same information is conveyed by relationships $d \,\bar{\in}_{q_1}\, R$, ..., $d \,\bar{\in}_{q_m}\, R$ where q_i stands for a context such that $\text{val}_{q_i}(d) = n_i$. All these connected facts may be expressed with the use of one statement $\bar{d} \in R$, if this statement is interpreted in contexts which are included in the set $Q = \{q_1, q_2, ..., q_m\}$. Formally, a pattern p is a triple (d, R, Q), where d is a template, R a relation, and Q a set of contexts. The pattern d can also be interpreted as $\text{val}_q(d) \in R$ for any q from Q. However, very often we are unable to define the family of contexts Q explicitly. A more effective way of determining the set Q is therefore needed.

We shall determine the sets $\forall'$ and $\exists'$ by setting the following restrictions. Let a template d contain only one indirect reference in the form of x, assuming values from a set X. Then:

$$(x, X, d) \in \forall' \text{ iff } \forall y \in X \ \text{val}_{C(\{(x,\, y)\})}(d),$$
$$(x, X, d) \in \exists' \text{ iff } \exists y \in X \text{ such that } \text{val}_{C(\{(x,\, y)\})}(d).$$

Let us explain how the relations $\forall'$ and $\exists'$ can be used by looking at the example of the following triple:

$$z = (x, \{\text{MERCURY, VENUS, EARTH, MARS}\}, [\text{'ORBIT'}\ x\ \text{'SUN'}]).$$

Then $z \in \forall'$ if, and only if,

$$\forall p \in \{\text{MERCURY, VENUS, EARTH, MARS}\}\ \text{val}_{C(\{(x,\, p)\})} ([\text{'ORBIT'}\ x\ \text{'SUN'}]).$$

Therefore, we can also write that $z \in \forall'$ if, and only if,

$$\forall p \in \{\text{MERCURY, VENUS, EARTH, MARS}\}\ (\text{'ORBIT'}\ p\ \text{'SUN'}).$$

Now we define the relations $\bar{\forall}$ and $\bar{\exists}$ which remove the restrictions set before:

$$(x, X, G, d) \in \bar{\forall} \text{ iff } \forall y \in X\ \text{val}_{C(G \cup \{(x,\, y)\})}(d),$$

where G is the connecting set. Analogously,

$$(x, X, G, d) \in \bar{\exists} \text{ iff } \exists y \in X\ \text{val}_{C(G \cup \{(x,\, y)\})}(d).$$

The relations $\bar{\forall}$ and $\bar{\exists}$ make it possible to extend quantifications by means of adding new variables to the actual connecting set G. In the simplest case the set G may be empty.

3.3.2 Representation of Continuous Changes

In Sect. 3.2.4 we introduced the relations R^* and R^{**} and showed how they could be utilized to express history. For instance: the fact that "Boris had a car from the time t_1 to t_2" may be written down in the following way:

$(t_1, t_2, \text{BORIS, CAR}) \in \text{TO HAVE}^{**}$.

This is in fact an abbreviated form of the more exact statement

$(\bar{\forall}, t, I, \emptyset, [\text{'TO HAVE}^{**}\text{'}\ t\ \text{'BORIS' 'CAR'}])$,

where I is the interval (t_1, t_2). The relation R^{**}, although convenient for expressing a relation which is invariable in an interval I, cannot represent a relation which depends on time. One possible solution to this problem is to specify the time dependence of d in a quantificational statement $(\forall, t, I, \emptyset, d)$. For instance, the continuous movement of a robot (*ROB*) from the point 0 to the point 100, with a velocity of 10m/s, starting at moment t_1, may be represented by the quantificational statement:

$(\bar{\forall}, t, I, \emptyset, d)$, where I is the interval $[t_1, t_1 + 10)$,
and $d = [\text{'AT}^{*}\text{'}\ t\ \text{'}ROB\text{'}\ \langle\text{Multiply 10}\ \langle\text{Difference}\ t, \text{'}t_1\text{'}\rangle\rangle]$.

3.3.3 The Notion of Process

Practically speaking, it is impossible to code explicitly the whole chain of changes (see Sect. 3.2.4) which occur in the course of a nonempty time interval. Although a human being usually does not know much about time changes, he or she is still able to perform various tasks fairly well. This fact indicates that in order to operate successfully, the system does not need to possess all information concerning time changes. We assume that people group particular sets or sequences of changes into blocks. These blocks will be called "processes".

A chain of changes (i.e., a sequence of time changes) may be taken to be the result of certain processes which took place during a certain time interval. A process can be regarded as a description, characterizing or explaining a particular set of time changes. A process can also be taken to be an account of the differences between successive states.

3.3.4 The Simplest Processes

By "the simplest processes", we mean those that can be represented in the form of linear sequences of statements (without branching).

All the simplest processes can be divided into two categories: instantaneous and sustained scripts (IScr and SScr). *Instantaneous scripts* are used for modeling changes which take place in the outer world in the form of a process without any duration. The IScr describes the fact of a change (the result of the change) but not the process of the change. *Sustained scripts* represent changes in the form of a continuous process dependent on time. The IScr may be represented by a 4-tuple (p, i, d, a), where p denotes the set of parameters characterizing the process, i the set of template statements which determine the conditions that have to be fulfilled for the process (i.e., the script) to be initiated ("excited"), *d* the set of template statements which cease being true after the process is accomplished ("deletion statement"), and *a* the set of template statements which become true as a result of the process being accomplished ("addition statements"). Using SIS to denote the set of all instantaneous scripts, we can express the fact that a 4-tuple is an element of the set of instantaneous scripts in the form of the statement $(p, i, d, a) \in \mathrm{SIS}$. All calls for instantaneous scripts form the set CIS. A call for a concrete script may be denoted by $(S, t, G) \in \mathrm{CIS}$, where S is an instantaneous script (an element of the set SIS) and t is the time of the call, i.e., of assigning the values indicated in the connecting set G to the parameters of S.

Let us illustrate the above by means of an example. Let us consider a micro-world consisting of a one-dimensional space, a robot, ROB_1, and two elevations, h_1 and h_2, located at fixed points in the space: x_1 and x_2 respectively. The robot is able to move in the space (along the ground) and to climb the elevations. We shall describe, in terms of the IScr, the process by which a robot c climbs off the ground onto an elevation w, located at a point denoted by a coordinate r.

CLIMBING = ({*c*, *w*, *r*}/* *p* – list of parameters */ /* then follows the list of conditions necessary for the process to be initiated (*i*) */
{['ELEMENT' *c* 'ROBOT'] /* *c* is an element of the set of robots */,
['ELEMENT' *w* 'ELEVATION'],
['AT' *c r*], /* *c* is located at the point with coordinate *r* */
['AT' *w r*], ['ON' *c* 'GROUND'], /* *c* is on the ground */
['SELECTION' *c* 'CLIMBING' *c w*]} /* then follows a deletion statement – *d* */
{['ON' *c* 'GROUND']}, /* then follows an addition statement */
{['ON' *c w*]})

The sense of the script CLIMBING is obvious. Note that the text marked by /*... */ is a commentary, intended to help the reader understand the sense of the operators. The script contains three parameters: a robot, an elevation onto which-the robot is to climb, and the coordinate of a point at which this climbing is to be performed. The conditions for initiating the process are that the coordinates of the robot and of the elevation coincide, that the robot is on the ground, and that it "wishes" to climb the elevation. As the result of accomplishing the script one statement is deleted ("the robot is on the ground") and one is added ("the robot is on the elevation"). It should be borne in mind that a script does not describe any actual changes in the surrounding world. What a script actually describes is the type of changes. To draw an analogy with the language Algol-60, we can say that a script corresponds to a procedure statement (and not to a procedure call). A call for a script is performed with the use of the actual information that determines the form of a particular change. For instance, if the script CLIMBING(ROB_1, h_2, x_2) is called at the moment of time t_0, we shall obtain, in accordance with the above-mentioned scheme of CIS:

$$(\mathrm{CLIMBING}, t_0, (c, ROB_1), (w, h_2), (r, x_2)) \in \mathrm{CIS}\,.$$

In practice it is advisable to introduce a separate relation for each script – for the script CLIMBING, for instance, the relation R-climbing. One may consider time t' to be an inexplicit parameter of any instantaneous script. When a script is called, the time of its initiation is assigned to t'. Thus, we can write: $G \in R$-climbing if, and only if, the script CLIMBING is initiated at the moment t_0 with the values of its parameters specified by the connecting list G. For the example considered above we can write:

$$\{(c, ROB_1), (w, h_2), (r, x_2), (t', t_0)\} \in R\text{-climbing}.$$

Sustained scripts (SScr), like instantaneous ones, may be represented in the form of a set of n-tuples. Let us denote the set of all sustained scripts by SSS. This set includes as its elements 4-tuples of the form (p, i, f, D), where p and i have the same meaning as they had in the case of the IScr, f denotes a set of template statements which determine the conditions for terminating the process, and D stands for a set of templates d which express the SScr's passage in time. The essential difference between an SScr and an IScr is the fact that an SScr is characterized by duration of time. An SScr is initiated at the initiation time t_i and is terminated at the moment t_f at which the conditions of termination are fulfilled, i.e., the SScr develops in the course of a time interval $[t_i, t_f)$. Any template d is interpreted as a pattern $(\overline{\forall}, t, I, V_g, d)$, where t is time assuming values from the interval $I = [t_i, t_f)$ and V_g is a connecting set.

Let us describe, in terms of an SScr, the movement (MOVEMENT) of a robot in the microworld introduced above:

MOVEMENT = ({c, v, x_i} /* list of parameters */
{['ELEMENT' c 'ROBOT'], ['ON' c 'GROUND'], ['AT' c x_i],
['LESS =' x_i x_{max}], ['SELECTION' c 'MOVEMENT' c v],
['LESS =' v v_{max}]}, /* conditions of initiation of the process */
{['¬ SELECTION' c 'MOVEMENT' c v], ['AT' c x_{max}],
['¬ ON' c 'GROUND'],
['LESS =' x_i x_{min}]}, /* conditions for terminating the process */
{['AT*' t c ⟨add x_i ⟨multiply v ⟨difference t t_i⟩⟩⟩]} /* action which is performed by the robot */)

The parameters of this script have the following meaning: c – the robot, v – the velocity of the robot, v_{max} – the robot's maximum permitted velocity (this parameter should be specified "tacitly"), x_i – the coordinate of the point at which the robot starts its movement, x_{min} – the minimum coordinate in the microworld (specified "tacitly"), x_{max} – the maximum coordinate in the microworld (specified "tacitly"). The conditions for initiating the process are the following: the robot should be located at the point where it has to start its movement, the coordinate x_i should lie inside the interval $[x_{min}, x_{max}]$, the robot should "want" to move, and the velocity of the robot should be permissible, i.e., it should be less than the maximum velocity. The movement of the robot is described by the template d, which may be interpreted in the following way:

($\overline{\forall}$, t, I, V_g ['AT*', t c ⟨add x_i ⟨multiply v ⟨difference t t_i⟩⟩⟩])

i.e., $y = x_i + v(t - t_i)$. A negative value for the robot's velocity corresponds to movement from right to left, while a positive value denotes movement from left to right. A call for a sustained script may be defined as a 4-tuple (s, t_i, t_f, G), where t_i and t_f stand for the times of initiation and termination of the process, and s and G have the same meaning as before, in the case of a call for an instantaneous script.

3.3.5 Complex Automatic Processes

The two types of process considered above were of the simplest kind. The vast majority of changes which occur in the surrounding world can be expressed as a combination of the simplest processes; such combinations are called automatic processes (AP). Their name is derived from the resemblance between these processes and so-called abstract automatons (Glushkov 1962). Let AP be the set of all automatic processes. An element *ap* of this set can be represented by a 5-tuple

$$ap = (C, K, c_s, C_F, P) \in \text{AP}$$

where C is the set of states, K the set of lines which connect states, $c_s \in C$ an initial state of the automatic process *ap*, $C_F \subset C$ the set of final states, and P the set of parameters characterizing the process *ap*. The state of a process *ap* can be denoted by $c = (N, D_c)$, where N is the name of the state c and D_c stands for the set of patterns which characterize this particular state. Two different states cannot have the same name, but they may be characterized by identical patterns. Any particular *ap* terminates after the transition into a state $c \in C_F$ has been performed. All states from the set $C_F \cup \{c_s\}$ take the form $c = (N, D_c)$ where $D_c = \emptyset$. Any particular line of an *ap* ($k \in K$) may be represented by a 5-tuple $k = (c_x, c_y, i, d, a)$. If a template statement i is inputted into *ap* the process changes its state from c_x to c_y and template statements (d, a) appear on output. All the variables which are used in template statements i, d, a are elements of the set P. Let *ap* be in a state c. Suppose that n lines begin at c – these will be denoted by $k_1, ..., k_n$. For any $j \in \{1, 2, ..., n\}$ let $k_j = (c, c_j, i_j, d_j, a_j)$. Being in the state c, the *ap* analyzes the set of template conditions i_j. The conditions i_j are mutually exclusive; i.e., it is impossible to fulfill several conditions i_j simultaneously. The transition proceeds from c along a line k_j for which all conditions i_j are fulfilled. At the same time, statements d_j are deleted and statements a_j are added.

Let us see how instantaneous and sustained processes can be represented in the *ap* formalism. A graphical representation of an instantaneous process is shown in Fig. 3.1. The letter i denotes the initial conditions, and (d, a) stands for the output statements which appear when the automatic process changes its state from the initial one to the final one. Figure 3.2 represents a sustained process. We shall connect this representation with a 4-tuple $(p, i, f, D) \in \text{SSS}$ which we introduced before in order to describe an SScr: p corresponds, as before, to the set of parameters P; i, as before, is denoted by i; j is a set composed of only one element – a disjunction of conditions determined by element f; D corresponds to D_x. The

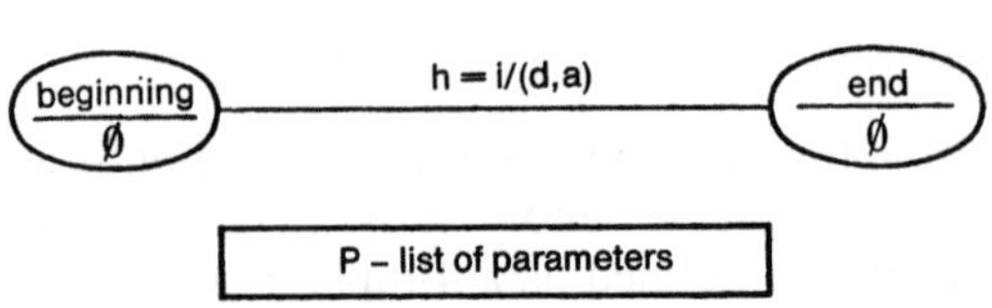

Fig. 3.1. An instantaneous process in the form of an automatic process

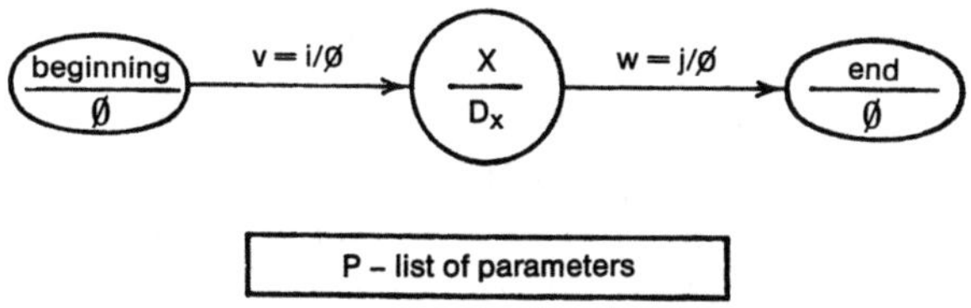

Fig. 3.2. A sustained process in the form of an automatic process

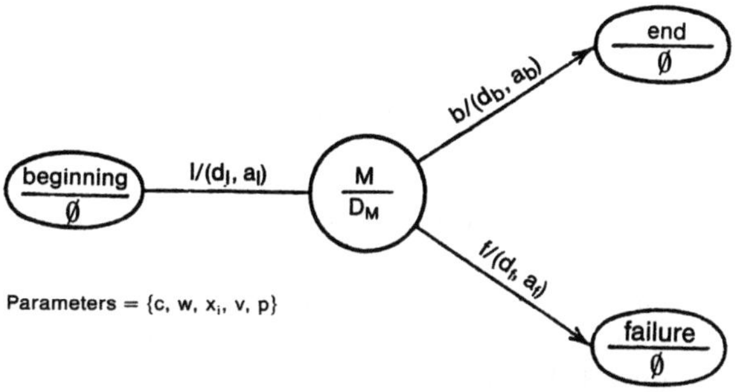

Fig. 3.3. The automatic process "taking a taxi"

correspondence between j and f requires some explanation. In an SScr, f denotes the set of conditions of termination, while in an *ap* it is the set of conditions of initiation. Since the conditions of initiation are linked by a conjunction mark and the conditions of termination by a disjunction mark, to represent f by j one has to write all statements included in f in the form of one disjunctive statement.

Figure 3.3 represents an automatic process performing an action which in a natural language is normally called "taking a taxi". Let us assume that in the microworld described above the elevations have been replaced by waiting taxis. In order to "take a taxi" a robot should move (MOVEMENT) so as to be located at the same point as a taxi, it should "want" to get into this taxi, and it should perform the action of getting into this taxi (CLIMBING).

TAKING A TAXI = (C, K, (∗ beginning ∗, ∅), (∗ end ∗, ∅), P) ∈ AP, where

C = {(∗ beginning ∗, ∅), (∗ M ∗, D_M), (∗ end ∗, ∅), (∗ failure ∗, ∅),

D_M = {['AT*' t c ⟨add x_i ⟨multiply v ⟨difference t t_1⟩⟩⟩]},

K = {((∗ beginning ∗, ∅), (∗ M ∗, D_M), l, d_l, a_l),
((∗ M ∗, D_M), (∗ end ∗, ∅), b, d_b, a_b),
((∗ M ∗, D_M), (∗ failure ∗, ∅), f, d_f, a_f)}

Let us specify the statements connected with the lines (see Fig. 3.3):

l = {['ELEMENT' c 'ROBOT'], ['ELEMENT' w 'TAXI'],
['ON' c 'GROUND'], ['AT' c x_i], ['LESS =' x_i x_{max}],
['SELECTION' c 'MOVEMENT' c v], ['LESS =' v v_{max}]

$d_l = a_l = \emptyset$

b = {['AT' c x_i], ['AT' w p], ['EQUAL' p x_i],
['SELECTION' c 'CLIMBING' c w], ['LESS =' x_i x_{max}],
['ON' c 'GROUND']

d_b = {['ON' c 'GROUND']}
a_b = {['ON' c w]}
f = {['OR' ['LESS =' x_i x_{max}], ['LESS =' x_{max} x_i],
['AND' ['¬ SELECTION' c 'MOVEMENT' c v],
['¬ EQUAL' p x_i], ['AND' ['¬ SELECTION' c 'MOVEMENT' c v],
['EQUAL' p x_i], ['¬ SELECTION' c 'CLIMBING' c w]]}
$d_f = a_f = \emptyset$

3.3.6 Extended Automatic Processes (EAP)

Automatic processes may be extended in several directions. One possibility is to introduce a special type of line – IMMERSION. This direction of extending the automatic processes was proposed by Woods in his study of extended transition networks (Woods 1970). The line IMMERSION IMMER $[X, G]/(d, a)$ connects two states c_i and c_j and is interpreted as follows: An automatic process (ap_1) memorizes the name of the state c_i and moves on to another automatic process X (a subprocess). G is a connecting set. If the subprocess X is successfully accomplished the supervisory program returns to the state c_j of the process ap_1. Let us note that the line IMMER is equivalent to the notion of a procedure call in automatic programming languages. Another peculiarity of EAP is the introduction of special states: OR, $\rightarrow AND$, $\leftarrow AND$, and I. The transition to the state OR is performed in the usual way but an ap cannot stop at this state – it must proceed to one of the states connected with OR (the state OR does not model any actual changes in the surrounding world). Since a transition from OR to any other state connected with it is possible, an ap in this case resembles a nondeterministic algorithm (Floyd 1967). Thanks to the state OR, we are able to model random processes, such as flipping a coin to come down heads or tails. The states $\rightarrow AND$ and $\leftarrow AND$ usually occur in pairs. The transition to the state $\rightarrow AND$ is performed in the usual way, while the exit from it is performed along all lines beginning at $\rightarrow AND$. The state $\leftarrow AND$ "collects" all paths created by the state $\rightarrow AND$. The supervisory program does not exit the state $\leftarrow AND$ until all the conditions determined by the lines entering it have been fulfilled. The use of AND lines, together with the line IMMER, makes it possible to activate several subprocesses simultaneously. Figure 3.4 illustrates an example of an EAP – man's usual morning activities. The lines $\rightarrow AND$ and $\leftarrow AND$ are expecially convenient when dealing with nonlinear plans (Sacerdoti 1975). The state I (from "instantaneous")

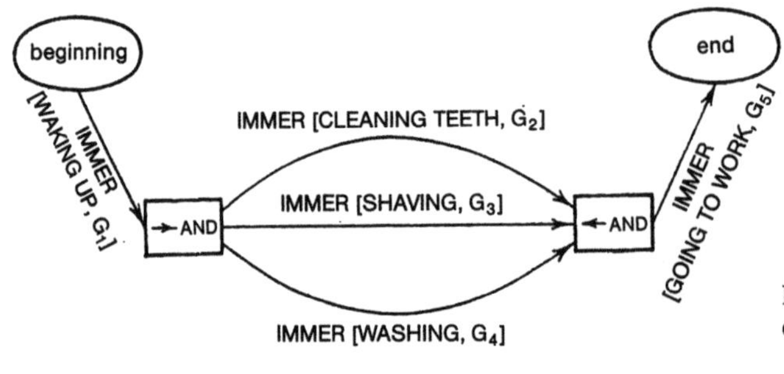

Fig. 3.4. An example of an extended automatic process

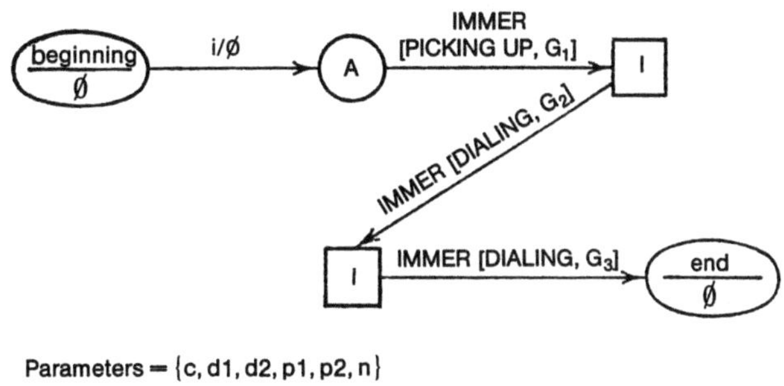

Fig. 3.5. An example of using instantaneous states

is characterized by the fact that a process cannot stop at this state. If no transition to the following state is possible, a process is considered to have failed. How the state I may be used can be demonstrated with the help of the example "dialing a telephone number" (see Fig. 3.5). We assume that a robot (c), calling from a telephone (p_1), obtains a connection with another telephone (p_2), which is located at a point n. Telephone p_2 has a two-digit number – d_1d_2. Generally speaking, the process of "dialing a telephone number" consists of the subprocess "picking up the receiver" (PICKING UP) and two subprocesses "dialing a number" (DIALING). The meanings of the variables used in Fig. 3.5 are:

$$
\begin{aligned}
\mathrm{i} \ &= \{[\text{'ELEMENT'}\ c\ \text{'ROBOT'}], [\text{'ELEMENT'}\ p_1\ \text{'TELEPHONE'}],\\
&\quad [\text{'ELEMENT'}\ p_2\ \text{'TELEPHONE'}], [\text{'AT'}\ c\ n], [\text{'AT'}\ p_1\ n],\\
&\quad [\text{'AT'}\ p_2\ n], [\text{'}\neg\text{BUSY'}\ p_1], [\text{'NUMBER'}\ p_2\ d_1d_2],\\
&\quad [\text{'SELECTION'}\ c\ \text{'DIALING'}\ p_2]\}\\
G_1 &= \{(c, *\, c), (p, p_1), (n, *\, n)\}\\
G_2 &= \{(c, *\, c), (p, p_1), (n, *\, n), (d, *\, d_1)\}\\
G_3 &= \{(c, *\, c), (p, p_1), (n, *\, n), (d, *\, d_2)\}
\end{aligned}
$$

Thus, we have shown how knowledge of changes in the surrounding world which, from the human point of view, are connected with each other can be organized in the form of blocks. By distinguishing portions of information connected in blocks, we can simplify the interaction between man and a dialogue system.

3.3.7 Categories, Rules, and Hierarchical Taxonomy

Another way in which people systematize their knowledge is by structuralizing it in a hierarchical system of classification. Such a system provides a mechanism for abstracting, for removing superfluous information, and for reconstructing information that is lacking ("tacit"). A hierarchical classification system divides all entities into several categories (classes). Entities which are in some sense similar are grouped together, allowing us to consider them all, as opposed to each of them separately. The system is hierarchical – in other words, some categories are subcategories (lower categories) of more general categories (supercategories or higher categories). The lower a category, the greater is the similarity between its elements. This "similarity" exists by virtue of the fact that any category has specific properties which characterize each of its particular members. It is not obligatory for a hierarchical system to have a treelike form. Supercategories need not be mutually exclusive.

The notion of category is the central concept in a hierarchical system of classification. A *category* may be defined as a set whose elements are entities that accord with a rule R (test T or predicate P). In general, a category can be determined by several different rules R. This applies in the situation where different intensions (different rules) determine the same extension (set of entities). The category PARALLELOGRAM may serve as an example here. It may be defined by either of the following rules, h_1 or h_2:

1. A quadrilateral whose opposite sides are parallel
2. A quadrilateral whose opposite angles are equal

We shall represent a rule h by an $(n+1)$-tuple $h = (d, x_1, x_2, ..., x_n)$. Let

$(z_1, z_2, ..., z_n) \in H^h$ iff $\mathrm{val}_{C(\{(x_1, z_1), ..., (x_n, z_n)\})}(d)$ true.

We say that entities $y_1, y_2, ..., y_n$ obey (fulfill, observe) a rule h if, and only if, $(H^h, y_1, y_2, ..., y_n)$ is a true statement. Let us write, using the notation just introduced, the category of entities colored red: $h_1 = (d, x)$, where $d =$ ('TO BE RED' x). H^{h_1} is the set of objects colored red. An entity z obeys the rule k_1 if (H^{h_1}, z) is a true statement. The following important fact should be emphasized: rules and quantificational statements have much in common. They both utilize a template (see Sect. 3.2.5) which contains variables. Quantificational statements (QS) quantify these variables (and, consequently, inexplicitly assign values to them) before the template is calculated. A QS expresses the truthfulness of a template statement for any such assignment of values to variables. A rule, however, does not quantify and does not assign values to the variables of the template that corresponds to this rule. These values of a rule's variables are assigned by some external mechanism.

A category (K) and the rule (h) which defines it can be connected by the following most important relations: necessity (n-rule), sufficiency (s-rule), and necessity and sufficiency (ns-rule). A rule is an ns-rule if a fact $z \in K$ is possible if, and only if, (H^h, z) is true. A rule is an n-rule if a fact $z \in K$ entails (H^h, z). A rule is an s-rule if (H^h, z) entails $z \in K$.

Let us define the simplest form of a rule. This is called "an attribute". Let K and J be sets of entities such that each element of K corresponds to an element of J which characterizes this element of K. We can then say that elements of K possess an attribute (property) a. The attribute a (which we shall denote by 'a') may be considered a binary relation A which is a subset of $K \times J$; i.e., for $x \in K$ one can find $y \in J$ such that $(x, y) \in A$. If $(x, y) \in A$ then y is called $*$'a'x, i.e., a value of the attribute a of the entity x. This very definition means that an attribute (being an invariable formal relation) has a unique value and cannot change. Elements of one category may be considered to possess common attributes yet to differ as to the values of these attributes. An example of attributes applicable to physical objects is, for instance, "mass" or "form". For a particular event, e.g., EXCHANGE, the following attributes may be pertinent: "salesman", "purchaser", "what is bought", "what is sold", etc. Linguists call these attributes "semantic cases" (Fillmore 1968).

3.3.8 Metarules and Predictions

We shall explain the essence of the notion of a metarule (M-rule) by the example of a situation where "one object is located on another object in the course of a certain time interval". This situation may be described in terms of the relation ON**. Elements of this relation are of the form (t_1, t_2, A, B). Each such 4-tuple corresponds to a particular situation: "the object A is located on the object B in the course of the time interval $[t_1, t_2)$". Let us note that each 4-tuple corresponds to the values of four attributes. From the practical viewpoint, it is advisable to have an intensional description of a relation (in contrast to the extensional form in which relations are usually described in mathematics). An intensional description of the relation ON** could run as follows: The relation ON** is a subset of $T \times T \times P \times P$. The values of the first two attributes should be elements of the set T (time), while the values of the last two attributes should be elements of the set P (physical objects). Rules like those described above will be calles "r-rules" (restricting rules). These rules indicate what attributes characterize a given category, the types and ranges of possible values of each attribute, etc. The problem of coding such rules will be examined in Sect. 3.5.7.

M-rules enable a system to predict properties of entities which do not appear explicitly in an input utterance. These predicted properties may direct (speed up) analysis of the input utterance. What is more, utilizing the predicted properties, the system may locate the lacking entity in the context of the dialogue which is stored in the SNL. Apart from the values of attributes, M-rules may be extended to describe their presumed values – this makes it possible to assign proper values "tacitly" if the information is incomplete (Minsky 1975). "Tacit" assignments are particularly important in solving problems connected with understanding and planning (see Sect. 3.5.7).

3.3.9 Abstracting

By the term "abstracting" we mean the process of focusing attention on the most important aspects of entities, ignoring details. One form of abstracting consists in direct use of a classification system. If everything we know about an entity z is that it is an element of a category K, then the n-rules, ns-rules, and M-rules connected with this category convey abstract information about z. This form of abstracting is used when detailed information about z is lacking.

Another form of abstracting is the so-called cutting off of branches. This form can be explained in the following way. Let $z \in K_1$ and let K_2 be a subcategory of K_1; i.e., K_1 corresponds to a higher level. A piece of information concerning z may be explicitly assigned to z itself, but more general information may be connected with K_2 and K_1. The process of abstracting the notion of z consists in ignoring the information specific to z and retaining only that part of the information which is conveyed by the fact that z is also an element of the category K_2. Then the process of abstracting can be continued by considering information from K_1. The form of abstracting described above is not caused by lack of information – it is called "abstracting z in relation to K". As we have already observed, in hierarchical taxonomy subcategories of a category K need not be mutually exclusive; i.e., it is possible that $z \in K_1$ and $z \in K_2$, where K_1 and K_2 are categories of the same level. This property allows us to examine one object from different angles. For example, we can consider a generator an electrical device (K_1) or a mechanical device (K_2).

Abstracting performed with the use of "rules of decomposition" is the third form of abstracting we shall consider (Hendrix 1975a). This is sometimes called "splitting branches". The two above-mentioned methods of abstracting have an important disadvantage: they are not sufficiently flexible. Indeed, if an entity z is abstracted in relation to a category K, all information that is more specific than the properties connected with K will be lost, while all the properties connected with K and its supercategories are, of necessity, known in any case. In contrast to the two preceding methods, "splitting branches" enables us to investigate the taxonomic "tree" from various angles, according to the rules of decomposition connected with each category. Several rules of decomposition (i.e., several branches) may be connected with one category – the name of the method, "splitting branches", is derived from this particular fact. For example, one rule of decomposition makes it possible to single out an electrical component of a generator, whereas another rule singles out a mechanical component. In order to obtain "full" knowledge, both rules have to be used. Rules of decomposition have been successfully applied to problems connected with planning (Sacerdoti 1974).

The method of "splitting branches" allows us to consider entities at various levels of detail, which is necessary for an SNL to be able to answer questions. A problem that arises here is the following: What level of detail should be chosen in formulating an answer? One of the suggested solutions to this is to choose the same level as that of the question. If the question is, for instance, "How can a picture be fixed to a wall?", a suitable answer is: "It can be nailed." If, however, the question were "How can a picture be nailed to a wall?", the same answer would no longer be suitable. The answer should now be something like "By using a hammer and nails". It should be stressed, however, that this method of choosing the proper level cannot be considered a general solution to the problem. In order to solve the problem the system should understand the objectives, intentions, and abilities of the user who is asking the questions. In other words, it should take into account a model of the user (see Sect. 4.5).

3.3.10 Unification of Processes and Taxonomy

The use of processes in defining categories of entities provides the most obvious evidence of the existence of a relationship between the two forms of knowledge indicated in the title of this section. Such a relationship becomes evident when one uses ns-rules which state that a given entity A is an element of a category K if, and only if, the entity A represents changes expressed by a certain process. It should be noted that many entities which are not events in the usual sense of the word may nevertheless be defined (at least in part) in terms of processes. For instance: *an island* – a piece of land *surrounded* by water, *a blanket* – an item of bedclothes used to *cover* the body, etc. This type of relationship between an entity X and a process Y max be expressed as a rule of correspondence (c-rule): "X follows a procedure coded by process Y". A relationship between X and Y may also be specified by the rule of checks (ch-rule): "The procedure coded by process *Y* may be successfully applied to *X*."

Categories, as has been shown, may be defined by processes – however, the contrary can also be the case. For instance: IMMER [*X*, *G*], used in a certain process, may state that the transition along this line is possible only if an event from category *X* occurs. The process of abstracting that we discussed above in terms of categories is also related to processes (in the sense that processes can be examined at various levels of detail). The mechanism of IMMER lines is one of the ways in which the process of abstracting can be carried out for processes.

3.4 Classification of Methods of Representing Knowledge

We previously defined a method of representing knowledge as an internal (machine) language of a conversation system, used by it to represent facts (see Sect. 3.1). The essential requirements which should be met by the internal language of a conversation system have also been specified above (see Sect. 2.2), as well as in several other works (see Winograd 1975; Popov 1977, 1978b). The problem of selecting a method of representing knowledge is usually reduced to an examination of the "balance" between declarative and procedural representations (DR and PR). However, systems which possess solely declarative knowledge – or solely procedural knowledge – do not exist. Until quite recently, attempts were made to justify the opinion that one of these approaches was superior to the other (Hewitt et al. 1973; McCarthy and Hayes 1969). The difference between DR and PR corresponds to the difference between "KNOWING WHAT" and "KNOWING HOW". In the PR approach, one assumes that intellectual activity is equivalent to knowledge of the surrounding world, built into programs, i.e., knowledge of "how" some entities or other may be used. In the DR approach, however, one assumes that knowledge of certain entities ("KNOWING WHAT") does not have any deep relation with the procedures used to process these entities. Intellectual activity is based on a certain universal set of procedures which process facts of all kinds, and on a set of particular facts describing a particular domain of knowledge.

3.4.1 Declarative Representation

DR, as compared to PR, has one essential advantage. This is that in using DR one is not forced to indicate how a particular fragment of knowledge should be used. Simple statements may usually be used in more than one way. It therefore seems inconvenient to specify in advance all possible ways in which they may be used (as is required by PR). This property of DR ensures its flexibility and efficiency, as it makes it possible to use the same facts in many different ways.

In the DR approach, knowledge is considered to be a set of independent facts. This makes it possible to modify and extend knowledge simply by means of deleting or inserting statements. In the PR approach this problem is much more complex, as one has to take into account the way in which a given statement may be used. A conversation in a natural language is usually conducted in the declarative form, i.e., people's utterances concern facts rather than procedures describing the use of these facts. Obviously, this is because people tend to economize on effort in the course of a conversation – a single fact can be used in a great deal of ways.

3.4.2 Procedural Representation

It is known that there are many entities which can be conveniently represented in the form of procedures, although it is almost impossible to give a purely declarative representation of them. It is easier, for instance, to represent the actions of a robot in its surroundings in the form of procedures, as PR allows us to overcome (in part; see Sect. 2.2.3) the so-called frame problem (see Rafael 1971), which is characteristic for DR. On the other hand, the use of PR is connected with the "side effect" problem (Sridharan and Hawrusik 1977). PR, in contrast to DR, makes it easy to represent knowledge of the second order, which is necessary to express facts describing the use of facts. PR – again in contrast to DR – makes it possible to take into account, in a simple way, the peculiarities of a particular area of subject matter. These peculiarities may be given, for instance, in heuristic knowledge, which it is difficult (or impossible) to express by the universal procedures of DR. The importance of what has been said here becomes apparent if one bears in mind that it is heuristic – not universal – knowledge which effective deductive reasoning is based upon.

3.4.3 Frame Representation

Winograd (1975) showed that both DR and PR may be represented as points of the spectrum "modularity (decomposition)/interaction". Representation of knowledge in the form of predicate calculus of the first order may serve as an example of modularity (see Popov and Firdman 1976, Sect. 3.5). In this representation, the initial data are considered axioms, while the task to be performed is regarded as a statement, the truthfulness or falseness of which is to be proven with the help of axioms and rules of reasoning. Axioms are considered to be the maximum decomposition of knowledge. Indeed, every axiom is true if no dependence on its interaction with the rest of knowledge is taken into account. On the other hand, a program (if no special restrictions have been imposed on it) is an obvious example of interaction. Indeed, in the course of performing any part of a program (a subroutine) "side effects" usually appear – these provide an interaction with other parts of the program. Interactions (versus decomposition), which occur in all programs, result in the fact that it is very difficult (or even impossible) to understand the sense of a program if one does not know in what situation it is to be used, and when and how its results are to be utilized.

From the point of view of the spectrum "decomposition/interaction", the flexibility and efficiency of DR are the consequence of a division of knowledge into "WHAT" (facts) and "HOW" (universal procedures). The ease with which DR may be modified is a direct result of the independence of declarative statements from the procedures in which they are used. On the other hand, the PR approach is a more natural way to express strong and comprehensive interactions between the blocks knowledge is divided into. In order to make use of the advantages of both DR and PR, we have to develop a formalism which would enable us to use decomposition without sacrificing the possibilities connected with interactions.

It should be stressed that efficiency is not the only factor which determines the choice between DR and PR; certain other factors exist as well. The incompleteness of knowledge of the surrounding world, for instance, makes it impossible to describe every phenomenon in the form of procedures, and the strong interdependence between some other phenomena rules out the possibility of describing them adequately with the help of declarative representation.

Traditional semantic networks are located more to the right in the spectrum "decomposition/interaction" than the language of predicate calculus, i.e., their properties are more similar to interactions; consequently, they lose the property of "ease of learning". However, the declarative statements which constitute semantic networks are still largely independent. This makes the process of interaction more complex. Indeed, this independence results in the need to express all information connected with a statement in the statement itself. In contrast to networks, a great proportion of information in programs concerns not a particular statement (language operator) but the whole program (subroutine). In classic semantic networks, interactions between different parts of knowledge can be expressed by means of absolute addressing only, while procedures may utilize indirect and relative addressing and are able to perform interactions in the form of "side effects".

An attempt to develop a representation which would combine the advantages of both decomposition and interaction was made by Minsky (1975), who introduced the so-called frame representation (FR). It should be borne in mind that FR (like DR and PR) is not a concrete language used to represent knowledge, but rather a sort of general concept which can be put into practice in different ways in such particular languages as KRL (Bobrow and Winograd 1977a, b), FRL (Goldstein and Roberts 1977), and K-NET (Fikes and Hendrix 1979). Before describing a particular language, let us determine the principles of FR. We shall follow Minsky's original work here (1975).

A *frame* is a structure of data (declarative representation) used to represent a certain standard situation. With every frame one associates a variety of information (including procedures), such as how a given frame may be used, what the expected results of accomplishing this frame are, or what one should do if these results are different from those expected.

A frame may be represented in the form of a network. The "upper levels" of a frame are fixed (invariable) and represent facts which are always true and situations which are to be described by this particular frame. The "lower levels" end in terminals (slots), which are filled by concrete information when the frame is called. Thus, there is an analogy between the slots of a frame and the formal parameters of the procedures of programming languages. In our opinion, the essential difference between slots and formal parameters (as they are treated in programming languages) consists in the fact that a frame contains a description of its structure in terms of semantics (not syntax) and in metaterms. Every slot is accompanied by a description of the requirements which have to be met in determining the concrete meaning of the slot. In the simplest case, these requirements can be reduced to an indication of the semantic categories to which the meaning of the slot should correspond. In more complex cases, the requirements may concern the relationships between the actual meanings (values) of several slots.

Related frames create a system of frames. The system contains description of the interdependences (of cause and effect, time, etc.) between constituent frames. To express these interdependences, the frames have a set of slots which are common to all of them. Having these relationships explicitly expressed, it is possible to predict the transition from a state A (described by frame A) to another state dependent on A – state B (described by frame B), and to accomplish this transition effectively, i.e., without recalculating all the parameters characterizing B, but only those which change their value or have not been calculated before.

The phenomenological usefulness of the frame representation results chiefly from the fact that it takes into account suppositions (predictions) and expectations. Some standard (typical) initial values may be assigned ("tacitly") to the slots of a frame. This makes it possible, with the use of similar frames, to analyze situations where information about many details is lacking. Standard values, assigned "tacitly", are not rigidly connected with the corresponding slots – they may be replaced by better values if such values are found in the course of processing a given situation. The use of the concept of "tacit knowledge" often makes it unnecessary to use quantificational statements.

Systems of frames, in turn, are organized as an information retrieval network. This property of a system of frames is utilized when an attempt to determine a consistency between a given situation and a given frame fails, i.e., when it turns out to be impossible to assign to the slots of the frame values which would meet the requirements connected with these particular slots. If this is the case, the network proposes some other frame.

Let us note that from the point of view of the concepts we introduced before (a data-directed process and a goal-directed process – see Sect. 2.2.5), the notion of a frame successfully solves the problem of goal direction (i.e., "downwards") but rather poorly that of data direction (i.e., "upwards"). This can be explained in the following way. If a given frame (F) has already been chosen (i.e., the goal is established) then F contains considerable information which can be used to direct the process (for instance, "understanding" an input text concerning F); on the other hand, a frame itself cannot help in determining, on the basis of the text being processed, whether it is precisely this particular frame that should be called up.

3.4.4 Analysis of the Existing Methods of Representing Knowledge

Frame representation is the generally accepted method of representing knowledge. However, as we have already observed, FR is a general concept rather than a well-defined representation. We ourselves find it necessary to choose a frame representation which is based on declarative representation with procedural connections (DRPC). A similar approach was used in KRL (Bobrow and Winograd 1977a, b); however, this differs from ours in several respects.

First, the language of KRL is an external language, i.e., it is designed to record knowledge by the user (not by the designer of an SNL). The language which will be described in Sect. 3.5 is an internal (not external) language of the logical level (in contrast to the physical level, i.e., the level of machine representation). Although an external language plays an important role in knowledge representation, in Sect. 3.5 we shall focus our attention on an internal language – for the following reasons:

1. The main goal of this book is to examine the algorithmic principles of the process of conversation in a natural language. Therefore, we are chiefly interested in internal representation.
2. Throughout this book we always assume that a dialogue system possesses all the information which is necessary for the process of conversation to be accomplished. Since both the space here available to us and the author's knowledge are limited, we shall not consider the problem of how this information appears in the system. To be complete, our picture should be supplemented with a description of the language of external knowledge representation and of the process of transforming the external representation into the internal one. This problem, however, is by no means an easy one. To view this in proper perspective, let us note that the solution to this problem would be equivalent to a solution to the problem of learning – and this problem is still far from being solved.
3. This author is convinced that it is a natural language that should be used as an external language (in the future, at least). Otherwise, we can hardly expect to be able to "teach" the system a sufficient amount of knowledge. However, the problems which arise here are not only difficult but even insoluble if an SNL is to deal with a large, or variable, area of subject matter. If the subject matter is sufficiently narrow, knowledge may be inserted into the system by the designers of the SNL, using symbolic languages whose structure is more rigid (more formalized) than that of KRL.

Second, in order to achieve the maximum compactness of knowledge representation (which is absolutely necessary for systems of real-life complexity), we propose not one language of knowledge representation but rather several (see below): languages designed for A-networks, C-networks, D-tables, and a system dictionary.

Third, the description of knowledge is realized in the form of networks (as in the K-NET language) and not in the form of lists (as in KRL). This ensures better effectiveness of methods of access, as well as better clarity of representation. However, the proposed language of networks may, if necessary, be expressed in the form of list structures (see Sect. 3.5.11).

In this author's opinion, the choice of declarative representation as the basis of knowledge representation is justified by at least the following factors:

1. A conversation in a natural language is conducted mainly in declarative form (see Sect. 3.4.1).
2. Declarative representation ascertains a fact, but does not indicate any way in which this fact might be used (in contrast to PR); therefore, DR is more

suitable for considering knowledge at various levels of abstraction and from various angles, depending on the objectives and tasks to be performed with the help of this knowledge.
3. Since knowledge of the world is always incomplete, it is impossible to obtain a procedural description of all possible phenomena.

Of the above-mentioned factors, this author believes the second one to be particularly important. This is because "understanding", which is a part of the process of conversation, is determined by the participant's objectives; it is not something "absolute". It should be stressed that choosing declarative representation is not equivalent to solving the problem – different forms of declarative representation are known: predicate calculus language (PC), list structures, semantic networks, and "tabular" (relational) language (Codd 1970).

The following shortcomings of the PC language can be mentioned (Popov and Firdman 1976):

1. Difficulties (ambiguities) arise during translation of sentences from an NL into the first order formulae of the PC.
2. Difficulties arise in attempting to make provision for partial knowledge of the subject matter.
3. There is a lack of effective procedures for the second and higher order calculations.
4. There is a lack of interdependence (interaction) between the formulae of the PC.

The most important shortcomings of the tabular language are the following:

1. Quantificational statements cannot be represented.
2. There is a lack of explicitly expressed semantic relationships between concepts in the tabular representation.
3. Because of this lack of relationships, it is necessary to observe a strictly defined order of all participants in events and states (i.e., the order given in a row of a table) – even if many of them are unknown or unnecessary. This leads to substantial redundancy when representing information of a particular type.

Let us note that tabular representation is nonetheless an extremely effective (compact) method of representing partial information.

The representation proposed here will be based on DR in the form of semantic networks. The most important merits of such a choice are the following:

1. The interrelations between the entities constituting a network are expressed explicitly. This simplifies the problem of access to the necessary information.
2. Semantic networks are well suited to representing the informal sentences occurring in an NL.

Traditional semantic networks have several shortcomings, however. For example, it is difficult to represent quantificational statements and variable events in terms of such networks. Their power of expression is also insufficient (as compared with formal logic). However, we intend to show that by expanding the language of semantic networks we can overcome many of these deficiencies. We do not claim that the language of expanded semantic networks makes it possible to represent the surrounding world in all its diversity. Nevertheless, we shall demonstrate that it can serve as a very useful tool, enabling us to represent the entities which are used in contemporary SNLs. As we have already observed, there is no way in which the world, in all its rich variety, can be represented here. Thus, for want of anything better, we have chosen semantic networks as our base, letting ourselves be guided by Sir Arthur Eddington's wise saying: "What my net can't catch isn't fish".

3.5 Representing Knowledge About the Model of the Surrounding Environment

3.5.1 General Structure of Knowledge Representation

It is advisable to divide knowledge about the surrounding environment into parts according to the differing internal structure of knowledge and the fact that different parts of knowledge are necessary at different stages of processing an utterance. We shall distinguish three such parts: N-networks, C-networks, and D-tables. An *A-network* (abstract network) is used for storing information about the set of all possible states of the subject matter. The information is expressed in terms of general concepts, events, and characteristics. An A-network is used as a method of eliminating the inexplicitness of an input utterance (i.e., of making this utterance understandable), and of making it consistent – as regards the form of representation – with the representation used in the C-network of the system. As a first approximation, an A-network may be considered to be a labeled, oriented graph. The vertices of this graph correspond to words or word combinations and the lines correspond to the semantic relations which connect these words. We shall describe A-networks in more detail further on.

A *C-network* (concrete network) contains concrete facts (events or states) which are known to the system. These are represented in the format of an A-network. The existence of a relationship between objects in the C-networks *must* (not *may*, as is the case with an A-network) entail the existence of a corresponding relationship in the world which is being modeled. In A-networks, the vertices correspond to concepts existing in the real world; in C-networks they denote concrete objects. Like an A-network, the C-network may also be considered to be a labeled, oriented graph. However, in all real systems, the number of concrete facts substantially exceeds the number of abstract concepts; therefore, it is very advisable to store C-networks in a more compact form. The list of participants and their roles in a given event or state represented in a C-network are specified by the A-network. Hence, it is not necessary for semantic relationships connecting events (or states) with participants in these events (or states) to be explicitly indicated in a C-network.

D-tables store values which characterize concrete events or states, i.e., what usually interests the user who is conversing with the system. The information contained in a D-table and the structure of the table itself depend strongly on the area of subject matter and on the use to be made of the system. If, for instance, a system is to give information about documents, the D-tables may contain the texts of these documents (the symbols by which they can be referred to are then stored by the C-network). If a system stores information about an enterprise's economic performance, the D-tables contain the planned and actual values of parameters which characterize events and states at different periods of time. The above-mentioned examples show that the storage capacity of D-tables is usually much greater than that of C-networks (to say nothing of A-networks); therefore, in order to make D-tables effective, a different representation is used for them than for C-networks. From the point of view of data retrieval and processing, it is convenient to represent D-tables in the form of relational data bases (Codd 1970). In this section we shall focus our attention on a description of A-networks, as it is these which play the most "intellectual" role in the DRPC.

3.5.2 Primary Components of Network Notation

The base elements of network representation are labeled vertices and lines. The vertex of a network represents an entity from the set U (see 3.2.1). The lines of a network also correspond to entities (which code the interrelations between two participants) occurring in a situation which does not depend on time. The last limitation imposed on lines is a consequence of the following: A line may only be determined by three parameters – the name of the line, the initial vertex, and the final vertex. Therefore, it can model a situation which depends on not more than three aspects. A situation, however, may be characterized by the type of situation, by the participants in this situation, and by the time interval during which the given situation takes place. The type of situation is defined by the name (label) of the line; the two other parameters specify the participants in the event and the time interval (let us note that in order to define the time interval we should specify two values). Hence, if an event is to be described by a line, it cannot be dependent on time. It should be noted here that the names of lines ('*a*') which originate from any vertex (event) can be considered attributes ('*a*') of this particular event (see Sect. 3.3.7). It should be stressed that all vertices of a network must have different names (labels), while lines, although also labeled, do not necessarily have to have different names. In Fig. 3.6 a fragment of a semantic network is depicted. The information conveyed by this particular fragment is: "During time interval $[t_1, t_2)$ Mikhail possessed a ZHIGULI-25-15" [*Zhiguli* – name of a Russian car; trans. note]. Mikhail is an agent (owner) in the event P_1. Mikhail is an element (*e*) of the set PERSON. ZHIGULI-25-15 is an element of the set CARS. The event P_1 is an element of the set of all events POSSESSING which, in turn, is a subset (*s*) of the set SITUATIONS, etc. Let us notice that any number of pieces of information may be assigned to an event with the use of originating lines. In accordance with the type of originating line, events may be classified into different relations which, in turn, may be grouped into various types of "situations" (for instance, POSSESSING, IMPLICATIONS, UTTERING, etc.). Any event may be represented in the form of a formal relation (R), but one should remember that the event and R are not equivalent. Thus, the event P_1 which is shown in Fig. 3.6 may be represented in the form of the n-tuple (see Sect. 3.2.4)

(POSSESSING**, t_1, t_2, MIKHAIL, ZHIGULI-25-15)

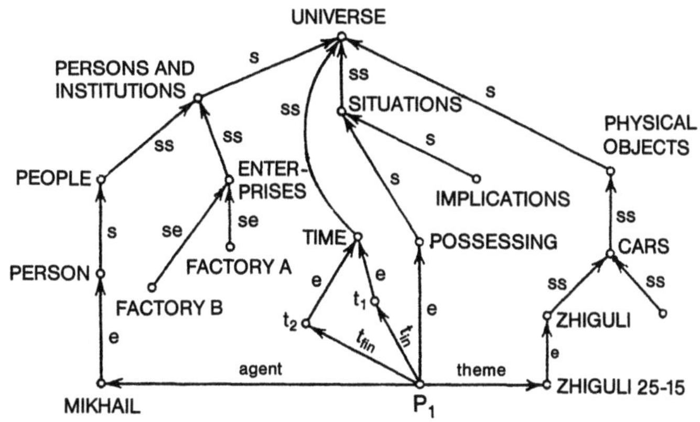

Fig. 3.6. Fragment of a semantic network

which is not the event itself, and this n-tuple may be false. Representation in the form of an n-tuple (in contrast to network representation) does not explicitly specify the roles performed by the participants in an event. The following point seems to be relevant here: machine representation should model an entity itself (an event E, for instance) not a mathematical model (i.e., a relation R). A mathematical model, however, may be used to formalize relationships between modeled entities.

3.5.3 Hierarchical Taxonomy

The lines "e" (element) and "s" (subset) which were used in Fig. 3.6 express the taxonomy of concepts the vertices correspond to. The importance of taxonomy lies in the fact that many sets are characterized by properties which are common to all elements of the given set (see Sect. 3.5.7). In networks, therefore, these properties are connected not with particular elements, but rather with a vertex corresponding to the whole set. The line "s" indicates the relation "to be a subset". Since the majority of subsets do not intersect one another, it is advisable to introduce a special type of line "ss" ("separate subset") for such nonintersecting subsets. Thus, a line "ss" from a vertex x to z indicates that a set represented by the vertex x is a subset of a set represented by the vertex z, and that x does not intersect any other subset represented by a vertex r connected with z by the "ss" line. In the network depicted in Fig. 3.6, for instance, the sets x (= PEOPLE) and r (= ENTERPRISES) are both subsets (*ss*) of the set z (= PERSONS AND INSTITUTIONS), and these two subsets have no common elements. The relation "se" may be introduced in an analogous way. In Fig. 3.6 the vertices FACTORY A and FACTORY B are separate elements (the relation "se") of the set ENTERPRISES.

3.5.4 Network Spaces

There is an important difference between traditional semantic networks and expanded semantic networks: the latter may be divided into subnetworks (i.e., spaces). It is also possible to establish relationships not only between vertices, but also between spaces (Hendrix 1975a, b). Each line and each vertex of an A-network is an element of at least one space. Let us note that the concept of a space is analogous to the notion of parentheses in mathematical notation. The spaces of a network may be arranged to form a tree of spaces. The vertices of such trees correspond to the spaces themselves, while the lines correspond to relations of "visibility". An example of a space tree is depicted in Fig. 3.7. In this tree, the space P_6 (a space descendant) "sees" only the vertices and lines from its space ancestors P_4, P_2, P_0; all the other spaces are "invisible". The relation of "visibility" makes it possible to group spaces in ordered sets – "perspectives". Perspectives are used to limit the number of network entities which are "visible" to a procedure working with the network. Usually, only hierarchically grouped spaces are included in a perspective. In the following examples we shall use several assumptions concerning the way in which spaces are represented: (a) vertices and lines belonging to one space are enclosed in a polygon (usually this is a rectangle); (b) it is assumed that each figure is enclosed in a certain space of a higher (outer) level which is omitted from the figure for the sake of simplicity; (c) a line belongs to the space where there is the name of this line; (d) if a space P_i (or, more precisely, the polygon it is enclosed in) lies inside a space P_j, P_i is considered to be a descendant (inner level), i.e., P_j is "visible" to P_i. The space P_i may be treated as a "supervertex" contained in P_j. The property of "invisibility" makes the operation of retrieval in the network more effective. If, for instance, concrete information is being sought, information from quantificational statements and rules is invisible, as it is contained in spaces which surround these statements and rules.

To close this section we shall say a few words about the problem of the computer representation of networks which are built of spaces. A network may be represented in the form of three lists (of spaces, of vertices, and of lines). The list of spaces includes, for each given space, a list of all spaces visible to it, together with a list of the vertices and lines of this particular space. The list of vertices includes the name of the space each vertex belongs to, and the list of lines leading to and originating from this particular vertex. The list of lines includes the name of the space each line belongs to, and the names of the vertices which are connected by this particular line. Let us note that all the aforementioned lists vary in the course of processing (they are created and removed).

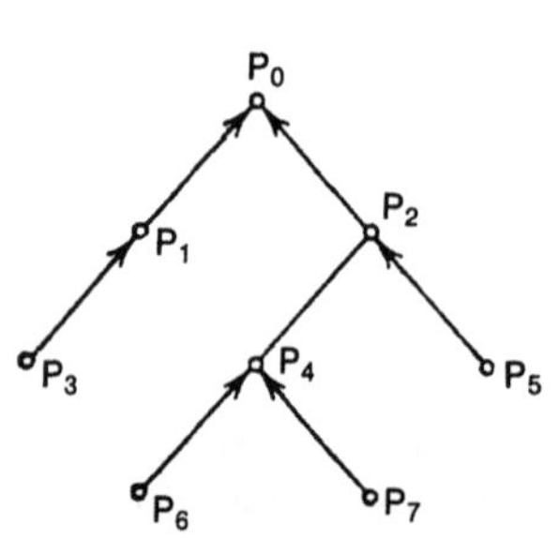

Fig. 3.7. Example of division of a network into spaces

3.5.5 Negations, Disjunctions, and Implications

Of the whole variety of logical connectives we shall be considering only negation, disjunction, and implication: $\neg$, $\vee$, $\rightarrow$. Let us recall that negation, either with disjunction or with conjunction, forms a complete system of logical connectives (Mendelson 1964). However, we shall also include implication in our considerations, as this is a useful tool for representing quantificational statements in A-networks. No additional means are required to represent conjunctions in networks; in accordance with the rules of constructing networks, all vertices and lines are tacitly connected by conjunction marks. Figure 3.8 represents the conjunction of two events. Other logical connectives are quite a different matter. In order to

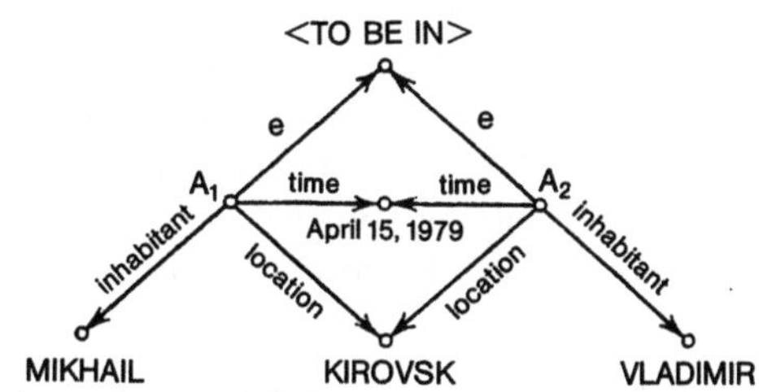

Fig. 3.8. Network representation of conjunction of two events

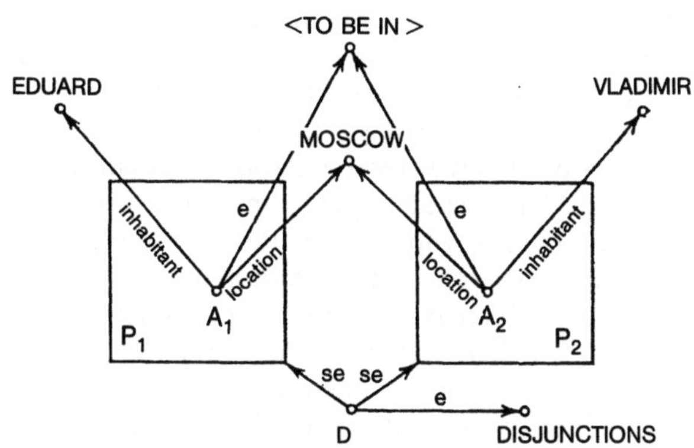

Fig. 3.9. Network representation of disjunction of two events

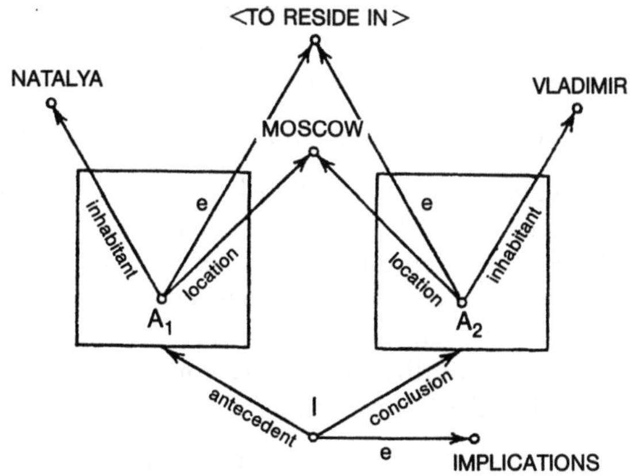

Fig. 3.10. Network representation of implication

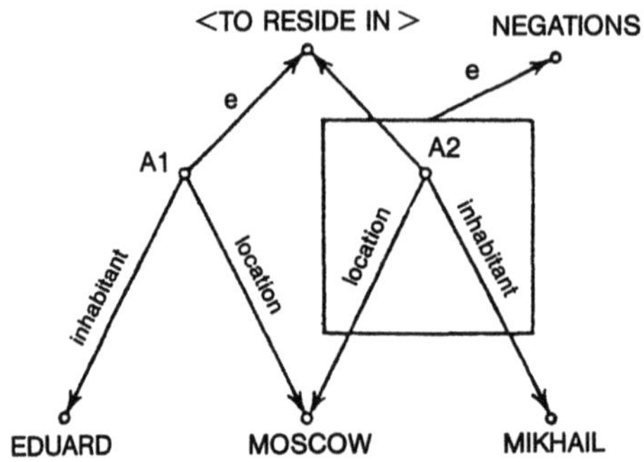

Fig. 3.11. Network representation of negation of an utterance

represent them, we can use network spaces. Figure 3.9 shows the possible representation of a disjunction. The vertex D in this figure is interpreted as the statement that at least one of the two spaces P_1 and P_2 actually exists. Implication is depicted in Fig. 3.10 ("If Natalya lives in Moscow, then Vladimir lives in Moscow, too"), and negation (of the statement "Eduard lives in Moscow and Mikhail does not live in Moscow") in Fig. 3.11.

3.5.6 Network Representation of Quantificational Statements

In Sect. 3.3.1 we introduced the notion of patterns of situations which are coded in the form of quantificational statements. Quantificational statements enable us to represent in an effective way sets of situations and quantificational utterances of a natural language (e.g., "All factories consume energy"). Let us consider the problem of effective representation of quantificational statements in semantic networks. The first attempts to approach this problem were rather clumsy. Then Hendrix (1975a) proposed a method for coding quantificational statements – this method, with some modification, is the one we shall be adopting. In the above-cited work, Hendrix analyzed several other methods (Shapiro 1971; Kay 1973; Woods 1975; Schubert 1975) and compared them with his own, which he demonstrated to be the best of them all.

Binding by existential quantifiers in an A-network is performed automatically, as the occurrence of an entity X (a vertex or a line) in a space P is considered a statement about the existence of X in P. Figure 3.12 shows an example where the statement $(\exists x \in X)\, P(x)$ is represented. A universal quantifier may be expressed with the aid of negation and an existential quantifier, i.e.,

$$(\forall x \in X)\, P(x) \equiv \neg\neg\, ((\forall x \in X)\, P(x)) \equiv \neg\, ((\exists x \in X) \neg\, P(x)).$$

A fragment of an A-network with the universal quantifier expressed by the existential quantifier and negation is depicted in Fig. 3.13. From the point of view of logic, this representation is exact. To a human being, however, this is not intuitively obvious (this is particularly so when certain quantifiers are "immersed" in each other). Therefore, we shall use another representation for the universal quantifier; it is more comprehensible to a human being if it is transformed in the following way:

$$(\forall x \in X)\, P(x) \equiv \forall x\, ((x \in X) \rightarrow P(x)).$$

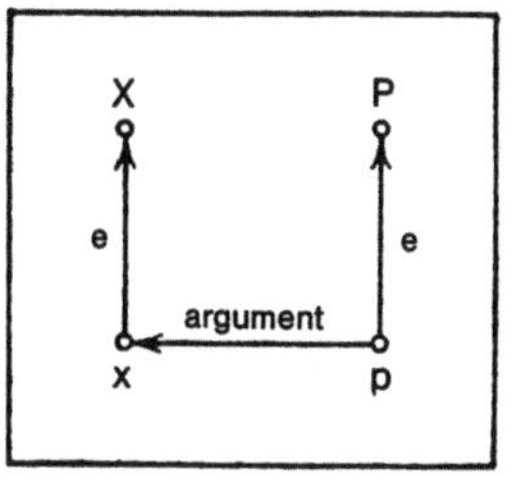

Fig. 3.12. Network representation of the existential quantifier for the statement $(\exists x \in X)\, P(x)$.

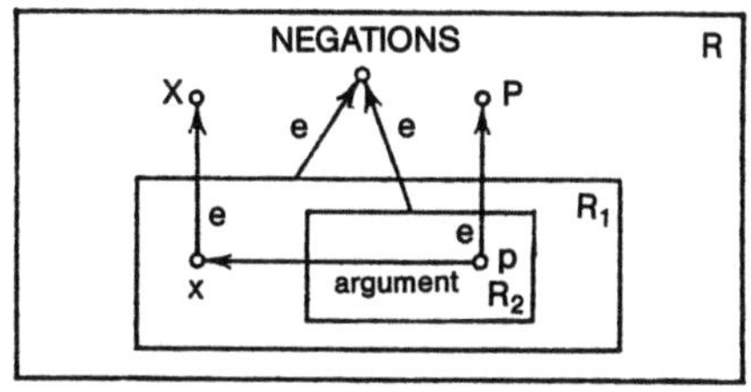

Fig. 3.13. Network representation of the universal quantifier with the aid of negation and the existential quantifier

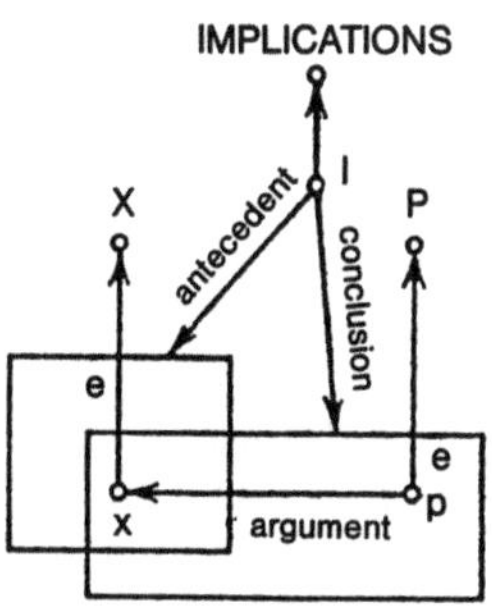

Fig. 3.14. A-network representation of the universal quantifier

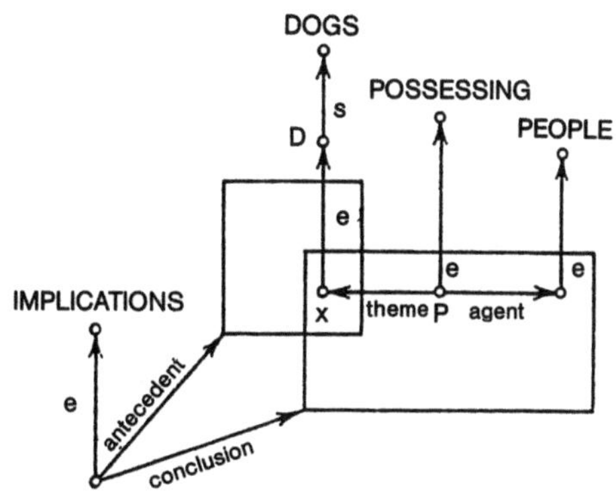

Fig. 3.15. A-network representation of the quantifier "some"

In other words, any universal quantifier may be represented by an implication in which the antecedent determines the type of variable the quantifier applies to, and the consequent (conclusion) expresses the statement corresponding to the action of this universal quantifier. A universal quantifier differs from normal implication in that the universal variable (i.e., the variable bounded by the universal quantifier) occurs in both the space of the antecedent and the space of the conclusion. Figure 3.14 shows an example (in which the expression $(\forall x \in X)\, P(x)$ is represented in an A-network with the use of implication). Note that we need not consider "chains" of quantifiers (quantifiers which are immersed in each other) if an expression occurring in the area of action of a quantifier is an implication. Indeed,

$$(\forall x \in X)(Q(x) \rightarrow R(x)) \equiv (\forall x)((x \in X) \rightarrow (Q(x) \rightarrow R(x)))$$
$$\equiv (\forall x)(((x \in X) \wedge Q(x)) \rightarrow R(x)).$$

Any "chain" of quantifiers may be achieved by inserting implications in the spaces of the conclusions of other implications. For instance:

$$(\forall x \in X)(\exists y \in Y)(\forall z \in Z)\, P(x, y, z)$$
$$\equiv \forall x((x \in X) \rightarrow (\exists y)((y \in Y) \wedge (\forall z)((z \in Z) \rightarrow P(x, y, z)))).$$

Examples of certain particular quantificational statements will be studied in Chap. 6 (Fig. 6.12).

A natural language contains the whole spectrum of quantifications from universal quantifiers to existential quantifiers. As examples, we might mention such quantifiers as "a certain", "a few", "many", "the most". Each of these may be expressed with the help of certain special methods. It turns out, however, that universal and existential quantifiers may suffice. Figure 3.15, for instance, represents the sentence "Some dogs have masters (i.e., owners)". The network in the figure states that for any $x \in D$, x has a master. But D is defined as a subset ("s") of the set DOGS. D is "some dogs" from the set DOGS, and all dogs (x) from this subset have masters. Strictly speaking, the quantifier "some" implies that the set D is not the null set – this fact should somehow be reflected in the network. For the quantifiers "a few" or "many", the "size" of a set D – compared with the size of the set it is included in – should be indicated (not necessarily by absolute numbers).

3.5.7 Rules and Categories

The simplest method of representing a hierarchical classification in a network is by utilizing the lines "s" and "ss" (also "e" and "se"). These lines were described in Sect. 3.5.3. A more complex method of classification requires the use of rules determining categories (see Sects. 3.3.7 and 3.3.8). Let us therefore consider the problem of how rules may be represented in a network. It has already been stressed that representing rules and representing quantificational statements have much in common (see Sect. 3.5.7). This will become apparent after we have considered the examples given below.

Let us consider the representation of r-rules in an A-network (see Sect. 3.3.8). Rules of this kind are widely used in the process of understanding input sentences in an NL. These rules impose restrictions on the forms of entities which should be referred to by the participants in a particular event. In Fig. 3.16 we give an example of the r-rule (introduced by the line "restriction") for the event POSSES-

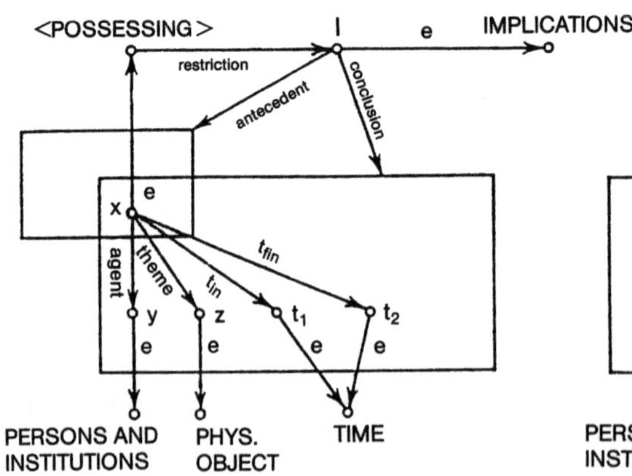

Fig. 3.16. Representation of the r-rule for the event POSSESSING

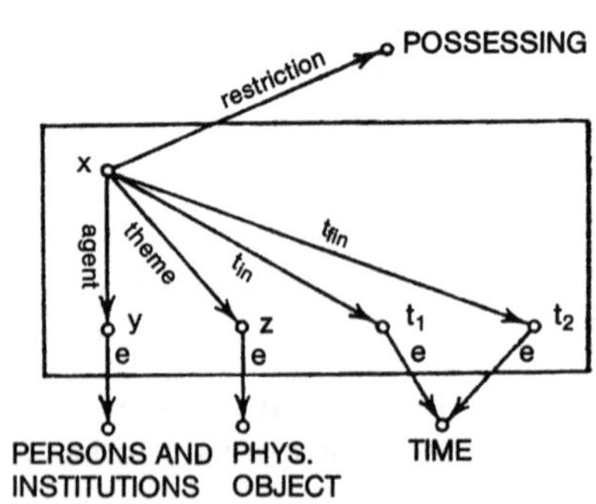

Fig. 3.17. Simplified notation of an r-rule

SING. The rule indicates that every situation POSSESSING should be characterized by an agent, a theme, t_{in}, and t_{fin}. In addition "an agent" must be a person or institution, "a theme" must be a physical object, and t_{in} and t_{fin} must be elements of the set TIME. Applying r-rules at the stage of semantic analysis (see Sect. 5.4) makes it possible to reject incorrect versions of interpretation submitted at the stage of syntactic analysis. For the sake of simplicity, we shall use a simplified form of representation of r-rules (not taking into account the real machine representation). The simplified form of representation of the r-rule for the event POSSESSING is given as an example in Fig. 3.17.

3.5.8 Representation of Higher-Level Structures

Besides the above-mentioned methods of representing logical connectives, quantifiers, and rules, an A-network may be utilized for coding other, higher-level structures. For instance, network spaces may be effectively applied for representing hypothetical worlds and contexts, for planning, for expressing disjunctions, implications, and negations, for coding various levels of abstraction, etc. Figure 3.18 gives an example of a network representation of the following hypothetical situation: "Vladimir wants to own a car". In this representation, the notion of space is not used; as a consequence, the representation has at least two substantial deficiencies: (a) the car A is not in fact a variable, as it should be, but rather a concrete element of the set CARS; (b) the event P (possessing) is represented as an actual (not hypothetical) element. Thus, in this representation, the event P cannot be distinguished from really existing events. The same event may be represented in a method which is free from these two deficiencies (Fig. 3.19).

Other examples of higher-level structures are representations of interrogative sentences and of focus. Representation of interrogative sentences in an A-network will be considered in Chap. 5, where examples will also be given (see Figs. 5.8 and 5.9). Focus (i.e., context) will be considered in Sect. 6.3.

3.5.9 A-Network Representation of a Process

The concept of process was introduced in Sect. 3.3. The set of all calls for a process A constitutes a category which can be defined by the rule: "An event falls

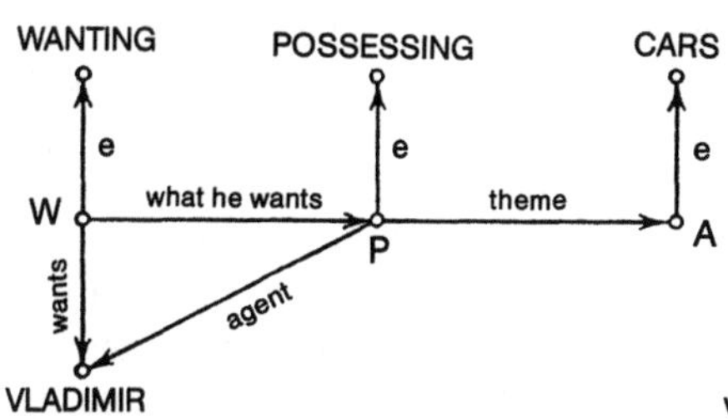

Fig. 3.18. Network representation of a hypothetical world; space not used

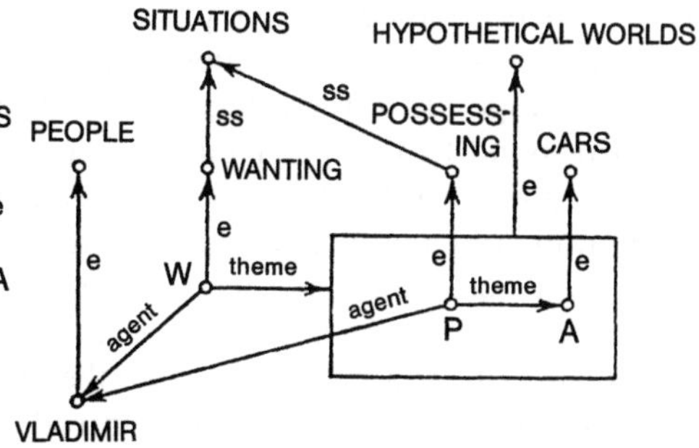

Fig. 3.19. Representation of a hypothetical world; space used

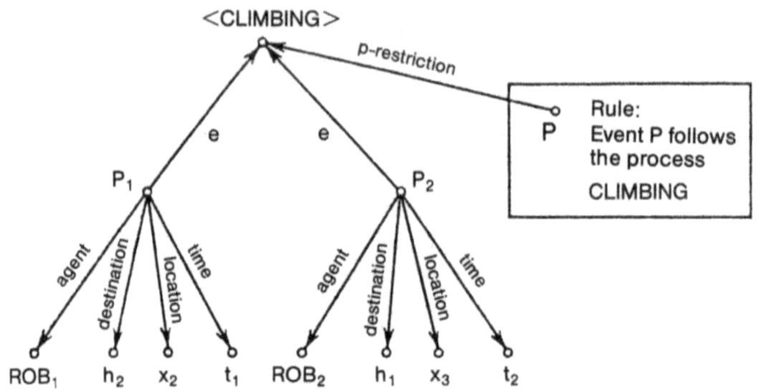

Fig. 3.20. Interrelations between the category of an event, the process characterizing the event, and the assignment of the event

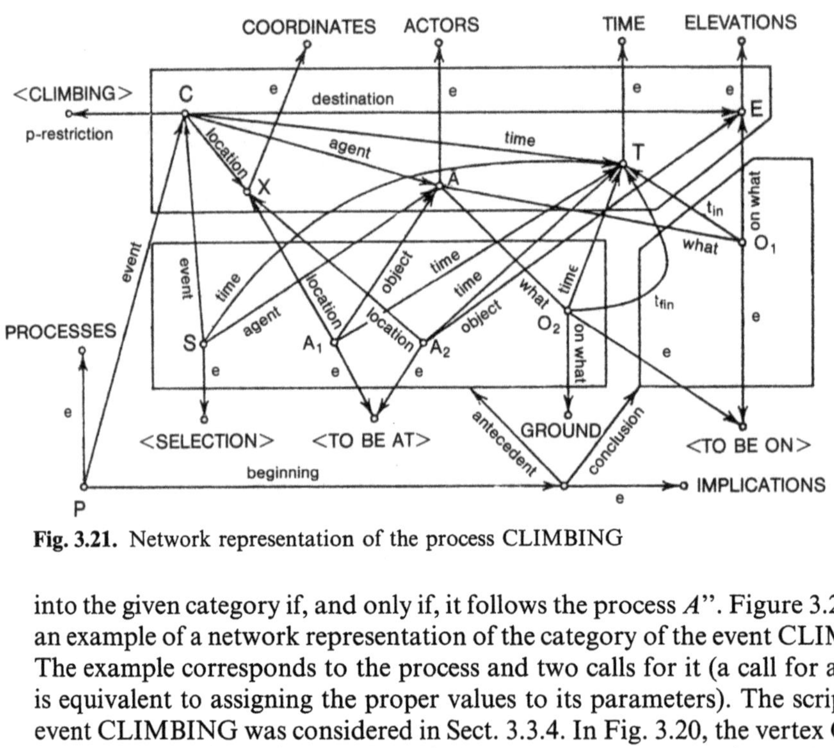

Fig. 3.21. Network representation of the process CLIMBING

into the given category if, and only if, it follows the process *A*". Figure 3.20 shows an example of a network representation of the category of the event CLIMBING. The example corresponds to the process and two calls for it (a call for a process is equivalent to assigning the proper values to its parameters). The script of the event CLIMBING was considered in Sect. 3.3.4. In Fig. 3.20, the vertex CLIMBING corresponds to the category of all events CLIMBING. The vertices P_1 and P_2 correspond to two particular calls (assignments) for the event CLIMBING. The category CLIMBING is determined (by an r-rule) with the use of the line "p-restriction" (an analogue of the line "restriction", used when describing processes). The structure of the process introduced by this rule is shown in Fig. 3.21. A process represented in a network is characterized by the conditions for initiating the process (the space introduced by the line "antecedent"), by the conditions for terminating the process (the space introduced by the line "conclusion"), and by the rule of the description of the process (the space introduced by the line "p-restriction").

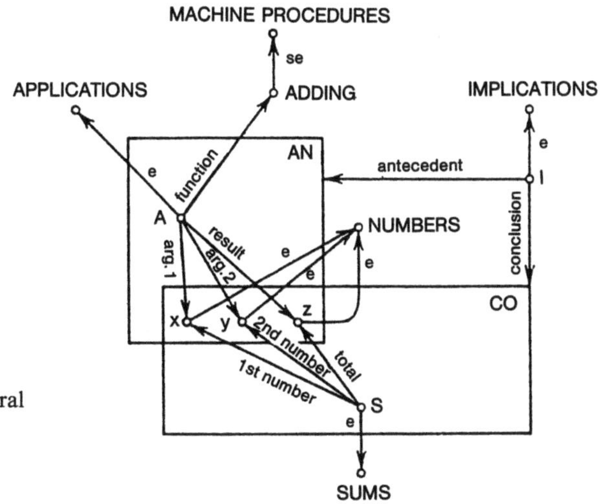

Fig. 3.22. Example of procedural accretion in an A-network

3.5.10 Procedural Accretions

In solving many concrete problems it not infrequently turns out that semantic networks alone do not provide the most convenient and effective means of performing a particular task. Consequently, in the system of understanding, knowledge is expressed not only in the form of networks, but also in the form of relational data bases or of procedures. The mechanism of procedural accretion is introduced to A-networks to ensure a link between the network and other (external) knowledge sources. The link between a network and external knowledge sources is represented in the form of "theorems" (i.e., implications containing universally quantified variables). Figure 3.22 shows an example of a representation of such a "theorem". The interpretation of this theorem is as follows: If the function ADDING is successfully applied to a certain set of arguments which correspond to the descriptions given in the space of the antecedent (*A*), then the arguments and the result returned by the function may be used to create relations and objects which correspond to the descriptions indicated in the space of the conclusion (*C*). The theorem shown in Fig. 3.22 indicates that application of the function ADDING (which is a machine function) may be used to produce a new example of the relation SUMS in the network. Thanks to this theorem, it is not necessary to store in the knowledge base all possible examples of the relation SUMS in their explicit form. When a system encounters the problem of adding two numbers together, then, with the aid of this theorem, the mechanism of inferring (see Sect. 6.4) will formulate a call for the function ADDING and will give the result in the form determined by the relation SUMS.

3.5.11 Linearization of Network Notation

Computer representation of network structures is substantially simplified if we introduce linearization of network notation, i.e., if the network is transformed into a list. The linearized language for A-networks, called LAN (linearized A-

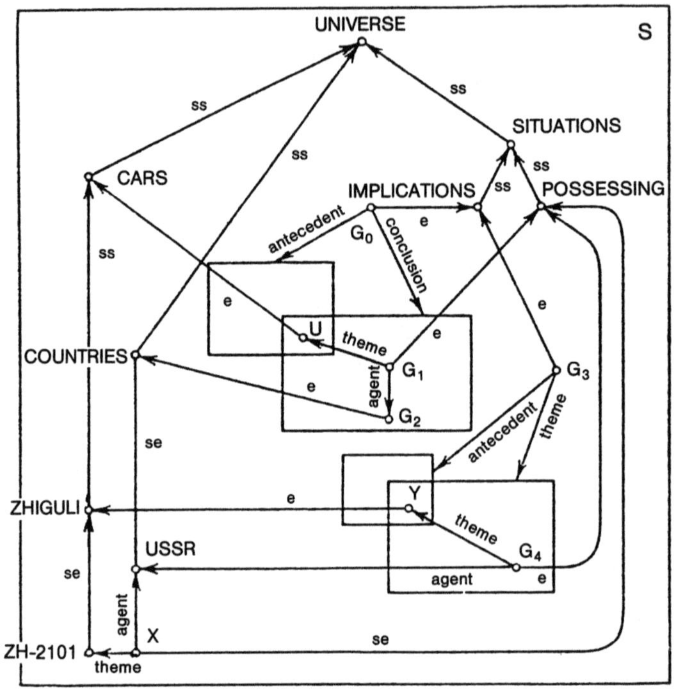

Fig. 3.23. Fragment of an A-network used to illustrate the use of the language LAN

Table 3.1 Linearized counterpart of a fragment of a network in LAN

(!SPACE S	1	(IMPLICATION	15
/UNIVERSE/	2	(/U (EL.CARS)/)	16
/SITUATIONS (IS UNIVERSE)/	3	(/-(EL.POSSESSING)	17
/IMPLICATIONS (IS SITUATIONS)/	4	{(theme U)	18
/POSSESSING (IS SITUATIONS)/	5	(agent (EL.COUNTRIES))}/))	19
/CARS (IS UNIVERSE)/	6	(DET.SIT.	20
/ZH-2101 (EL.ZHIGULI)/	7	POSSESSIN	
/ZHIGULI (IS CARS)/	8	(POSSESSOR PROPERTY)	21
/COUNTRIES (IS UNIVERSE)/	9	/(EL.POSSESSING)	22
/U.S.S.R. (EL.COUNTRIES)/	10	{agent POSSESSOR}	23
/X (EL.POSSESSING)	11	{theme PROPERTY}/)	24
{agent U.S.S.R.}	12	(IMPLICATION	25
{theme ZH-2101}/	13	/Y (EL.ZHIGULI)/	26
(SWITCH TO SE)	14	(⟨POSSESSING U.S.S.R. Y⟩)))	27

network), has a syntax resembling that of the language KRL (Bobrow and Winograd 1977a). In order to convey some idea of the language LAN, let us consider the fragment of a network shown in Fig. 3.23 and its linearized counterpart in LAN (see Table 3.1).

The function (! SPACE LABEL $e_1, e_2, \ldots, e_n$) is called by the first operator and forms a space. The first argument of this function is the name (label) of the created space; the rest of the arguments correspond to the context of this space.

The first of these arguments, [UNIVERSE], is transformed in the course of processing into (! VERTEX UNIVERSE). The result, generally speaking, is of the form (! VERTEX nonoblig. name e_1, $e_2, \ldots, e_n$). At the same time, in the current space (S) a new vertex is created: a nonobligatory name is assigned to it and the expressions $e_1, \ldots, e_n$ are calculated (these have been left out in this example). The third line creates the vertex labeled SITUATIONS and calculates the expression (IS UNIVERSE), which creates the line "ss" leading from SITUATIONS toward UNIVERSE. The following three lines are processed analogously. The seventh line creates the vertex ZH-2101 and the line "se" from ZH-2101 to the vertex ZHIGULI. Lines 8, 9, and 10 are processed analogously to the foregoing lines. The eleventh line creates the vertex X, connected with POSSESSING by the line "se", and then forms the lines: "agent" (to U.S.S.R.) and "theme" (to ZH-2101), which both originate from X. The expression in line 14 indicates that from now on the functions IS and EL create the lines "s" and "e" instead of "ss" and "se". The function IMPLICATION has two arguments: the list of expressions which are used to create structures in the space of the antecedent (this is given as the first argument) and in the space of the conclusion. The IMPLICATION from line 15 creates, in the space of the antecedent, the vertex U with the line "e" leading to CARS. The labels of vertices in the conclusion space are determined by the translator which processes the operators of the language LAN. The created vertex (G_1) is an element ("e") of the set POSSESSING; U plays the role of a "theme" and G_2 that of an "agent" (G_2 is a newly created vertex connected with the vertex COUNTRIES by the line "e").

The function DET.SIT. does not create any structures. It determines the simplifications which will be considered permissible in the following operators. In our example DET.SIT. redefines the names of the participants in the situation POSSESSING. Angle brackets $\langle$ and $\rangle$ are used when a situation is being concretized. The first argument inside brackets indicates the name of a situation, the rest of the arguments denote the participants in this situation.

4 The System's Knowledge About the Language and the Participants in the Conversation

4.1 Connected Text and Linguistic Concordances

Let us define a discourse (i.e., a connected text) as a set of two or more sentences which are interdependent as regards their sense. These sense connections are ensured by at least the following forms of linguistic concordances: aspectual-temporal, anaphoric, stylistic, modal, agreement of presuppositions, etc. Interdependence between sentences may be attained using both linguistic and extra-linguistic (situational) methods. The situational methods which make it possible to achieve an interdependence between sentences can be determined with the help of the mechanism of inferring (see Sect. 6.4) and scripts (see Sects. 3.3 and 3.5). Of the linguistic methods of expressing interdependence between sentences, we shall be examining the phenomena of anaphoric references and of ellipsis.

Every statement in a dialogue (or any discourse) may contain information of two different kinds: "old" information, i.e., information already introduced in the preceding sentences, and "new" information, i.e., information introduced by the given statement. To understand a statement in a discourse means to be able to determine, for every concept used in that statement, whether this concept has to be treated as a "new" one or as an "old" one. If it is "old", it is necessary to establish which of the concepts introduced earlier it refers to. If it is "new", a corresponding object must be found (or inserted) in the knowledge possessed by the system. Because of different methods of processing, we usually distinguish between nominal references (NR) and pronominal references (PR). In order to decipher any NR or PR, the process of retrieval must be used. In the case of an NR, the situational context and global text context (i.e., the preceding sentences of a discourse) play an essential role, whereas the local context is practically irrelevant. In the case of a PR, the situation is exactly the opposite. Since a pronoun itself usually does not convey any semantic information, what is essential in this case is the local text context, i.e., the linguistic context of the sentence currently being processed, or of the sentence directly preceding it. We can therefore say that deciphering an NR is a global semantic process, while deciphering a PR is more local and more "syntactic". There are, however, certain exceptions where deciphering a PR is also a global semantic process.

Pronominal references always correspond to entities which have been explicitly indicated in the text. Nominal references occur in more diverse ways. The simplest form of an NR occurs when a notion is indicated explicitly in the form in which it was introduced before. For instance: "I work in a factory. *The factory* is near my house". A more complex situation arises in the case of "partially coinciding" references. There are two possibilities here: (a) an initial notion is more concrete than the reference to it (for example: "In the year 1942 I was working in the Kirov factory. Despite all the difficulties of war time, *the factory* managed to fulfill its plan"); (b) an initial notion is less concrete than the reference to it (e.g., "I have sent my clothes to the cleaners. *The blue coat* will be ready tomorrow"). Probably the most complex case arises when the system encounters a reference to an object which has not been explicitly indicated in the preceding text but which is closely related to an object explicitly mentioned. For instance: "I entered Petrov's office. The first thing I noticed was the bright blue floor". Note that the word combination "bright blue floor" should not be considered a "new" object. It is obvious that a particular floor, i.e., the one in Petrov's office, is meant in the second sentence. Thus, in this case the reference is based on the situational context.

The essential difference between sentences constituting a discourse and isolated sentences consists in the presence of elliptic constructions in discourse sentences. A construction is called *elliptic* if some of its elements are omitted but may be unambiguously reconstructed by a participant in the dialogue. Such a reconstruction of an omitted element can be accomplished either by a reference to the textual context (usually the local context) or by a reference to the situational context. In the sentences given below, the first and second are examples of the former, while the other two illustrate the latter.

1. An apple tree bears apples and a pine tree, cones (it bears cones).
2. Will you be able to come? I hope I will (be able to).
3. How did you manage to get out (of prison)?
4. Would you like some more (tea)?

Paducheva's book (1974, Chap. 7) may be recommended to those interested in studying these questions in more detail.

The ellipsis may be reconstructed either with the use of the context of a given sentence (examples 1, 3, 4) or on the basis of the context of the preceding sentences (example 2). Elliptic constructions may occur at the level of a sentence, of a nominal group, or of a verbal group (examples 5, 6, and 7 respectively).

5. What tool did you use to tighten the bolt? A wrench (To tighten the bolt I used a wrench).
6. Do you like the cake? Yes, I'd like some more (cake), if you don't mind.
7. Have they read this book? Petrov has read it, but Ivanov hasn't (read it).

Note that ellipsis is a more local phenomenon than reference. Local context is always sufficient to reconstruct ellipsis. Note as well that not only semantics but also syntax plays an important role in the course of reconstructing ellipsis. The presence of ellipsis and the place in the sentence where it occurs are often expressed by a disturbance in the correct syntactic structure of the sentence (see Sect. 5.3).

4.2 Knowledge About the Language of Conversation

In this section we shall classify our knowledge of the Russian language. We shall also distinguish the main aspects of this knowledge which are necessary to design a system capable of conversing with the user in the natural Russian language. Because of the extreme complexity of any natural language, and because of the limitations of space we are confronted with here, we shall confine our considerations to the general structure of knowledge about the language; in other words, what we intend to do is to give an elementary introduction to the problem (on the basis of the Russian language). Such an approach to linguistics is in our opinion justified for two reasons. First, the designers of SNLs tend to have a rather superficial knowledge of the complex nuances of an NL, despite the fact that they speak it fluently. The vast majority of the nuances of a natural language are not noticed by the speakers of the language. This leads to baseless oversimplifications during work on designing a conversation system. The price for these oversimplifications is paid later, at the stage of using the system in practice. Second, the description of an NL given by linguists is not suitable for the designers of an SNL. Linguists aim at describing the whole language, without any limitations. In addition, as a rule, they simply describe the phenomena they have noticed while studying the language. Thus, their investigations are not directed at applying these phenomena (expressed by linguists in the form of filters) to the analysis and synthesis of phrases in NL.

In terms of the problem of conversation, it would be very interesting to study how a natural language can be utilized to express this or that concrete piece of information concerning reality. Obviously, such a description of a natural language (as yet not produced by anybody), which could be called a "semantic" description, would be geared toward answering the following question: In what way do native speakers of a given language carry out analysis (i.e., understanding) and synthesis (i.e., formulation) of texts? Below we shall briefly describe the Russian language, referring whenever we are able to elements of semantics. It should be borne in mind that what follows is only a general outline and by no means a detailed description of the Russian language.

4.2.1 The General and the Individual

Thanks to the research conducted by linguists, it is now obvious that it is impossible to describe a language in "general" terms only; we have to refer extensively to the individual properties of concrete lexemes and the ways of combining them. The general properties of a language are expressed by the rules of grammar of this language, while individual ones are expressed in the form of the information contained in the dictionary entries corresponding to particular lexemes. By the term "grammar" we mean a set of rules which govern the construction of lexical units from morphemes (morphology), and of utterances and parts of utterances from lexical units (syntax). During the act of speech, the appropriate rules are selected in accordance with the sense which is to be expressed. The main task is to select those rules which express as directly as possible the correspondence between the "contents" and "mode of expression", i.e., between the sense (represented in the model of reality) and the particulars of the outward appearance of the language units being formulated. In this author's opinion, the ultimate goal in describing a language is to find rules of constructing the text which, at the same time, play the role of rules of analysis and synthesis of senses. We would like to stress that the fact that we treat individual properties as distinct from grammar does not reflect the insufficient development of grammar but stems from the specific features of natural languages.

The syntactic properties of lexemes of natural languages can be divided into individual and categorical ones. By *categorical properties* we mean properties common to the entire morphological class of lexemes and reflected in rules of grammar. Thus, for instance, in the Russian language any noun (A) may possess as its attribute an adjective (B) which agrees with A as to gender, number, and case; any noun in the genitive case may play the role of an attribute of another noun of any gender, number, and case. Since the *individual properties* of lexemes cannot effectively be provided for in rules of grammar, they are indicated in a dictionary. Examples of such individual properties of a lexeme are the relations of government characteristic for this particular lexeme, or its lexical functions (see Sect. 4.3.3). In accordance with what has been said, our knowledge of a language may be divided into general knowledge, represented in the form of grammar, and individual knowledge, represented in the form of dictionary information (see Sect. 4.3).

4.2.2 The Sentence

A sentence may be defined as the smallest unit of speech which is grammatically correct (i.e., obeys the "norms" of the abstract language system adopted). It expresses a fact (facts) from the model of reality (a state, event, etc.) and the general relation between what is uttered and that reality. This *general interdependence* includes a relation between what is uttered and reality (the notion of modality) and also the passage of what is being uttered in the framework of specified time (the notion of syntactic time). Linguists distinguish between *objective modality* (i.e., the relation between what is uttered and reality) and *subjective modality* (i.e., the relation between the speaker and his utterance). It should be stressed that the connections between facts are expressed explicitly in the model of reality; however, not all aspects of these connections are explicitly expressed in a discourse conducted in a natural language. Serious research into these phenomena has only been undertaken by linguistics quite recently, and the results which have been obtained in this field are therefore still fairly modest. However, at a high level of abstraction, we can distinguish the following forms of connections (which are evident in accordances of various kind): aspectual-temporal connections, modal, stylistic, and anaphoric connections, and agreements of presuppositions. In the broadest and most comprehensive way, sense connections are expressed by using anaphorism and sets of presuppositions accompanying every sentence. All these forms of concordance constitute the system of attributes of a sentence as part of a discourse (as against a pseudosentence – see Sect. 1.3.3). Let us note that the description of forms of sense concordance in a sentence of a discourse is obviously the task of sentence syntax (unfortunately, this still requires further study by linguists). Information about reality is represented by a multidimensional construction in the model; in a natural language, however, this information is conveyed by the one-dimensional (linearly ordered) line of a text. In connection with this fact, one of the tasks of rules of grammar is to establish the appropriate linear order of words (lexemes). This task is preceded by the task of determining the boundaries of a sentence and determining its type. The point here is that sense connections between facts from reality can be expressed with the help of a different number of sentences; moreover, they can be distributed in sentences in various ways. We still know very little about how and on what basis human beings make this choice from among all the possibilities available to them. In other words, we know very little about why this or that structure of a discourse is chosen and what other structures are possible. As far as sentence structure is concerned, a detailed classification of it exists; nevertheless, we do not know much about why a person chooses this or that type of sentence (see Valgina 1973).

A sentence, as a unit of speech, is formulated in accordance with a specific task of communication. Thus, its grammatical structure depends on the tasks of a goal-directed utterance. The notion of the grammatical structure of a sentence assumes that we can distinguish, as constituent parts of the sentence, certain components; these are called clauses and word combinations. Adopting the grammatical structure of a sentence to correspond to communicative tasks (by including it in this or that speech situation) is called the *actual division* of this sentence. The units which appear during this division are called the *theme* (i.e., what has been given, the stem) and the *rheme* (i.e., what is new, the nucleus). What is known is the *theme of the utterance*, what is being communicated is the *rheme* – it is for the sake of this that the sentence has been formulated. Both the theme and the rheme may contain both the main and secondary parts of the sentence. Their distribution between the theme and the rheme is determined by the communicative task at hand. The following example should help the reader to understand the difference between actual and grammatical divisions. Let us consider the following sentence: "Will Nikolai come tomorrow?" By itself, this sentence cannot function as a meaningful act of speech, since it is not clear what it is that is actually unknown to the person posing the question: Is it Nikolai that is involved (or is it someone else?), will he come (or will he not?), will this be tomorrow (or some other day?)? During an act of speech, the rheme (i.e., what is new) can be distinguished by the use of logical stress; e.g., "Will Nikolai come *tomorrow*?" In this sentence "Will Nikolai come" is the theme (what is already known), while "tomorrow" is what is new (the rheme). Let us note that in terms of grammatical division this sentence is composed of a subject, a predicate, and an adverbial modifier.

To a considerable extent, the grammatical classification of sentences reflects semantic information. In accordance with the character of the relation to reality expressed by a sentence (objective modality), we can distinguish two types of sentences: *affirmative* ones and *negative* ones. In accordance with the goal of an utterance and the intonation linked to this goal, sentences can be divided into *narrative, interrogative,* and *hortatory* ones (each of these may become an exclamatory sentence if given the appropriate emotive coloring). Depending on the number of predicative units (actions or states of the model of reality) sentences fall into two categories: *simple* (having one predicate) and *complex* (having more than one predicate).

Obviously, all this cannot be taken to be a complete and detailed description of the syntax and morphology of the Russian language. The following books are recommended to readers interested in the questions raised in this section: Maslov 1975; Valgina 1973; Kubriakova 1974.

4.2.3 Word Combinations and Clauses

The problem of sentence structure cannot be considered to have been solved entirely (see Valgina 1973, p. 17). Not aspiring to strictness or completeness, we shall consider a sentence to be one or more word combinations connected with one or more predicative forms (verb, short-form adjective, verbal substantives, participle, adverbial participle), or as one separate word combination. In our approach a word combination does not include any predicative forms except verbal nouns. Thus, a *word combination* is an association of autonomous words; the association is created on the basis of sense and grammar. In degenerate cases, a word combination may contain only one word. The vast majority of linguists consider a word combination to be the result of joining together several words; we, however, take a different view: to us, a word combination is the result of the division (segmentation) of a sentence. This approach is still encountered rather rarely, although it is becoming increasingly more popular (Zvegintsev 1976, p. 90). We can say that a word combination is produced by the first segmentation of a sentence into parts conveying certain units of sense. Consequently, words are produced by the second segmentation of a sentence and morphemes by the third. Generally speaking, the differences between the segments produced by the first, second, and third segmentations can be reduced to the different degrees of concretization of their meanings. Let us consider the following sentence: "My older brother skis very well on his slalom skis". The segments resulting from the first segmentation are the following: *my older brother, skis very well, on his slalom skis.* The segments resulting from the second segmentation are: *my, older, brother, to ski, on, his, skis.* Comparing the segments of the first and second segmentations, we can easily see that the latter (which are words) possess a more general meaning, i.e., their meaning is not put in the narrow framework of the segments of the first segmentation. The meaning of a unit of the first or second kind consists of its *lexical meaning*, i.e., the sense content specific for this particular word or word combination, and its *grammatical meanings*, i.e., the grammatical categories assigned to a word or word combination. Lexical meanings are determined by extralinguistic reality and remain linked to this reality. This connection does not exist in the case of grammatical meanings, where the freedom of choice characteristic for lexical meanings is lost. When using a word, a speaker is obliged to choose one particular grammatical meaning from among all those potentially possible (in the given language). What is "obligatory" here and what is not is specific to the language. However, this does not influence the "comprehensibility" of languages. Even if among the obligatory meanings (in a given language) the one necessary for expressing a particular piece of information is lacking, this may still be expressed by lexical means, i.e., by a nonobligatory meaning.

The classification of word combinations is based on the notion of combinability (see Apresyan 1974, p. 61). We shall not describe the complete classification of types of word combinability in terms of all their features. We shall confine ourselves to those that will later be relevant for our purposes. Let a word *A* be connected, directly or indirectly, with a word (or word combination) *B*. By the morphosyntactic combinability of word *A* (or the morphosyntactic restrictions imposed on the combinability of *A*), syntactically connected with word *B*, we mean information concerning the part of speech or syntactic status of *B*, and the grammatical (in particular prepositional-nominal) form that *B* should take. As an example, let us consider the different morphosyntactic restrictions on the non-exact synonyms *oshibat'sa* (*adresom*) – *pereputat'* (*adres*) [to mistake (an address) – to confuse (addresses); trans. note].

By the lexical combinability of *A* (the lexical restrictions imposed on the combinability of *A*) we mean information regarding what word *B* (or class of words B_1, ..., B_n) can be syntactically connected with *A*. For instance, the word *oshibat'sa* may be lexically combined with only a few substantives such as *adres, dom, dver', nomer, etazh* [address, house, door, number, floor]. These nouns have to be specified by being listed explicitly; it is impossible to define them according to any semantic feature. Yet the verb *pereputat'* although closely related to *oshibat'sa* in meaning, can be combined with various other words as well, such as *kniga, shlapa, data, dolzhnost'* [book, hat, date, position].

By the semantic combinability of *A* (the semantic restrictions imposed on the combinability of *A*) we mean information regarding what semantic features a word *B* should possess to be syntactically connected with *A*. It is reasonable to consider the semantic – not lexical – restrictions on *A* only in certain particular situations, where any word *B* that possesses a specific semantic feature can be combined with *A*. For instance, the verb *perevozit'* [to transport, to carry] can only refer to physical objects of limited size (such as lathes, spare parts, horses, etc.).

Let us note that in defining dictionaries the specific features of morphosyntactic, lexical, and semantic combinability are commonly treated (quite unwarrantedly) as peculiarities of a word's lexical meaning (on this subject, see Apresyan 1974). Information about combinability is highly individual, and consequently can be described only in a dictionary – not in the grammar of a language – in the form of lexical functions and models of government (see Sect. 4.3.3).

In considering the ways in which syntactic connections are formally expressed in the Russian language, such concepts as government, concordance, and parataxis are usually introduced, as well as subordination and coordination (conjunctional and nonconjunctional) (Maslov 1975). The task of syntactic connections is to express, by means of natural language, the actually existing relationships between entities in the model of reality. It is a characteristic of the Russian language (and of most other languages as well) that semantic relationships are usually expressed inexplicitly, or even completely concealed.

At this point we shall close our description of sentences and word combinations. Obviously, this has not been a complete description of the Russian language. In order to ensure that readers are aware of what questions were not raised at all, let us mention some of these: the order of words in a sentence, similar parts of a sentence, isolated parts of a sentence, parenthetic and inserted constructions, allocutions, conjunctive constructions, complex sentences, incomplete sentences, elliptic sentences, etc. (see Valgina 1973; Maslov 1975).

4.2.4 Parts of Speech

Morphology involves the study of words. It is a well-known fact that the borderline between morphology and syntax is by no means clear cut. This is because the grammatical meaning produced by modifying the form of a word can only be revealed if its syntactic function in a sentence and word combination is taken into account.

In order to distinguish certain general features of various words, they are classified into parts of speech. When we speak of parts of speech, we assume that the grammatical grouping of lexical units of a language has taken place, i.e., that groups of words have been defined on the basis of certain common grammatical features which they possess. There is no one generally accepted opinion on this subject in linguistics (see Maslov 1975, p. 201). Words are usually divided into two categories; syntactic and full (autonomous). Both of these categories include several parts of speech.

Full words are subdivided into nominative and substitutive words. Nominative words include nouns, adjectives, verbs (and verboids), adverbs, and numerals. Substitutive words are mainly pronouns. By *syntactic words* we mean prepositions, conjunctions, and particles (Maslov 1975).

Gender, number, and case are the main grammatical categories assigned to every noun. Neither these categories nor others used further on will be described in detail here (readers undoubtedly remember these things from their schooldays). Nouns are declined by case and number. Full-form adjectives are declined by gender, number, and case. Short-form adjectives are declined by number (*krasen, krasny* [singular and plural short forms of the adjective *krasniy*: red; trans. note]) and, in their singular forms, by gender (*krasiv, krasivo, krasiva* [masculine, neuter, and feminine short forms of the adjective *krasiviy*: pretty; trans. note]). Cardinal numerals are declined by case; they have neither gender (except for the numerals *odin, dva, oba, poltora* [one, two, both, one and a half]) nor number (except for the numeral *odin* [one]). Cardinal numerals cannot be qualified by adjectives. Ordinal numbers are declined by gender, number, and case, agreeing with the noun they refer to. The following grammatical categories are assigned to verbs: tense, mood, voice, aspect, and person. The set of all inflectional forms of a verb is called a conjugation. Gender and number are often considered to be included in the category of person; in the following, however, we shall treat gender and number as distinct grammatical categories (and not as part of one category – "person").

The following verboids occur in the Russian language: infinitive, participle, and adverbial participle. Verboids combine the characteristics of a verb with those of other parts of speech. Participles, for instance, combine the characteristics of a verb with those of an adjective. Like verbs, they have voice, aspect, and tense. Again, like verbs, they can be transitive or intransitive. At the same time they have gender, number, and case, and may occur in short or full forms. In this regard, therefore, they resemble adjectives. An adverbial participle combines the characteristics of a verb with those of an adverb. Like an adverb, it cannot be conjugated and is used in a sentence as an adverbial modifier. Like a verb, an adverbial participle is characterized by transitiveness (intransitiveness), voice, and aspect.

4.2.5 The Word and Its Composition

A word and its composition are the subject matter of morphology. The notion which plays the most important role in this branch of linguistics is that of a morpheme. Morphemes are produced by the third segmentation of a sentence (the first producing word combinations and the second words). By *morpheme* we mean the minimum unit of a language with fixed content (sense, meaning), which cannot be broken down into smaller parts possessing this property (Maslov 1975, p. 164). Many linguists believe that the meaning (sense) of a morpheme is primary and can be defined directly from its referent, whereas the meanings of words, word combinations, and sentences are derived from the meanings of morphemes. In this author's opinion (see also Zvegintsev 1976), precisely the opposite is the case. Morphemes (and words as well) get their meanings (senses) "from above", as a result of the successive segmentations into words, and words into morphemes.

The most important here are the so-called segmental morphemes, i.e., parts of words. These may be divided into two large classes: *roots* and *affixes*. These classes are counterposed as regards both the character of the meaning they express and their function within the word. The roots of autosemantic words have independent lexical meanings which are usually similar to the lexical meanings of the words containing these roots. For instance, the word *ruka* [a hand] contains the root *ruk*, which coincides with the lexical meaning of the word *ruka*, plus the affix *a*. Affixes do not have *independent* lexical meanings; their meaning is determined by their word-formative role (*gor-(a)*, *gor-(ets)*, *gor-n-(iy)*, *gor-ist-(iy)* [a mountain, a highlander, mountain (adjective), mountainous; trans. note]), their inflexional role (*gor-a, gor-oy, gor-y* [nominative, instrumental, and genitive cases of *gora*: a mountain; trans. note]), their formal-structural role (*ruk-o-moynik* – connecting vowel *-o-* [*ruk* – from *ruka*: hand, *moynik* – from *mit'*: to wash, *ruk-omoynik*: a soap dispenser; trans. note]) or their formal-classifying role (*wyruch-i-(t')* – conjugation marker *-i-* placed before the infinitive marker – *t'* [*wyruchit'*: to rescue, to help; trans. note]). According to their location in relation to the root, affixes are divided into *prefixes*, placed before the root, *postfixes*, placed after the root, and *interfixes*, placed between roots (*bur-e-lom* [*bur* from *buria*: storm, *lom* from *lomat'*: to break (up), *burelom*: fallen wood; trans. note], *les-o-rub* [*les*: wood, *rub* from *rubit'*: to chop, *lesorub*: a logger, woodcutter; trans. note]).

In the Russian language, postfixes are divided into suffixes and endings. By *ending*, we mean a postfix placed at the very end of a word and usually not followed by any other postfix (with the exception of the reflexive postfix – *sa/s'*). This expresses the syntactic connection with other words. Thus, we talk of case, personal, and (for verbs) sexuated endings. On the other hand, the postfix placed at the end of a comparative adverb is not regarded as an ending (*sil'n-ee* [more strongly]). All postfixes which do not fall into the category of endings are called *suffixes*. These may be placed at the very end of a word, or may be followed by other postfixes. The sole exception here is the reflexive postfix *-sa/s'* which is always

placed at the very end of a word, even after the ending. There is as yet no commonly accepted terminology for this particular postfix in Russian grammar. For our purposes, inflexional affixes are of the greatest interest, as these express relations between words. They usually terminate a word – they can be followed only be a reflexive postfix. The form of an affix determines the morphological information which can be assigned to the given word. However, we should bear in mind that this information may be ambiguous. Thus, for instance, the inflexive affixes *-aya, -'e, -v* (which occur in such words as *osnovn-aya* [main, chief (feminine); trans. note]), *stat-'e* [article (locative case); trans. note], *prinia- v* [anticipatory participle from *priniat'*: to accept; trans. note]) convey the following information:
purposes, inflexional affixes are of the greatest interest, as these express relations

-aya – adjective, nominative case, singular number, feminine gender
-'e – noun: (a) dative case, singular number, feminine gender,
or (b) locative case, singular number, feminine gender
-v – anticipatory participle

Most Russian words possess many word forms. Thus, for instance, nouns are declined through six cases and two numbers (in all, $6 \times 2 = 12$ forms); adjectives by case, number, and gender ($6 \times 2 \times 3 = 36$ forms); verbs are conjugated by number, person, tense, mood, aspect, and voice (about one hundred forms); participles by number, case, gender, tense, voice, and aspect. The diversity of word forms makes it inexpedient to store all of them in a dictionary. It makes more sense to store only one form of a word: its stem, i.e., the word minus its inflexional and word-formative affixes.

4.2.6 The Category of Number

Some of the morphological categories mentioned above require more detailed consideration. This applies above all to those which possess analogues in the field of semantics, i.e., the categories of number, tense, and aspect. The category of number seems obvious. If, however, we study the problem of expressing this in a natural language, we encounter several nuances. In the Russian language, the category of morphological number is, in principle, divided into plural and singular. However, not all words possess both forms. For example, the word *sani* [a sleigh] only has a plural form, while *nieft'* [oil] only exists in the singular. Hence, it is necessary to distinguish between words which possess only one form and those which can occur in either the singular or the plural; i.e., we have to distinguish three types of words: those that possess both numbers, those that possess the singular number only, and those that possess the plural number only.

In an NL, the morphological number of a word *A* is not always determined by the actual number of objects involved (the latter determines the semantic number). This applies even in cases where *A* possesses both singular and plural forms. Thus, for instance, we have (a) 101 *zavod* or 2 *zavoda* – several objects are involved in both cases, but the word *zavod* is in the singular [*zavod*: a factory. In Russian, a numeral ending with 1 is followed by the nominative singular, one ending with 2, 3, or 4 is followed by the genitive singular, and in all other cases the noun following is in the genitive plural. The noun *zavod* possesses both singular and plural forms; trans. note]; (b) *odni sani* – here the word *sani* is in the plural, although only one object is referred to [*odni sani*: one sleigh]; (c) *5 tonn ugla* – here the word *ugla* is in the singular, although it is used with the numeral 5 [*5 tonn ugla*: 5 tons of coal; trans. note].

4.2.7 The Category of Tense

We have already made certain observations about representing time in the model of reality. A natural language possesses the same types of time orientation of an event – absolute and relative. Each can be expressed by both lexical and grammatical means in the Russian language. The chief lexical means of expressing absolute time orientation are nominal groups (usually accompanied by prepositions); *letom 1975 goda* [in the summer 1975], *s 1 dekabrya* [from the 1st of December], *v techenie marta* [during March], *do 1940 goda* [until 1940], *po oktabr'* [up to and including October], etc. Such expressions as *v techenie* and *za* [in (e.g., *in* two weeks' time); trans. note] indicate a time interval; *s* or *nachinaya s* [as of] indicate the left-hand limit of an interval; while *do, po,* and *k* [by, toward] indicate the right-hand limit of an interval. Relative time orientation may be expressed by the use of the following lexical means:

1. Prepositions which express the relation of anteriority (*posle, po* [after, on (e.g., *on* arrival); trans. note]), of simultaneity (*vo vremia, v period, v protsessie, pri, nariadu s, odnovriemienno s,* etc. [during, while, in the course of, when, at the same time as, simultaneously with]) and of posteriority (*do, pered* [until, before]).
2. Temporal conjunctions which express temporal relations between verbs in principal and subordinate clauses. These relations, again, may be relations of anteriority (*kogda, kak tol'ko, posle tovo kak,* etc. [when, as soon as, after]), of simultaneity (*kogda, poka, do tekh por poka, po mere tovo kak* [when, while, for the time being, meanwhile]), and of posteriority (*do tovo kak, pered tem kak, do tekh por poka, poka,* etc. [by, before, till until]). As can be seen from the above examples, the conjunction *kogda*, for instance, may express either simultaneity or anteriority. This homonymy can be resolved when the aspect of the verb in the subordinate clause is taken into account [*aspect* – the nature of the action of a verb as to its beginning, duration, completion, or repetition and without reference to its position in time; trans. note]. The perfective aspect indicates anteriority here, while the imperfective signifies simultaneity. Analogously, the conjunctions *poka* and *do tekh por poka* express simultaneity if the aspect of the verb in the subordinate clause is imperfective, and posteriority if it is perfective.
3. The verbs *predshestvovat'* and *sledovat'* (*za*) [to precede and to follow].

There are also certain verbal word forms that can express the time orientation of an action (in this case we talk of a grammatical expression of time orientation). Thus, several forms of verbs, participles, and adverbial participles possess this property. On the other hand, infinitives and verbal substantives, included in the verbal paradigm, do not convey any time information. In accordance with their ability to express various time relations, the temporal forms of a verb can be divided into the present, past, and future tenses (morphological tense). In the

Russian language, morphological tense may be expressed in various ways: by the use of aspectual prefixes (*delayet – sdelayet* [is doing – will do; *delayet* is in the imperfective aspect, while the addition of the prefix *s* changes it into the perfective aspect transforming the present into the future tense; trans. note]), of affixes (*delayet – delal* [is doing – was doing], *derzhashchiy – derzhavshiy* [present and past participles of the verb *derzhat'*: to hold; trans. note]), and of analytical forms of verbs (*delayet – budet delat'* [is doing – will be doing; trans. note]). There are certain restrictions imposed on the combinability of temporal and aspectual characteristics in the Russian language (see Sect. 4.2.8). It must be stressed here that morphological tense does not directly reflect "semantic tense" (see Sect. 3.2.3). For instance:

1. *V tekushchem godu zavod stroit noviy dom.*
2. *V 1970 godu soobshchalos', shto zavod stroit noviy dom.*

[1. The enterprise is building a new house this year. 2. In 1970 it was reported that the enterprise was building a new house. In Russian there is no sequence of tenses in reported speech as there is in English; therefore the verb *stroit'*: to build, is used in the present tense in both sentences; trans. note]. In the first example *stroit* [is building] expresses the absolute present tense, while in the second it is used relatively. Generally speaking, the time meaning of the temporal form of a verb (absolute or relative) depends both on its morphological characteristics (morphological tense, aspect) and on the syntactic structure of the sentence. In the above we considered the time orientation of an event. However, time orientation may be applied to any characteristics of an event or concept (Winograd 1972), even if this is not expressed explicitly in an NL. For instance:

1. Many rich men made their fortunes during the Depression.
2. Many rich men lost their fortunes during the Depression.

In the first sentence, *rich men* refers to those who are rich now, while in the second it refers to those who were rich before the Depression. Thus, the adjective *rich* like any other attributive characterizing a state, assumes an implicit temporal reference. Similar problems arise if we describe states which are true or false depending on time. These states may be expressed not only by adjectives, but also by nouns (e.g., if we replace *rich men* by *millionaires* in the above examples) or by nominal groups.

4.2.8 The Category of Aspect

The morphological category of "aspect" has three values: *perf* ("the perfective"– what did he do (once)?), *imperf* ("the imperfective" – what was he doing?, what did he use to do?), and $\overline{asp}$ (indefinite aspect). In the last case, a word form may be considered to be related to both the perfective and imperfective aspects. Thus, for instance, *rekonstruiroval* [(he) reconstructed, was reconstructing] answers both the question "What was he doing?" and also "What did he do (accomplish)?" The category of morphological aspect is assigned to the following parts of speech: verbs in a personal form, infinitives, adverbial participles, participles, and short-form adjectives (if derived from a verb, e.g., *vypolnien* [accomplished] but not *krasen* [red]). With respect to the category of "aspect", every Russian verb falls into one of the following two classes: (a) verbs with a normal paradigm (as regards "aspect"); (b) verbs with an anomalous paradigm. Verbs from the first class possess both perfective and imperfective forms and are not affected by "aspectual homonymy"; i.e., if two forms of a verb refer to different aspects they cannot be exactly identical (e.g., *delat'* (imperf) and *sdelat'* (perf) [to do]). Verbs from the second class can be subdivided into verbs with "aspectual homonymy" (for instance, *rekonstruiruyet* (asp) [(he) reconstructs]) and verbs which occur in one aspect only: either the perfective (*poyti, zarabotat'* [to leave, to begin working]) or imperfective (*sushchestvovat', uchastvovat'* [to exist, to participate]).

In the Russian language, certain restrictions are imposed on the combinability of the temporal and aspectual characteristics of a word form: word forms of "perfective aspect" do not possess a "present tense". Moreover, in the process of morphological analysis, the value of the category "tense" depends on the value of the category "aspect". Consequently, any ambiguity (homonymy) as to the category "aspect" may result in ambiguity as to the category "tense". Thus, for instance, since the aspect of the word form *rekonstruiruyet* is indefinite, there is also ambiguity here as to its "tense" (*he is reconstructing now* or *he will reconstruct (sth.) next year*). Several factors determine the "aspect" of a verb. The transition from one aspect to the other very often results in formal modifications to a verb. Such transitions can be performed in the following ways:

1. With the help of prefixation (*delat'* (imperf) – *sdelat'* (perf) [to do])
2. By modification to elements of the stem (*ugnat'* (perf) – *ugonyat'* (imperf) [to drive on, to expel])
3. By the use of equivocal aspectual affixes (*oslabet'* (perf) – *oslabevat'* (imperf) [to weaken])
4. With the help of unequivocal aspectual affixes (e.g., *-iva-*, *-yva-*, etc.)

In the first two cases, "aspect" may be assigned to the stem of the word; thus, in the course of morphological analysis, this is taken directly from the dictionary. In the third case, suffixes convey certain aspectual information for a specified set of "aspectual pairs" only – for other pairs the meaning of these suffixes may be the opposite. Information about aspect can therefore be obtained by assigning (in the form of rules) information about the aspectual suffixes specific to a given stem to that stem. In the fourth case, suffixes make it possible to assign unequivocal aspectual information to a word. The above-mentioned four ways of differentiating the aspectual values of words encompass all verbs except for "dual-aspect" ones (asp) and those related to them where aspect is determined by stress (*nasípat'* (perf) – *nasipát'* (imperf) [to fill (with a granular substance)]). Deciphering such aspectual homonymy of verbs is the task of syntax and semantics, not of morphology. We have considered the notion of morphological aspect. "Aspect", however, also conveys semantic information. As yet linguists have no one definitive view on the semantics of verbal aspect. When referring to aspect, linguists mean the ability of a verbal word form to express not only events (actions or states) but also certain characteristics of these events. As has already been indicated, all verbal word forms can be divided into two classes, called the perfective and imperfective aspect. These classes are characterized by a set of mutually exclusive values. The main difficulty which arises in investigating the category of aspect is to specify those values which are specific to either class. Bondarko's work (1971) is recommended to readers who would like to study the problem of aspect further. In his work, Bondarko distinguishes the following semantic values of aspect:

1. Concrete-actual (*On poluchil pis'mo* [He received a letter])
2. General-actual (*Ya vstrechal yevo u znakomikh* [I used to meet him at my friends'])
3. Total (*Shofer dva raza povernul nalevo* [The driver turned left twice])
4. Boundless-iterative (*On yezdit na rabotu avtobusom* [He goes to work by bus])
5. Constant-continuous (*Volga vpadaet v Kaspiyskoe more* [The Volga empties into the Caspian Sea])
6. Potential-qualitative (*Moy drug pishet stikhi* [My friend writes poetry])

Thus, for instance, in the sentence *On igraet na skripke* [He plays (is playing) violin], the verb *igraet* is in the imperfective. There are, however, two possible interpretations of the verb; both conform to the imperfective aspect. One value of the imperfective aspect used here describes an action which is just taking place (at this moment) while the other expresses potential ability to perform the given action (He can play the violin). In constructing a Russian phrase correctly, it must be borne in mind that some contexts require a definite aspect – perfective or imperfective – to be used. Thus, in the phrase *On chasto igraet na skripke* [He often plays the violin] the verb must be in the imperfective (*sigral* [the perfective form of the verb *igrat'*: to play; trans. note] is unacceptable here). The vagueness of the semantics of verbal aspect gives rise to serious difficulties both in the course of the semantic interpretation of the morphological characteristics of "aspect" during analysis and in determining the value of "aspect" during synthesis. We possess no general solution to this problem as yet. Below (see Sect. 4.3.2) we shall describe a considerably simplified solution. We shall proceed from the following supposition concerning the semantics of aspects: At the semantic level, the morphological category of "aspect" corresponds to the category of "duration" (see Sect. 3.2.3) which can be considered to be the semantic category of "aspect". In the representation of the surrounding world, we distinguished (see Sect. 3.2.3) two types of events: those spread over time (the value of the characteristics "duration" = "interval") and those at particular instants (the value of "duration" = "point").

4.3 Representation of Individual (Dictionary) Pieces of Knowledge About Language

As we have already indicated, knowledge about a language can be divided into the general (grammar) and the individual (the latter corresponds to information about the characteristics of concrete lexemes given in a dictionary).

The most natural way of representing individual knowledge is in declarative form. The formulation of a complete grammar of an NL in declarative form (i.e., in the form of rules of grammar) would be of interest only if a universal algorithm of analysis existed applicable to any particular grammar. Indeed, this would make it possible, without changing the algorithm (program) of analysis, to exchange rules of grammar for one another in order to select the most acceptable one. The grammar of the Russian language belongs to context-dependent grammars (i.e., it falls into the first type of grammar in Chomsky's classification). This means that no such universal algorithm can be developed for the grammar of the Russian language. Variations of grammar rules inevitably influence the algorithm of analysis (Chomsky 1966, p. 165). Moreover, even if such a universal algorithm were to be constructed, due to the complexity of the grammar of an NL it would prove to be far too overdeveloped compared with an algorithm of analysis designed for a concrete grammar. The above considerations inescapably lead us to the conclusion that the advantages of a declarative representation of grammar (i.e., representing grammar in the form of a set of rules for a pseudouniversal algorithm of analysis), as compared with procedural representation, are in fact illusive. By this we do not mean that the use of one of these variants, including the mixed variant, is impossible. We would like to stress, however, that a procedural representation is in our opinion more comprehensible to readers. This is because it encompasses both grammar rules and also the manner in which these are applied. A declarative representation, in contrast, separates grammar from the manner in which it is used. In describing the Russian language, we shall use mainly the mixed representation. Individual knowledge about language will be represented declaratively, whereas grammar (in principle) will be represented procedurally. Due to limitations of space, it is impossible to describe the Russian language (even a limited version) in full detail. Therefore, only a general outline will be given below.

This section is devoted to a description of that part of knowledge about language that can conveniently be represented in declarative form. To begin with this involves a description of the form in which the results of the grammatical processing of a sentence can be represented, and a description of the structure of a dictionary which stores individual knowledge about language. The proposed structure of this dictionary is to a considerable extent similar to that already developed and described in detail by linguists (Apresyan 1974; Mel'chuk 1974a; Apresyan et al. 1978). The dictionary stores information concerning the morphology, syntax, and – to some extent – semantics of concrete words (lexemes) and word combinations. In line with the successive stages of processing, we shall distinguish declarative morphological, declarative syntactic, and declarative semantic knowledge.

By declarative morphological knowledge about the language we mean the following:

1. A list of parts of speech and morphological information characterizing each of them
2. A list of Russian affixes and information about their combinability
3. Morphological information about concrete lexemes

By declarative syntactic knowledge about the language we mean the following:

1. A list of possible syntactic relations between the words of the sentence being processed
2. Information about the grammar of the Russian language (in the form of syntactic filters – see Sect. 5.3)
3. The syntactic component of the model of government connected with concrete lexemes
4. The lexical functions of concrete lexemes

By declarative semantic knowledge about the language we mean the following:

1. A list of the possible semantic relations between the lexemes of the sentence being processed
2. Information about semantic groups of words
3. The semantic component of the model of government connected with concrete lexemes
4. Definitions of lexemes and discriminative networks (see Sect. 7.2)

By declarative pragmatic knowledge about the language we mean the following:

1. Information about classes of lexemes (i.e., metaknowledge of individual lexemes)
2. Metaknowledge about the structure of a dictionary entry and about restrictions imposed on the language of conversation
3. Information about the semantic associations of concrete lexemes
4. Information about the modal component of the meaning of a lexeme
5. References which establish the interdependence between the lexemes of the language and the subject matter represented in the semantic network.

The above-mentioned morphological, syntactic, semantic, and pragmatic information is insufficient to process every Russian text. This is a consequence of the following:

1. It is extremely difficult to develop a full (linguistic) model of the Russian language.
2. It is extremely difficult to realize such a model in the form of a computer program which would process, correctly and within a reasonable time limit, every text in an NL.
3. The lack of restrictions results in a tremendous amount of information concerning every word stored in the dictionary. This makes the process of inputting this information into the system and the process of debugging practically impossible. For instance, in the system which is now being constructed at the "Informelektro" institute, the dictionary information about every individual word occupies up to ten pages of typescript (Apresyan et al. 1978, p. 38).

All the above-mentioned facts do not mean that we should abandon attempts to design a system capable of understanding a natural language in its full complexity. The point, however, is that such attempts are still at the experimental stage due to the extreme complexity of the problem, whereas systems with certain appropriately selected restrictions may already be of practical use. Readers interested in a more detailed linguistic description of the Russian language are referred to the following works: Apresyan et al. 1978; Korovina et al. 1977; Yomdin et al. 1975; Yomdin and Pertsov 1975; Savvina, 1976.

4.3.1 Restrictions Imposed on the Language of Conversation

As has already been pointed out (see Sect. 2.1), in order to design an effective conversation system we have to impose certain restrictions on the style of the language of conversation (so-called business prose), as well as on the subject matter the system is designed to deal with. These restrictions are of an essential character; they result from the insufficient development of linguistic models and from the extreme complexity of the problem of designing the system's mathematical and information software. In addition to these essential restrictions, we shall introduce others which flow from the following requirements:

1. To describe, at a sufficient level of concretization, all the stages of processing Russian texts
2. To confine the size of this book to reasonable limits

Consequently, only those parts of speech which turn out to be relevant during analysis of an input text (see Chap. 5) are listed in Table 4.1. This table presents the morphological information that will be assigned to parts of speech. It can be

Table 4.1. Parts of speech relevant to analysis of an input text

Part of speech	Grammatical categories (names of their values)
Noun (nn)	Gender (m, f, n, ḡ), number (sn, pl), case (nom, acc, gen, dat, ins, loc), animateness (anim, inan, ā)
Full-form adjective (fadj)	Voice (pass, act, v̄), tense (past, pres, t̄), gender (m, f, n, ḡ), number (sn, pl), case (nom, acc, gen, dat, ins, loc), animateness (anim, inan, ā), aspect (perf, imperf, $\overline{\text{asp}}$)
Short-form adjective (sadj)	Voice (pass, act), tense (past, pres, fut), gender (m, f, n, ḡ), number (sn, pl), aspect (perf, imperf, $\overline{\text{asp}}$)
Verb (ver)	Voice (pass, act), tense (past, pres, fut), gender (m, f, n, ḡ), number (sn, pl), aspect (perf, imperf, $\overline{\text{asp}}$)
Infinitive (inf)	Voice (pass, act), gender (m, f, n, ḡ), number (sn, pl, n̄)
Adverbial participle (advpar)	Voice (pass, act), tense (past, pres), aspect (perf, imperf, $\overline{\text{asp}}$)
Adverb (adv)	Type: nonqualitative (nqual), qualitative (qual)
Cardinal numeral (cnum)	Type: "1", "2", "5", fraction (fracn), indefinite (indefn), nominal (nom)
Pronoun (pr)	Class: possessive (poss), demonstrative (dem), reflexive (ref), reflexive-attributive (ref-att), of the third person (3p); case (nom, acc, gen, dat, ins, loc, c̄), number (sn, pl, n̄), gender (m, f, n, ḡ)
Conjunction (con)	Type: coordinating (coor), subordinating (subor)
Preposition (prep)	Case (acc, gen, dat, ins, loc)
Particle (part)	Type: interrogative (introg), negative (neg)
Syntactic unit (synunit)	–

seen from the table that, for instance, "mood" and "person" are not considered. "Mood" is always assumed to be the indicative, and "person" is assumed to be the third person. Such restrictions do not cause any noticeable inconvenience for the user and consequently can be used in real SNLs.

4.3.2 Declarative Morphological Knowledge of the Language (the Morphological Zone of the Dictionary)

As we have already indicated, most Russian words (lexemes) possess numerous word forms. Either the stem of a lexeme or all its word forms may be stored in the dictionary. Each of these methods of representation has its own advantages and disadvantages; the choice of one or the other possibility is usually based on the use to be made of the particular system (see Sect. 5.2). In the following, we shall assume that the dictionary contains, as a rule, only the stems of lexemes, not all their word forms. Thus, an entry in the dictionary of stems comprises a heading zone (containing the stem), a morphological zone, and a syntactic-semantic zone. Since certain Russian words are not inflected at all (e.g., number, symbols, brackets, prepositions) or are inflected irregularly, it is convenient to have – in addition to the dictionary of stems – a dictionary of ready-to-use word forms as well. The structure of the dictionary of word forms resembles that of the dictionary of stems, except for the fact that the former stores word forms (not stems) and contains full (not partial) morphological information on each word form. In the case of the Russian language, the size of the dictionary of word forms is considerably smaller than that of the dictionary of stems. Consequently, a word which is being processed is checked in the dictionary of word forms first, and then, if it is not found there, the affixes are removed (at the stage of morphological analysis) and the stem thus remaining is sought in the dictionary of stems.

Table 4.1 contains the restrictions imposed on the morphology of the language of conversation. Let us explain the contents of this table. There is a certain special catagory in the table, labeled $\bar{\text{g}}$, $\bar{\text{v}}$, etc. This category has been introduced for the following reasons: It sometimes happens in the Russian language that if a word possesses a certain value of one category, the value of another category is indefinite. For instance, plural adjectives have no definite gender. It is to mark such cases that we have introduced the above-mentioned "special" category. Since a few such categories exist, they are identified by the first letter(s) of the name of the category with a bar above the letter. Thus, for instance, the full-form adjective *bol'shiye* [greater (plural)] is accompanied by the following morphological information (MI-line): fadj, $\bar{\text{v}}$, $\overline{\text{asp}}$, $\bar{\text{g}}$, pl, nom.

The value $\bar{\text{g}}$ of the category "gender" is assigned to plural words (not substantives), to verbs in the present and future tense, to active infinitives, and to infinitives ending in *-sa*.

We shall include participles (full- and short-form) as adjectives (full- and short-form). This deviation from the principles of the Russian language is acceptable because the difference between participles and adjectives will be expressed not by identifying them as different parts of speech, but by the fact of whether a word is (in the case of participles) or is not (in the case of adjectives) accompanied by a model of government (see Sect. 4.3.3). Since participles have been included as adjectives, the characteristics of the latter must be extended to include voice and tense. The value $\bar{v}$ of the category "voice" and $\bar{t}$ of "tense" will be assigned to "true" adjectives (i.e., adjectives which are not derived from a verb, and consequently do not possess any model of government). The value $\bar{a}$ of the category "animateness" will be assigned to full-form adjectives if they are not in the accusative case. The value $\bar{n}$ of the category "number" will be assigned to active infinitives and to passive infinitives ending in *-sa*. The value $\overline{asp}$ of the category "aspect" will be assigned to dual-aspect stems.

Ordinal numbers will be treated as full-form adjectives not derivable from a verb. The type of numeral characterizes the manner in which a noun is brought into agreement with a cardinal numeral. For instance: *odin stanok, nol' stankov, dva stanka, piat' stankov* [one, zero, two, five lathes]. The type of numeral is determined by the final two digits. Numerals ending in 1 (but not 11) are of type "1", those ending in 2, 3, and 4 (but not 12, 13, 14) are of type "2", and all other numerals are of type "5". Thus, for instance, the numerals 101, 1, and 21 are of the type "1" (101 *stanok*, 1 *stanok*, 21 *stanok*), 5, 10, and 112 are of the type "5" (5 *stankov*, 10 *stankov*, 112 *stankov*), and 22, 2, and 103 are of type "2" (22 *stanka*, 2 *stanka*, 103 *stanka*). As an example of a fraction we may cite 1/3, of a nominal numeral – 30%, of an indefinite numeral – *mnogo* [many].

The essential information which is needed to identify stems is contained in the table of affixes of the Russian language. All affixes are grouped in two tables: the table of inflexional affixes (endings) and of word-formative affixes (suffixes). Inflexional affixes, in turn, are grouped according to parts of speech. For every affix, the corresponding morphological information (MI) is indicated in the table. It should be stressed that many affixes are characterized by more than one MI. Thus, for instance, in the case of ending *-ey*, the following information may be assigned to a word form:

1. Adjective	gen, sn, f, $\bar{a}$	(*sredney*) [medium]
2. Adjective	dat, sn, f, $\bar{a}$	(— " —) [— " —]
3. Adjective	ins, sn, f, $\bar{a}$	(— " —) [— " —]
4. Adjective	loc, sn, f, $\bar{a}$	(— " —) [— " —]
5. Noun (type of stem – 4, 6, 7)	ins, sn, f, $\bar{a}$	(*matritsey*) [matrix]
6. Noun (type of stem – 8, 9, 15)	gen, pl, $\bar{g}$, $\bar{a}$	(*misheney*) [target]
7. Noun	acc, pl, $\bar{g}$, $\bar{a}$	(— " —) [— " —]

The following information is assigned to the ending *-to*: short-form participle, pass, sn, n, perf; and to the ending *-ya*: advpart, pres, act, $\bar{g}$, imperf. The suffix *-ashch-* conveys the information: participle, pres, act, imperf, and the suffix *-in-*: participle, past, pass, perf. Information about aspect is assigned only to unambiguous aspectual affixes (see Sect. 4.2.8). As we see, on the basis of an affix several MI-lines may often be assigned to one word form. Removing such homonymy is one of the main tasks of the morphological zone of the dictionary.

The morphological zone corresponding to a given stem should contain information about part of speech, the grammatical meaning of the stem, and its inflexional type. The type of information concerning grammatical meaning depends on the part of speech concerned (noun or verb). For nouns, it is advisable to indicate their gender, number, and animateness. For verbs, we indicate voice – always active (act), always passive (pass), either active or passive (a/p) – and aspect. The inflexional type must be identified in the case of nouns; this indicates the declension (see Table 4.2).

Information about aspect may be assigned to a stem by the use of marking or rules. The stem of a verb in a dictionary is characterized by the following markings concerning aspect: perf (perfective), imperf (imperfective), perf/imperf (may occur as a perfective or imperfective verb), and $\overline{\text{asp}}$ (dual-aspect stem, i.e., ambiguous). One should bear in mind, however, that a marking does not necessarily provide an unambiguous definition of the actual aspectual type of the stem (see Sect. 5.2).

If the stem of a verb is of the perf/imperf type, supplementary information is given about rules which make it possible to determine the actual aspect of a word form at the stage of morphological analysis. In order to clarify the nature of these rules, let us introduce certain definitions. The maximum structure of a verbal word form can be represented in the form $V = S_0 + S_1 + S_2 + S_3 + S_4$, where S_0 = the stem of the verb (together with a prefix); S_1 = the aspectual suffix (this may be lacking, i.e., $S_1 = \emptyset$); S_2 = either the participial suffix or the personal endings of the verb in the present and past tenses, the endings of adverbial participles, of short-form participles, and of the infinitive; S_3 = the nominal inflexion of full-form participles, lacking for the other forms of the verb; S_4 = the reflexive participle. Since we are interested in "aspect", we shall deal only with segments S_1 and S_2.

Table 4.2. Morphological types of nouns

Examples	Protsess, brat	Gramm	Nomyer	Matritsa	Stupnya, stat'ya	Ideya	Liniya
	1	2	3	4	5	6	7
nom, sn	∅	∅	∅	a	ya, 'ya	ya	ya
acc, sn	a	∅	∅	u	yu, 'yu	yu	yu
gen, sn	a	a	a	y, i	i, 'i	i	i
dat, sn	u	u	u	ye	ye, 'e	ye	i
ins, sn	om, yem	om	om	yey, oy	yey, 'ey	yey	yey
loc, sn	ye	ye	ye	ye	ye, 'ye	ye	i
nom, pl	y, i, 'ya	y, i	a	y, i	i, 'i	i	i
acc, pl	y, 'ev	y, i	a	y, i	i, 'i	i	i
gen, pl	ov, yev, yey, 'ev	∅	ov	∅	yey	iy, ', ∅	iy
dat, pl	am, 'am	am	am	am	yam, 'am	yam	yam
ins, pl	ami, 'ami	ami	ami	ami	'ami, yami	yami	yami
loc, pl	akh, 'akh	akh	akh	akh	'akh, yakh	yakh	yakh

The rules indicated above may be divided into two groups. The rules of the first group involve a comparison of the contents of segment S_1 with the members of an aspectual pair (perfective-imperfective). Knowing the contents of segment S_1 corresponding to the word form being analyzed, and comparing this with the possible contents of segment S_1 corresponding to the aspectual pair (these contents being specified in the rule), we can then determine "aspect". Certain rules of this group are superfluous as the cases they involve are too specific. The second group of rules applies to verbs with the marking perf/imperf. The actual aspect of such verbs is determined on the basis of the contents of segment S_2; the rules of this group check whether these contents belong to the affixes of personal endings of the present tense. Since, in our approach, the use of the 1st and 2nd person is restricted, it is chiefly 3rd-person endings of the first conjugation that are meant here (*-yet, -yut*).

The total number of rules of the first and second type does not exceed ten (assuming the agreed restrictions on the input languages are taken into account). To save time, we shall mention only two of these as examples. Rule No. 1, belonging to the first group, reads: If segment S_1 of a given word form contains *– a-* or *-ya-* then "aspect" = imperf. For instance: *izmier-ya-t'* but *izmier-i-t'* [to measure – imperfective and perfective aspects respectively; trans. note], *resh-a- t'* but *resh-i-t'* [to solve].

Rule No. 3, from the second group, states: If segment S_2 = *yet* or *yut*, then "aspect" = imperf, otherwise – $\overline{\text{asp}}$. For example: *razrez-a-yet* (imperf) [(he) cuts], but *razrez-a-l* ($\overline{\text{asp}}$) [(he) cut]. In the latter case, the "aspectual homonymy" is caused by the neglect to stress – in spoken language *razrězal* is perfective while *razrezál* is imperfective.

Table 4.2. (continued)

Mishen'	Zaboy, ugol'	Sanatoriy	Telo	Derevo	Vremya	Polotentsye	Polye, ust'ye	Vliyanye
8	9	10	11	12	13	14	15	16
'	y, '	iy	o	o	ya	ye	ye, 'ye	ye
'	y, '	iy	o	o	ya	ye	ye,'ye	ye
i	ya	ya	a	a	i	a	ya, 'ya	ya
i	yu	yu	u	u	i	u	yu, 'yu	yu
'yu	yem	yem	om	yem	yem	yem	yem, 'em	yem
i	ye	i	ye	ye	i	ye	ye, 'ye	i
i	i	i	a	i, 'ya	a	a	ya, 'ye	ya
i	i	i	a	i, 'ya	a	a	ya, 'ye	ya
yey	yey, yev	yev	Ø, ov	Ø, ov, 'ev	Ø	Ø, yev	iy, yey	iy
yam	yam	yam	am	am, 'am	am	am	yam, 'am	yam
yami	yami	yami	ami	'ami, ami	ami	ami	yami, 'ami	yami
yakh	yakh	yakh	akh	akh, 'akh	akh	akh	yakh, 'akh	yakh

4.3.3 Declarative Syntactic Knowledge of the Language (the Syntactic Zone of the Dictionary)

The following syntactic relations (SYR) between words will be distinguished here: predicative (PR), completive (1C, 2C, 3C, 4C, 5C), adverbial (ADVB), attributive (ATTR), quantitative (QUANT), homogeneous (HOM), negative (NEG), and auxiliary (AUX). It is easy to demonstrate that this set of syntactic relations is by no means exhaustive, i.e., it does not encompass all the possible interrelations of sense which may be expressed by syntactic relations. It can be shown (Apresyan et al. 1978, p. 15) that 30–40 syntactic relations are needed to ensure that it is possible to describe any scientific or technical text (making no provision for the semantics of the subject matter). In view of this fact, we shall expand our set of syntactic relations somewhat by introducing certain modifications to the types of SYR mentioned above. Thus, for instance, we shall introduce markings like PRcom (predicative-comparative), 1Ccom, ADVBcom, ATTRcom, etc. Since the set of syntactic relations that we shall be considering nevertheless remains incomplete, we are not in a position to describe the analysis or synthesis of all Russian texts: certain restrictions must be imposed on these texts.

Declarative syntactic knowledge of the language may be subdivided into individual and categorical knowledge of grammar. Individual knowledge is stored in the dictionary, while categorical knowledge, in the form of filters (see Sect. 5.3), is connected with procedural knowledge (the stage of syntactic analysis).

The syntactic properties of word forms are expressed in their ability to enter into certain semantic relations with certain other word forms. Information about the individual syntactic properties of the word forms corresponding to a given dictionary entry is stored in the dictionary's syntactic zone. The dictionary is organized in such a manner that a single entry contains information about several word forms derived from a given stem (all of them, in ideal cases). A stem may have several syntactic and semantic homonyms. Words which are written identically but have different meanings are called semantic homonyms. For instance: *otpravleniye* [dispatch and departure]. The homonyms *vyes* 1 (from *vyes-it'* [to weigh]) and *vyes* 2 (from *vyes-y* [scales]) are examples of syntactic homonyms in the case of the stem *vyes*.

The syntactic component of the model of government is an essential factor in establishing the SYRs between the word forms of a sentence. The model of government (MG) is considered to be a separate zone of a dictionary entry. It contains syntactic and semantic information on a given lexeme. The number and semantic contents of "points" of the model of government corresponding to a given word (i.e., the syntactic-semantic valences) depend on two factors: the number and nature of actants in a situation denoted by the given word (these actants are called the *semantic valences* of a word) and the number and nature of subjects and objective complements which depend on a given word and are actually observed in a text (these are called the *syntactic valences* of a word). Thus, the MG of a word contained in the dictionary combines the syntactic and semantic valences of this word.

The actants in a situation can be determined by means of semantic analysis of the situation (Apresyan 1974, p. 99), i.e., by means of lexicographic interpretation of the word. The following example will make this clearer. Let us consider the situation "to punish" (the words *to punish* or *punishment*). It is reasonable to speak of this situation existing only if the following actants can be specified: *A, B, C,* and *D,* where *A* is the person who committed the misdeed *B*, and *C* is the person who inflicts an injury *D* on *A* with the aim of making *A* (or other people who commit similar misdeeds) mend his ways and refrain from committing a misdeed like *B* in the future. If even one of the actants indicated above is lacking, and/or the roles of these actants do not correspond to the ones indicated, the words *to punish* and *punishment* cannot be used in this situation. It should be stressed that the number of semantic valences in an MG does not depend on the number of dependent objective complements connected with this MG (the example of the word *to punish* suggests such an inference). Thus, the Russian verb *promakhnut'sa* [to miss one's target] has four semantic valences: *who* (the actor), *at what* (the target), *from what* (the weapon – not obligatory), and *with what* (a fist, a bullet, etc.). Only the first of these valences is usually expressed in the Russian language. For instance, the phrase *On promakhnulsa po banditu pulyey* [he missed the bandit with a bullet] is incorrect. However, the verb *ne popast'* (a synonym of *promakhnut'sa*, i.e., possessing the same semantic valences) admits all four syntactic valences (*on ne popal iz rogatki v okno*) [he missed the window with his slingshot]. For a more detailed study of this question readers are referred to the book by Y.D. Apresyan mentioned above. The word forms of the following parts of speech may possess a model of government (one or several): verb, short-form adjective, infinitive, adverbial participle, full-form adjective (derived from a verb, i.e., a participle), noun (usually verbal), and preposition. The word forms of other parts of speech (numeral, adverb, conjunction, pronoun, participle, and syntactic unit) do not, as a rule, possess a model of government.

The MG of a word form *A* may be represented in the form of a table, each column of which – whether it is syntactically realizable or not – corresponds to one semantic valence of *A*. The MG of *A* may additionally contain a column which does not correspond to any semantic valence of the word *A*, but characterizes the arrangement of a semantic valence of another word *C*, syntactically dependent on *A*, which constitutes a strong objective complement of *A*. We shall distinguish a syntactic component (MGSY) and a semantic one (MGSE) of the MG of a word *A*. The syntactic component determines the morphological properties that syntactic valences of *A* should possess. The first column indicates the morphological characteristics of a word which can be connected with *A* by the predicative SYR, the second – by 1C, the third – by 2C, etc. For every other column, the semantic component determines: (a) the semantic categories that the word forms of a sentence should possess in order to perform the role of semantic valence; (b) the semantic relations that correspond to syntactic relations (from the MGSY).

It is quite obvious that different homonyms of a stem may possess different MGSYs (the word *vyesit'* [to weigh] possesses an MGSY while *vyesy* [scales] does not possess one at all). On the other hand, one homonym may possess several MGs which constitute a so-called group MG. That one homonym may have several MGs stems from the fact that not all individual properties of a word form can be realized simultaneously in one phrase. For instance, the word form *nachal* [(he)

Table 4.3. Group model of government for the verb *kolotit'* [to thump]

A (agent)	T (theme-object)	I (instrument)	P (struck part of the object)
Noun, nom	2.1 S_{acc} 2.2 *po* (followed by S_{dat}) 2.3 *v* (S_{acc})	3.1 S_{ins}	4.1 *po* (S_{dat})
Animate object	2.1 animate or physical object 2.2 inanimate object (part of another object or sufficiently large object) 2.3 obstacle		Part of the body of object T

began] may possess, as its objective complement (in the 1C syntactic relation), a noun in the accusative case (*nachal stroitel'stvo* [(he) began building]), or an infinitive (*nachal stroit'* [(he) began to build]). In one phrase a noun in the accusative case and an infinitive cannot be connected in the 1C SYR with the verb *nachal.*

Table 4.3 shows an example of the group model of government for the verb *kolotit'* [to thump]. The verb has three valences and its MG is represented by a four-column table. The semantic valences of the verb *kolotit'* are the following: who (the agent – A), what (the theme – T), and with what (the instrument – I). For instance: *Ivan* (agent) *kolotit Petra* (theme) *kulakom* (instrument) [Ivan (A) thumps Peter (T) with his fist (I)]. There may in fact be two, three, or four syntactic valences for this verb (*Ivan kolotit Petra kulakom po spine* [Ivan thumps Peter on the back with his fist]). Strictly speaking, *po spine* [on the back] may also be treated as an object. *Petra* then qualifies the words *po spine*, i.e., *Petra* is an objective complement which expresses a semantic valence not of the verb *kolotit'* itself but of its object.

The following characteristics may be used in the columns of the syntactic components of an MG:

1. Parts of speech (nouns, full-form adjectives, infinitives, numerals) with the concrete case involved indicated (except for the infinitive)
2. Concrete lexemes (usually prepositions). If a preposition may be followed by nouns in various cases, the concrete case in question is explicitly indicated, e.g., *v* (acc) or *v* (loc).
3. A concrete lexeme which introduces a subordinate clause. We use the following notation in this case: (SUB *shto*) [*shto* – that]. For instance: *Petrov schitayet, shto on khoroshiy rabotnik* [Petrov thinks that he is a good worker].
4. Lack of a candidate for a given column will be denoted by ∅. We shall also sometimes be using another, more compact notation for the MGSY. The information contained in a table will be expressed in the form of a line. The MGSY of the verb *kolotit'*, for instance, will then read: 1. S_{nom}; 2. (2.1 S_{acc}) ∨ (2.2 *po* (dat)) ∨ (2.3 *v* (acc)); 3. S_{ins}; 4. *po* (dat) [*po*, *v* = prepositions; trans. note].

Strictly speaking, the syntactic component of the model of government corresponds not to a lexeme but rather to its concrete word forms. All the word forms corresponding to one lexeme may possess one common MGSY if the lexeme is a noun, preposition, or full-form adjective; however, for other lexemes this does not hold true. It is frequently the case that different MGSYs can be reduced to one, or a few so-called *nuclear models of government* (for dictionary entries corresponding to a verb or to a short-form adjective). Some word forms of the sentence being processed may possess both a *standard individual MGSY* (IMGSY), derivable from the nuclear MGSY, and a *nonstandard IMGSY*, i.e., an MGSY which cannot be derived from the nuclear MG and must therefore be included in the dictionary. Thus, nuclear MGSYs (NMGSY) and nonstandard individual MGSYs must be indicated in a dictionary entry (fortunately, the latter are not great in number). Thanks to this approach, it is possible for one dictionary entry (corresponding to a verb) to describe simultaneously verbs, infinitives, adverbial participles, full-form adjectives with an MG (participles), verbal nouns, and short-form adjectives.

As the NMGSY for a dictionary entry corresponding to a verb, linguists usually choose the MGSY of the word form morphologically characterized as "active verb, past tense, neuter, singular", and for an entry corresponding to a short-form adjective, the MGSY of the word form morphologically characterized as "short-form adjective, neuter, singular". The standard individual MGSY of a concrete word form is obtained from the NMGSY by way of a transformation based on the morphological information conveyed by the word form, and on the form of the NMG. A fragment of the list of transformations is shown in Table 4.4. The total number of lines in the list is over fifty. The following example explains how the table is used. In a dictionary entry corresponding to a verb, we find the following NMGSY assigned to the stem of the word *soobshchalo* [to inform, to let know (singular, neuter, past tense); trans. note]: +PR (nn, nom); 1C (nn, acc), 2C (nn, dat) (as in *Pyotr soobshchil Nikolayu telefon Ivana* [Peter informed Nikolai about Ivan's telephone call]). The sign "+" indicates that establishment of an SYR in this column is obligatory. Let us assume that the word form *soobshchayut* [they inform] has been encountered in the course of processing a text. At the stage of morphological analysis, the stem *soobshch* is distinguished and the following MI-line is then assigned to it: ver, act, pres, pl. Referring to the table of transformations (first line) we see that the NMG should be transformed into an IMG by removing the "+" sign at the predicative SYR. Hence the IMGSY takes the form: PR (nn, nom); +1C (nn, acc); 2C (nn, dat), which reflects the possible existence of the sentence *Nikolayu soobshchili telefon Ivana* [They informed Nikolai about Ivan's telephone call].

If the word form considered is *soobshchen* (*Telefon Ivana soobshchen Nikolayu Petrom* [Nikolai was informed about Ivan's telephone call by Peter]), then the MI-line of the NMGSY should be transformed into the following IMG (third line in Table 4.4): +PR (nn, nom); 1C (nn, ins); 2C (nn, dat). Note that the passive voice is accompanied by the transposition of semantic categories and semantic cases (of the first and second columns of an MG); i.e., the PR now concerns the semantic categories (and semantic case) of the person whom the information is about, not the person who is informing. It is 1C which concerns the person who is informing.

A group MGSY stores information about several nuclear MGSYs. Not all combinations of pieces of morphological information from different columns form permissible MGSYs. For example, the MGSY of the word *arest* [arrest]

Table 4.4. Fragment of list of transformations based on morphological information conveyed by word form and on form of NMG

Characteristics of MI-line corresponding to the word-form	Characteristics of nuclear MGSY	Characteristics of the obtained individual MGSY different from those of NMGSY
1. Ver, act, pl	+PR (nn, nom) +1C	PR (nn, nom)
2. Inf, Advpar, Fadj } act	Any characteristics	PR (∅)
3. Ver, pass	+1C (nn, acc) +1C (nn, gen)	+Pr (nn, nom) 1C (nn, ins)

reads as follows: 1. nn, ins; 2. (2.1 nn, gen) ∨ (2.2 *sredi* [among] (gen)); 3. (*za* (acc) ∨ *po obvinenyu v* (loc) [for]). In this MGSY, 2.2 and 3 cannot occur simultaneously, i.e., the phrase *aresty sredi studentov za narushenye*... [arrests among students for offenses...] is incorrect, while *aresty studentov za narushenye*... [arrests of students for offences...] is correct. Indications that concern such restrictions on a given MG will be called *bans* (proscriptions). Bans may be divided into obligatory and facultative ones. We have already introduced the sign "+", which indicates that an SYR is obligatory in a given MG.

We say that the *i*-th valence of a word *A* is *syntactically facultative (obligatory)* if a sentence containing the word *A* but with the *i*-th valence not provided is correct (incorrect). Thus, for the verb *soobshchat'*, the first and second valences (who informs, and about what) are obligatory, while the third (who is informed) is facultative. A word may possess two or more syntactically facultative valences. The following types of relations between them may then be introduced: the relation of collateral/non-collateral subordination, of separability/inseparability, and of quasiobligation (Apresyan 1974). We say that *n* syntactically facultative valences of a word *A* are quasiobligatory if at least $n - k$ valences ($n > 2, k < n$) must necessarily be provided in any correct sentence which contains the word *A*. Facultative valences are *collaterally subordinated/not collaterally subordinated* if they can/cannot be provided simultaneously. The facultative valences *x* and *y* of a word *A* are separable/inseparable if either of them can/cannot be provided in a sentence when the other is not. When valences *x* and *y* are separable, the relation $A \xrightarrow{x} B$ is permissible without $A \xrightarrow{y} C$ (and inversely). The facultative valence *x* of a word *A* is *inseparable* from the valence *y* if providing *x* is impossible without providing *y*, i.e., if $A \xrightarrow{x} B$ is not permissible without $A \xrightarrow{y} C$.

We shall introduce the notation *K* (1, 2) (or *K* (1.2, 3.1), etc.) for the relation of quasiobligation. This means that one of two valences has to be provided. Let us consider the word *krasnet'* [to blush]. This has the following MG: 1. nn, nom; 2. *za* [for (of)] (gen); 3. *pered* [in front of] (ins). Hence, we should add *K* (2.1, 3.1). In fact, the second and third valences are facultative, except that one of them (no matter which) has to be provided.

If two valences are *not collaterally subordinated* we write *c* (1.1, 2.3). If this symbol does not occur, collateral subordination is tacitly assumed. Thus, the word *grekh* [sin] with the MG: 1. (1.1 nn, gen) ∨ (1.2 fadj); 2. (2.1 *protiv* [against] (gen)) ∨ (2.2 fadj); 3. nn, gen must be accompanied by the restriction *c* (1.*, 3.1), where the asterisk indicates that either 1.1 or 1.2 can be placed here. Indeed, the phrase *evo grekh prelyubodeyanya* [his sin of adultery] is incorrect, while *grekh Pavla* or *grekh protiv religii* [the sin of Pavel, a sin against religion] are quite correct. In order to indicate "inseparability" we shall use the notation $O(1.1, 2.1)$. If this symbol does not occur, "separability" will be tacitly assumed. Thus, for the above-mentioned word *arest*, the MG should be supplemented by $O(1.1, 2.1)$, because 1.1 is possible only if accompanied by 2.1, i.e., the phrase *aresty politsyey robochikh* [arrests of workers by the police] is correct, while *aresty politsyey za spekulatsyu* [arrests by the police for profiteering] is not. Analogous bans can also be introduced for an MGSE.

The MG of a word A conveys information about the morphosyntactic combinability of A (see Sect. 4.2.3). Information about the lexical combinability is expressible in terms of *lexical functions* (Zholkovsky 1974; Apresyan 1974). Let X be the set of all words. For any $x\,(x \in X)$ a lexical function (LF) – e.g., f – determines a set of words (or of word-combinations) $y_i = f(x)$ (where $y_i \in X$), such that for any x_1 and x_2 ($x_1, x_2 \in X$) the following statement is true: if $f(x_1)$ and $f(x_2)$ exist, then the sense relation between $f(x_1)$ and x_1 and the sense relation between $f(x_2)$ and x_2 are identical.

There are two types of LFs: LF conversions and LF parameters. A *lexical conversion* is a function which transforms a given word x into another word y whose lexical meaning (in the semantic representation) coincides, in whole or in part, with that of x. At the same time, the syntactic properties of x and of y may be substantially different. It is obvious that lexical conversions are extensively utilized in paraphrasing, i.e., they provide a means of lexical synonymy in the broad sense of the term. Lexical conversions comprise: proper synonyms (Syn), conversions (Conv), and syntactic derivatives (S_0 – noun, A_0 – adjective, V_0 – verb, Adv_0 – adverb), i.e., derivatives from another part of speech that fully retain the lexical meaning of the original word. We shall not describe all these lexical functions here (for more on this, see the literature quoted above); we shall confine ourselves to giving a few examples that should clarify matters.

Syn (aggression) = attack
$Conv_{21}$ (to be afraid (1, 2)) = to frighten
(to be afraid: who is afraid (1), of whom (2); to frighten: who frightens (2), who is frightened (1));
$Conv_{321}$ (to buy (1, 2, 3)) = to sell
(to buy: who buys (1), what (2), from whom (3); to sell: who sells (3), what (2), to whom (1));
S_0 (to embroider) = embroidery
A_0 (to learn) = learned
A_0 (space) = spatial
Adv_0 (politics) = politically
Adv_0 (language) = linguistically
V_0 (game) = to play
V_0 (aggression) = to attack

It should be stressed that a derivative $X_0\,(Y)$ and Y need not form a pair of words similar in appearance but belonging to two different parts of speech (e.g.,

S_0 (to embroider) = embroidery). The two words may be completely different in external appearance (e.g., V_0 (aggression) = to attack). Other lexical functions related to lexical conversions include Anti (antonym) and Gener (generic word). As examples of these functions we can mention Gener (tennis) = game, or Anti (to close) = to open.

A *lexical parameter* is an abstract, typical meaning expressed (like grammatical meaning) by a fairly large number of words. In contrast to grammatical meaning, however, the lexical parameter is expressed in different ways for different words, i.e., the way in which it is expressed depends substantially on the word in question. The majority of lexical parameters can be considered analogues of verbs, nouns, and adjuncts (adjectives and adverbs). The most important verbal lexical parameters are the following: Oper_i, Func_0, Func_i, and Labor_{ij}. In order to explain their meaning, let us consider a situation *C*, where – for the sake of simplicity – there are only two participants (i.e., semantic actants), *A* and *B*. *A* will be called the first participant, and *B* the second. Let all three words, *A*, *B*, and *C*, be nouns. In Russian, to construct a phrase describing the situation *C* with its participants *A* and *B*, a verb must be used. This verb can be chosen in various manners: (a) a verb for which *A* is the subject, *C* the direct object, and *B* the indirect object; (b) a verb for which *B* is the subject, *C* the direct object, and *A* the indirect object; etc. The aforementioned parameters express just these various possibilities of choosing a verb. Figure 4.1 shows the scheme of a situation *C* and of the interrelations between various components of this situation.

Oper_i is a semiauxiliary verb connecting the name of the *i*-th participant in the situation, which is the subject, with the name of the situation itself, which is the object. Thus, Oper_1 has the name *A* as its subject and *C* as its direct object; Oper_2 has *B* as its subject and *C*, as before, as its object; Oper_0 stands for an impersonal Oper (i.e., one with no subject).

Func_0 is a semiauxiliary verb meaning "to take place". The name of the situation plays the role of a subject here. Func_i is a semiauxiliary verb which connects the name of the situation – its subject – with the name of the *i*-th participant, its object. Thus, Func_1 has the name of the situation *C* as its subject and *A* as its object; for Func_2 *C* is the subject and *B* the object.

Labor_{ij} is a semiauxiliary verb connecting the name of the *i*-th participant (subject) with the name of the *j*-th participant (the first object), while the name of the situation *C* is the second object. Thus, Labor_{12} has *A* as its subject, *B* as its first object, and *C* as its second object.

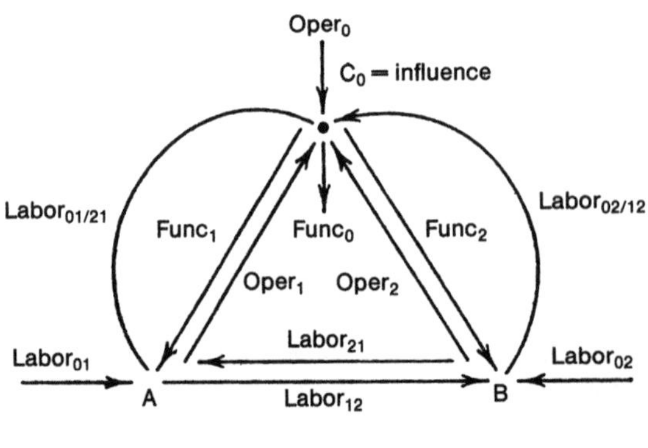

Fig. 4.1. Scheme defining lexical parameters

Let the situation C be C = (the influence of participant A on participant B). We thus have the following lexical parameters: $\text{Oper}_1(C)$ = to exert (A exerts influence on B); $\text{Oper}_2(C)$ = to be subject to (B is subject to the influence of A); $\text{Func}_0(C)$ = to take place (A's influence on B takes place); $\text{Func}_1(C)$ = to come from (the influence on B comes from A); $\text{Func}_2(C)$ = to extend (A's influence extends to B); $\text{Labor}_{12}(C)$ = to subject (A subjects B to his influence). It should be stressed that the parameters Oper_i, Func_i, Labor_{ij} are semantically empty. Their role is entirely syntactic: to dissociate a verb from a noun which conveys the whole sense.

Most of the other verbal lexical parameters have autonomous lexical meanings and usually correspond to verbs. We shall divide these into participants and nonparticipants in a situation. The following are parameters for nonparticipants in a situation: Caus (causative), Liqu (liquidative), and Perm (permissive). The name of a nonparticipant in a situation should be the subject of Caus (= to cause a certain situation to begin to take place). Liqu (= to prevent a certain situation from taking place) is equivalent to "Caus not", while Perm (= not to prevent a situation from taking place) is equivalent to "not Caus not". Let us give some examples: Caus (school) = to build, Caus (sweater) = to knit, Caus Oper_1 (power) = to empower, Liqu (to sleep) = to wake, Liqu Oper (power) = to liberate (sb. from sb. else's power), Perm (examination) = to admit (sb. to an examination), Perm Func_1(trouble) = to avert.

Let us pass on to the verbal parameters for participants in a situation. These are: parameters with a phase meaning – Incep (= to begin), Cont (= to continue); parameters with an aspectual meaning – Perf (= to perform an action which is denoted by the name of a situation), Real (= to realize the requirement laid down in the meaning of the name of a situation), Result (= to be a result of an action); parameters with a causative meaning – Caus_i (= the i-th participant in a situation causes...), Liqu_i(= Caus_i not), Perm_i (= not Caus_i not); and the parameter Manif (= to make manifest). Let us cite a few examples of these verbal parameters: Incep (to sleep) = to fall asleep, Cont Oper (calm) = to keep, Cont Func_0 (smell) = to be discernible, Result Perf (to lay down) = to lie, Result Real_1 (to study) = to know, Caus_1 Func_1 (power) = to gain (power over sb.), Liqu Real_2 (memory) = to erase (sth. from memory), Perm_2 Func_2 (beating) = to suffer, endure (a beating), Caus_1 Manif (valor) = to exhibit (valor).

The essential lexical parameters constituting analogues of nouns are S_{inst}, S_{loc}, S_i, S_{mod}, S_{res} (typical names of the instrument of a situation, the location of a situation, the i-th participant in a situation, the mode of acting, and the result of a situation) and Figur (a graphic, figurative representation of a situation). All these parameters are connected with verbs only. Let us look at some examples: S_1 (examination) = examiner, S_2 (examination) = examinee, $S_1\text{Oper}_1$ (aggression) = aggressor, S_{inst} (to think) = brain, S_{loc} (battle) = battlefield, S_{mod} (to go) = walk, S_{res} (conference) = conclusions (of a conference), S_{res} (to report) = report, S_{fig} (conversation) = the thread (of a conversation).

The analogues of adjectives (Magn, Bon, A_i, Able_i) and of adverbs (Adv_i) are referred to as adjunctive parameters. Magn (= high magnitude) can be combined with various parts of speech: Magn (search) = thorough, Magn (to sleep) = soundly, Magn (to wound) = critically, Magn (white) = dazzlingly, Magn (healthy) = perfectly. Bon (= good) is applied to nouns and verbs: Bon (chance) = lucky, Bon (to buy) = cheaply. A_i denotes a typical name of the i-th participant in a situation, and $Able_i$ a potential i-th participant: A_i (moustaches) = moustachioed, A_2 (to know) = well known, $Able_i$ (to soak) = permeable. Adv is a typical adverb, semantically connected with the name of the i-th participant in a situation.

To end our description of lexical functions, we would like to emphasize that they are used to describe *lexical combinability,* not semantics.

4.3.4 Declarative Semantic Knowledge of the Language (the Semantic Zone of the Dictionary)

Semantic relations between lexemes, established in the course of processing a given sentence, correspond to the relations which take place between the vertices of a semantic network. Let us note that each choice of a name for such relations and for vertices indirectly imposes certain restrictions on the subject matter dealt with by the input and output languages of an SNL.

Above we described the notion of an MG. We also indicated that the MG comprises two components: syntactic (MGSY) and semantic (MGSE). For every column of an MG, the semantic component should indicate (see Table 4.3): (a) semantic categories characterizing the actant of a situation (the semantic valence), which corresponds to the given column, and (b) the name of the semantic relation which connects a situation determined by a word A with an actant corresponding to the given column.

The semantic component of the MG of a word A (semantic categories) conveys information on the semantic combinability of this word (see Sect. 4.2.3). If a lexeme does not possess an MG, the corresponding semantic zone in the dictionary contains a list of semantic categories characterizing this lexeme. Semantic categories are treated as semantic components of the component analysis (see Sect. 1.2.2). Since the shortcomings of component analysis indicated in Sect. 1.2.2 mean that it cannot be considered a universal semantic method, it should be stressed that the semantic categories of the MG of a word A should not be considered to form the sense of the word A, but should rather be regarded as a means of speeding up and directing the process of analysis or synthesis. In the simplest systems, an MG and a list of semantic categories may play the role of defining a word.

By the *meaning (sense)* of a word, linguists usually understand its definition. However, as we indicated in Sect. 1.3.3, the meaning of a word can be established only after its context has been taken into account. Thus, a dictionary definition cannot fully explain meaning. This does not mean that a definition is completely useless. Our point is that a definition is not equivalent to a word's sense (as in our understanding of the term *sense*). We shall thus specify the purposes for which such definitions will be used (for the sake of brevity, we are talking of *definitions of words* – usually it is word groups, not individual words, that are defined):

1. To distinguish a word (or word group) A from another word B (i.e., to find a canonical representation during analysis, and to choose a concrete word when

constructing a sentence (during synthesis) – see discriminative networks, Sect. 7.2)
2. To express information used when implicative and synonymic transformations are performed
3. To express a meaning in concise form, i.e., to replace "part" of a meaning by a single word
4. To retrieve information from a semantic network
5. To enable the system to answer the user's questions when asked what it understands by a certain word (the aspect of metaknowledge)

The language in which definitions are expressed is likely to be identical to the one used to represent the model of reality. The following requirements should be met in defining lexical meanings:

1. The lexical meaning of a word should be defined in terms of simpler meanings (to avoid tautology). In practice, this means that every lexical meaning *A* should be expressed in terms of at least two other lexical meanings *B* and *C*.
2. The lexical meanings *B* and *C* should be such meanings as are necessary and adequate to define *A*.
3. Differences in the outer form of two words *A* and *B* should not necessarily entail different forms of definitions for *A* and *B*. This requirement, although quite obvious, is often not met.
4. We do not normally define an individual word, but rather an expression of the *XPY* form, where *P* is the word to be defined, and *X* and *Y* are variables which incorporate the given expression into a sentence or word combination.

The first requirement means that a definition is expressed – not necessarily directly – in terms of interrelations between elements of a small set of *elementary meanings EM* (which are not defined). Elementary meanings need not have literal analogues in a natural language. We should emphasize that it is not necessary to express a definition in terms of EMs alone. However, it is necessary that the definition of the lexical meaning of *A* be expressed in terms of metanotions (not of words in the NL), which should be simpler than *A* and, in particular, may belong to the set of elementary meanings. Thus, it is possible – but not obligatory, as many authors assume – for a lexical meaning to be expressed by EMs; this possibility need not be expressed explicitly and is realized as a result of the mechanism of inference (see Sect. 6.4).

Let us explain the need for the second requirement by using an example. Let the verb *to finish* be defined as *to cease*; i.e., these two verbs are semantically equivalent. An SNL will then not distinguish the utterance "He finished working" from "He ceased working", although these two utterances are obviously different: the first assumes that the work has been accomplished, the second does not. Thus, the SNL will perceive synonymy where this does not exist. On the other hand, if *A* and *B* are synonyms, but *A* is defined as *BC*, the system will not register synonymy where this does exist.

If the third requirement were not fulfilled, the process of carrying out implicative and synonymic transformations could be considerably impeded. For instance, if *builder* is defined as "a person who builds...", then *surgeon* should be defined as "a person who operates", because the relation (to operate: surgeon) is exactly the same as the relation (to build: builder). In defining dictionaries, *surgeon* is usually given as "a doctor who is a specialist in surgery". In order that a word be defined correctly, it should be placed in the corresponding word-formative series of thematically connected words.

The fourth requirement (to define an expression *XPY* rather than an individual word *P*) stems from the fact that in many cases – such as words possessing an MG, certain adverbs and pronouns, modal words and particles, predicates involving negation, etc. – it is impossible to define the meaning of an isolated word (Apresyan 1974). For instance, the verb *to allow* should not be defined as "not to cause not being able to" since it is not clear whose action – that of the subject or of the object of a sentence – is negated by the second "not". We should therefore say: "*A* allows *B* to do *X*" = "*A* does not cause *B* not to be able to do *X*".

It can easily be demonstrated that all the requirements specified above must of necessity be satisfied. In constructing successive definitions, starting from elementary meanings and then moving on to more and more complex ones, the links connecting a given lexical meaning with all related meanings become evident and constitute the hierarchical structure of the language's lexical-semantic system. This lays the basis for formulating rules of synonymic and implicative transformations and for constructing various semantic word groups.

For instance, let the verb *to inform* be defined as follows: "*A* informs *B* about fact *C*" = "A person *A* causes another person *B* to know fact *C*". The explicit indication of the semantic relationships between *to inform, to cause,* and *to know* allows us to perform the following transformations: "*A informs B* about fact *C*" ⇒ "*A* knows about *C*" or "*A informs B* about fact *C*" ⇒ "*B* knows about *C*".

Let us consider how the definition of a word (or an expression) can be utilized in the process of information retrieval in a semantic network. As far as this author is aware, this problem has never been posed up to now. Let us explain what is involved here by the following example. Let us suppose a system has been told a few short tales. Then it is asked to say whether any of the tales were about *envy*. In order to answer this question, the system should be able to compare this word with the sense of the texts. Let the word *envy* be defined as follows: "*X* envies *Y* his *Z*" = "*X* does not possess *Z*, *Y* possesses *Z*, *X* feels negative emotions caused by the fact that he does not want *Y* to possess *Z* but wants to possess *Z* himself". This problem can be solved – or, strictly speaking, reduced to another problem, already solved – in the following way. The definition of the word can be represented by a frame with appropriate descriptions of the words *X*, *Y*, and *Z*. Then the problem is reduced to the problem of identifying the frame that corresponds to *envy* (which exists in the system's knowledge about reality and is activated during the processing of the input texts) with the linguistic definition of the word *envy* (represented by a frame of a similar name). Let us note that this approach to the problem is quite reasonable, even if the word *envy* has not been used in the texts of the tales. We are not yet prepared to discuss this question in greater detail. However, we would like to point out that at present, in all systems we know of, this problem is resolved by the simple device of ignoring it. Generally speaking, the problem can be reduced to projecting a definition (in the form of a frame) onto the system's knowledge of the surrounding environment (in the form of a frame or of a network of frames).

There is one more role played by definitions that we would like to call readers' attention to. In the course of a dialogue with the user, they may be employed to formulate answers to questions of the type "What does the system know about the transportation system?" It is advisable to require that all the information contained in an answer to such a question be expressed in terms of the system's metaknowledge. This enables the system to extend its explanations by making them more detailed according to the user's needs or demands. It must be emphasized that the process of defining words is a very complex one, based to a considerable degree on heuristic methods. Apresyan (1974, p. 99) distinguishes the following methods that may be of use when formulating the definition of a word *A*:

1. A complete analysis of the typical situation that *A* refers to. This analysis should include an enumeration of the features or actions on participants in the situation, as well as descriptions of the relationships connecting these participants. This may be regarded as a ramified analogue of an MG. In fact, an MG can itself play the role of a word's definition in the simplest systems.
2. An analysis of a paradigmatically connected group of words containing the word *A*. According to Apresyan, such groups can be constructed from non-exact synonyms (e.g., *to help – to facilitate; to disturb – to impede*), antonyms, thematically connected words, etc. If it is established that *to help* is to *to facilitate* as *to disturb* is to *to impede*, and if other such relations are determined, then the description of one word leads to a *uniform* description of the whole group of words.
3. An analysis of a syntagmatically connected group of words. This is carried out with the aim of distinguishing the proper meaning on the basis of characteristics of combinability. *Meaning* and *combinability* must be precisely differentiated, lest we include in the meaning of a word the semantic components not of this particular word, but of a word it is combined with. For instance, the word *bark* should be defined as "a sharp and loud sound" rather than "the sound that dogs make". The latter definition stems from the fact that these two words – *bark* and *dog* – are very often associated with each other.
4. An analysis of negative material, i.e., of various errors and mistakes made in the process of speech

Apresyan (1974, p. 107) describes patterns of definitions which he developed on the basis of the heuristic methods mentioned above. These methods make it possible to attain a much higher degree of correctness in definitions. The ability to function as human beings do would be the final criterion of the correctness of the model as a whole. However, the problem of how this ability is to be achieved is by no means a trivial one and requires further investigation.

4.3.5 Pragmatic Knowledge About the Language

In addition to the proper lexical meaning, various other features may be associated with a particular word, from semantic associations (i.e., connotations) to the modal components of meaning (i.e., the modal framework of an utterance) which are connected not with a concrete situation but with any situation that might arise during a conversation. These are all included in what linguists call *pragmatics*. The common feature that they all possess is that they characterize the relation between a speaker or addressee and the reality described by a given sign. In addition to what we have already indicated, any knowledge about knowledge which helps direct the process of comprehension and/or of planning will also be considered to be included in pragmatics.

Semantic associations (connotations) reflect such extralinguistic factors connected with a word as custom and generally accepted manners of using the objects in question. For instance, the word *flash* is associated with such notions as rapidity, light, etc. Hence, in the pragmatic zone of the dictionary entry we have *flash 1* = "a sudden short blaze of light", with indication given of the semantic associations of "rapidity", "brightness", and so on, while the next entry is *flash 2* = "a first short news report, received by telegraph, radio, etc." with the note "as *flash 1* as to the connotation of rapidity". Despite the fact that such comments do not enter directly into the semantics of a word, they are of great importance, as in many cases they produce the basis for determining the manner in which the word enters into comparisons and similes ("as quick as a flash"), metaphors, derivative words, etc. As a matter of fact, what is associative and pragmatic in one lexical meaning may become essential and semantic in another. Thus, for instance, the words *servant* and *butler* are to a great extent synonymous; their connotations, however, are different, which becomes particularly apparent when we consider metaphorical meanings such as that conveyed by the expression *a servant of the people*.

The modal component of a meaning (i.e., the modal framework) expresses the speaker's, listener's, and observer's assessment of a situation. Linguists recommend that this component be directly included in the definition of a word (i.e., in the semantic zone). For example: (a) "*even A acted*" = "others acted; *A* acted; the speaker did not expect that *A* would act"; (b) "*only X*" (as in *He is only fifty*) = "*X*, and the speaker considers this to be little"; (c) "*already X*" (as in *He is already fifty*) = "*X*, and the speaker considers this to be a lot".

A reference to an observer – as opposed to the speaker, the listener, or a participant in the events being described – is implicitly included in such expressions as "to come from" or "to come out from behind". The use of the former does not depend on the location of the observer in relation to the moving object. The observer may say, "He is coming from the railway station", whether he himself is or is not at the railway station. However, if the sentence is "He came out from behind the fence", the location of the observer is not arbitrary: had he himself been behind the fence, he could not have seen the person appear, but rather would have seen him disappear.

The pragmatic zone of a dictionary also contains information that may be used in order to direct the processing of a sentence and expose ambiguities. This information concerns such semantic classes as action predicates, state predicates, phase predicates, empty predicates (i.e., verbs with the meaning of the lexical functions Oper, Func, and Labor), copulative, functional, and modal predicates, notions, characteristics, the values of characteristics, and so on. All this information is extensively used by the system to direct the processes of analysis and synthesis. Let us note that all the aforementioned classes belong to the metanotions known to the system and used in the descriptions of semantic networks.

The pragmatic knowledge about language described above is an individual form of knowledge, i.e., it is peculiar to a given lexeme. It is also advisable, however, to consider general pragmatic knowledge, which contains that part of the metaknowledge of the natural language expressible in the form of knowledge of the structure of the dictionary and of tables, in the form of active knowledge of the forms of restrictions imposed on the language of conversation, and in the form of information about the degree of importance of this or that piece of information for analysis and synthesis of texts.

Knowledge of the structures of the dictionary and tables enables the system to carry out automatic checks (regarding format) on a new piece of information about the NL. Therefore, the user need not know these structures. This type of knowledge includes the following: The system knows that individual information about the NL is stored in the dictionary, whereas the general information is in the form of rules of grammar and morphological tables of affixes. The system possesses knowledge about these rules and about the structure of the dictionary and of tables. The system knows, for example, that the dictionary comprises morphological, syntactic, semantic, and pragmatic zones; it also knows the format and purpose of each of these. The system is able to express this knowledge in the natural language. Thus, the system is able to check whether the user has made any mistakes in inserting a new piece of information into the dictionary (e.g., the user might have forgotten to indicate information about one of the zones or made some error in format). Because of this knowledge, the system can obtain the necessary information about words it does not know by posing questions to the user (even if the user is not familiar with the structure of the dictionary).

The active knowledge of restrictions imposed on the language contains a list of these restrictions and information which allows the system to check whether these are being observed. Owing to this knowledge, the system can foresee the reasons for possible failures and thus avoid them – alone, or with the aid of the user. For example, the system knows that the input language comprises projective, interrogative, and isolated sentences in the NL. Let us now suppose an attempt to understand a sentence *A* has failed. The system can easily verify that this sentence is indeed isolated and interrogative (as it ends with a question mark). It can then conclude that the failure was caused by the fact that the sentence was not projective. If it is unable to state whether the sentence was in fact projective, it may ask the user for help (explaining to him, if necessary, what the word "projective" means).

Knowledge of the degree of importance of a certain piece of information about an input text is used by the system when it encounters contradictions in the information obtained at different stages of processing. Let us assume, for instance, that the MG of a certain word requires an accompanying noun to be in the accusative and to correspond to the semantic categories "undertaking" or "location". However, the input sentence contains only one noun in the accusative, and this corresponds to neither of the indicated categories. In these circumstances, if the system knows that semantic categories are more important than morphological information, it will be able to continue processing the sentence (as a safeguard, informing the user about the problems it has encountered and the manner in which they have been resolved).

A dictionary entry corresponding to a lexeme (a stem) ends with references to the vertices of the abstract network which correspond to the interpretation of the meaning of every homonym of the lexeme that exists in the network.

4.4 Knowledge About the System Itself: Methods of Representing This Knowledge

Knowledge about the system itself may be divided into *passive knowledge* and *active knowledge*. By active knowledge we mean knowledge used by the system in the course of its work. By passive knowledge we mean information which is known to the system and may be communicated by it, but which is not used during its work. Active knowledge is subdivided into *simple knowledge* and *metaknowledge*. By metaknowledge of A we mean active knowledge which is "actively" possessed by the system, i.e., the system "knows that it knows A". In other words, the system is capable not only of using the knowledge A directly, but also of investigating A, discussing it, and abstracting it.

Passive knowledge includes information that the system possesses about itself which is supplied to users not familiar with the system. It is convenient to store this knowledge in the form of instructions. For systems of real-life complexity, these instructions may prove very cumbersome. It is therefore advisable that they should be supplemented with a "list of contents" which may be shown to the user on the display. In this way every user can choose those instructions that are of the greatest interest to him. The instructions should contain at least the following information about the system: (a) the name of the system; (b) a description of the language of conversation (the description should be accompanied by examples); (c) a detailed description of the stored vocabulary and facts corresponding to a given area of subject matter; (d) information about the system's abilities; (e) information about the principles of the system's operation and its structure; (f) the parameters of the system. Any piece of information yielded by the system, but not used by it during its work, may be included in the passive knowledge.

In this section we shall concentrate our attention on the system's metaknowledge. The metaknowledge contains information about WHAT the system knows (what knowledge it possesses "actively") and HOW this knowledge is organized (i.e., represented). The metaknowledge can be divided into *static* and *dynamic components*. By *static metaknowledge* we mean metaknowledge which does not vary in the course of the system's operations, while by *dynamic metaknowledge* we understand metaknowledge which does vary. In accordance with the type of information being described, the metaknowledge is divided into metaknowledge of the system itself and metaknowledge of reality (the language, the dialogue, the surrounding environment, the user). The metaknowledge of reality contains information on:

1. The language and structure of the dialogue, the restrictions imposed on the language of the conversation, type of dialogue, and the structure of the repre-

sentation of the dictionary and of the grammar of the language of the conversation
2. The surrounding environment (the subject matter) known to the system, and the structure of the representation of knowledge in data and in the abstract and concrete networks
3. The user and the method of representing knowledge about him

The metaknowledge of reality has been described in the sections devoted to the representation of the knowledge of reality (see Sects. 3.4, 3.5, 3.6).

As a rule, existing systems work in the regime of constant surroundings (not varied by the system), i.e., in the regime of a static world. Dynamics is attained by introducing new data without the system's knowledge. This restriction, although rather rigid, does not mean that systems designed to work in this regime are of no practical use. A static world is permissible for information retrieval systems, reference systems, and question-answer systems. Generally, however, we should not confine ourselves to static metaknowledge when representing the knowledge of the system's operations. This is because static metaknowledge, by definition, does not reflect possible changes in the state of the system or in transformations of an input text.

Let us move on to a description of the knowledge of the system itself. This knowledge is necessary in order to (a) explain to the user the actions undertaken by the system, and (b) organize the system's work efficiently (i.e., quickly and with as few mistakes as possible).

We shall proceed from the supposition that in order to perform the tasks indicated the system should be able to determine the following information:

1. The state of the system. What is the objective (objectives) of the system during the processing of an input text, i.e., what is it aiming to achieve? What is the current state of the system? How has the system reached this state? Why has the system reached this particular state (i.e., as a result of what rules)? What is the system going to do now?
2. The state of the text being processed. (a) What is the value of a certain parameter or meaning? For example: "What is the gender of the *i*-th word?", "Has a nominal group containing the words *i*, *j*, and *k* been found?", "Was the interpretation of a given nominal group successful?", "Has the information indicated in the question been found in the data base?", etc. (b) How (with the help of what inferences) has the value of a given parameter been obtained? For example: "How has the answer to the input question been obtained?" (possible answer: "It has been found in the data base", "It has been calculated on the basis of such-and-such a formula", etc.), "Why is the word *A* in the masculine gender?" (answer: "On the basis of information about this word stored in the dictionary").
3. The data employed. What data have been employed in order to determine a parameter or specify its value? Why were these particular data employed? Why were the data concerning *X* not employed?

In order to perform these tasks, information on the following is required (see Sects. 2.4, 2.5): (a) how the system functions and how it is organized; (b) the knowledge sources and how they can be described in the form of rules; (c) the algorithm of the work of the metainterpreter; (d) how goals are determined (goal formation).

4.4.1 Information About the Participant's Activities

In the course of a conversation between the user and the participant (the system) the context of the conversation is created. This involves: (a) the input text at various stages of processing; (b) the sequence of the participant's states; (c) a list of data which have been used (activated) in processing the input text. The task facing the participant here is to determine the value of various attributes (parameters) of the current context. If the participant is for any reason unable to determine the value of a parameter, he should ask the user about this value. This allows a system designed on the basis of the model of a participant in the conversation to make use of the user's assistance in order to perform its task. If the system (participant) is to be able to act in accordance with the user's directions, provided to it in the course of processing ("observing what is imposed"), certain requirements have to be fulfilled. These requirements concern both the organization of the system as a whole and the principles of the operation of its parts (stages). In fact, at every stage input and output texts should be expressible in terms of metaknowledge (i.e., they should be "comprehensible" to the system). In a system based on the TEXT-SENSE-OBJECTIVE model, knowledge of the system's own activities is expressed in the form of 4-tuples comprising an object, an attribute, a value, and a coefficient of specificity (CS). The CS is represented by a number from the interval $[-1, 1]$. It measures the degree of credibility assigned by the system to the proposition that the object's attribute possesses the value indicated. The reason for introducing the CS is to make it possible to represent indefinite knowledge about the surrounding world (this knowledge may be expressed by utterances such as: "*A* assumes *B*", "*C* is questionable", etc.). Consequently, an attribute may have several values simultaneously (even mutually exclusive ones). The most important advantages of this approach are its versatility and simplicity. The latter is of paramount importance, as it enables the participant to investigate its own knowledge. Besides the form of 4-tuples, knowledge of the surrounding world may be expressed in the form of lists and tables, organized in such a way as to make them suitable for use in productions. It is convenient to represent several facts in the form of lists and tables; this form often allows us to reduce the number of rules necessary.

4.4.2 Knowledge About Knowledge Sources and About the Structure of Rules

In order to be able to explain its activities, the system (i.e., the participant) should understand the semantics of all rules that are used. These semantics may be defined by describing the meaning of every rule in a form comprehensible to the metainterpreter. Alternatively, the meanings of rules can also be specified by ensuring that the operators of the language which these rules are written in are comprehensible to the metainterpreter. The advantages of the second approach become particularly apparent when the number of rules is very large. In the first approach, we have to give a complete description of new rules that are added or existing ones that are modified. In the second approach, however, there is no need to change anything, provided the new rules are also expressible using the operators of the language adopted. Thus, if a system is to be used to resolve a problem from the real world – which always involves a large number of rules – the second approach is preferable.

Knowledge of the functioning of the KSs is expressed in the form of production rules. These describe the prerequisites for activating a given KS and its presumed (not actual) actions in terms comprehensible to the user. The aim of this approach is to express knowledge about KSs in concise terms (i.e., more abstract ones), free of the endless concrete details of programming languages. Given that knowledge of KSs constitutes metaknowledge, it must be so arranged as to ensure its compactness and simplicity. The latter is achieved by describing only the most important and most meaningful aspects of the actions of KSs and of the prerequisites for these actions. The existence of metarules of KSs reduces the system's task in describing its own actions to indicating which of these rules (or their parts) have been employed, and why. The compactness of the rules facilitates their use in planning and seeking solutions.

These rules (productions) consist of an antecedent and actions. The antecedent describes the situation, taking the form of a list specifying the conditions necessary for the situation to take place. If an antecedent is true, the production is carried out. Before the true or false character of an antecedent is verified, the system attempts to determine the values of all parameters mentioned in this antecedent. If there is a parameter whose value cannot be determined, or if the expression integrating the conditions in this antecedent is false, the antecedent itself is concluded to be false. In order to derive the value of an antecedent from the conditions, we shall use the logical symbols **and* and **or*, which are the many-valued analogues of the Boolean functions $\wedge$ and $\vee$. The conditions set in rules are represented by predicative functions ⟨predicate⟩, ⟨object⟩, ⟨attribute⟩, ⟨value⟩ which are given values from the interval $[-1, +1]$. The symbol **and* selects the minimum value from those which it connects; similarly, **or* selects the maximum value. An antecedent is considered true if its value exceeds a certain threshold value. This threshold value must be determined experimentally. In the system MYCIN, for instance, this value has been put at 0.2 (Davis and Buchanan 1977). If an antecedent is true, the action in question is carried out and the conclusion which is found has a coefficient of specificity equal to

$$\langle \text{CS antecedent} \rangle \times \langle \text{CS action} \rangle .$$

The relevant set of predicates, objects, and attributes must be determined for the given subject matters.

There is no need to use the same format (indicated above) for all predicative functions. These may be expressed by reduced descriptions (i.e., templates). The use of templates enables us to introduce new functions whose descriptions can be combined from the primitive functions (primitives) known to the system. Each primitive corresponds to a template with formal parameters, whose type is specified in the description of the template. The appropriate values, established on the basis of the given input text, are assigned to the formal parameters during processing. The primitives form the set of elements from which rules are constructed. The number of primitives is a question of tens, that of rules – of hundreds. The relatively small number of primitives makes it easier for the system to investigate its own rules.

It should be emphasized at this point that each rule is an isolated module of knowledge. The whole context required is specified in the rule's antecedent. This restriction is intended to make rules context independent, making it possible to add or modify one particular rule without worrying about all the consequences of such modifications. The simplicity of the structure of rules allows the system to investigate them by itself. In systems of real-life complexity, the number of rules is usually measured in hundreds. In order to guide the search for the rules relevant to the task at hand it is convenient to use metarules (M-rules). M-rules determine which groups of rules should be used prior to others, and which should not be used at all. In other words, M-rules make it possible to prepare a list of the relevant rules, and to arrange them in order. If necessary, we can construct a superior M-rule from M-rules (i.e., a rule of the second metalevel).

To conclude this brief description of rules, let us list the reasons which lead us to use the system of productions to represent the knowledge that a system has of itself, although not using this representation to describe reality (the language, the dialogue, the surrounding world). It is possible to represent knowledge in the form of productions only if the following conditions are satisfied:

1. The subject matter to be represented admits of a definite degree of formalization. This means that facts concerning the subject matter may be represented in the form of the set of base primitives, recognizable and comprehensible to the system.
2. The interrelations between primitives which correspond to the given subject matter should not be excessively ramified. The experience of work on the MYCIN system (Davis and Buchanan 1977) shows that rules which possess more than six conditions in their antecedent become impracticable. In other words, the number of factors which the performance of the action indicated in a rule is contingent on is in practice limited (although not in theory).
3. The mechanism adopted for processing the goal trees (AND/OR trees) requires that the conditions specified in an antecedent not set conflicting subgoals. If this requirement is not met, the final result will depend on the order in which the rules are processed.
4. Since the manner in which the rules are employed requires much time-consuming scanning, the number of rules that describe the given area of subject matter should not be too large. Experience of work on the MYCIN system (Scott et al. 1977) shows that this number, given existing methods of processing, should be on the order of a few hundred (MYCIN itself contains about 400 rules).
5. The following restrictions imposed by the system of productions should be accepted by the user: (a) the IF/THEN format is used for defining facts; (b) the mechanism of output (MODUS PONENS) used by the system is considered sufficient and convenient; (c) the ability to explain possessed by the system of productions is limited to giving references to rules or parts of rules.

The above-mentioned requirements make it clear that systems of productions should not be used if the knowledge about the surrounding world contains a very large number of facts, e.g., hundreds of thousands (as in information-retrieval systems or reference systems). However, systems of productions, being simple and context independent, can and should be used to represent dynamic subject matter whose states are analyzed by the system, i.e., in the representation of the knowledge the system has of itself.

4.4.3 Knowledge of the Work of the Metainterpreter

This knowledge (like the semantics of rules) can be given in the form of a description of the work of the metainterpreter or, alternatively, in the form of the operators of the given language. Moreover, knowledge of how the metainterpreter functions can be built into the system, i.e., it need not be defined in explicit form. A system may comprise several specialists, each of which is prepared to give answers to questions of a certain type. Each specialist knows how the part of the interpreting mechanism that corresponds to him works, and what knowledge he is able to employ. This is precisely the method of representing knowledge of the interpreter that should be used during the first stages of work with the system. In order to understand the rules, the system uses general knowledge about them possessed by specialists and represented in the form of descriptions of templates.

To illustrate the above, we shall show how this knowledge is used to construct semantic relations (SERs) in a nominal phrase (NP). An appropriate specialist investigates the rules (*X*) by which the system draws conclusions concerning the values of the parameter SER in the NP (e.g., SER. DEVERB, SER.NP, i.e., the programs constructing SERs for deverbative parts of speech and NPs). Then the specialist verifies the templates of all functions that have appeared in the part labeled ACTION of the rules *X*, and selects those rules which have the value "truth" (T). The same example is of help in illustrating the knowledge which is built into the knowledge possessed by a specialist. The specialist knows that the control mechanism has access to lists of rules that can be used to determine the meaning of any attribute. The specialist also knows that he should analyze only the right-hand side of rules (i.e., ACTION), because conclusions concerning facts are drawn by ACTION, while ANTECEDENT only uses facts. As we have already indicated, the ACTION of a KS reflects a presumed result, as opposed to an actual one. Thus, it is the specialist's task to formulate – on the basis of the actual results of the action of a KS (SER.NP in our case) – a metaresult, and to compare this with the presumed result. If the two results do not coincide, the metainterpreter looks for a rule that can overcome this incompatibility.

The metainterpreter memorizes the process of performing tasks in the form of a tree. Each vertex of this tree represents a goal and contains information about how the system has attempted to achieve this goal (a list of the rules that have been employed, a list of the questions that have been posed to the user, etc.). Every rule employed is accompanied by its result, i.e., success or failure (along with the reasons for failure). If any of the rules employed, e.g., the rule *A*, entailed the appearance of a new subgoal (as may happen, for instance, when the value of one of the parameters is unknown), then a new vertex is created in the tree. This vertex is a descendant of the vertex which used rule A. Depending on the character of the logical connections between the primitives from the antecedent, the vertex is of the type AND or of the type OR (Nilsson 1971).

4.4.4 Knowledge of Goal Formation

This knowledge is essential for the system to be capable of explaining its activities. The goal-formative component fulfills the following functions: it assesses the current state of the system, establishes the reasons for this particular state having been attained, and puts forward proposals regarding further action. The work of this component was described in Sect. 2.5. Here we shall concentrate on the knowledge of this component possessed by the system. The main purpose of this knowledge is to make the system "aware" of its own actions, which is of great importance as it enables the system to explain its actions to the user, and also facilitates the adding and modification of information (during both operation and debugging). Let us note here that the degree to which the system appears reliable to the user depends chiefly on the extent to which the user understands the actions undertaken by the system.

Let us assume that every question that the user poses to the system falls into one of the following categories: (a) questions about the actions of the system (AS); (b) questions about the static knowledge (SK) that the system possesses of itself; (c) questions about its dynamic knowledge (DK).

Dynamic knowledge encompasses questions about current actions (WHAT is the action), about WHY a particular action is being performed, and about HOW it can be accomplished. In order to answer the question WHAT, the system indicates the rule currently being processed, thus indicating what goal it is currently attempting to achieve. Since the process of obtaining an answer involves searching the AND/OR tree of goals, answers to questions such as WHY or HOW an action is being performed should take the following form: Every action performed (X) is connected by the system with a vertex (Y_1) of the tree of goals. An adequate answer to the question "WHY is Y_1 being performed?" will therefore contain information about the goal Y_0 (the supergoal of Y_1) for which Y_1 is a subgoal; an answer to the question "HOW is X being performed?" will indicate the goals Y_2, Y_3, etc., i.e., the subgoals of Y_1. The user can select the necessary degree of detail to be included in an answer by repeating the questions WHY and HOW. Let us clarify this with the aid of the following example. Let us assume a tree of goals has the form shown in Fig. 4.2: to achieve the goal "understanding the text" we have to establish the semantic relations (SERs) in the text; to establish the SERs we have to establish the syntactic relations (SYRs); to establish the SYRs we have to know the morphological information (MI); to obtain the MI we have to consult the relevant dictionary entry. Let us now suppose the answer given by the system to the question "WHAT is your current action?" is 1: "I am determining the semantic relations between the words of the input text". If the next question is "WHY are you doing that?" the system will then answer 2: "To understand the text". If, however, the next question is "HOW are you doing that?", the answer will be 3.1: "By establishing syntactic relations"; 3.2: "By establishing the semantic relations between the predicate SER.Pr and the nominal

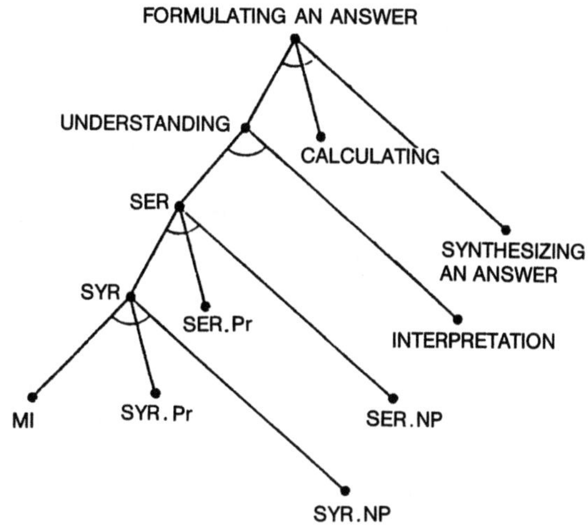

Fig. 4.2. Example of a tree of goals

phrases"; 3.3: "By establishing the semantic relations within the nominal phrases (SER.NP)". If the level of detail does not satisfy the user, he is free to change it. For instance, he may pose the question WHY and get a more general and abstract answer – 4: "To find the answer to the question". If a more detailed level is required, the user can then ask: "HOW is 3.2 being performed?", etc. It should be emphasized that a tree of goals may be either drawn from an analysis of rules or built into the metainterpreter (wholly or partially).

The question of static knowledge about the system itself is treated in similar fashion to the question of facts. The latter will be considered in detail in Chaps. 5, 6, and 7.

The problem of the system explaining its dynamic knowledge, i.e., the knowledge created in the course of processing an input text, is the most difficult and complex of all. It is therefore advisable to ensure that the user's questions regarding dynamic knowledge are restricted to the following kinds:

1. What are the ⟨attributes⟩ of the ⟨object⟩?
   a) What attributes characterize transport?
   b) Can transport be characterized in accordance with the type of goods conveyed?
2. What is the value of the ⟨attribute⟩ of the ⟨object⟩?
   a) What is the case of the word *Moskve*?
      [*Moskve* = the locative of *Moskva* (Moscow); trans. note].
   b) What is the semantic type of the word *transport*?
3. How did you determine the value of the ⟨attribute⟩ of the ⟨object⟩?
   a) How did you determine the case of the word *Moskve*?
   b) Why do you consider the words *transport* and *how much* to be connected by a semantic relation?
   c) What information from the dictionary have you used regarding the word *delivery*?

4. Why did you not consider the ⟨attribute⟩ as a characteristic of the ⟨object⟩?
   a) Why did you not consider the expression *how much* to refer to goods?

All the above-mentioned capabilities of explaining the system's actions and states are realized by means of the following operations: (a) the rule which is currently activated is communicated to the user (at his request); (b) the rules which have been activated while processing the input text are listed, and the relationships between these rules and the events indicated in the text are established; (c) data that have been used by particular rules are indicated. The functions of the system described above are designed to help the user assess the current state of the system and determine the reasons that have led to it. Using the results of this assessment, the user is able to modify an input text so as to avoid failures. Standard situations where failures are likely to occur, i.e., failures that can be foreseen by the system's designer, can be written in the form of rules of production.

To close our examination of the knowledge that the system possesses of itself, we would like to point out that the language in which the user converses with a system about its actions and states can be more restricted than the language used for a dialogue about the subject matter. Moreover, methods of processing utterances about the system's actions and states are usually simpler than those used to process utterances about the subject matter itself. Indeed, since the language is more restricted, it is often possible to employ a method based on the use of key words for analysis of input utterances (questions). This method does not require full semantic and syntactic analysis. Templates can be employed in order to perform synthesis. This simplified mode of processing was used in the MYCIN system (Scott et al. 1977).

4.5 Knowledge of the User

Knowledge of the user is primarily necessary for the system to be able to perform the following tasks: (a) understanding the user's objectives; (b) determining the level of an answer's generality/abstraction (the level of concretization); (c) determining aspects which are of interest to the user; making provision for permissible and obligatory uses of "tacit knowledge" in formulating an answer; (d) determining the proximity of facts the user is interested in to the points of discontinuity (see Sect. 2.4.1); (e) making provision for perlocutionary factors (see Sect. 1.1.3).

Let us note that, in general, knowledge of the user cannot be integrated with the model of the surrounding environment. This is because the system should be capable of working with users who are interested in different objectives and in different aspects and levels of concretization of the subject matter.

4.5.1 The Objectives of the User

The objectives of the user are determined by the system in a different way from its own goals. The system determines its actions on the basis of goals which are derived from rules, i.e., in accordance with the chain GOAL → PLAN → ACTION (by *plan* we understand a hierarchy of subgoals). In attempting to determine the user's objectives, the system "sees" only his TEXTS (ACTIONS), and on this basis it should create PLAN → OBJECTIVE. In other words, the system synthesizes its own actions, and analyzes those of the user. Consequently, to determine the user's objectives, the system does not employ a goal-oriented method to distinguish the relevant rules, but rather a data-oriented method (see Sects. 2.5 and 2.2.5).

The user's objectives are largely determined by the tasks he wishes to perform. Two classes of dialogue have been identified so far, distinguished according to the type of task facing the user: data base-oriented dialogues (DBOD) and task-oriented dialogues (TOD) (Grosz 1976, 1977a, b). The first class comprises dialogues involving the user conversing with a system which stores information about a given area of subject matter (information-retrieval systems, reference systems, etc.). Dialogues of the second class involve the user conversing with a system which is designed to perform certain tasks (e.g., a robot assembling components). These dialogues possess a more complex structure and are more difficult to analyze. In the following we shall focus our attention chiefly on dialogues of the first class. In contrast to the opinion voiced by Grosz (1976), we are convinced that not only TOD, but also DBOD possesses an internal structure. The ramified structure of a dialogue flows from the fact that the user's objectives vary in the course of a dialogue. Let us enumerate some of these objectives:

1. Obtaining the value of an attribute
2. Determining the scope of the knowledge possessed by the system
3. Understanding the reasons for a failure
3.1 Determining the current state of the system
3.2 Determining the sequence of actions that led to the failure
3.3 Determining the data used
3.4 Determining the results obtained
4. Correcting the input text
4.1 Correcting the user's own mistakes
4.2 Modifying the question to eliminate a difficulty encountered by the system
4.3 Imposing a proper understanding of an input text on the system
5. Making corrections to the knowledge possessed by the system

The most convenient way of expressing information regarding the user's objectives is to formulate it in terms of rules of incompatibility. In the "antecedent" of these rules we give a description of a concrete incompatibility between the presumed and the actual results – one encountered while processing a text. In the "actions" of the rules, we indicate the user's possible actions after the incompatibility has been removed. For example: the incompatibility that arises when one of the words of an input text is not in the dictionary may be represented in the form of the following rule:

IF: A word (*A*) from the text is not in the dictionary,
THEN: (a) pass over the word *A*, or (b) change the word *A*, or (c) add the word *A* to the system.

Each of these three actions is performed by a corresponding subroutine used for processing the given situation. The system selects one situation, basing itself either on a question to the user or on the user's subsequent actions. The question may, for example, be formulated as follows: "Should I pass over (P), change (C), or add (A) the word *A*?" In reply, the user quotes one of the letters – P, C, or A.

4.5.2 Determining the Level of Generality/Abstraction (Concretization) of an Answer

A full solution to this problem is not yet available, as this would require the system to have full information about the user's knowledge. For the time being, this does not seem feasible. However, partial solutions to this problem can be found. One of these is to give answers whose level of concretization is as close as possible to that of the question. This is a commonly employed method; however, it cannot be used in certain circumstances. Let us suppose the question is "Who did not fulfill the plan?" If the knowledge possessed by the system is sufficient, answers may be given in various forms: e.g., "Petrov", "Dept. No. 10", "The 'Progress' factory", "The Ministry of Food Processing", etc. The proper answer may be selected in such cases if the system knows what the user's own status as regards this hierarchy is, as this determines the level the user is interested in. Information about the user's status is utilized by the system when it interprets a question and chooses the appropriate level of generality of its answer. Status may be established on the basis of the user's identifier; alternatively, it may be defined by the user himself. A more general solution to this problem (though less convenient for the user) is for the user to select the level of concretization himself. The user is then able to change the level of concretization of an answer as and when he sees fit.

4.5.3 Determining the Aspects of a Situation of Interest to the User

Let us clarify what is involved here with the following example: Suppose the sytem possesses information about various aspects of one phenomenon. This kind of situation occurs when the system is designed to work with different users, or when it is programmed to store multiform information (an engine, for instance, can be described as a mechanical device or in terms of an electrical blueprint). Let the question posed to the system be, "In which desk is the physics textbook?" The possible answers to this question may differ as to how the desks are identified: e.g., "In the one by the window", "In Alexeevsky's", "In the head's", "In desk no. 205", "In the one with the patterns carved on it", "In the one the calendar is on", etc. The necessary condition to be fulfilled by an answer is that it be unambiguous. However, since the knowledge possessed by the system differs from that of the user, this condition may be satisfied from the user's point of view but not from the system's, and vice versa. Thus, it is obvious that in order to formulate an answer which will satisfy the user the system must know what is known by the user and what is not: Does this user know who Alexeevsky is?; Does he know Alexeevsky is the head?; Does he know where his desk is?; etc. If these things are not known by the user, the system must find another form of providing an answer. Let us note at this point that while an unambiguous identification of objects is a necessary precondition for conversation, the fulfillment of this condition is still not enough to ensure that the conversation achieves the desired goal. True, the answer "In desk no. 205" identifies the object in question unambiguously. But if the user has had no experience of stocktaking, he may find this answer extremely inconvenient.

The solution to the problem of determining the aspects of a situation that are of interest to the user requires indication of the user's knowledge to be given in the model of the user possessed by the system. In formulating an answer, the system should take the user's knowledge into account. It is advisable to represent the model of the user by the same method as that employed to represent knowledge of the surrounding world.

The problem of determining the aspects of a situation of interest to the user is related to the problem of permissible and obligatory "tacit knowledge" in answers. The essence of this problem is the following: Which pieces of "tacit knowledge" are obligatory (to avoid annoying the user by presenting him with redundant material) and which are permissible (not producing possible confusion)? The answers given by a specialist to the question, "What is electricity?", when talking to a little child, a schoolboy, a student, or another specialist, may serve as examples of the way in which the notion of "tacit knowledge" can be applied, with the model of the user being taken into account. For all practical purposes, the problem we have indicated in this section has yet to be studied by designers of SNLs. In our opinion, it is high time this problem were tackled.

5 Input Sentence Analysis

5.1 General Outline

The task of sentence analysis is to express intensionally the sense of a given sentence. This should be done in the terms used by the internal representation of the system. At subsequent stages of sentence processing, a concrete denotation (assuming this exists) is assigned to the intensional expression obtained, and information characterizing this denotation is determined. In the case of the Russian language, sentence analysis is traditionally divided into morphological, syntactic, and semantic analyses. We shall consider these three stages of sentence analysis in detail. It should be recalled here (see Sect. 2.4) that the system does not always observe the order of stages indicated above. Indeed, the activation of a given module (knowledge source) is a consequence of a particular situation which has appeared on the screen (see Sect. 2.5). Of all the potentially relevant KSs, it is those whose preconditions (antecedents) are fulfilled that will be activated. Let us recall that the choice of potentially relevant KSs, and of that KS (or several, in the case of a multiprocessor system) which will operate at a given moment, is based on the current objectives of the system. For instance, a typical list of objectives yielded by the goal-formative component may take the following form: (a) identifying words; (b) determining those which correspond to events; (c) distinguishing and processing nominal groups; etc. If no errors have been made, the above list corresponds to the following sequence of programs (established by the control component – CC):

1. The program applies the MA to all word forms that constitute the given sentence. Note that the MA may start to process word forms before the whole sentence has been inputted, i.e., sentence inputting and sentence processing may be performed simultaneously (at the stages of morphology, syntax, and – to a partial extent – semantics).
2. On the basis of objectives already established, the control component analyzes the results obtained by the MA. If any event (i.e., a word possessing a model of government) has been found, the CC calls the module of semantic analysis, which then processes the predicates (SEA.Pr). If no events are present in the sentence, the module of processing a nominal phrase (SYA.NP) is called.
3. The module SEA.Pr determines the roles of participants in the given event and indicates their possible characteristics.
4. The CC then calls the module of syntactic analysis, which processes predicative, completive, and adverbial syntactic relations (SYA.COMP).

5. The CC next calls the SYA.NP; i.e., nominal phrases (groups) are distinguished and the syntactic relations occurring in these phrases are determined.
6. The CC calls the SEA.NP to determine semantic relations which occur in the nominal phrase.

The system's further operations depend on whether the input sentence contains turns (nonstandard constructions) and subordinate clauses. The sequence mentioned above is not the only one possible. If any failure has occurred during the work of one of the modules, the order in which the modules are called will be changed. Let us suppose, for instance, that the MA is not able to identify one of the words in a sentence. The CC will then call the module of synthesis to carry out a dialogue with the user. The aim of this dialogue is to clarify what the system is to do to overcome the difficulty that has arisen. The user may select one of the following options: correcting the word which is causing the difficulty, telling the system to pass over this word, or modifying the whole sentence to avoid the use of a word which is not defined in the dictionary.

5.2 Morphological Analysis of Word Forms: Presyntax

By *morphological analysis* (MA) we mean processing word forms with no regard to context. A *word form* is that part of a text which lies between two blanks (punctuation marks are also considered word forms). The task of morphological analysis is to identify a word form and determine the complex of morphological information (CMI) which characterizes it. Generally speaking, a CMI is a set whose elements are morphologically homonymous MI-lines (i.e., pairs of stem and morphological information (MI)). The algorithm of the MA depends to an enormous extent on the method adopted for storing information in the system. There are two main methods of performing the MA: declarative and procedural. If the declarative method has been chosen (the declarative MA), the dictionary contains all possible word forms of words, each word form being accompanied by its own morphological information (MI). As a matter of fact, morphological analysis as such is not performed at all in this case, as the results of such analysis are stored in the dictionary itself. The only thing the declarative MA has to do, therefore, is to find a word form in the dictionary and copy the CMI that corresponds to it. Consequently, the declarative MA operates more rapidly than the procedural MA. On the other hand, use of the declarative MA entails storing all word forms corresponding to every stem. The number of all possible word forms corresponding to one stem may be fairly large (12 for a noun, 36 for an adjective, and for a verb – taking into account all deverbative forms – up to 100). This fact has two important consequences:

1. In constructing the dictionary the designer must define all the word forms of every word and provide each of these definitions with a set of corresponding MI-lines. Consequently, the preparation of the dictionary becomes an extremely laborious task (compared with the procedural MA). Let us note that different word forms from one lexeme should have one common syntactic zone, with one common semantic zone for each stem (as these zones are very

large). Therefore, each word form of a given lexeme should be furnished with a reference to the word form which has been chosen as the basic one.
2. The dictionary occupies a great deal of room in the machine's memory.

This book is devoted to conversation systems of real-life complexity. Such systems require very large dictionaries. Hence, in the following we shall focus our attention on an analysis of the procedural MA, since it requires the designer to devote much less time to preparing the information software. Variants of the MA which occupy an intermediate position, somewhere between the declarative and procedural approaches, are also possible.

The use of the procedural MA allows us to store only the stems of words in the dictionary. The procedural MA performs the following functions: it distinguishes the stem in a word form, it identifies this stem (looking it up in the dictionary and transforming it into a code which is then used at the syntactic and semantic stages), and it assigns the corresponding CMA to the given stem. For the sake of brevity, we shall investigate only one possible method of carrying out a morphological analysis of word forms taken from the Russian language – the so-called "reverse" method. Readers interested in other approaches, or in more detailed information on morphological analysis, are referred to Belonogov and Novoselov (1979). During its work, the algorithm of the procedural MA uses information from the morphological zone of the dictionary, and also from the table of affixes (see Sect. 4.3.2). It is convenient to divide the dictionary into two parts: the dictionary of stems (DS) and the dictionary of final word forms (DFF). The general structure of the MA consists of the following blocks: (a) the search for a word form in the DFF dictionary; (b) distinguishing the stem; (c) the search for the stem in the dictionary of stems; (d) word-combination processing; (e) presyntax.

The number of words which are either uninflected or irregularly inflected is not very large in the Russian language. For these words either the MA is absolutely superfluous (in the case of uninflected words), or it takes a nonstandard form (in the case of irregularly inflected words). Such words include prepositions, adverbs, uninflected nouns (e.g., *pal'to* [a coat]), punctuation marks, numbers, certain forms of verbs (*idti* [to go]), etc. These words are stored in the dictionary of final forms. The task performed by the first block of the MA involves checking whether the given word form of an input text is one of those stored in the DFF. If it is, the corresponding MI (together with the contents of the syntactic and semantic zones) is copied, and this brings the morphological analysis to an end. If this is not the case, the second block of the MA is put into action. Its work involves successively checking the possibilities of inserting, from right to left, various endings and suffixes in the word form being analyzed. To speed up the process of analysis, affixes containing more letters are added or removed first; the information about constituent smaller affixes is obtained not by means of a search, but with the aid of references. The "hierarchy" of affixes is as follows: affixes of full-form adjectives include those of nouns, affixes of verbs include those of nouns and of short-form adjectives, and affixes of nouns include those of short-form adjectives. Let us give an example. The affix *-yey* (*-ey*) (part of speech – adjective, e.g., *sredney* [form of the adjective *sredniy* – middle]) corresponds to four MIs: 1. gen, sn, f, ā; 2. dat, sn, f, ā; 3. ins, sn, f, ā; 4. loc, sn, f, ā, and to one reference to the affix *-yey* (*-ey*) (part of speech – noun, e.g., *matritsey* [form of the noun *matritsa* – a matrix]) with the MI: ins, sn, f for stem types 4, 6, and 7. The second form of reference can be demonstrated by the example of the affix *-yemu* (*-emu*) (part of speech – adjective, e.g., *srednemu* [form of the adjective *sredniy* – middle]). Two possible MIs are assigned to this affix: 1. dat, sn, m, ā, and 2. dat, sn, n, a, with a reference given to the affix *-u* (a constituent of *-yemu*). The affix *-u* corresponds to one MI for nouns with stems of the 4th type (acc, sn, f – *matritsu* [form of the noun *matritsa* – a matrix]), and two MIs for nouns with stems falling into types 1, 2, 3, 11, 12, and 14 (dat, sn, m, e.g., *protsessu* [form of the noun *protsess* – process] and dat, sn, n, e.g., *chislu* [form of the noun *chislo* – a number]).

The process described above results in determining one or several hypothetical stems (HS). Each HS is accompanied by one or more MIs. Hypothetical stems are then sought in the dictionary of stems. This part of the work is carried out by the third block of the MA. If an HS has been found in the dictionary of stems, and if the part of speech corresponding to this HS coincides with that corresponding to the dictionary stem (DS) – for nouns the concordance as to type of stem, animateness, gender, and number is also verified – this particular HS and the MI or MIs accompanying it are considered to be correct. If these requirements are not fulfilled, the HS is regarded as incorrect and is rejected. Once the correct stem has been found, the program memorizes not only the morphological zone of the corresponding dictionary entry but also the syntactic and semantic zones. This obviates the need for repeating the search for this word in the dictionary during the semantic and syntactic analyses.

The comparison that has been described above of an MI – obtained by using the table of affixes during morphological analysis – with information from the dictionary makes it possible to resolve the lexical homonymy of the stems of nouns. Such a comparison is usually sufficient to distinguish between homonymic stems, except in cases of full homonymy, i.e., when both the stems and affixes are homonymic. For example, it is impossible to distinguish between *luka* [a form of the noun *luk* – an onion] – gen, sn, m, and *luka* [a bend (in a river)] – nom, sn, f. In this case, the homonymy is resolved in the subsequent stages of analysis. For instance, an analysis of the word form *misheney* [target (genitive plural)] yields seven MIs. However, in comparing it with the morphological information from the dictionary, only one of these seven possibilities is selected.

A similar method of resolving homonymy (based on morphological types) can, in principle, be applied to verbal stems. However, this method proves less effective here. In the case of nouns, morphological types serve as a means of resolving the homonymy of affixes rather than the homonymy of stems. Verbs, however, do not possess homonymic affixes, so the system of morphological types is more complex. The difficulties that arise here are as follows: First, different affixes may correspond to the same morphological type (the suffixes *-iva-* and *-yva-* refer to the same type of verb, however: *ub-iva-t'* and *ub-yva-t'* [to kill – to diminish]). Second, there are affixes which do not determine the morphological type of a verb unambiguously (e.g., suffix *-a-* in *bezhat'*, as opposed to *bezhit* [to run – (he) runs], and in *veshat'*, as opposed to *veshayet* [to hang – (he) hangs]; the suffix *-a-* may thus occur as a marker of different types of verb). In order to overcome such difficulties, we can increase the number of morphological types of verbs. However, this method is inefficient. The most reasonable approach to the problem is to store stems in the dictionary together with the affixes assigned to them. To resolve a homonymy of stems, these affixes are compared with the one following the stem in the word form being processed. For example, two stems *ub* are stored in the dictionary. One of these is accompanied by the affix *-iva* (from *ubivat'* [to kill]), and the other by the affix *-yva-* (from *ubyvat'* [to diminish]). If the word *ubyval* [was diminishing] is encountered in an input text, the second of the two stems *ub* will be selected in the course of morphological analysis.

The problem indicated here can also be solved in a totally different way. If homonymy is encountered during the analysis of a word form *A*, the mechanism of synthesis can be brought into play. This involves forming various word forms on the basis of the stem (stems) and corresponding MIs (found during analysis). Those stems and MIs from which the word form *A* can be constructed by synthesis are considered to be correct. This method stands out as the most refined; moreover, it does not require any additions or corrections to the dictionary. However, it involves fairly intensive numerical effort. This method, which may be called "checking analysis through synthesis", is extensively used in systems designed to understand speech (as opposed to texts).

One of the tasks performed by the third block is to correct complexes of MIs (i.e., sets of MIs that are placed in correspondence with a given word form) obtained on the basis of the table of affixes. Thus, for instance, depending on the presence of the reflexive particle and on the voice of the verb in question (act, pass, act/pass – see Sect. 4.3.2) the characteristic "voice" can be corrected. Determining the aspect of a verb is particularly important here. As we indicated in Sects. 4.2.8 and 4.3.2, the "aspect" of a verbal word form is determined on the basis of aspectual affixes, the "aspect" of the stem, and the rules assigned to this stem. If the information conveyed by aspectual affixes is unambiguous (see Sect. 4.2.8), the aspectual properties of the stem and of the rules are not taken into account. However, a word form may not contain any unambiguous aspectual affixes; if this is the case, "aspect" is determined on the basis of the aspect of the stem (if it is "perf" or "imperf"), or, if the stem is of the "perf/imperf" type, on the basis of the rules assigned to it. It should be remembered that the presence of the mark "perf" or "imperf" accompanying a stem in the dictionary does not always determine its actual aspect unequivocally. Let us consider the pair of verbs *spisat'* (perf) – *spisyvat'* (imperf) [to copy out]. The stem *spis* may refer to either aspect. In imperfective forms, however, this stem is regularly followed by the unambiguous aspectual suffix *-yva-*. In this case, information about aspect that is assigned to the stem is not taken into account. If for a given word form the characteristic "aspect" has the value "perf", and the value of "tense" is "pres", then the value of the characteristic "tense" is replaced by "fut". [Perfective Russian verbs do not have a present tense; when standard present-tense endings are added to them, the future tense is produced; trans. note].

Let us demonstrate the work of the MA in more detail by considering the word forms *reshayet* and *reshitsa* [both from *reshat'* – to solve]. The following morphological information about the stem *-resh-* will be found in the dictionary of stems (see Sect. 4.3.2): part of speech – "verb"; stem possesses active and passive forms (act/pass); it corresponds to the "aspect" perf/imperf (*reshat'* (imperf) – *reshit'* (perf)); to determine aspect use rule no. 1. Since both word forms will not be found in the DFF, the second block of the MA will begin operation. First, the reflexive particle *-sa* and the ending *-yet* (*-it*) will be added. The MI corresponding to the ending *-yet* (*-it*) will then be found in the table of affixes: ver, pres, sn, ḡ, act. The ending will contain a reference to the empty ending -∅- for nouns with the stem types 1 and 3 (nn, nom, sn, m, ā; nn, acc, sn, m, inan – e.g., *teodolit* [theodolite]) and nouns with the stem types 4, 6, 11, 12, and 14 (nn, gen, pl, ḡ, ā; nn, acc, pl, ḡ, ā – e.g., *bit* [bit (as a unit of information)]).

For verbs, the suffixes *-a-* (for the first word form) and *-i-* (for the second) will be added. Thus, the whole procedure will yield the following hypothetical stems (HSs): (a) two stems will have been found for the first word form: *-reshayet-*, with an MI corresponding to a noun, and *-resh-,* with an MI corresponding to a verb; (b) the stem *-resh-* with a verbal MI will have been found for the second word form (nouns will not have been considered because of the presence of the reflexive particle *-sa*). The stem *-reshayet-* will not be found in the dictionary; it will therefore be rejected as incorrect. The stem *-resh-* will be regarded as correct because there is a concordance as to part of speech between the HS and DS. Since the stem is of the act/pass type, and *reshitsa* contains the particle *-sa*, the value "act" will be replaced by "pass" in the MI corresponding to the second word form. The stem *-resh-* is of the perf/imperf type, so information about "aspect" will be determined by using the rule connected with the stem. Applying rule no. 1 to the first stem (see Sect. 4.3.1), one obtains "imperf", and to the second – "perf". Since for the second word form the value of "aspect" is "perf", and of "tense", "pres", "tense" is changed to "fut". Thus, we will obtain the MI of the two word forms: *reshayet* – ver, pres, sn, ḡ, act, imperf; and *reshitsa* – ver, fut, sn, ḡ, pass, perf.

The fourth block transforms certain word forms, separated by a blank or by another word form, into one stem (the operation of "gluing"). This operation is carried out to make syntactic and semantic analysis easier. The operation is applied to word combinations and to verbs in "analytical form" (e.g., *budiet stroit'*, *byla postroyena* [will build, was built], etc.). All word forms which constitute a given analytical form of a verb are replaced by a "new" stem and the corresponding MI. The MI is constructed on the basis of information about the verb *byt'* [to be] and about the infinitive (or short-form adjective). [In Russian, the infinitive or short-form adjective is used to construct such forms as the future imperfective and passive voice; trans. note]. Consider, for instance, the analytical form *byt'* in the future tense + infinitive (e.g., *budiet stroit'sa* [will be built]), expressing the future tense of the verb, itself in the infinitive [i.e., *stroit'sa*]. The following transformations will then be carried out. The dictionary number of the infinitive *stroit'* [to build] will be assigned to the "new" stem. The MI will be defined as follows: ver (in line with the part of speech corresponding to *budiet*), pass (in line with the infinitive *stroit'sa*), with tense, gender, and number being determined in line with the verb *budiet* [fut, ḡ, sn; trans. note]. Thus, *budiet stroit'sa* will be replaced by *stroit'* – ver, pass, fut, ḡ, sn (i.e., an analogue of *postroit'sa*).

Let us move on to the question of "gluing" word combinations. By *word combination* we mean a rigidly fixed sequence of word forms, considered to convey one semantic notion. The dictionary entry corresponding to the stem (*X*) with which a given word combination begins contains the following information about all the word combinations beginning with *X*: (a) a list of all the stems constituting the word combination, and (if necessary) indications as to the part of speech, gender, number, and case of each stem; (b) the prop word of the word combination (i.e., the word on the basis of which the MI corresponding to this word combination is assigned). The dictionary entry that describes a word combination conveys information of the same kind as that relating to an ordinary stem. The "gluing" of word combinations is carried out as follows: First, all word forms are processed separately. Then, on the basis of a word form (*X*) which a word combination may begin with (this information is indicated in the dictionary), the system verifies whether the word forms following *X* correspond to those mentioned in the list of word combinations beginning with *X* (as regards part of speech, gender, number, case, etc.). If they do, information indicating that a given word combination is possible (although not obligatory) is then assigned to the first word of this word combination and transferred to the stage of syntactic analysis. If there is no such correspondence, this indicates that the given word combination does not occur in the sentence. This algorithm is complicated by the fact that words constituting a word combination need not form a group of consecutive words in a given sentence.

The MA is terminated by the block which we shall call "presyntax". This block prepares data used to facilitate syntactic analysis: 1. the number of a level is assigned to each word form in an input sentence; 2. words that are possibly dependent on preceding words are marked; 3. preliminary syntactic filters are used to remove redundant morphological information.

The first of the tasks mentioned above involves specifying, if possible, a level number for each word form. The word forms constituting a main clause are considered to be of zero level, whereas those of subordinate clauses and participial and adverbial-participial constructions (turns) belong to higher levels. Thanks to level numbers, syntactic analysis can be speeded up considerably, since only relationships between words of the same level have to be analyzed.

The second task involves the following: marking word forms that follow cardinal numbers (not of type 1), as such word forms are suspected of being dependent (see Sect. 4.3.2); memorizing the presence (or absence) of the particle *ne* [not], as this conditions the syntactic relation PRED (i.e., it requires a change of case from nominative to genitive); etc.

At the last stage of the MA the syntactic filters are employed; these check, for instance, whether adjectives agree with the nouns following them as to case, gender, number, etc. The use of syntactic filters makes it possible to remove redundant morphological information. For example, five MIs will be connected with the word form *territorii* [from *territoria* – territory]: gen, sn, f; da, sn, f; loc, sn, f; nom, pl; acc, pl, inan. However, if this word form is preceded by the preposition *na* (which requires the accusative or locative case), three of these MIs will be rejected. The remaining homonymy (*napadal na territorii piati gosudarstv* and *na territorii rayona* [he attacked the territories of five countries, on the territory of the region]) will be resolved with the help of syntax and semantics.

5.3 Syntactic Sentence Analysis

The task of syntactic analysis (SYA) is to establish the syntactic structure of an input sentence. The analysis is carried out on the basis of the morphological information obtained at the stage of the MA and information contained in the dictionary. Syntactic structure reflects the syntactic relations between words of a sentence. Since, generally speaking, the MA replaces words by sets of MI-lines, the SYA should establish the syntactic relations not between words (or word combinations) but rather between MI-lines (or sequences of MI-lines). The most commonly used methods for describing the syntactic structure of a sentence are (Popov and Firdman 1976, Sect. 7.2):

1. Describing it by means of component systems
2. Describing it by means of a dependency tree (i.e., a syntactic subordination tree).

Let us define these two methods.

5.3.1 Component Systems

Any nonempty sequence of word forms will be called a *chain*. By the length of a chain we mean the number of word forms constituting a given chain. The length of a chain ω will be denoted by $|\omega|$. Let ω, φ, η_1, η_2 be any chains picked at random. If $\omega = \eta_1 \ \varphi \ \eta_2$, then we are saying that the chain φ is included in the chain ω. A word form which is included in a chain is said to be a *point* in this chain. Let α and β be two points of the chain ω. Then $\omega = \eta_1 \alpha \eta_2 = \gamma_1 \beta \gamma_2$, and if $|\eta_1| < |\gamma_1|$, we say that α is to the left of β, or that β is to the right of α. This fact may be written in the form of the "inequalities" $\alpha < \beta$ or $\beta > \alpha$. Let α and β be two points in the chain ω, and let $\alpha \leqq \beta$. The set of all points γ, such that $\alpha \leqq \gamma \leqq \beta$, is defined as a *segment* of the chain ω. Let x be an arbitrary nonempty chain. The set C of segments of x is called a *component system* of the chain x if it fulfills two conditions:

1. It includes the segment consisting of all points of the chain x, and all one-point segments of x.
2. No two segments from C intersect, unless one is wholly included in the other.

Elements of C are called *components*. One-point segments are said to be *point* (or *trivial*) *components*.

In order to use a component system to describe sentences of a natural language, we usually introduce a *labeled component system*, i.e., a triple $\langle C, W, \varphi \rangle$, where C is a component system, W a set of labels, and φ a mapping of C in 2^W. The following example will explain this definition. Suppose that a chain ω has the form *agbacdef*. Let us define two different component systems, C_1 and C_2, of the chain ω. To represent them in a straightforward manner, we shall enclose each nontrivial component in parentheses. The left-hand and right-hand parentheses corresponding to one component are marked by the same label. Different pairs of parentheses are always marked by different labels. Integers can be used for labels. For example:

$$C_1 = \underset{1}{(}\underset{2}{(}\underset{3}{(}ag\underset{3}{)}b\underset{2}{)}\,ac\underset{4}{(}de\underset{4}{)}f\underset{1}{)}$$

$$C_2 = \underset{1}{(}a\underset{2}{(}g\underset{3}{(}b\underset{4}{(}a\underset{5}{(}cd\underset{5}{)}e\underset{4}{)}f\underset{3}{)}\underset{2}{)}\underset{1}{)}$$

A component system of a chain can be considered to express information about the syntactic structure of the sentence that corresponds to the given chain. The nontrivial components of a properly selected component system correspond to word combinations (see Sect. 4.2.3). As we see, a great many component systems can be determined for one sentence in a natural language; however, only certain of these will be "correct", i.e., acceptable from the point of view of the syntax of the given language. Several component systems can usually be put in correspondence with one sentence, each of them corresponding to a different interpretation of the sentence's meaning. This phenomenon is called *syntactic homonymy*. The component system of a sentence indicates what "level" a word combination is on, but it does not introduce any hierarchy of word combinations belonging to the same level. However, it is characteristic of sentences in a natural language that one intuitively "feels" that a given word combination is somehow "more important" than others. We can express this in the following way. Let C be a component system of a chain x. In each nontrivial component $A \in C$, we select, from among all the components included in A, one component A' that we call a *main* (*prop*) component. The set of all main components will be denoted by C' and is called a "*hierarchization*" of the system C. An ordered pair $\langle C, C' \rangle$ is thus a "*hierarchized*" *component system*.

5.3.2 Dependency Trees

Let x be any nonempty chain, and X the set of all points in x. A binary relation $\rightarrow$ on X, such that the graph $\langle X, \rightarrow \rangle$ is a tree, will be called a *relation of dependency* (*subordination*). The tree $\langle X, \rightarrow \rangle$ is then a *dependency tree* of x. The graphic representation of a dependency tree corresponding to a chain ω takes the form of the sequence of points which constitute ω; the points are located on one straight line. Let α and β be two points in the chain ω, and let $\alpha \rightarrow \beta$. We then draw an arc running from α to β. All such arcs will be drawn on one side of the line. If $\alpha \rightarrow \beta$, one says that α is a *governing point* (a "master"), and β a *subordinate point* (a "slave"). Figure 5.1 shows two different dependency trees for the chain *agbacdef*.

In analyzing Russian sentences, labeled dependency trees are usually employed. A *labeled dependency tree* of a chain x is a 4-tuple $\langle X, \rightarrow, Z, \psi \rangle$, where $\langle X, \rightarrow \rangle$ is a dependency tree of x, Z – a finite set of labels, and ψ is a mapping of the set of arcs of the tree $\langle X, \rightarrow \rangle$ in Z. The names of the syntactic relations which constitute the set Z were given in Sect. 4.3.

Let us note here that it is possible – at least in the case of the syntactic analysis of a Russian sentence – for a sentence that is undoubtedly homonymic (in terms

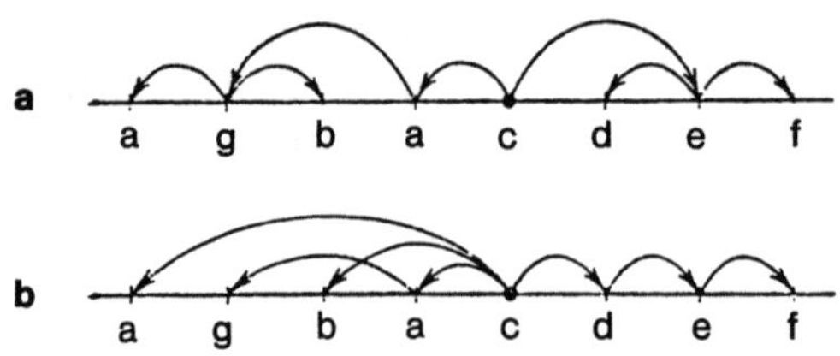

Fig. 5.1a, b. Examples of dependency trees: **a** projective, **b** nonprojective

of meaning) to admit of various "natural" descriptions in the form of dependency trees, but of only one description in the form of a component system. The converse can also be the case.

The class of dependency trees may be divided into two subclasses: projective and nonprojective trees. The vast majority of sentences in the Russian language fall into the first of these two classes, i.e., their dependency trees are projective. A dependency tree $\langle X, \rightarrow \rangle$ of a chain x (as well as the corresponding relation of subordination) is *projective* if for any three points α, β, γ of a chain the following implication holds: if $\alpha \rightarrow \beta$, and γ lies between α and β, then γ depends on α. In accordance with the generally adopted method of graphical representation of dependency trees, the fact that a given dependency tree is projective means that: (a) two different arcs cannot intersect and (b) a tree's root cannot lie under any arc. If the first condition is fulfilled but the second is not, we say that the given dependency tree is *weakly projective*. The sense of the two conditions mentioned above is that if a given word is syntactically related to another word in the sentence, it is also located close to it. The vast majority of sentences occurring in scientific or business Russian are projective. The syntactic structure of a projective sentence is much simpler than that of a nonprojective one (due to the proximity of syntactically connected words). For instance, a nominal group must be built of adjoining words – no gap in it is permissible. The effectiveness of the algorithm of syntactic analysis, which will be described below, is largely a consequence of the fact that we assume sentences to be projective. It should be emphasized, however, that nonprojective constructions may sometimes occur (although fairly seldom) in business language. These constructions are recognized by the algorithm of the SYA and processed by programs specially designed for this purpose.

It should be remembered that component systems and dependency trees characterize different aspects of the syntactic structure of a sentence. Component systems give an explicit description of word combinations but ignore the direction of connections (i.e., they do not differentiate between "master" and "slave"). Dependency trees, by contrast, make it possible to describe the direction of connections, but only between words. In many cases, however, it would be more natural to describe the structure of a sentence in terms of connections not only between words. Hierarchized component systems may prove useful here; nevertheless, it can be demonstrated (Gladky 1973, p. 293) that the potential of such systems is no greater than that of projective dependency relations (i.e., they are useful if for every word combination a corresponding prop word can be chosen in a sufficiently natural way). However, word combinations exist where it is impossible to select a prop word in a natural manner; for other word combinations such a choice, although possible, cannot be justified sufficiently. If, for instance, a construction contains homogeneous parts, there is no reason to consider this or that word to be a prop word; it is also natural to consider the external connections of an analytical form of a verb ("I will read") to refer to the word combination as a whole, since these forms are syntactically equivalent to simple forms. The same holds true for combinations of modal words and infinitives, and for constructions which possess certain standard lexical functions (e.g., Oper or Incep – see Sect. 4.3.3). An attempt to describe these constructions in terms of dependency trees leads to nonprojective trees. A partial solution to this problem may be obtained by "gluing" (see Sect. 5.2), performed at the stage of the MA.

In view of all that has been said above, it seems advisable to use a mixed representation of syntactic structure. Thus, we shall be using the so-called *generalized syntactic structure* (GSS). The GSS is capable of expressing the direction of connections. In this it resembles a dependency tree. However, in contrast to dependency trees, the GSS conveys information about word combinations which form groups of parts of a sentence (the subject group, the predicate group, the object group, the circumstantial modifier group, etc.). For the sake of brevity, all such groups will be called *nominal groups* (NG). The generalized syntactic structure expresses not only one variant of a dependency tree corresponding to the given sentence, but usually several variants which are homonymic (from the point of view of the SYA). This considerably decreases the number of returns from the semantic analysis to the syntactic one, and also the number of variants of sentence analysis generated during the SYA.

5.3.3 Principles of Designing the Algorithm of Syntactic Analysis

The method of filters (Kulagina 1973) is traditionally used to construct the syntactic structure (dependency tree) of a sentence in the Russian language. This method starts with the construction of all possible sets of connections (syntactic relations) between words. For most words, several possible connections may be found, with different governing words. Filters are then brought into operation, enabling us to reject many of these connections. Theoretically, the number of connections remaining should be equal to the number of words in the sentence (provided that "syntactically isolated" words do not occur in this particular sentence). However, in its pure form, the method of filters is not feasible in practical applications: the number of all possible connections between words is very large indeed, while the number of possible ways of selecting certain of them to form a dependency tree is discouragingly huge. Given the demands of practice, it is thus necessary to introduce methods which would enable us to guide and speed up the process of searching for correct versions of sentence analysis. The following means are employed in order to make our algorithm as effective as possible (Popov 1978c):

1. We make extensive use of global filters, which sift out words that cannot be connected syntactically.
2. The filters are employed during the process of choosing a chain, not after a concrete chain of pieces of morphological information – corresponding to a given variant of syntactic analysis – has already been chosen.

3. The analysis of an input sentence is guided by the "backtrack" method (Golomb and Baumert 1965), i.e., incorrect versions are not rejected but corrected (see Sect. 5.3.2).
4. If the SYA does not yield an unambiguous result, a generalized – not concrete – syntactic structure of the input sentence is transferred to the stage of semantic analysis (SEA; see Sect. 5.3.2).
5. Semantic information from the dictionary is also employed in constructing the syntactic structure of an input sentence (see Sect. 4.3.4).
6. Correct syntactic substructures for all possible variants of analysis are constructed only once (see Sect. 5.3.5).
7. The algorithm uses so-called parallel transition from the stage of SYA to the stage of SEA (see Sect. 5.3.8).

5.3.4 General Structure of the Algorithm of the SYA

This can be defined as follows:

1. Of all the possible methods of dividing up a sentence (or one part of it) into word combinations (i.e., nominal groups), successive methods are chosen, carrying out successive variants of the predicative, completive, and circumstantial SYRs.
2. For the chosen way of dividing up a sentence (or one part of it) into NGs, all possible variants of the SYR inside each NG are verified, i.e., a generalized variant of the NG analysis is determined.
3. If, after steps 1 and 2 have been carried out, SYRs are established for all words in the sentence (i.e., the syntactic filters remain undisturbed), the SYA is terminated and the SEA comes into operation. If the SYRs are not established, the algorithm returns to step 1 and a successive division of the sentence into NGs is chosen.
4. If the SEA fails to process the syntactic structure of the input sentence (or one part of it) transferred to it from the SYA stage, the algorithm returns to step 1.

Let us clarify some details of the algorithm of the SYA. We will base ourselves on the example of the following sentence:

V	*1976*	*godu*	*dva*	*zavoda*	*izgotovili*
1	2	3	4	5	6
[In	1976	year	two	factories	manufactured

dla	*rabochikh*	*stanki*	*iz*	*detalyey*
7	8	9	10	11
for	workers	lathes	from	components

uluchshennovo	*kachestva*	*s pomoshchyu*
12	13	14
of improved	quality	with the use

novovo	*oborudovaniya.*
15	16
of new	equipment].

Let us assume that the dictionary contains the following information about the syntactic MG of the verb *izgotovil* [(he) manufactured]: 1. nn, nom; 2. nn, acc; 3. *iz* (gen); 4. *dla* (gen); 5. (5.1. nn, ins) ∨ (5.2. instrumental prepositions); 6. (6.1. nn, ins) ∨ (6.2. prepositions of manner).

The information about semantic categories occurring in the MG of *izgotovil* is the following: 1. (factory ∨ person); 2. production; 3. (material ∨ production); 4. (factory ∨ person ∨ geographical area); 5. instrument; 6. method.

Let us assume that the dictionary contains the following information about the semantic categories of the words used in the above sentence: YEAR [3] – time; FACTORY [5] – enterprise, size, ...; LATHES [9] – production, ...; WORKER [8] – person, profession, age, ...; COMPONENT [11] – production, part, ...; QUALITY [13] – characteristic, ...; EQUIPMENT [16] – production, ...

Let us now describe the algorithm of the SYA.

5.3.5 Establishing the Predicative, Completive, and Circumstantial SYRs

The algorithm starts its work on an input sentence by distinguishing word forms which are not included in turns and/or subordinate clauses. These word forms constitute the main (zero) level of the sentence. From these it then selects the predicates, i.e., word forms possessing an MG. Next, from the syntactic zone of each predicate, the algorithm distinguishes and then processes – one by one – the corresponding group models of government (GMG; see Sect. 4.3.3). The reason some stems possess several group models of government is usually the homonymy of these stems. At the stage of the SYA, the analysis of one GMG corresponds to one stem homonym. Then, for each GMG, the corresponding nuclear models of government (NMG) are investigated, and for each such NMG the corresponding individual model of government (IMG) is constructed (see Sect. 4.3.3). In turn, for each IMG we have to determine a list of candidates which satisfy the requirements as to case, part of speech, and semantic category imposed by the corresponding MG. To shorten this list – and consequently, reduce the number of possible variants of the syntactic structure – the algorithm employs "sifting" filters. These filters remove all word forms that cannot play the role of "slave" of any predicate. For instance, the process of selecting word forms of the main level is an example of the operation of a sifting filter. In addition, filters remove adjectives (if they are not present in the IMG), word forms which follow prepositions (up to and including the first noun encountered; the semantic categories of this noun are then transported to the preposition), etc.

An input sentence may sometimes include word forms which change the cases required by the IMG. This must be taken into consideration when the list of candidates is drawn up. Examples of such word forms are cardinal numbers and word forms belonging to that part of speech we call the "negative particle". Cardinal numbers (which do not end in 1) change the case of the following noun from nominative and accusative into genitive. A negative particle preceding a predicate (strictly speaking – preceding a verb or short-form adjective) may change the case of a noun connected with the predicate by the syntactic relation PRED from nominative to genitive. When word forms that may produce a change of case are encountered, the algorithm of the SYA marks those word forms whose case may have been changed.

At this stage of its work, the algorithm removes homogeneous parts (except the first part of each homogeneous group) and memorizes information about the possible syntactic relation PRED, i.e., about incompatibility regarding number between homogeneous nouns in the singular and a verb in the plural.

The word forms which remain after "sifting" are then used to form arrays of candidates for each column of every IMG. In our example, the following words remain after applying the "sifting" filters: *zavod* (with a possible quantitative SYR indicated), *izgotovil, dla, stanki, iz, kachestvo, s pomoshchyu*. Information about candidates is then entered in the matrix (i.e., table) of an IMG. This information contains the number assigned to a word, the number assigned to an MI-line, a case, and semantic categories. Since not all individual syntactic properties of a word form have to be realized simultaneously in a given sentence, it is possible that some columns of the MG will remain empty, i.e., there will be no candidate corresponding to them. These empty columns are removed at the stage of correcting the matrix. The matrix obtained by the algorithm of the SYA for the example we are considering is shown in Table 5.1. To simplify matters, the numbers assigned to MI-lines and semantic categories have been omitted; only the numbers assigned to words are indicated in the matrix. In our example, the word *stanki* is not included in the first column of the MG [although its characteristic is nn, nom; trans. note] because of the incompatibility of its semantic categories; the word *zavod* is not included in the second column for the same reason.

When the correction of the matrix has been completed, the algorithm of the SYA carries out a consecutive analysis of all possible MGs and the corresponding columns of the matrix. All possible variants of determining the syntactic relations of each MG are then considered. The so-called maximum MGs are considered first. A maximum MG is one containing the maximum number of optional (nonobligatory) relations (see Sect. 4.3.3). When the maximum MGs have been analyzed, the algorithm examines MGs containing a smaller number of relations. We should remember here that to consider all possible variants of analysis, provision must also be made for MGs that do not contain various nonobligatory relations, although there are word forms corresponding to these relations in the matrix. In our example, only one maximum MG will be found after the matrix is corrected. This corresponds to columns 1, 2, 3, 4, and 6 in Table 5.1. A number of nonmaximum MGs will also be found (e.g., 1; 1, 2; 1, 2, 3; 1, 2, 4; etc.). These

Table 5.1. Matrix obtained by the algorithm of the SYA

	1	2	3	4	5	6	7	8
Number of column in MG	1	2	3	4	5	5	6	6
Syntactic zone of MG	nn nom	nn acc	*iz*	*dla*	nn ins	instr. preps	nn ins	preps of manner
Candidates	5	9	10	7	0	14	0	0

will not be analyzed, however, as the maximum MG yields the correct version of analysis for the sentence.

With the maximum MG already established, the algorithm analyzes all possible variants of determining the syntactic relations that satisfy the requirements imposed by syntactic filters. The algorithm also checks that none of the words has been used more than once. In our example, only one variant will be found in this manner. The algorithm must be able to perform the following two tasks when examining variants of determining syntactic relations:

1. Ensuring that all possible variants are examined
2. Doing this in an efficient way, i.e., avoiding full analysis of each variant

The first task can be formulated as a task of selection. Let $X_1, X_2, \ldots, X_n$ be n spaces of selection, and M_j the number of possible values of X_j. The task of selection here is to find a vector $(x_1, x_2, \ldots, x_n)$ (where $x_i \in X_i$) from the Cartesian product of the spaces $X_1 \times X_2 \times X_3 \times \ldots \times X_n$, with a certain criterion function for this vector $\Phi\ (x_1, x_2, \ldots, x_n)$ having its extreme value.

The number n may be interpreted here as $\sum_{i=1}^{K} n_i$ (where K is the number of words from the input sentence that possess an MG, and n_i is the number of actants corresponding to the i-th word with an MG). M_j is the number of word forms that fit the given column of the i-th word with an MG. There may be more than one extreme vector; the task at hand is to find the first for which all the syntactic relations can be established, and which can be interpreted at the stage of the SEA. In the case in question, the criterion function may assume either of two values: 1 (acceptable) or 0 (unacceptable). The straightforward method consists in examining all vectors in turn in order to find the first for which $\Phi(x_1, x_2, \ldots, x_n) = 1$. In the worst case, the algorithm must construct and examine the syntactic structure of an input sentence $M = \prod_{j=1}^{n} M_j$ times.

Let us now estimate the order of magnitude of M. Let an input sentence contain three words with an MG (only one for each word). This is quite realistic in sentences containing, say, 30 words. Let us assume that each of these three words possesses three actants and M_j = two candidates that correspond to each actant. Then $M = \prod_{j=1}^{3 \times 3} M_j = 512$; i.e., using the straightforward method means examining up to 512 variants of input sentence analysis. The number M may be much larger than that, since a word may possess more than one MG.

Our algorithm solves this problem by the backtrack method (Golomb and Baumert 1965). This method enables us to obtain a solution after less than M attempts; nevertheless, it remains exhaustive, i.e., it finds all solutions where $\Phi\ (x_1, \ldots, x_n) = 1$. We shall now briefly explain what is involved in this method. The components of the vector are determined one by one. Possessing a certain component, the algorithm uses a modified function $\Phi\ (x_1, \ldots, x_n)$ to check whether the vector obtained so far has any chance of being a possible solution. The effectiveness of this method lies in the following: if a partial vector $(x_1, x_2, -)$ has no chance of being a solution, then $\gamma = \prod_{j=3}^{n} M_j = M/(M_1 \cdot M_2)$ attempts can be avoided with no need for examing individual cases (in the above example, $\gamma = 512/4 = 128$).

The next stage of the work of the algorithm is to determine circumstantial relations. This concerns primarily adverbial modifiers of time and place. In order to determine circumstantial relations, the algorithm employs local syntactic filters, as well as the semantic categories PLACE and TIME. Let us note here that the stage of determining circumstantial relations is one where mistakes are particularly frequent, no matter which algorithm has been chosen. This stems from the fact that, in general, only semantics is able to determine whether a given nominal group is actually an adverbial modifier or an attributive adjunct. As an example, let us consider the sentence *Tetrad' lezhit v stole na chetyrekh nozhkakh* [The notebook is in a four-legged desk; lit. "The notebook is lying in a desk on four legs" – trans. note]. To determine whether *na chetyrekh nozhkakh* [on four legs] is an attribute referring to *stol* [desk] or an adverbial modifier of place referring to *lezhat'* [to lie] semantic methods have to be employed. In our algorithm, circumstantial relations have priority over attributive ones. The correctness of relations is checked at the stage of semantic analysis (SEA). If there is a mistake discovered at this stage, the syntactic analysis is repeated, with the next possible variant being analyzed.

Let us now return to our example. On the basis of semantic categories, the algorithm will identify the nominal group *v 1976 godu* [1, 2, 3] as an adverbial modifier of time. With the help of the syntactic filters, the algorithm will establish that the group *uluchshennovo kachestva* cannot be an adverbial modifier, since a circumstantial relation can refer to a noun with no preposition only if it is in the instrumental case.

5.3.6 Distinguishing Nominal Groups: Homogeneous, Attributive, Auxiliary, Quantitative, and Appositive Syntactic Relations

As we have already observed, the vast majority of sentences in business language are projective. Consequently, distinguishing nominal groups involves the assumption that nominal groups are built of adjoining words, i.e., that they are indissoluble. This assumption considerably reduces the number of possible variants of syntactic structure that have to be analyzed. Nonprojective sentences are identified by syntactic filters and processed by special programs. Nonprojective analytic forms of verbs may be processed and removed at the first stage of the work. Of the remaining nonprojective constructions, interrogative forms using the words *SKOL'KO* [how many/much] and *KAKOY* [what kind of] are most widespread in business texts, e.g., *Skol'ko zheleznodorozhniy transport perevez ugla v 1978 godu?* [How much coal did the railways carry in 1978?] The nominal group *skol'ko ugla* [how much coal] is broken up here. The syntactic filters will notice that the word *skol'ko* is not followed by a word in the genitive case (which *skol'ko* governs). The conclusions to be drawn from this fact are either that the sentence is incorrect or that a nonprojective construction has been used. The program for processing such constructions will therefore look for a word in the genitive case whose semantic categories correspond to the syntactic relations PRED or 1C. The following nominal groups will be distinguished in the example under consideration: 1. *v*

1976 godu; 2. *dva zavoda;* 3. *dla rabochikh*; 4. *iz detalyey uluchshennovo kachestva*; 5. *s pomoshchyu novovo oborudovanya.*

Generally speaking, syntactic relations can be established within a given NG in several ways. Different syntactic analyses of an NG are produced by the homonymy of word forms constituting this NG. Such homonymy occurs most often in the case of prepositions, substantivized nouns, and word combinations (since the word forms constituting a given word combination should also be investigated as if they did not belong to any word combination). The phrase *tsentr rabochevo rayona* is an example of a phrase which can be subjected to syntactic analysis in two different ways: 1 – ATTR → 2, 2 – ATTR → 3 [giving us the semantically ludicrous *the center of the worker of the region;* trans. note], and 1 – ATTR → 3, 3 – ATTR → 2 [giving us *the center of the working-class region;* trans. note].

Let us estimate the number of different variants of syntactic analysis which result from the fact that the analysis of an NG has not produced unequivocal results. Let an input sentence contain N nominal groups, with K words in each. By m_i we shall denote the number of variants of the analysis of the i-th nominal group (only one of which is correct). Thus, solely as a result of the ambiguity of the NG analysis, we obtain $\prod_{i=1}^{N} m_i$ possible variants of the analysis of the whole sentence. Let us bear in mind here that analyses of two different nominal groups are independent of each other. Thus, only $\sum_{i=1}^{N} m_i$ – instead of $\prod_{i=1}^{N} m_i$ – variants of analysis of all nominal groups have to be considered. This is precisely what is achieved by our algorithm of the SYA. In order to perform this task, what is actually transmitted to the stage of the SEA is not one concrete variant of the syntactic analysis, but rather a general structure containing all alternative analyses of each NG (for which there is more than one variant) for the given variant of completive SYRs, and all alternatively variants of circumstantial SYRs. Let us note that different variants of circumstantial SYRs result in different variants of SYRs in an NG.

The algorithm for determining SYRs in an NG is fairly simple. Attributive relations are established between a "master", i.e., a noun, and a "slave", i.e., an adjective without an MG, and adjective with an MG (a participle), an attributive adverb, or a noun. For adverbs and adjectives without MGs the attributive relations can be established with relative ease. Nouns present greater difficulties. In many cases, the syntactic filters make it possible to find the correct relation (e.g., on the basis of the fact that a noun is in the genitive case). In addition, there is a semantic filter which establishes an attributive (not circumstantial) relation if a noun is in the instrumental and is parametric (e.g., weight, volume, thickness, etc.). For instance: *Detal'tolshchinoy 3 cm lezhit na stolie* [A component 3 cm thick is lying on the table; *tolshchinoy:* the instrumental case of the word "thickness"; trans. note].

All other SYRs in an NG can be established fairly easily. Prior to establishing all the SYRs mentioned above, the algorithm checks whether all the requirements imposed by the syntactic filters are satisfied. At this stage, the algorithm establishes homogeneous syntactic relations. The limits of a homogeneous group are determined with the help of the semantic filters, on the basis of commas, conjunctions, parts of speech, case, and number. The homogeneous SYRs give only a preliminary idea of the character of the homogeneous connections. This is then made more precise at the stage of the SEA.

5.3.7 Syntactic Relations in Subordinate Clauses and Turns

When the syntactic relations at the main level of an input sentence have been established, the algorithm moves on to establishing the relations that exist between word forms from the main level and those from turns (nonstandard constructions) and subordinate clauses. If there is an adverbial-participial construction, the adverbial participle is connected by a predicative relation with a word form connected with a main verb by the relation PRED. Semantic and syntactic filters are employed if a sentence contains more than one verb. The primary purpose of the semantic filter is to connect an adverbial-participial construction with the "main" predicate (the semantic type of the predicate – modal, empty, phase, or main – is indicated in the dictionary). Then a homogeneous relation (of the type $\wedge$) is established between the predicates of the turn and those of the principal (main) clause. Infinitive constructions are processed analoguously. The only difference is that a homogeneous relation between predicates is now of the type $\rightarrow$, the arrow pointing toward the infinitive. The participle from a participial construction is connected by a predicative relation with a noun that precedes the turn and agrees with the participle according to the requirements imposed by the filters. Agreement of gender, number, and case is usually required. Predicates from the principal clause and a participial construction are connected by homogeneous relations of the type $\wedge$.

The syntactic relations that connect a main clause with a subordinate clause can be of the following three types: (a) those specified by a corresponding MG (PRED or completive), (b) circumstantial ones, or (c) attributive ones. Since the restrictions imposed on the input language limit it to sentences with no more than one subordinate clause, connections between the principal and the subordinate clause can be established with no great difficulty.

The work of the SYA ends with the establishment of the syntactic relations that exist between the word forms of a turn and those of a subordinate clause. Turns of the first level are processed first (i.e., turns which are connected with word forms of the main level). Turns of higher levels are then analyzed. Relations inside turns and a subordinate clause can be established in the same manner as those inside the main clause.

5.3.8 Interdependence Between Syntactic and Semantic Analyses

The SEA and SYA are performed by the algorithm in parallel, i.e., the SEA starts work as soon as the first correct syntactic structure of an input sentence, or some part of it (possibly a general syntactic structure), has been obtained by the SYA. The complete syntactic structure, or a part thereof, is transmitted from the SYA to the SEA. The SEA processes this structure and memorizes the results of its analysis in the matrix of relations (MR) and the matrix of nominal groups

(MNG). Three results of processing are possible: (a) the analysis of a relation or an NG is not carried out (NCO); (b) the analysis is carried out successfully (S); (c) the analysis ends in failure (F). The SYA analyzes the state of the MR (in constructing syntactic relations), or of the MNG (when dividing a sentence into nominal groups). If, for SYRs or NGs obtained by the SYA, the matrices contain information about a failure discovered by the SEA, the next variant of the syntactic structure is analyzed by the SYA. If the given SYR or NG is analyzed for the first time (or if it is rechecked and found to be correct by the SEA), the SYA goes ahead with its normal work.

5.4 Semantic Analysis of a Sentence (SEAS)

The stage of the SEAS marks the end of the process of constructing an intensional expression of the sense of a sentence. The representation of a sentence obtained at the stage of the SEAS will be called a *semantic graph of a sentence* (SGS). The SGS may be considered an explicit representation of the sense of a sentence. The SGS, like the knowledge possessed by the system, is expressed in terms of extended semantic networks (see Chap. 3). On input to the SEAS, a sentence takes the form of a general syntactic structure (i.e., a generalized tree of analysis). This structure contains:

1. An unequivocally selected homonym of every word possessing an MG (i.e., a concrete group MG), and unequivocally established predicative and completive SYRs (i.e., candidates agreeing with the concrete individual MG).
2. Alternative variants of circumstantial relations
3. Alternative limits of nominal groups and alternative variants of analysis for each nominal group
4. Information about the number and gender of each word from the input sentence; this information is then used during the semantic processing of pronouns.

It is convenient to divide the SEAS into two stages: the construction of an unstructuralized semantic graph of the sentence, and the subsequent structuralization of this semantic graph.

5.4.1 Construction of the Unstructuralized Semantic Graph of a Sentence

The task of this substage is to select a semantically meaningful variant of syntactic analysis (i.e., to distinguish that part of the general syntactic structure which does not contradict the abstract knowledge possessed by the system), to construct an unstructuralized semantic graph corresponding to this variant, and to identify quantifiers (see Sect. 5.4.4). It is convenient to divide this substage once again, into the processing of words with an MG, and the processing of nominal groups, i.e., words which do not possess an MG. This subdivision flows from the fact that the semantic contents conveyed by words with an MG and by nominal groups are different – the methods used to process them must therefore be different, too. The semantics of words with an MG are largely determined by a meaning specified in the MG, not by context. This enables semantic information about a word with an MG to be given in the dictionary. Information from the abstract network may be of use here, but only in verifying the correctness of a choice made at the stage of semantic analysis. Semantic relations which connect words from a nominal group (words without an MG) are generally determined by context. In order to discover these relations, knowledge about the surrounding world (a semantic network) has to be brought to bear.

Let us clarify this idea by using the following example. If a word possesses an MG (e.g., the word *KUPIL* [(he) bought]), then the dictionary contains information – in the form of this MG – about ways in which this particular word can be connected with other words (e.g., *who bought* – a noun in the nominative case, an organization, a person, etc.; *what did he buy* – a noun in the accusative case, a physical object, etc.). However, if a word does not possess an MG, e.g., the word *GAZOVIY* [gas (adjective)], its connections with other words depend on context, and consequently cannot be indicated in the dictionary. Indeed, the semantic connections are completely different in such nominal groups as: *gazoviy zavod, gazovaya plita, gazoviy ballon*, and *gazoviy sharf* [gasworks; gas stove; gas cistern; a fine, lightweight scarf]. The corresponding semantic connections are, respectively, TO PRODUCE, TO CONSUME, TO CONTAIN, and TO COMPARE WITH REGARD TO WEIGHT.

5.4.2 Processing Words with an MG

Different words with an MG influence a sentence in different ways. If we confine ourselves to business texts, we can distinguish at least three main groups of predicates. These are predicates of action, functional predicates, and empty predicates. Predicates of action characterize states of objects which exist in real life and are observable in the world that is being modeled. For example: DELIVERING, PASSING, CARRYING, PRODUCING, etc. These states are characterized by the time at which they are accomplished and by the fact that they are either already accomplished or have still to be (i.e., these states either exist or are merely projected). A predicate will be termed a *predicate of action* if it contains a reference to the semantic network in which the sense of this predicate is indicated, together with the set of notions that may play the role of actants in the given context (see Sect. 3.5). The semantic categories of an MG, by their very nature (see Sect. 4.3.3), represent generalized information in the dictionary about "typical" candidates for the roles characteristic of the given situation. This information is transferred from the semantic network to the dictionary with the aim of making the system's work more effective. Thanks to this, variants of the syntactic analysis which do not meet the requirements imposed by semantic categories can be rejected on the basis of information from the dictionary (without a search of the network). Theoretically, it is possible for the semantic categories of an MG to convey exactly the same information about an event as that contained in the network. In practice, however, information contained in an MG is usually more general (less concrete) than in the network. This is why a complete semantic analysis cannot always be carried out on the basis of dictionary information alone. Let us note that the transfer of semantic information from the network to the dictionary need not be performed "manually" (i.e., by a human being); it may be carried out automatically by the system itself.

Functional predicates are operators which relate to predicates of action. Their role is to indicate what operations predicates of action have to undergo during the given sentence processing. They include, for instance, TO FULFILL, TO DECREASE, TO EXCEED, etc. Functional predicates have no representative in the semantic network. They select the right procedure for processing a predicate of action (at the stage of processing). For instance, the procedure corresponding to the functional predicate TO EXCEED should involve a comparison between the actual value of a parameter and the value that was planned, with the system able to answer a question posed to it on the result of such a comparison (DID FACTORY X EXCEED ITS PLANNED PRODUCTION OF LAMPS?).

Examples of *empty predicates* include copulas (TO BE, IS), empty verbs (TO CARRY OUT), phase verbs (TO BEGIN, TO TERMINATE), modal verbs (CAN, SHOULD), etc. These verbs either do not possess any real semantic content (i.e., none whatsoever, or none in the given area of subject matter), or they convey information not about an action itself, but about its stage of development (TO BEGIN, TO TERMINATE). Thus, no vertices of the network are placed in correspondence with empty predicates.

From the above, very incomplete classification we can see that the processing of empty and functional predicates consists in reconstructing the syntactic structure. This reconstruction includes the removal of an empty or functional predicate, and the transfer of the syntactic relations that connected this predicate with other parts of a sentence to the predicate of action. It is virtually impossible to perform this task in the case of the Russian language with no limits imposed on it. To tackle this problem, we have to employ the lexical and semantic rules of paraphrasing (Mel'chuk 1974a, Chap. 1). We shall not go into the details of this here; we shall confine ourselves to giving one explanatory example. Figure 5.2a shows the syntactic structure of a sentence before (*dotted line*) and after (*solid line*) reconstruction.

From the point of view of the SEAS, the reconstruction is equivalent to transforming the original sentence into the sentence THE FIRM SHIPPED TEN LATHES (Fig. 5.2b). In order to carry out the transformation shown in Fig. 5.2, the corresponding algorithm has to ascertain that the empty predicate is the lexical function $\mathrm{Oper}(S_0(C_0))$, and that the given sentence contains $S_0(C_0)$, which

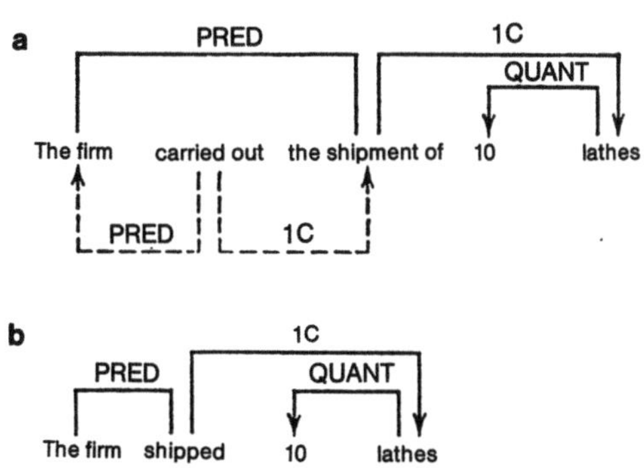

Fig. 5.2 a, b Example of reconstruction of the syntactic structure of a sentence

can be replaced by C_0. In our example, CARRIED OUT is $\mathrm{Oper}_1(S_0(C_0))$, THE SHIPMENT is $S_0(C_0)$, and CARRIED is C_0.

Prior to replacing syntactic relations by semantic ones, events have to be brought into canonical form, i.e., various synonymic ways of expressing a given event in the natural language must be replaced by one "standard" form. Generally speaking, this can be done by means of the lexical functions Syn and Conv (see Sect. 4.3.3). For instance, the words "to produce", "to turn out", "to manufacture", etc., are reduced to one form – "to produce". Note that the notions of Syn, Conv, etc., may depend on the particular subject matter under consideration. The reduction to one "standard" form is performed in the following way: Each derivative form ("to turn out", "to manufacture") contains a reference to the canonical form ("to produce"), and the canonical form is provided with a reference to the vertex of the semantic network that corresponds to the set of events TO PRODUCE (see also Sect. 4.3.5). In a similar manner, all the words of a sentence represented in the semantic network are put into correspondence with the vertices of the network. Then, for relations (strictly speaking – triples, i.e., homonym-relation-homonym) that are processed for the first time (the corresponding value in the matrix of relations: NCO – see Sect. 5.3.8), the syntactic relations – predicative, completive, and adverbial (circumstantial) – that refer to a predicate of action are replaced by semantic relations. For predicative and completive relations this can be done on the basis of the semantic zone of an MG; it can then be verified using the semantic network. If a word has several homonymic semantic meanings, the semantic network allows the system to choose one of them. If, however, all possibilities have been rejected by the semantic network, i.e., if none of the candidates for predicative and completive relations obtained at the stage of syntactic analysis are of the semantic types indicated in the restrictive rule corresponding to a given event, then the algorithm returns to the SYA stage and begins to process the next alternative variant. The result of the verification carried out by the semantic network is entered in the matrix of relations (this result being either S (success) or F (failure); see Sect. 5.3.8). Figure 5.3 shows a semantic representation of the sentence "The firm shipped lathes". The representation has been obtained using the restrictive rule shown in Fig. 5.4. Because of the "tacit knowledge" typical of any natural language, it may turn out to be useful to re-establish the actants of an action which are not explicitly indicated in a given sentence. This may be done using restrictive rules. What is basically involved in this process of re-establishment is the following: Let us suppose that some actants of a predicate of action remain empty, i.e., there are no appropriate candidates for them in the given sentence. In this case, certain entities indicated in the restrictive rule are placed in correspondence with these actants. An example is shown in Fig. 5.3: The "instrument" TRANSPORT and the "source" and "destination" PLACE are added on the basis of the relevant restrictive rule. The reason it is advisable to fill in "empty" actants is that this procedure facilitates the process of interpreting the semantic structure. In the optimum situation, the number and the contents of the descriptors characterizing an input sentence should correspond to the number and the contents of those describing a given fact in the data base. The lack of such a correspondence will make the process of retrieving the desired piece of information much more complicated, if not impossible.

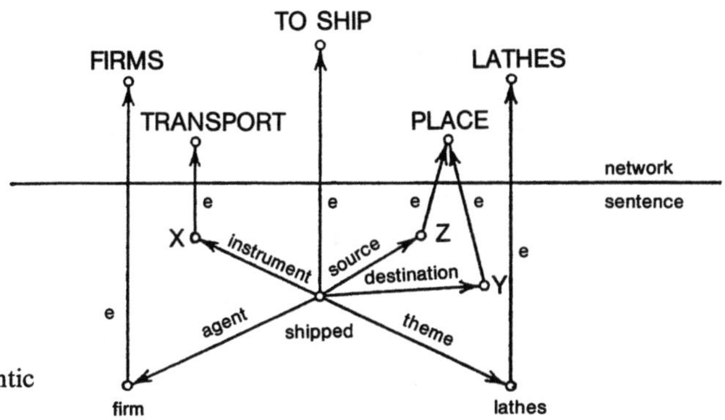

Fig. 5.3. Example of a semantic representation of a sentence

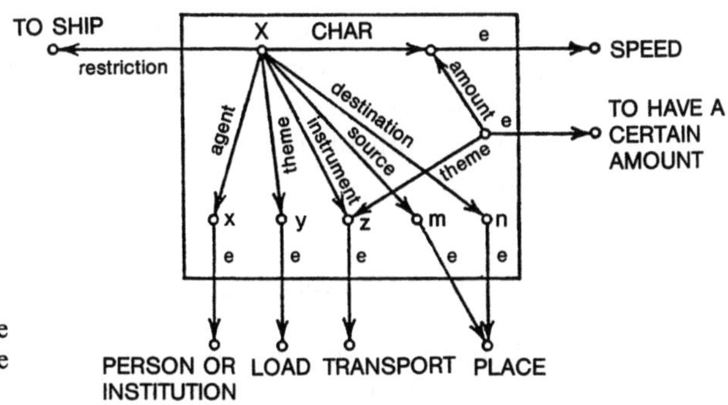

Fig. 5.4. Representation of the restrictive rule for the predicate TO SHIP

The process of replacing circumstantial syntactic relations by corresponding semantic relations is the most complex and ambiguous part of processing words with an MG. In describing the syntactic analysis, we observed that a characteristic feature of the Russian language is the lack of reliable syntactic filters which could make it possible to differentiate between circumstantial (adverbial) relations and attributive ones. We also indicated that in cases where doubt arises, the SYA constructs both ADVB and ATTR relations. Thus, the SEAS has to confirm (or reject) a circumstantial relation, and, if confirmed, reject the ATTR relation and replace ADVB by the corresponding semantic relation. If an ADVB is not confirmed, it is simply removed and the SEAS goes ahead with its work. Confirming or rejecting an ADVB relation is performed by means of a comparison between the semantic types indicated by the relation CHARACTERISTIC in the restrictive rule corresponding to a given predicate of action, and the semantic categories of the prop word of the adverbial modifier in question. Let us consider the sentence "At what average speed do the railways carry (ship) freight?" The SYA here will yield the adverbial modifier "at what average speed". This will be confirmed at the stage of the SEAS, because the rule corresponding to the predicate TO SHIP (see Fig. 5.4) contains the characteristic SPEED. However, let us now examine the sentence *Stol s dvoma yashchikami perevozili na gruzovike* [The desk with two drawers was carried (shipped) by truck]. In this case, the syntactic analysis will yield the adverbial modifier *s dvoma yashchikami* [with two drawers]. This will be rejected by the SEAS, because "drawers" are not a characteristic of the event TO SHIP (see Fig. 5.4). This "adverbial modifier" will therefore be eliminated, giving us the nominal group *stol s dvoma yashchikami* [the desk with two drawers].

From the point of view of the SEAS, processing an "attribute" of a word with an MG is practically identical to processing an adverbial modifier (with the exception of quantifiers – see Sect. 5.4.4). For instance, in the sentence *Chemu ravna srednaya skorost' perevozok zheleznodorozhnevo transporta?* [What is the average speed of transport (of shipments) by rail?], the word *skorost'* [speed] is linked to the predicate *perevozok* [of transport] by an attributive SYR but is processed in the same way as in the preceding sentence, where it played the role of an adverbial modifier.

At the final stage of processing words with an MG, the algorithm unites, if necessary, several adverbial groups into one. For instance, in the sentence "Irene lives in a big house on the seventh floor", two adverbial groups will be found during the SYA. However, it is advisable to join these two groups into one during the SEAS, as they are both adverbial modifiers of place, one of them being more precise than the other.

5.4.3 Nominal Group (NG) Processing

After words with an MG have been processed, the generalized syntactic structure of the sentence (or of one part of it) is broken up into several subtrees, which in business texts generally take the form of NGs. In the method we have adopted for breaking up sentences into nominal groups, words with an MG are not included in these groups.

Before NG processing begins, nonprojective constructions are united into one NG. Let us take as an example the sentence *Skolko zavod perevez ugla?* [How much coal has the firm transported?; lit. How much the firm has transported of coal?; trans. note]. The SYA will mark this sentence as a possible candidate for a nonprojective construction, since the word *zavod* [firm] is not in the genitive case as required by the word *skol'ko* [how much]. The SEAS will thus have to find a word which ensures concordance as to semantic categories and meets the syntactic requirements that are set (i.e., a word in the genitive). Then a corresponding NG can be created (in our example, *skol'ko ugla* [how much coal]). The nominal group thus created is then processed in the usual way, like any other NG.

NG processing, as opposed to the processing of words with an MG, has one important distinctive feature, namely, it results in the creation of new vertices in the semantic network. The principal stages of this processing are as follows:

1. Characteristics not indicated explicitly in a sentence are uncovered on the basis of the semantic network.
2. An appropriate homonym is selected using the relevant part of the semantic network.
3. The NG is translated into an internal representation identical to a semantic network, i.e., syntactic relations are replaced by semantic ones.

We shall distinguish the following word groups which lack an MG: concepts, characteristics without an MG (e.g., *weight, duration, trademark*), the values of characteristics, prepositions, and numerals. In terms of syntactic analysis, the only possible syntactic relations referring to nominal groups are attributive, auxiliary, quantitative, homogeneous, negative, and appositive. The processing of attributive relations is particularly difficult. These relations connect words which may be characteristics, notions, or values of characteristics. The complexity of processing attributive relations is a consequence of the fact that these particular relations are the main method of expressing "tacit knowledge" in a nominal group (in the Russian language, at least). For instance, "gas cistern" means "a cistern – containing – gas", "red ball" means "a ball – color – red", etc. Deciphering "tacit" characteristics is carried out on the basis of the semantic network, where semantic interrelations between entities are explicitly indicated. The most complex situation in processing an attributive relation arises when it is the predicate that is expressed "tacitly". For example, *Vse izdelia zavoda X za 1-y kvartal 1978 goda byli otpravleny na BAM* [The entire output of factory *X* for the 1st quarter of 1978 was sent to the BAM; BAM = Baikal-Amur Trunk Railroad (currently under construction); trans. note]. The nominal group *izdelia zavoda X* [output of factory *X*] means "factory *X* – to produce – output". After this piece of "tacit knowledge" has been exposed, the algorithm returns to the stage of processing words with an MG (SEAS [MG] and SYA) in order to determine the semantic relations connecting the predicate "to produce" with the words "factory *X*" and "output". Let us note that after this return to the SYA and SEAS(MG) a revision of circumstantial relations will also be performed. Indeed, before the predicate "to produce" was exposed, the predicate "sent" was the only word with an MG, i.e., the adverbial modifier "for the 1st quarter of 1978" could be syntactically linked to this particular predicate alone.

The task performed at this stage is not just a question of replacing syntactic relations with semantic ones by exposing semantic relations which are not explicitly indicated in the natural language. It is also a question of selecting that variant of the syntactic analysis of an NG that is confirmed by the semantic network. Figure 5.5 shows two alternative variants of the syntactic analysis of the NG *v tsentre rabochevo rayona* [in the center of the working class region; see Sect. 5.3.6; trans. note]. The second, incorrect version is denoted by the dotted line. The incorrect version will be rejected by the semantic network since no direct link will be found between *v tsentre* [at the center] and *rabochevo* [of the working-class (adj) *or* of the worker]. Let us note, however, that there may be an area of subject matter for which both variants are, in principle, correct. In such cases all alternative variants of the semantic representation of the given NG are transferred to

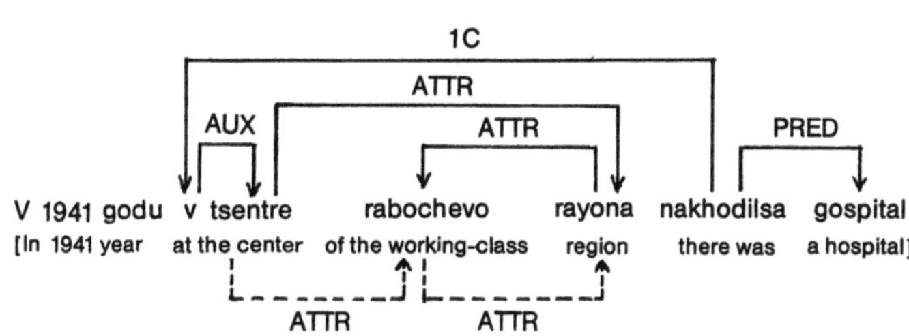

Fig. 5.5. Alternative analyses of a nominal group

the stage of interpretation. This stage selects a variant which agrees with an event already found during interpretation (and, in the case of a connected text, with an existing context). If the processing of a nominal group does not make it possible to find a characteristic that links two syntactically connected word forms, this nominal group and the syntactic relation connecting these two word forms are marked as being incorrect, and information about this fact is entered in the matrices MR and MNG (see Sect. 5.3.8).

To end this description of the process of constructing a nonstructuralized semantic graph, we would like to draw readers' attention to one last matter. At this stage, all quantifiers are marked and information is memorized about which word they refer to and which NG they are elements of (assuming the given quantifier belongs to some NG). We shall now move on to an outline of the substage of structuralizing a semantic graph. In fact, this substage can sometimes be omitted. This can be done when the given subject matter does not require the presence of quantificational statements in the input language. Should this be the case, the semantic graph is transferred to the stage of interpretation in the form of a nonstructuralized graph in which interrogative words are marked.

5.4.4 Structuralizing a Semantic Graph

This substage entails structuralizing the semantic graph (SG) obtained at the preceding stages. Structuralization involves determining – for a given SG – higher-level predicates, the way in which these are "immersed" in each other, and their scope of operations. Since the vast majority of these predicates can be considered quantifiers (in the broad sense of the term), we shall also call this substage the *stage of quantification*. The need to structuralize (quantify) a sentence can be explained as follows: Sentences in a natural language express statements (or questions) concerning the properties of entities or the relations between entities. The simplest way of naming entities is to use their proper names (e.g., "The war of 1904 – 1905 shook Russia"). However, it is obvious that the number of proper names in a natural language is much smaller than the number of all individual objects. Thus, in order to name these objects, we are forced to use expressions. These expressions are not in themselves the proper names of any individual entities; nevertheless, they play the role of proper names in the linguistic or extralinguistic context (e.g., "The young man came out of the neighboring house"). Apart from such sentences, where concrete entities are named in one way or another, there is also the very important class of sentences which express statements that do not individualize entities. These sentences contain various quantifiers (e.g., "All men are mortal"). Their sense "completeness" is ensured not by the context they appear in, but by the presence of quantifiers which single out certain entities as against others. In terms of syntax, every quantifier falls into one of the following categories: (a) quantifying adjectives – *vsakiy, vse, kazhdiy, kakoy-nibud', nekotoriy, nikakoy, kakoy by to ni bilo, kakoy-to, kto-to, nekto, nekiy*, etc. [these adjectives are translated into English as *any, all, every, each, whatever, some, a, nobody, somebody, anybody*, and so on, depending on context; trans. note]; (b) quantifying nouns – *vso, kto-nibud', kto- libo* [*everything, anyone, someone, whoever* – again depending on context]; (c) quantifying adverbs –

vsegda, inogda, kogda-nibud', kogda-libo [*always, sometimes, one day, ever*]; (d) quantifying verbs – *sushchestvuyet, imeetsa, yect', net* [*there exists, there is, to be, there is no*]; (e) phraseological combinations – *kakov by ni bil, shto by ni, gde by ni, kogda by ni,* etc. [*whoever, whatever, wherever, whenever*].

Thus, the task of quantification is to determine the types of quantifiers involved, the order in which they are to be considered, and the way in which their scopes of operations are "immersed" in each other. The type of quantifier introduced at the stage of quantification is determined only by quantifying words which occur in the given sentence. An order in which quantifiers are to be considered is determined by a constant weighting assigned to them and by the syntactic structure of the sentence being processed (principal clause, subordinate clause, nonstandard constructions, immersed constructions, immersed nominal groups). Leaving aside – for the time being – the details involved in determining the order of quantifiers (see Sect. 5.4.5), we shall describe how the stage of quantification functions. It is difficult (if not impossible) to determine the scope of operations of quantifiers before the stage of the semantic processing of the whole sentence. This flows from the fact that the quantifiers assigned to one NG usually influence other NGs, too. Moreover, the scopes of operations of many quantifiers are strongly influenced by other quantifiers occurring in the sentence being processed. To give some idea of how the stage of quantification functions, we shall consider the following simple question: *Yavlaetsa li izgotovitelem lubovo stanka marki M7 zavod X?* [Is factory *X* the manufacturer of every lathe with trade mark M7?]. The nonstructuralized semantic graph of this sentence is shown in Fig. 5.6. If we compare it with the SG of the sentence "Factory *X* produces lathes with the trade mark M7", we notice two differences. One of these involves the quantifier ∀, which appears as a consequence of the use of the word *luboy* [every; any]; the other is the appearance of the quantifier YN (YES/NO) which corresponds to the particle *li* [interrogative particle requiring answer of the yes/no type; trans. note]. After quantification, the question assumes the form shown in Fig. 5.7. The space

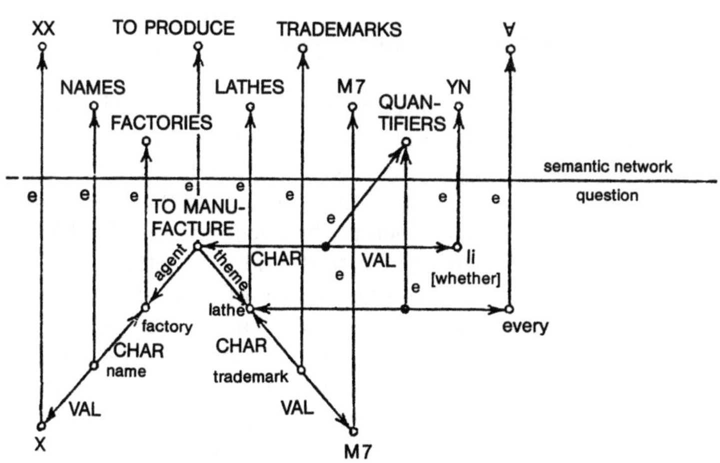

Fig. 5.6. A nonstructuralized semantic graph

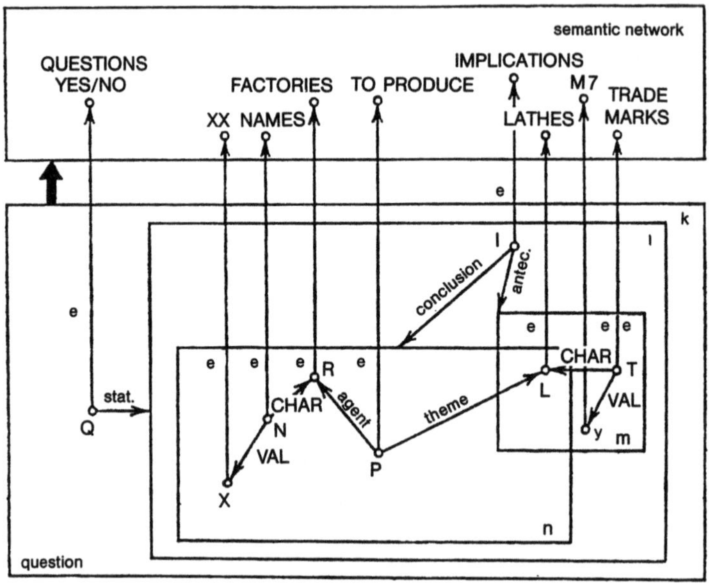

Fig. 5.7. A structuralized semantic graph

k here corresponds to the space of the initial question. It contains a direct indication that the question is of the YES/NO type. The statement expressed in the question, the true or false nature of which is to be determined, is represented by the space *l* ("For any *C*, if *C* is an element of the set LATHES, and if it has the trade mark M7, then *C* has been produced by factory *X*"). In different notation this statement may be expressed as follows:

$$(\forall y)\ ((y \in \text{LATHES}) \wedge (\text{TRADE MARK}\ (y, \text{M7})) \rightarrow$$
$$\rightarrow \text{PRODUCE}\ (\text{FACTORY}\ X, Y)).$$

Let us recall that the universal quantifier is expressed by an implication (see Sect. 3.5).

Processing the question consists in calling successive quantifying functions (Q-functions). First, the YN-function is called (see Sect. 5.4.5). This creates a structure corresponding to the YN question, i.e., it creates the vertex *Q* with two lines running from it ("e" and "statement"), and the space *l*, which represents the substance of the sentence. Then the ∀-function is called. This creates the vertex *I*, the spaces *m* and *n* connected with it, and the vertex *L* (i.e., a variable that the quantifier ∀ refers to) which is an element of both spaces, of *m* and of *n*. Then all the words connected with the vertex *L* ("lathes") are processed. Since there is no other quantifier explicitly expressed in the sentence, the existential quantifier ∃ is introduced "tacitly". The corresponding ∃-function simply copies the other words of the NG which includes the word "lathes", transferring them from the nonstructuralized SG to the space *m*. The other vertices of the sentence undergo an analogous operation. They are all copied down in the space *n*.

5.4.5 The Order in Which Quantifiers are Processed

Let us recall that by the term *quantifier* we mean any higher-level predicate. Consequently, in addition to the standard quantifiers, we also take this word to mean negations, types of question, etc. The ways in which quantifiers are expressed in the Russian language, together with the corresponding Q-functions and weightings, are given in Table 5.2. Note that for homonymic words only one quantifying meaning is mentioned in the table. The values of the respective weightings should be considered rather approximate; they can be made more precise on the basis of experimental data. Readers interested in further details on this problem are referred to the book by E.V. Paducheva (1974).

As we have already observed, a quantifier may take the form of a quantifying word (*luboy, vsakiy, sushchestvuyet, li,* etc. [*any, every, there exist,* interrogative particle]), or may be rooted in the structure of the sentence (PLN-NUMBER, PLN- DEF, YN, WH, etc.). The notation used in Table 5.2 is straightforward. We shall explain the meaning of some abbreviations. By the quantifier WH, we mean the structuralization induced by the use of such interrogative words as *KTO, SHTO, KOMU, CHEMU, KAKOY,* etc. [*who, what, to whom, to what, which*; precise English equivalents depend on context; trans. note].

The quantifier YN is introduced by the particle *LI* in an interrogative sentence, or by an interrogative sentence with no interrogative word (e.g., "You know Petrov?"). The quantifier PLN-NUMBER is introduced by the plural number (PL) of a nominal group in which the number of elements is explicitly indicated (e.g.: "five factories", "101 lathes"). The quantification induced by PLN-NUMBER is different from that induced by the universal quantifier. Let us take the following sentence as an example: "Factory Y has produced 50 lathes". The meaning of this sentence may, for example, be expressed like this: "50 is the number of elements in the set S. Then $x \in S$ if, and only if, x is a LATHE and x has been produced by factory Y".

The quantifier PLN-DEF is introduced by a reference to a defined (DEF) nominal group (i.e., an NG which is projectable onto context) in the plural. For

Table 5.2. Ways of expressing quantifiers in the Russian language

Quantifiers	Q-functions	Weightings of quantifiers
Luboy [any, every]	$Q \cdot \forall$	7
Vsakiy [every, each]	$Q \cdot \forall$	6
Vse [all]	$Q \cdot \forall$	2
Sushchestvuyet [there exist]	$Q \cdot \exists$	0
Nekotoriy [a, a certain]	$Q \cdot \exists$	1
Kakoy-libo [any]	$Q \cdot \exists$	1
Nyet [there is no]	$Q \cdot \neg\exists$	4
Nikakoy [no, none]	$Q \cdot \neg\exists$	2
PLN-NUMBER	$Q \cdot \mathrm{Set}$	1
PLN-UNDEF	$Q \cdot \exists$	0
PLN-DEF	$Q \cdot \forall$	3
Li (YES/NO)	$Q \cdot \mathrm{YN}$	8
WH (Who/What etc.)	$Q \cdot \mathrm{WH}$	5

example: "Each of these factories was built in the years of the first 5-year plan". The quantifier PLN-DEF here means "Any of the elements of the set 'these factories' was built in the years of the first 5-year plan".

The quantifier PLN-UNDEF is introduced when there is no quantifying word and the case in question cannot be included in the categories PLN-NUMBER and PLN-DEF. For example: "Factory *Y* produces lathes". This quantifier is treated as the existential quantifier: "There exist lathes that are produced by factory *Y*".

The form of a sentence which is obtained after processing depends on the order in which Q-functions are applied. The rules that are employed to determine this order are, roughly speaking, as follows:

1. The construction (nominal group, predicate) containing the quantifier with the highest weighting is processed first.
2. If there is more than one quantifier in a nominal group, the outermost is processed first.
3. If two quantifiers in nominal groups have the same weighting, the one further to the left (i.e., nearer to the beginning of the sentence) is processed first.

In order to understand how the weightings assigned to quantifiers influence the final result of an analysis, let us consider two examples:

1. *Kto postroil vse X?* [Who built all the *X*s?], and
2. *Kto postroil kazhdiy (vsakiy) X?* [Who built each (every) *X*?].

The word *vse* [all] has a weighting of 2 (see Table 5.2), *vsakiy* [every] – 6, and *kto* [who] – 5. Thus, *kto* is "stronger" than *vse*, and the first sentence can be structuralized, for example, like this: Who is the builder *Y* such that for any $x \in X$ he built *x*?" The graph corresponding to this sentence is shown in Fig. 5.8. On the other hand, *vsakiy* is stronger than *kto*; consequently, the second sentence will be structuralized like this: "For any $x \in X$, who built *x*?" (see Fig. 5.9).

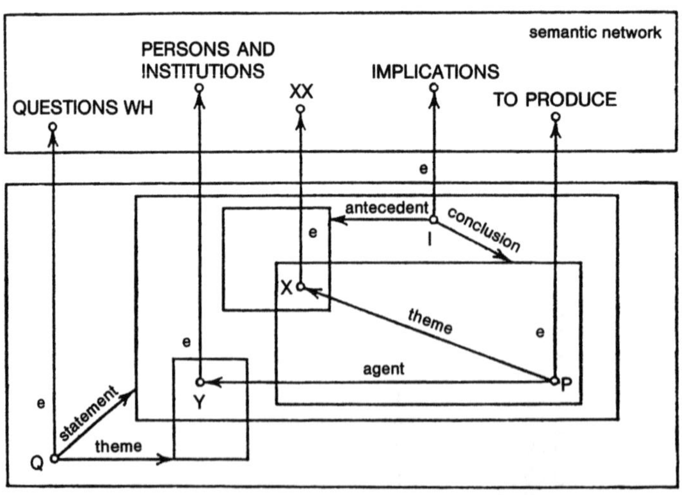

Fig. 5.8. The structuralized graph corresponding to the sentence "Who built all the *X*s?"

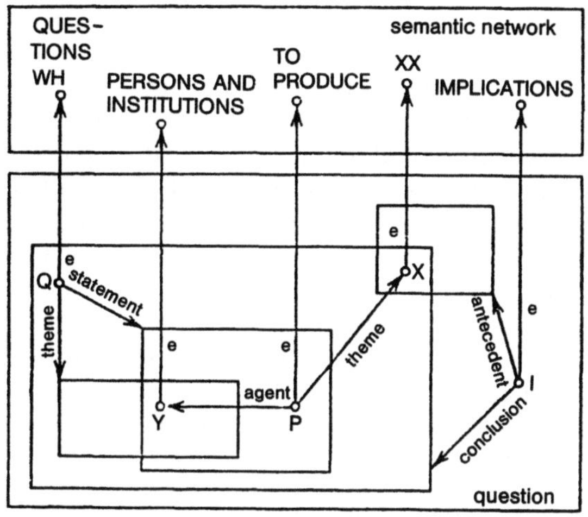

Fig. 5.9. The structuralized graph corresponding to the sentence "Who built every *X*?"

To close this section, let us observe that the approach to the problem of structuralizing a sentence described above should be regarded only as the first step toward resolving this complex problem. Indeed, we have disregarded such important factors as making a quantifier's weighting dependent on its location in a sentence (this weighting is usually greater when a quantifier is the first word in a sentence), the ambiguity in meaning of quantifying words, and the structuralization of a sentence that can be induced by syntactic constructions (dependent and coordinative clauses, and participial, adverbial-participial, and infinitive constructions, etc.).

5.4.6 Formation of the Semantic Categories "Aspect" and "Tense"

At the semantic level, the morphological category of "aspect" is interpreted, in accordance with the restrictions we have adopted (see Sect. 4.2.8), in an extremely straightforward manner: imperf "aspect" corresponds to the value of the characteristic "duration" equal to "interval", and perf "aspect" to the value equal to "point". In the case of aspectual ambiguity, the correct aspect can be determined by considering the verbal form in the context of the whole sentence. Thus, the aspectual ambiguity of an infinitive can be removed if the infinitive is accompanied by phase verbs (e.g., *Predpriyatye nachalo obsledovat'* (imperf) *sostoyanye transporta* [The enterprise began to examine the state of its transport]). The aspectual ambiguity of the verbal form may also be removed if it is accompanied by "repeated adverbial modifiers" (*ezhegodno, regularno, postoyanno*, etc. [*annually, regularly, constantly*]). For example: *Predpriyatye regularno obsledovalo* (imperf) *transportniye sredstva* [The enterprise regularly examined its transport facilities].

The semantic interpretation of the category of "tense" is a more complicated problem. The morphological category of "tense" is projected either directly onto the semantic "tense" (i.e., morphological "tense" corresponds to real "time"), or onto deep predicates which may be called BEFORE (preceding), TOGETHER (occurring simultaneously), and AFTER (following). The rules that govern the interpretation use information about the morphological characteristics of a word form (part of speech, tense, voice), about its position in the syntactic structure of the sentence, and about the individual semantic properties of a given lexeme. Since it is impossible to describe here in full detail all the rules of the semantic interpretation of the category of "tense", we shall confine ourselves to those rules that concern a word form predicate included in a subordinate part of a compound sentence.

Rule 1. This rule is employed if a word form *Y* is a "slave", according to the syntactic relation 1 COMPL, of an active predicate (*X*) in the principal clause, or if it is a "slave", according to PRED SYR, of a passive predicate in the principal clause:

1.1 If *Y* (verb pres.), then (*X* TOGETHER *Y*), i.e., *X* and *Y* occur together (simultaneously).
1.2 If *Y* (verb past), then (*Y* BEFORE *X*).
1.3 If *Y* (verb fut.), then (*Y* AFTER *X*).

Rule 2. This rule is employed if a word form *Y* is a "slave" of the final conjunctions *shtoby* or *dla tovo shtoby* [*to, in order to; for... to*] (the morphological "tense" of a predicate in a subordinate clause is always PAST in this case):

2.1 *Y* (verb past) → (*Y* AFTER *X*)

For example: *Dla tovo shtoby zavod osvoil (Y) novuyu tekhnologyu proizvodstva, yemu budut predostavleny (X) dopolnitelniye sredstva* [For the firm to introduce (*Y*) new production technology, it will be granted (*X*) additional funds; *osvoil* is in the past tense; trans. note].

Rule 3. In all other cases the morphological "tense" of *Y* coincides with its semantic tense.

For instance: *Zavod, kotoriy proizvodit stanki M7, v proshlom godu zavershil rekonstruktsyu kuznechnovo tsekha* [The factory which produces M7 lathes completed the modernization of the forging shop last year].

6 Connected-Text (Discourse) Processing

6.1 General Structure

The following tasks should be performed when processing a discourse: (a) establishing and explicitly expressing the interdependence between the sentences in the discourse and (b) carrying out the interpretation of the connected text. The connectedness of a text, i.e., of a sequence of sentences, can be obtained by both linguistic and extralinguistic methods. The main linguistic methods that can be used to express an interdependence between sentences are references and ellipses (see Sect. 4.1). We take these to be linguistic methods, as they are expressed in the form of language. This does not mean, however, that to establish a referent (i.e., the entity meant when a reference was made) or to reconstruct what was omitted in an elliptic construction it will suffice to employ syntactic methods alone. Extralinguistic methods encompass all phenomena that are not expressed (or virtually not expressed) in language form ("tacit knowledge" – see Sect. 1.1.6).

We shall consider the question of how the linguistically expressible interdependencies between the sentences of a discourse can be revealed in Sect. 6.2, and to some extent in Sect. 6.3. The same problem, as regards extralinguistic interdependencies, will be examined in Sect. 6.3 (with the use of context) and in Sect. 6.4 (with the use of the mechanism of reasoning). Connected-text processing ends with the stage of interpretation (see Sect. 6.4), in the course of which the following tasks are performed: First, we have to reveal the interdependencies between the facts mentioned in a discourse and the concrete pieces of information possessed by the system. In order to do this when facts from a discourse do not directly coincide with information contained in the system's knowledge, we have to employ certain deductive operations. The second task performed at the stage of interpretation is the processing proper of an input text, i.e., the inference or derivation of an answer in the case of a question, or the unification of information from the discourse with that in the system's knowledge in the case of affirmative sentences. These problems will be studied in Sect. 6.4.

6.2 Determining the Linguistically Expressible Interdependencies Between Sentences in a Discourse

6.2.1 The Problem of References

Reference is the most important means of representing a linguistically expressible interdependency between sentences in a discourse (see Sect. 4.1). The problem of identifying references can be divided into two subproblems: (a) establishing where in the context we should seek the entity (i.e., referent) that is denoted by the given reference; (b) establishing how to determine that a given referent and the given reference correspond to each other. The simplest solution to the first of these two subproblems is to search for the referent in preceding statements (of a certain proximity) (Chafe 1972). This approach has been used in the systems developed by Winograd (1972) and Norman et al. (1975). However, this method has the serious deficiency that the user does not know how to determine the number, i.e., proximity, of preceding sentences that have to be taken into account when looking for the initial notion (i.e., referent). In practice, this shortcoming considerably prolongs the time spent on the search, and leads to errors in identifying references. Grosz (1976) has shown that a dialogue is not linear and has a structure corresponding to that of the task performed in it; consequently, the method of identifying references by a retrograde search must lead not only to tremendous outlays of time but, even worse, to errors in identifying referents. As Grosz demonstrated, the solution to the problem of references requires knowledge of the structure of a dialogue (on the basis of the structure of the task being performed), and the proximity factor should also be taken into account (see Sects. 6.2.3 and 6.3).

The solution to the second subproblem is elementary for simpler forms of references, i.e., when the referent and reference coincide, and extremely difficult when they do not. The complexity of the problem stems from the fact that when referring to an entity introduced earlier, people do not indicate all the properties of this entity; on the contrary, to make the dialogue more concise, they have a tendency to diminish the amount of information directly used in the given reference. An examination of real-life dialogues shows that when choosing the form of a reference, people usually take the following two factors into account: (a) the utterance should be of minimum length, and (b) the listener should have to spend only the minimum amount of time looking for the referent that corresponds to the speaker's reference. When both these factors are considered, people usually do not give the minimum amount of information needed to find the referent for the given reference, as this would slow down the process of the listener (reader) looking for the referent, and thus increase the total time of the dialogue. Additional, superfluous information is given to facilitate the listener's search for a referent. The problem of correspondence between a referent and a reference can also be expressed using descriptions. This can be done as follows: When entities are encountered in a text, an understanding system (either human being or computer) assigns them a set of descriptions that characterize them ($N_1, N_2, \ldots, N_k$). When analyzing a reference X, the understanding system selects those descriptions that do not contradict the description M_x.

The structure of a dialogue determined on the basis of the structure of the task being performed enables us, in looking for a referent, to consider only those entities which are used in a current subtask (subdialogue), or in subtasks (subdialogues) in which it is included. When a subtask has been accomplished, the entities that were used to perform it cannot be used in the next references. Using this structure of a dialogue makes it possible to speed up the process of identifying references, since the search is carried out in only one part of the text, not in all of it. In order to illustrate what we have just said, let us consider a treelike

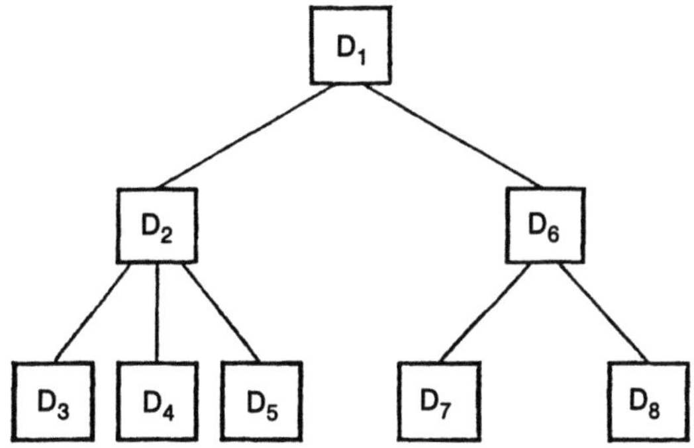

Fig. 6.1. Example of a structure of a dialogue

structure of the process of performing a task (Fig. 6.1). The ordinal numbers of the blocks in the figure correspond to the order in which the subdialogues appear in the text being processed. When the subtask (i.e., subdialogue) D_5 is being performed, the focus of attention includes subtasks D_2 and D_1 (the search starts with the nearest subdialogue – in this case, D_2), and references can be made only to entities from D_1 and D_2, not to those from subtasks D_3 and D_4. Correspondingly, from D_7 one can make references to entities introduced in D_6 and D_1, but not to ones from D_2, D_3, D_4, or D_5. Let us note that a structure of a dialogue is used not only to speed up the search for a referent; it also helps to avoid errors during this process. The role of a structure of a dialogue is particularly important in the case of nominal references (NR) in the plural. Let us suppose a notion X^1_{sing} – in the singular – is used in a dialogue, and then the same notion appears again, but in the plural (X^2_{pl}). When the reference X^3_{pl} is encountered, it is therefore unclear, if we do not know the structure of a dialogue, whether this refers to both previous appearances of X (i.e., X^1_{sing} and X^2_{pl}), or just to the latter. However, if the structure of a dialogue is known, this problem can be overcome.

Let us now explain the notion of accomplishing a subdialogue, and what is involved in removing the entities introduced in this subdialogue from the focus of attention. In the case of NRs, the entities introduced in a subdialogue can be removed immediately after this subdialogue is accomplished. However, in the case of pronominal references (PR), the situation may be different. The problem here is that in a natural language there is often a need to link two adjacent subdialogues (X and Y). For instance, let us assume certain objects have been found in the subdialogue X, and an operation involving these objects in the subdialogue Y. Under these circumstances, in order to make a reference from Y to X, the entities introduced in X should be removed from the focus of attention, not as soon as the subdialogue X is accomplished, but during analysis of the subdialogue Y, adjacent to X. The most natural method of expressing such references is to use PRs, not NRs. For example:

Teacher: Find four red cubes.
Pupil: ....
....
Pupil: I have found all four red cubes.
Teacher: Good. Now build a tower out of *them*.

In the last sentence of the above example, it is not only possible, but in fact necessary, to use the pronominal reference "them" (or "out of those cubes"). Indeed, the use of a nominal group in place of "them" would be more appropriate if some other four cubes were meant. [The problem under discussion here is one not found in English, where the use of the definite article "the" removes all ambiguity; trans. note]. The above example demonstrates that to identify references it is necessary to take both the structure of a dialogue and the proximity of sentences into account. A solution to the problem of references – using the notion of the focus of attention – will be considered in Sect. 6.3.

6.2.2 Reconstructing Ellipsis

Focus provides not only a semantic tool for identifying references, but also a syntactic and semantic tool for interpreting sentences that contain elliptic constructions. We have already observed that the reconstruction of ellipsis is based on local context, i.e., on the preceding part of the given sentence (if it is not a simple sentence) or on the preceding sentence (see Sect. 4.1). Dialogues that include a sequence of statements (sentences) X, Y, Z, where Y and Z are elliptic sentences which may be reconstructed on the basis of the full version of sentence X, do not contradict the above-mentioned statement about local context. Indeed, when ellipsis from Y has been reconstructed, Y is then known in its full form (without ellipsis), and the reconstruction of Z is carried out not on the basis of X, but of Y. Processing elliptic sentences comprises the following stages: (a) detecting the presence of ellipsis; (b) searching the local context containing the preceding statement (sentence) for constructions similar to those in the elliptic sentence; (c) constructing a full sentence by inserting an elliptic construction into the preceding statement.

The presence of ellipsis is usually manifest in a violation of the correct syntactic structure for a given sentence. Figure 6.2 shows a few examples of this: 1. lack of a connected dependency tree (Fig. 6.2 – 1a); 2. obligatory valences of a word with a model of government not being filled (Fig. 6.2 – 2a); 3. the appearance of weak projectiveness (see Sect. 5.3.2) instead of just projectiveness (Fig. 6.2 – 3a).

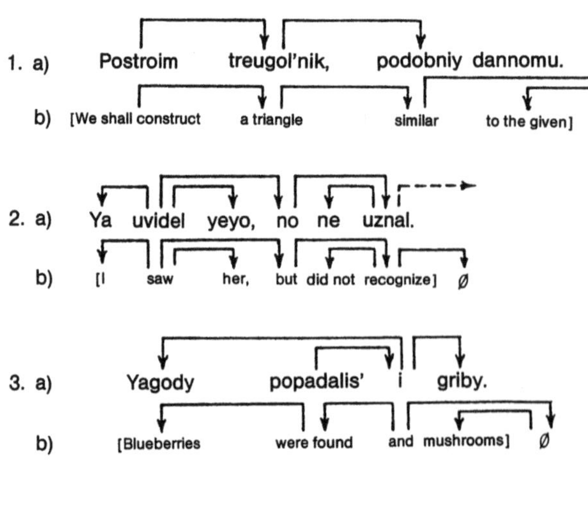

Fig. 6.2. Examples of elliptic sentences. [These sentences are perfectly correct in Russian; trans. note]

The problem of violations of syntax is examined in detail in a book by Paducheva (1974). However, the presence of ellipsis is not always connected with a violation of the syntactic structure of a sentence. For example, the sentence, "What is the length?", is syntactically complete, yet semantically incomplete. In such cases, ellipsis can be reconstructed only during semantic analysis and interpretation.

Establishing what has been "omitted" in a sentence containing ellipsis requires the use of both syntactic and semantic filters. The task performed by syntactic filters is to determine the level of ellipsis involved (see Sect. 4.1) and to identify constructions from the preceding sentence which resemble this ellipsis. The level of ellipsis can usually be inferred from the violations of the syntactic structure. Similarities with preceding constructions are detected by comparing the gender, number, and the case of the prop word in the elliptic group with those of nominal groups in the preceding sentence. We shall not consider syntactic filters in detail here, but shall confine ourselves to pointing out that their use allows us to simplify and speed up the stage of semantics. Sometimes, however, syntactic methods alone are capable of resolving all ambiguities. For example:

1. a) *Nikolay otpravil pis'mo Pyotru.* [Nikolay has sent a letter to Pyotr].
   b) *Sidorov?* (i.e., Is it Nikolay Sidorov who has sent a letter to Pyotr?) [The surname *Sidorov* is in the nominative case, and therefore cannot be associated with *Pyotru*, which is in the dative; trans. note].
2. a) *Nikolay otpravil pis'mo Pyotru.*
   b) *Sidorovu?* (Is it Pyotr Sidorov Nikolay has sent a letter to?) [This time, *Sidorovu* is in the dative; trans. note].

Generally speaking, however, semantic information is needed to reconstruct ellipsis. Let us consider one of the most widespread forms of ellipsis occurring in dialogues, when one nominal group plays the role of a question or an answer. For example:

Q1: *Zavod A izgotovil stanok B?* [Has factory *A* produced lathe *B*?]
A1: .... (answer)
Q2: *A kompressor C? (Zavod A izgotovil kompressor C?)*
[What about compressor *C*? (Has factory *A* produced compressor *C*?)]
A2: .... (answer)
Q3: *A zavod D? (Zavod D izgotovil kompressor C?)* [What about factory *D*? (Has factory *D* produced compressor *C*?)]

In terms of syntax, the elliptic construction Q2 can be put into correspondence not only with the word combination Y_1 ("lathe *B*") but also with the word combination Y_2 ("factory *A*" – giving us "Has compressor *C* produced lathe *B*?"). The choice of the first variant (the correct one) can be made by analyzing the semantic similarity between the word combination and the elliptic construction (Q2: Y_1 and Q2: Y_2). If knowledge is represented in the form of a semantic network, the semantic similarity may be determined on the basis of the hierarchy of relations "e" (an element of a set) and "s" (a subset). A vertex X (from an elliptic sentence) is most similar to the vertex of vertices Y_i (from the preceding sentence) for which the following statement holds: Y_i and X are both elements of a common set M, and M does not contain any other vertex Y_j $(i \neq j)$. In other words, the vertex X is semantically most similar to a vertex Y_i if the pair made up of X and Y_i has a common ancestor (defined by lines "e" and "s"), which is expressible in terms of a less abstract notion (vertex) than that corresponding to any other pair (X, Y_j), where $j \neq i$. In the above example, the closest similarity occurs in the case of X (i.e., Q2) and Y_1, as their common ancestor ("product") is a less abstract notion than the common ancestor of X and Y_2 ("physical object"). In other words, the set M of entities corresponding to the vertex "product" does not contain entities that correspond to the vertex Y_2.

Let us suppose a candidate Y_i from the preceding sentence has already been chosen. It is then replaced by X, and the sentence thus obtained undergoes semantic analysis and interpretation. Let us note that to carry out the substitution whereby an elliptic construction (EC) is inserted into the preceding sentence (PS), the latter often has to be subjected to some transformation. Let us consider the following dialogue:

PS: *Kakoy instrument vy ispol'zuyete dla zakreplenya korpussa?* [What tool do you use to tighten up the frame?]
EC: *Gayechniy kluch.* (*Dla zakreplenya korpusa ya ispol'zuyu gayechniy kluch.*) [A wrench. (I use a wrench to tighten up the frame.)]

The following two transformations have to be carried out to insert the EC into the PS: (a) the transformation of the form of the PS from interrogative to affirmative, and (b) replacement of the pronoun *vy* [you] with *ya* [I], and bringing the verb into agreement with the latter [*ispol'zuyete* – *ispol'zuyu* – "to use" in the second person plural and first person singular respectively; trans. note]. We would recommend Grosz's book (1977a) to readers interested in studying methods of reconstructing ellipsis in more detail.

6.2.3 The Structure of a Dialogue

Barbara Grosz (1976) was one of the first to notice the influence that the structure of the task being performed during a dialogue exerts on the structure of the dialogue itself. She demonstrated that the structure of a dialogue reproduces the structure of the task which constitutes the subject of the dialogue. In other words, a dialogue splits into subdialogues that correspond to subtasks, distinguished in the course of performing an initial task. The correspondence indicated above plays a crucial role in determining the context in which a given input sentence should be interpreted. Grosz distinguishes two main subclasses of helping dialogue: a dialogue oriented toward performing a task (DOT), and a dialogue oriented toward retrieval in the data base (DOR). A detailed analysis of real-life dialogues led Grosz to conclude that the influence of the structure of a task is particularly noticeable in dialogues of the DOT type, while less pronounced in those of the DOR type. As an example of a dialogue of the first type, Grosz mentions a dialogue between an instructor and an apprentice attempting to solve a certain problem (e.g., assembling a compressor). Grosz includes in dialogues of the second type those that occur when a user wants to obtain a piece of information of interest to him stored in a computer. In our opinion, the division of dialogues into two distinct subclasses can be traced to the fact that up to now the problems solved during conversations between man and machine have been tasks of a very elementary nature (microtasks). As a matter of fact, what is involved in them is actually the microtask "find the value of the parameter that is of interest to the user", with this value either stored in the computer explicitly, or capable of being derived from the stored information by means of the simplest calculations. In other words, the tasks performed so far have in fact no structure at all, while the dialogue, as a rule, consists of one question and one answer. In asking the system to provide a certain piece of information, the user does not, at present, inform the computer what macrotask he intends to perform, although he is undoubtedly engaged in a task more complex than just establishing the value of a single parameter. If it were possible to obtain assistance from the computer in performing a macrotask, the structure of this task would certainly be reflected in the structure of the dialogue between man and machine. Moreover, for systems of real-life complexity, even the process of performing a microtask often splits up into several subtasks (a point not noticed by Grosz because the conversations she studied were with systems of an experimental character). For example, a dialogue occurring during the performance of the microtask X might comprise the following subdialogues:

1. Eliminating a syntactic error made by the user when formulating the microtask X
2. Eliminating terminological ambiguities
3. Projecting the microtask X which the user is interested in onto the knowledge possessed by the system (e.g., the system informing the user that it does not possess the piece of information he is seeking, or the user discovering during the course of his conversation with the system that the latter possesses information on subjects related to the one he is interested in, thus causing him to modify his input sentence).

What we have just said does not signify a rejection of Grosz's research; in fact, it substantiates her conclusions regarding the influence of the structure of a task on the structure of a dialogue, not only in the case of dialogues oriented toward performing a task, but also for those oriented toward retrieval in the data base. Obviously, the structure of the DOR type of dialogue is at present much simpler than that of the DOT type. This is precisely why, at present, machine realization of DOT dialogues can, in our opinion, be considered only at the purely theoretical level, not at the level of designing systems with practical applications. However, developing systems capable of conducting DOR dialogues in a natural language to resolve real-life problems is a question not only of theory, but also of practice. We shall now briefly consider the question of determining the structure of a dialogue. We shall not differentiate between DOT and DOR dialogues; nevertheless, the reader should bear in mind that determining the structure of DOT dialogues is – at the present stage – a much more complex task.

The thematic structure of a dialogue (see Sect. 4.1) is determined on the one hand by knowledge about the structure of the task to be performed, and on the other hand, by distinguishing linguistic constructions in the dialogue that indicate the segmentation of this dialogue. The structure of DOT dialogues is more varied, which reflects the diversity of tasks performed by dialogues. The structure of

DORdialogues is much simpler; in fact, they all perform the same task – "retrieval of the value of a parameter". The structure of this task is very simple, and all the subtasks involved may be known to the system. There are a limited number of these subtasks. They include the following:

1. Identification of a notion by the user ("What do you mean by average speed?")
2. A subdialogue designed to obtain assurance that the knowledge about an area of subject matter possessed by both the system and the user coincide. For instance, before inquiring about the values of the parameters of a given object, the user checks the structure of the system's knowledge about a certain subsection of the subject matter ("What kinds of transport are known to the system?", "What period of time does this information relate to?").
3. A subdialogue designed to clarify the user's error
4. A subdialogue designed to explain why the system was not able to process an input sentence
5. An introductory subdialogue concerning the system's potential, its limitations, and its thematic orientation

A subdialogue can be identified in a text on the basis of natural language statements which "open" or "close" subdialogues. Certain phrases in Russian indicate the opening or closing of a subdialogue quite explicitly; e.g., *zatem, tepier', yasno, itak, zakonchit',* etc. [*then, now, it is clear* (that), *so* (thus), *to conclude*]. However, there are also words which can perform several functions; moreover, in order to open or close a subdialogue, not one but two statements may be used:

Q: What should I do now?
A: Remove the engine.

The most complicated situation arises when a subdialogue is opened or closed inexplicitly. For instance, a subdialogue may be inexplicitly closed by the explicit opening of another subdialogue – this is particularly frequent.

To close this brief examination of the structure of a dialogue, we would like to emphasize that the stage of designing a concrete SNL should be preceded by a detailed study of real-life dialogues concerning the given area of subject matter. The experience gained during this study will be of considerable help in designing the system.

As we have already observed (see Sect. 4.1), apart from the thematic structure there is also another important feature characteristic of dialogues (at least those between human beings): the so-called macrostructure. Many phenomena related to macrostructure are absent from present-day dialogues between man and machine owing to the limitations imposed on the language of conversation. However, it should be stressed that knowing *why* the user is carrying out a given subdialogue – i.e., what objectives he has – is of great importance in establishing a "mutual understanding" between the user and the system.

6.3 Context and Its Role in Discourse Processing

A conversation consisting solely of isolated (unconnected) sentences would be quite impracticable, even in the case of a very narrow area of subject matter. The reasons for this are the following: In order to conduct such a conversation, the user would have to express all the relevant information in one sentence (question or answer) in an unambiguous manner. To do this for an area of subject matter taken from real life the user would have to know all the aspects of a given fact that needed to be presented to the system. This is impossible. In any case, even if the user knew all these aspects, it would be extremely difficult to construct a sentence in a natural language conveying information about a large number of diverse questions. A conversation in the form of isolated sentences could not be sufficiently compact, as each sentence in it would have to convey all the information required explicitly (not "tacitly"). If a connected text is used, the above problems disappear. However, processing a connected text poses various other problems for an SNL. The problem of interpreting a sentence from a connected text (i.e., a discourse) is one of placing that individual sentence in context. If not related to context, an individual sentence from a discourse may have several different meanings, or it might be totally incomprehensible. The interpretation of a concrete sentence from a connected text depends on both the preceding sentences (the *textual context*) and the situation the sentence appears in (the *situational context*). The situational context does not usually occur in a text in explicit form because of the "tacit knowledge" characteristic of any natural language. It is recreated by the participants during the process of comprehension. One might say that the division into textual and situational contexts reflects the manner in which a context is formed – explicitly (textually), or inexplicitly (situationally). Taking into account the tasks that have to be performed in analyzing a discourse, it is also convenient to distinguish global and local context. *Global context* corresponds to the general thrust of a text and to the circumstances surrounding it. Global context serves as a basis for choosing the most appropriate meaning of a homonymic word (e.g., "nucleus": 1. the central portion of a galaxy; 2. a cellular organelle; 3. the central portion of an atom; 4. the peak of energy in the utterance of a syllable; etc.). This type of context also makes it possible to identify nominal references, i.e., to establish what notions introduced in the preceding part of the text are being referred to by a given notion. Global context selects that part of the general knowledge possessed by the system which is relevant in understanding the current sentence of the dialogue; i.e., it selects from the homogeneous structure of the knowledge the vertices and lines which lie within the focus of attention of the user conducting the dialogue. *Local context* corresponds to the several sentences which directly precede the one being processed. Local context makes it possible to uncover "tacit knowledge" in sentences containing ellipsis.

In point of fact, what is usually called "the context of an utterance" is actually a set of restrictions focusing attention on the notions occurring in the discourse. We shall use the term *focus of attention* (or simply *focus*) to refer to knowledge obtained on the basis of context.

6.3.1 The Requirements to Be Satisfied in Representing Focus of Attention

A representation of the focus of attention should ensure that the following functions are fulfilled: (a) knowledge is differentiated according to its degree of relevance; (b) both the explicit and inexplicit entities of the text are brought into focus; (c) focus varies dynamically (shifts) in line with changes in the subject raised during the discourse.

Of the three functions mentioned above, the first would seem to be the most important. Focus should be able to spotlight those entities which are most relevant in understanding the discourse being processed. This ensures the easiest (quickest) access to the most important information. The second function indicated above signifies the capacity to focus not only on those entities which have been explicitly mentioned in a discourse, but also on those that may be associated with them and on possible references to them in the following part of the discourse. The third function necessitates a mechanism for shifting focus. A shift in focus may result either from gradual changes in the surrounding environment over a period of time or from a rapid change in the theme of a dialogue. Not only entities may change in focus – the angle from which they are viewed may vary, too. For instance, in the process of describing an engine, it may first be treated as a mechanical device, then as an electrical blueprint.

In the next two sections we shall consider separately the representations of explicit and inexplicit focus. *Explicit focus* involves entities of indisputable relevance in interpreting the sentence being processed, as they have been explicitly indicated in the preceding part of the discourse. *Inexplicit focus* involves entities which are likely to be relevant, as they are closely related to those explicitly mentioned in the preceding part of the discourse. The following two dialogues illustrate the difference between these two concepts:

(D1) A1: Fasten the poster to the wall with tacks.
B1: Where are the tacks?
(D2) A2: Fasten the poster to the wall.
B2: Where are the tacks?

The words "poster", "fasten", and "wall" are in explicit focus in both dialogues. The word "tacks", however, is in explicit focus in the case of dialogue D1, but in inexplicit focus in D2. The division into explicit and inexplicit foci is based on the following considerations. First, the total number of inexplicitly indicated entities in a discourse is enormous; the vast majority of them, however, are never used in a reference occurring in any subsequent part of the discourse. Failure to differentiate between explicit and inexplicit entities would thus reduce the system's efficiency in selecting relevant entities (i.e., it would prolong the time needed for retrieval). Second, the category of inexplicit focus facilitates carrying out shifts in focus, as references to inexplicit entities are regarded as signs that such a shift in focus may be necessary.

6.3.2 Representation of Explicit Focus

Explicit focus may be represented using network spaces (see Sect. 3.5). When we examined network spaces previously, we introduced the relations of "visibility"

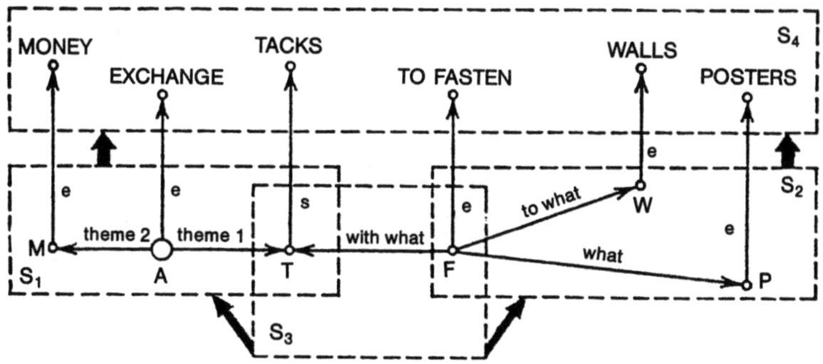

Fig. 6.3. Example of a network divided into focal spaces

and "invisibility". "Visible" spaces can form what we called a "perspective". The notion of spaces has so far been used to represent quantifiers and hypothetical worlds, and for abstracting. In the following, we shall reserve the term "logical spaces" for these types of spaces. Spaces connected with the notion of focus will be said to be *focal spaces* (FS). Thus, one and the same network divides up into two different sets of spaces – one used in quantification and the other in focusing. In diagrams, we shall use a broken line to denote focal spaces and a continuous line to denote logical spaces. Focal spaces as a method of describing focus of attention were first introduced by B. Grosz (1976). We shall follow her approach to the problem of representing focus. Focal spaces will be used to select entities that are relevant in understanding a discourse. They form a hierarchy which reflects the structure of a discourse. This form of organizing FSs is necessary to carry out shifts in focus (see Sect. 6.3.5).

Figure 6.3 shows a fragment of a network divided into four focal spaces: S_1, S_2, S_3, and S_4. The hierarchy of the spaces is marked by the continuous arrows connecting them. Each space has its own "perspective", i.e., an ordered set of spaces "visible" from that given space. For instance, in the case of space S_4 this is just (S_4), while in the case of space S_3 it is (S_3, S_2, S_4). Perspective determines the angle from which a certain entity is viewed. For example, from the spaces (S_1, S_4), the set of tacks (*T*) is "visible" only as a participant in the operation of exchange *A*, while from (S_3, S_2, S_4) it is viewed as the instrument for fastening *P* to *W*. These two perspectives provide two alternative ways of viewing *T*. From the perspective of (S_2, S_4), *F* is "visible" as the event which involves fastening *P* to *W*, with the instrument (tacks) unspecified. From (S_3, S_2, S_4) *F* is seen in a more concrete light. Thus, the division into focal spaces makes it possible to view entities occurring in one dialogue in a number of different ways. If an entity occurs twice, in two different subdialogues, then the corresponding vertex or line of the network will appear in two different focal spaces. The capacity to focus on different features of an entity makes possible differentiated access to the entity, and consequently to the arrangement of facts concerning this entity.

There are two rules governing representation of a notion in a focal space. First, if a notion is in a focal space, then information about what kind of notion this is should also be contained there. Information about the kind of notion involved may take the form of information about the aspect of focusing or may consist in a reference to additional information about this notion. In terms of the network representation, this means that if a notion is in focus, then so are the lines ("element" – "e" and "subset" – "s") running from it. Second, if a line of a notion which is in a certain situation (e.g., "tacks" is the theme of the event "exchange") is in focus, then the situation itself (the event "exchange") should also be.

A shift in focus during a dialogue results in the creation of new focal spaces. At each point in a discourse, only one focal space is "active", although there may be several "open" focal spaces. An *active FS* corresponds to the focus of attention at the current point in a dialogue. *Open FSs* are those which were active before and, containing some unfinished subjects, may consequently become active again (when the dialogue returns to these unfinished subjects). The relationships between focal spaces are determined by the structure of the dialogue under consideration (strictly speaking, by the structure of the task which is being performed by the dialogue, see Sect. 4.1). When focus shifts, the focal space thereby created is always open; it is closed when the sentence being processed indicates a change of subject.

6.3.3 Representation of Inexplicit Focus

In order to be able to represent inexplicit focus, we have to solve the problem of which information relating to a notion in explicit focus should be brought into inexplicit focus. The solution depends on the knowledge possessed about the notion and the participants' expectations. In addition, we have to specify the amount of information that is to be associated with a given notion, as well as how many levels of association are to be considered. The problems just mentioned still require further detailed study. Here we shall confine ourselves to a brief description of one possible approach.

The problem is straightforward in the case of physical objects: if such an object is brought into explicit focus, its parts (or subparts) should be brought into inexplicit focus. A more complex situation arises when we deal with events. A subevent now becomes directly analogous with a part. If, however, an event is brought into inexplicit focus, it seems advisable to bring not only corresponding subevents, but also the participants in these subevents into focus. To this end, subevents and participants in these subevents should be indicated in the representation of the corresponding event. The representation of the event "fastening a poster to a wall" is shown in Fig. 6.4. The logical space S_1 contains all entities from the data base. The set A_2 = (TO FASTEN. POSTER. WALL) is a subset of all events TO FASTEN. The line "restriction" (see Sect. 3.5), running from A_2 to A_1, introduces a description of the semantic cases of the event TO FASTEN and the restrictions imposed on entities corresponding to these cases. The vertex A_3 is a descriptor of the event A_2. Of all the lines running from A_3, it is the line "structure" that will be of the most interest to us here. "Structure" introduces the space of structure (S_3), containing the structure of the division of event A_2 ("to fasten") into two subevents, B_1 and B_2, corresponding to the events TO ATTACH and TO FASTEN WITH TACKS. The lines "foll" ("follow") indicate the order of the subevents. A sequence of subevents may be either ordered (as in the

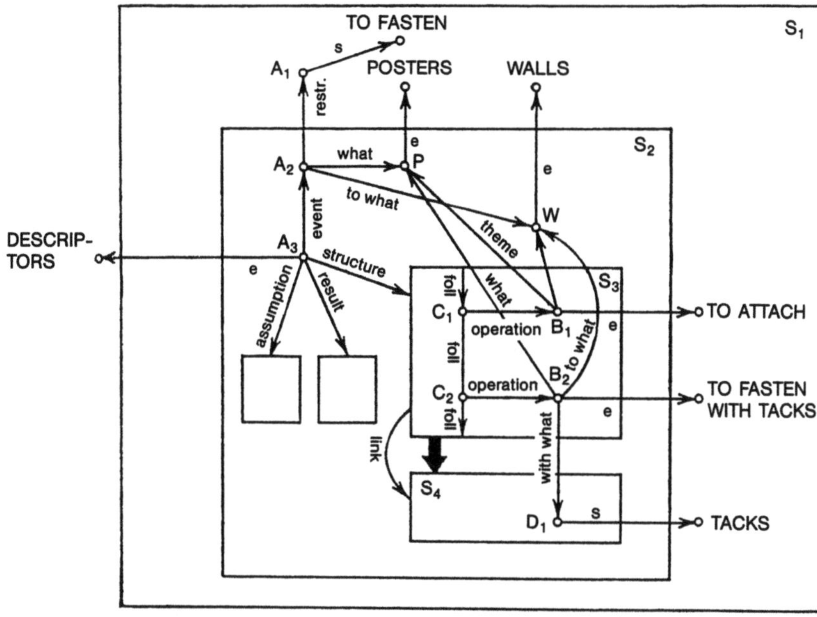

Fig. 6.4. Representation of an event oriented toward inexplicit focus

diagram) or partially ordered. The line "link" links spaces S_3 and S_4. The space S_4 (a joint space) includes the vertex that corresponds to the subset D_1 of the set TACKS. D_1 is a participant in event B_2. When an event of fastening a poster to a wall is brought into explicit focus, the corresponding subevents B_1 and B_2 and the subset D_1 are brought into inexplicit focus. Generally speaking, a joint space (in our example – S_4) contains all participants in events who have not been mentioned as participants in the main event. The inexplicit focus on an event comprises the perspective corresponding to the space of structure and the joint space. It is used to interpret (nominal and pronominal) references to objects and events. For instance, a nominal reference to TACKS in dialogue D_2 will be sought in the inexplicit focus created by the event TO FASTEN.

6.3.4 The Role of Focus in Matching

Retrieving an entity from memory is one of the most widespread operations for knowledge-based systems. For systems that use networks to represent knowledge, the *operation of matching* plays a key role in the process of retrieval. This operation consists in matching a fragment of a network containing variables with the general semantic network. During the process of matching, retrieval can be carried out when context is lacking only if certain local restrictions are taken into consideration. The main use of focus is to limit retrieval on the basis of information from the discourse (i.e., on the basis of global information). The process of matching will be described later (Sect. 6.4). Here we shall confine ourselves to clarifying certain details which will be of help in understanding the role of focus

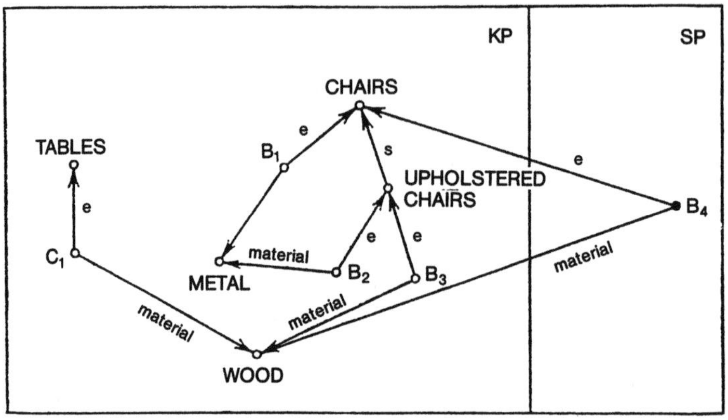

Fig. 6.5. Example of matching a sentence perspective (SP) with a knowledge perspective (KP)

in this process. The process of matching uses two logical (not focal) perspectives: *sentence perspective* (SP) and *knowledge perspective* (KP). SP is the set of spaces containing sentences being processed which are being matched. KP is the set of all pieces of information used in the matching. The process of matching consists in attempting to link each entity (i.e., vertex or line) from the corresponding SP with an element in the KP. The number of calculations that are needed to carry out this process depends on two factors: first, on the order in which entities from the SP are matched with the KP; second, on the way in which an element (X) from the KP is selected to correspond to a given entity (Y) from the SP. Generally (without focus), various candidates correspond to one Y, and local information is the only information accessible for guiding retrieval.

Figure 6.5 shows the example of the SP for the phrase "wooden chair" along with its corresponding KP. The process of matching should establish a correspondence between vertices B_4 and B_3. First the system matches the line B_4-material-WOOD with the line B_3-material-WOOD and infers that B_3 is an element of the set CHAIRS (by following the line "e" from B_3 to UPHOLSTERED CHAIRS, and then the line "s" to the vertex CHAIRS). As a result, a new line is created in the KP: B_3-e-CHAIRS. Next the line B_4-e-CHAIRS will be put into correspondence with this newly created line. This ends the process of matching vertex B_4 with B_3. We mentioned that two factors determine how many calculations are required. In our example, the choice of an entity from the SP (either the line B_4-material-WOOD or B_4-e-CHAIRS) corresponds to the first of these two factors; the choice between the candidates from the KP (B_3-material-WOOD and C_1-material-WOOD, both being suitable for matching with the selected entity B_4-material-WOOD from the SP) illustrates the second factor. A connection established between an entity from an SP and an element of the corresponding KP is not immediately in final form. It becomes more precise during subsequent stages of processing.

When focus is not taken into consideration, the above choices can be made only on the basis of local information. Thus, for the case illustrated in Fig. 6.5, the choice between the two options open to us – linking B_4 along the line "e" or along the line "material" – can be made on the basis of the fact that the number of "e" lines converging on the vertex CHAIRS is smaller than that of "material" lines converging on the vertex WOOD. In other words, we have to specify what should be sought: (a) a CHAIR whose characteristics coincide with those of the vertex B_4 (i.e., the material WOOD), or (b) an entity made of WOOD, whose characteristics correspond to B_4 (i.e., the entity is an element of the set CHAIRS). One of our aims in introducing focus is to guide the process of matching on the basis not of local information, but rather of global information about the discourse.

Focus may be used to determine the order in which candidates are checked during matching. This makes it possible to reduce considerably the number of calculations required. The entities (vertices and lines) that are contained in a given focus limit the process of matching to a consideration of only those elements of a KP which are relevant in the given dialogue. The process of matching in which focus is employed to limit retrieval will be referred to as *focal matching* (FM). In addition to SP and KP, the process of FM utilizes focal perspective (FP) and the list of entities contained in a given focus (LECF). Focal perspective contains the set of vertices and lines which are in focus. The process of FM differs in explicit and inexplicit matching. If a focus is explicit, the focal perspective can be either one active space or the perspective of all open focal spaces. In the case of inexplicit focus, the focal perspective consists of the inexplicit focal spaces corresponding to all the entities contained in the explicit focus (for instance, the perspectives of structure space and of connection space corresponding to each event are used). An LECF contains those entities from an SP which are connected with elements of a focal space. An example of how the list of entities contained in a focus is used is the requirement that the referent of a nominal reference should be included in the focus. This requirement corresponds to a focal matching where the LECF contains the vertex of the SP corresponding to the prop word (i.e., nucleus) of the nominal group.

The inclusion of entities from an SP in the focus strongly limits retrieval in a KP. The entities for an LECF are considered to be the first candidates from an SP to participate in matching. If matching has been completed successfully, this allows us to limit the other entities from an SP. If the matching of entities from an LECF fails, we can try matching without the use of focus.

Focal perspective makes it possible to establish the order of elements from the KP used for initial matching with chosen entities from the SP. Each step in the work of the algorithm of matching starts with selecting elements of an FS which are relevant first for direct matching (entities from an SP are connected with entities explicitly indicated in the KP), and then for inference matching (with the use of general rules of inferring which generate new elements in the KP). Consequently, focus influences the order in which deduction is applied (see Sect. 6.4) in the process of establishing correspondence.

Figures 6.6 and 6.7 illustrate how focus is used to reduce the number of candidates that have to be considered during the process of matching (Fig. 6.6 refers to a KP, and Fig. 6.7 to an SP). The KP in Fig. 6.6 contains several chairs: C_1, made of wood (in focus F_1); C_2, made of wood (in focus F_2); C_3, made of metal (in focus F_2); and C_4, made of metal (out of focus). The SP in Fig. 6.7

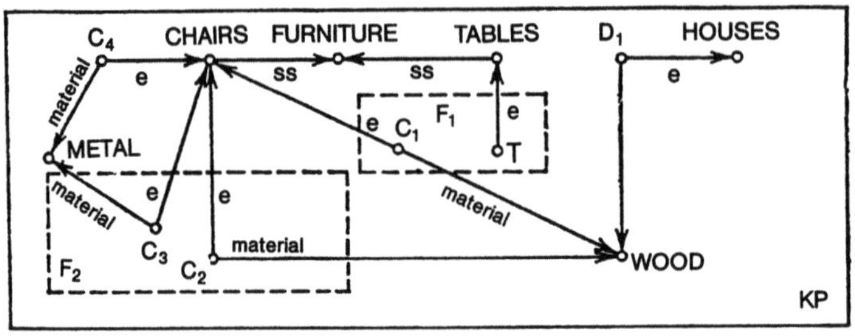

Fig. 6.6. Example of a knowledge perspective (KP) with two focal spaces

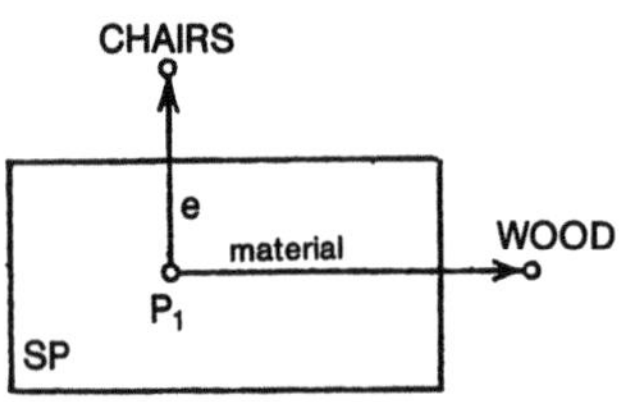

Fig. 6.7. The perspective of the phrase "wooden chair"

contains the structure corresponding to the phrase "wooden chair". If we attempted to match the KP with the SP without the use of focus, it would be necessary to regard as a candidate corresponding to P_1 either all vertices connected by an "e" line with the vertex CHAIRS (C_1, C_2, C_3, C_4), or all vertices connected by a "material" line with the vertex WOOD (D_1, CHAIRS, C_2); this depends on which of these two sets is the smaller. The use of focus allows us to reduce the amount of time spent on making a choice. If the focal space F_1 is employed, only the vertices C_1 and T will have to be considered. The vertex T will be rejected, as it is not connected, either directly or indirectly, with the vertex CHAIRS. If the focus F_2 is used, only the vertices C_2 and C_3 have to be considered; the latter, however, will be rejected since it is not connected with the vertex WOOD. The effect achieved by using a focus can be enhanced considerably if inferring is used in establishing correspondence. For instance, it is possible to reject an entire rule with the use of focus, whereas without it entities governed by this rule are rejected separately, one by one.

6.3.5 Shifting Focus: Use of Focus to Identify References

To complete our description of focus we shall now consider the problem of how focus can be changed (i.e., shifts of focus). A shift of focus can be indicated explicitly in a discourse (e.g., "I have accomplished this stage", "What should be done now?", "Let us change the subject"), but it is usually expressed inexplicitly. What it is that indicates a shift of focus depends on the participants' objectives (the macrostructure of the dialogue, see Sect. 4.1) and on the subject (task) of the dialogue (i.e., the structure of the dialogue). Let us concentrate on the widespread type of dialogue where the subject concerned involves the performance of a task (see Sect. 4.1). The structure of dialogues of this type, reflecting as it does the structure of the task at hand, is the main indicator of a shift of focus. In most systems developed so far (Winograd 1972; Norman et al. 1975; Walker et al. 1976) the structure of a dialogue is not taken into consideration, i.e., it is assumed that the discourse is linear (structureless). However, to limit retrieval – e.g., when looking for the referent of a nominal reference – scanning only covers a fixed number of preceding sentences. This means, in fact, that only the most recently encountered notions are brought into focus. For dialogues of the type we are now considering, a shift of focus occurs every time an old task is completed or a new one begins. When a reference to a subtask is encountered in a dialogue, a new active focal space (*Y*) is created; this is included in the current active focal space *X* (which becomes an open focal space). Once the subtask has been performed, the corresponding space *Y* is closed and the old space *X* (i.e., the higher-level space) becomes active again. These processes can also be "immersed" into one another. Any word combination can indicate the need for a shift in focus: a nominal group, a verbal group, or an attributive group. However, although an individual word combination may indicate the need for a shift, in order to determine the form of this shift the whole sentence has to be analyzed. For example, while an isolated nominal group (*X*) may indicate the need for a shift to a certain task, the same *X*, treated as a constituent part of a verbal group, may indicate a shift to a different task. Let us give an example of the interrelation between shifting focus and retrieving the referent of a nominal reference. Grosz (1977a) gives a detailed description of the interaction between different types of word combinations during the process of shifting focus.

The manner in which a nominal group may indicate a shift of focus will be illustrated by the example of a dialogue between an instructor and an apprentice who is to assemble a compressor (Grosz 1977a). Figure 6.8 shows the hierarchy of subtasks that the process of assembling a compressor can be divided into. The representation of information about the structure of the task in the form of a semantic network is shown in Fig. 6.9. The continuous lines in Fig. 6.8 indicate the hierarchy of tasks, while the broken lines represent the chronological order in

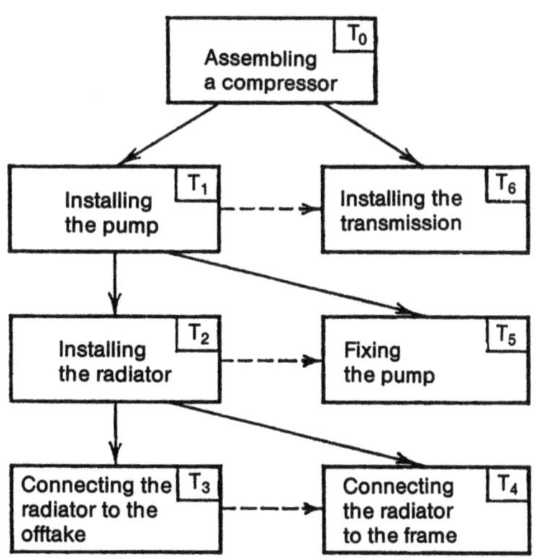

Fig. 6.8. Example of a hierarchy of tasks

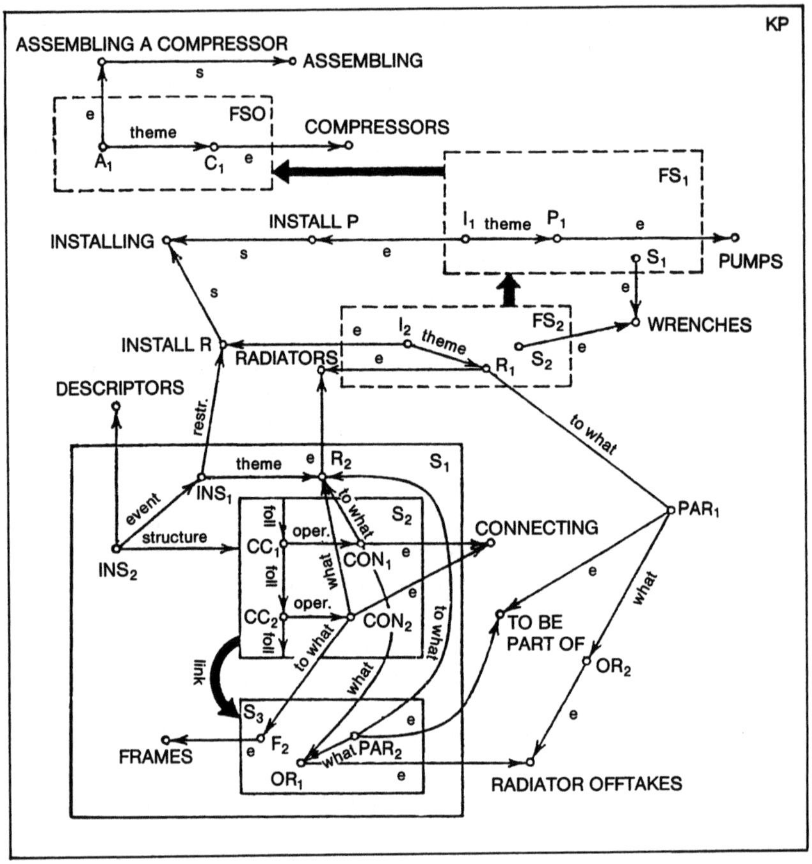

Fig. 6.9. An example of shift of focus induced by a nominal group

which these tasks should be performed. Let us suppose that at a given moment in time task T_2 (installing the radiator) is being carried out. The focal spaces FS_0, FS_1, and FS_2 correspond to the subtasks T_0, T_1, and T_2 respectively. FS_2 is an active focal space. The perspective (FS_1 and FS_0) is a hierarchy of open focal spaces. Nominal references to an object contained in the active focal space or in either of the open focal spaces do not induce a shift of focus. Referents are sought in the active focal space, and then, if not found there, in the open focal spaces. Phrases such as "this radiator", "the wrench just mentioned", etc., refer to objects from FS_2; these references will not lead to a change in focus. Phrases such as "the given pump" or "this compressor" will be analyzed first in FS_2, then in FS_1 and FS_0. These will not induce a shift in focus either. In the phrases just quoted, the words "this", "the given", and "just mentioned" stress that these phrases do not refer to *any* radiator, *any* pump, or *any* wrench; they refer to the concrete radiator, pump, or wrench just mentioned in the text. Let us note that in contrast to Russian, where such qualifications require full words (e.g., *etot, upomianutiy* [this, the mentioned]), in the English language the same function is fulfilled by the definite article *the*, which precedes the given word. In comparison with Russian, therefore, references in the English language can be identified much more easily.

References to a new task (of a parallel or higher level) or to a subtask of the task at hand induce a change of focus. In the example in question, the space S_1 (see Fig. 6.9) contains a description of the process of installing a radiator (INSTALL R). The structure space (S_2) is the inexplicit focus for the vertex INS_2. It shows that the installation of the radiator is carried out in two stages (tasks T_3 and T_4 in Fig. 6.8). The first stage consists in connecting the radiator to one of its parts – the offtake. In the situation shown in Fig. 6.9 the radiator offtake is not included in explicit foci (i.e., in the active and open spaces). Thus, the nominal reference "radiator offtake" indicates the possibility of a shift of focus to task T_3. If the remaining part of a sentence containing this nominal reference does not contradict the proposed shift, a new focal space (FS_3) will be created, lower than FS_2 in the hierarchy. The sentence "Connect the radiator offtake to the radiator" may serve as an example of a sentence that does not contradict the shift; on the other hand, the sentence "The offtake is broken" does contradict it. Note here that a shift of focus may entail both defining certain new entities and identifying certain real entities corresponding to hypothetical entities in inexplicit focus. For instance, if focus is shifted to task T_3, OR_2 (the radiator offtake) is brought into focus. If the phrase "the radiator offtake just mentioned" is now encountered, it will be identified with OR_2 (i.e., the new focal space will contain the vertex OR_2). As we can see, the use of focus makes the process of identifying nominal references considerably different from the previous process of seeking referents by exhaustive scanning of the preceding part of the discourse.

6.3.6 Other Applications of Focus

In addition to those already mentioned, the following problems should be resolved by the system if it is to understand a dialogue. First, a choice must be made: should information deduced by the system be memorized, or should it be reconstructed all over again when it is needed? In the ideal situation, information should be stored for as long as it is needed and then erased from the system's memory (forgotten). Second, every entity can be considered from a number of different angles. The problem here is how to determine which of these angles is appropriate in a given discourse. Focus may be employed to solve both of these problems. In the first case, the role of focus consists in the following: Let us assume the system has come to a certain conclusion (e.g., that the vertex X under consideration is connected with a certain vertex Y). Information about this conclusion may be added to the current focal space (for the above example, this means that a line connecting X with Y is added to the focus). The information is kept there until the given focal space is closed. In this way, the use of a focal space provides easy access to relevant information, while allowing the system to "forget" this information as soon as it has become irrelevant.

The second problem stems from the necessity of examining a notion N from several different angles. The use of focus makes it possible to distinguish one particular angle that is appropriate in the given discourse. Lines running from entities in focus to those out of focus ensure that access to the most relevant information is given preference during the process of matching. The fact that access to various pieces of information is differentiated does not mean that a given notion can be considered from only one angle. Focus only influences the order in which different angles are considered.

6.4 Interpretation of an Input Text: Inferring

This section will be devoted to a description of that component of an SNL designed to retrieve and infer information (as determined by the input text) from the knowledge possessed by the system. Retrieval and inferring constitute a reaction on the part of a system to the input text. The range of possible reactions is extremely broad, and is determined by the system's "intellectual prowess". In the simplest variant, the system is able to understand the input text literally and to determine the facts required by retrieval from its own knowledge and by inferring and calculations. In more developed variants the system should: take into account its own objectives and views as well as the user's; consider how the input text influences its own need; formulate its own objectives and perform actions which lead to these objectives being achieved; and consider how its own actions and the user's will influence future states of the surrounding world. The capabilities of the systems that exist at present are not so extensive. Nevertheless, in this section we shall be examining how these capabilities might be acquired.

At the stage of interpretation, the input text is represented by a statement (X). If an input sentence is a general question (e.g., "Does factory A produce lathes B?"), then X (or $\neg X$) is sought in the system's knowledge. If an input sentence is a particular question (e.g., "What products are produced by factory A?", i.e., ($\exists y \in$ PRODUCTS) TO PRODUCE (FACTORY A, y)), then the system's task is to find those values of variables where the statement X holds true. Note that a question put to the system need not take the form of an interrogative sentence (e.g., "Inform me as to the speed of a TU-135 airplane").

6.4.1 General Structure of the Process of Interpreting and Inferring (PII)

Information indicated in an input text may be stored in the system in different forms. First, in explicit form – in the form of a *concrete* fact represented in the semantic network. Second, in inexplicit form – in the form of knowledge different from the semantic network, such as files from which information is accessible by certain specialized procedures connected with certain vertices of the network. Third, in the form of *general* statements – inexplicit, nonconcrete statements memorized as theorems in the semantic network. The work of the PII depends on the form in which the system stores information indicated on input. In order to extract information that is relevant to a given input text from the system, it is generally necessary to employ deductive reasoning. We shall use so-called natural inferring as a deductive mechanism (Bledsoe 1971; Bledsoe et al. 1972). It should be emphasized that there are other methods of inferring, such as the formal one (Nilsson 1971), that based on blurred sets (Yezhkova and Pospelov 1977, 1978), etc. In natural inferring, two network structures are used to represent input – one corresponds to the input sentence and the other to the system's knowledge. The mechanism of inferring views the input as a pattern and attempts to find examples of such a pattern in the system's knowledge. In other words, an input is considered to be a theorem that is to be proved by definition, i.e., by connecting the pattern's variables with concrete elements of the system's knowledge. For instance, the question "Who produces lathes *B*?" will be transformed into the theorem:

$(\exists x)$ TO PRODUCE (x, LATHES B).

An answer takes the form of a list of connections (x, FACTORY A), and may be obtained either by retrieving or inferring, or with the aid of specialized procedures – dependent on the form in which the system stores information. Let us assume, for instance, that the user has posed the question: "Which factory produces lathes with the brand name *B*?", and the system stores, in explicit form, the fact j that "Factory *A* produces lathes with the brand name *B*". In this case, simple retrieval from the set of all facts "to produce" will suffice to answer the question. Let us now suppose, however, that this fact is not represented in the system's knowledge in the form of a concrete statement, but in the form of the theorem i: "All roughing lathes are produced by factory *A*", and the fact $(j+1)$: "Lathes with the brand name *B* are roughing lathes". An act of deduction will then have to be carried out to answer the question; during this act, the theorem i and the fact $(j+1)$ will both be employed. If neither this theorem nor this fact is known, but the system stores the theorem $(i+1)$: "The function PRODUCER (X, Y) determines the one who produces (Y) by what is produced (X)", then the answer may be obtained by calling the function PRODUCER (LATHE B, y).

The perspective of the sentence being processed (SP) and the knowledge perspective (KP) are both inputted to the PII stage. The SP is a statement that may be regarded as a pattern (with variables from the SP) matched with the KP. Successful matching produces a list of pairs, with each element of the SP being put into correspondence with an element of the KP. For instance, Fig. 6.10 shows the form of the SP and KP for the question: "What lathes are produced by factory *A*?" In analyzing this KP, the system will examine elements of the set TO PRODUCE (P_1 and P_2) which are connected by an "agent" line with FACTORY *A*, and by a "theme" line with vertices which, in turn, are connected by an "ss" line with the set LATHES. Every vertex connected by a "theme" line with the subset (P_1, P_2) of the set TO PRODUCE will constitute an answer to the initial question. The PII component generates answers to an input text in the form of a list containing connections for each element of the SP. When one answer has already been found, the PII component may repeat its action, thus obtaining another answer (if one exists). An answer is formulated in the form of a list of pairs. The first part of the first pair bears the name ANSWER. As a result of the operations of the PII, the following values may be assigned to this variable: YES, NO, UNKNOWN. The value YES is assigned when a counterpart to each element of an SP has been found. The value NO is assigned when it has been proved that there is an element of the SP that cannot be put into correspondence with any element of the KP. In all other cases the variable ANSWER is given the value UNKNOWN.

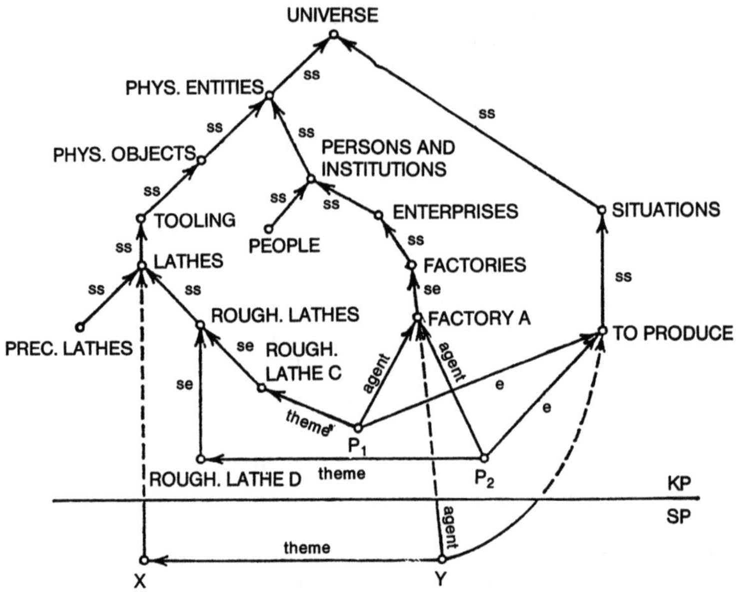

Fig. 6.10. The knowledge perspective (KP) and sentence perspective (SP) for the question: "What lathes are produced by factory *A*?"

It has already been indicated that the work of the PII depends on the form in which the system stores information. An example of interpretation, using the sentence "Which enterprise produces precision lathes of the type *C*?", is depicted in Fig. 6.11 (space SP_1). To obtain an answer, it is necessary to retrieve a fact stored explicitly in the system. The work of the PII results in the creation of the following pairs, each consisting of an element of the SP_1 and a corresponding element of the KP: 1. the line "Y_1 – theme → PREC. LATHE *C*" and the line "P_1 – theme → PREC. LATHE *C*"; 2. the line "Y_1 – agent → X_1" and the line "P_1 – agent → FACTORY *A*"; 3. the line "Y_1 – e → TO PRODUCE" and the line "P_1 – e → TO PRODUCE"; 4. the vertex Y_1 and the vertex P_1; 5. the vertex X_1 and the vertex FACTORY *A*. The answer to the question posed is: X_1 = FACTORY *A*. Let us note that to obtain this answer it was necessary to infer that "FACTORY *A* – e → ENTERPRISE". This inference is based on the properties of the relations "ss" (separate subsets) and "se" (separate elements). Such inferences, built into the process of retrieval, will not be considered to constitute examples of inferring (although in fact they do), as we want to distinguish them from inferring based on theorems.

An example of interpreting the sentence "Which enterprise produces roughing lathes of the type *D*?" is also shown in Fig. 6.11 (space SP_2). To answer this question it is necessary to make an inference on the basis of the theorem: "Factory *B* produces all roughing lathes" (i.e., "only FACTORY *B* produces roughing lathes"). This theorem will be found using the line "e" running from vertex P to the vertex TO PRODUCE. The process of unification, i.e., of substituting concrete values for variables (see Popov and Firdman 1976, Sect. 5.2), allows us to

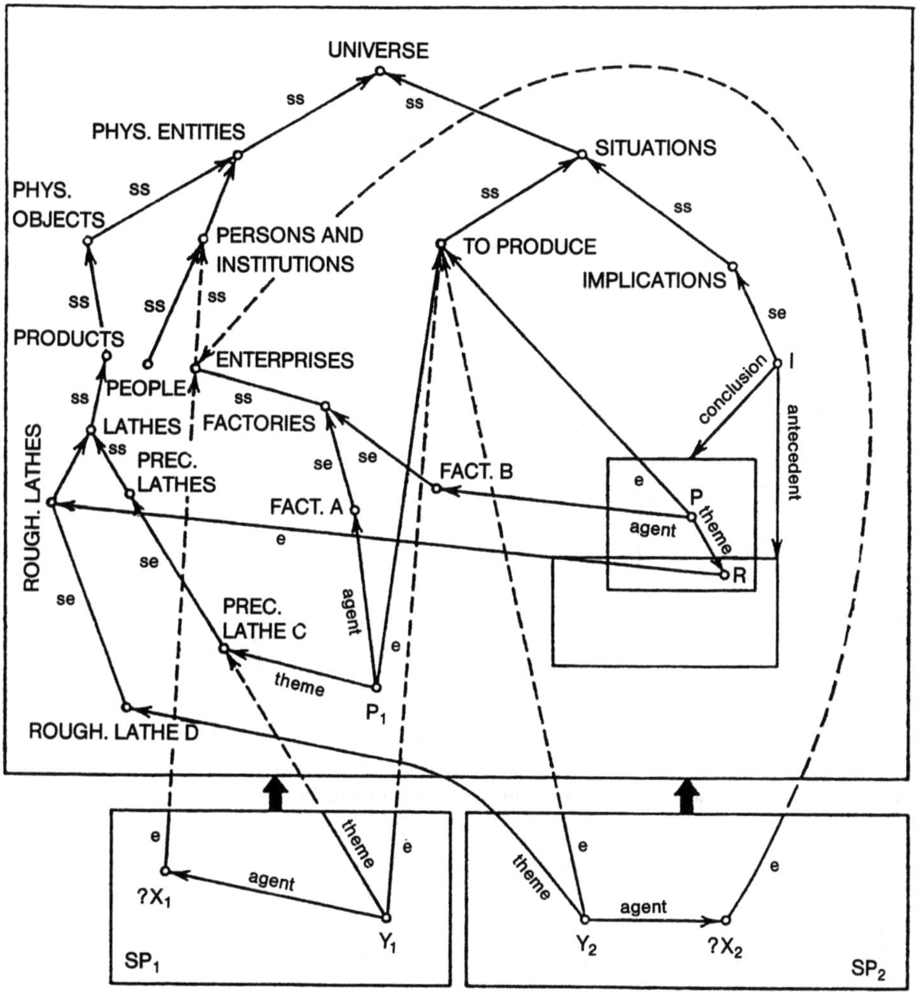

Fig. 6.11. Interpretation of two sentences (SP_1 and SP_2). SP_1 – retrieval; SP_2 – retrieval and inferring

determine that the relevant example of the theorem involves substituting the value ROUGH. LATHE *D* for the variable *R* (subjected to universal quantification). The theorem states that: "If it can be proven that ROUGH. LATHE *D* is an "e" of the set ROUGH. LATHES, then a new element of the situation TO PRODUCE exists". To establish the truthfulness of the antecedent, a new subtask is created. Performing this subtask results in the creation of a new situation belonging to TO PRODUCE and connected with Y_2. This provides a link between X_2 and the vertex FACTORY *B*. Another way of interpreting the same sentence ("Which enterprise produces roughing lathes of the type *D*?") is shown in Fig. 6.12. In this case, the information required to formulate an answer is stored in inexplicit form and can be found using the specialized procedure

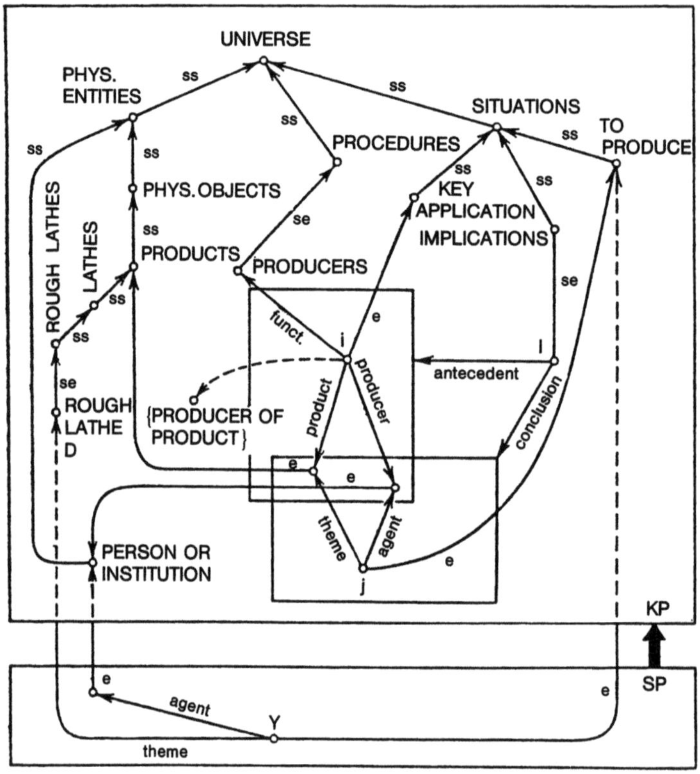

Fig. 6.12. Interpretation of sentence using specialized functions

PRODUCERS (*X, Y*). Retrieval of the required information is carried out with the help of the theorem which states that the specialized procedure PRODUCERS may be employed to obtain information about an element of the set TO PRODUCE. The use of this theorem is similar to the use of the theorem from the preceding example (Fig. 6.11, the space SP_2). The theorem creates a subproblem, which is an example of the theorem's antecedent. The procedure PRODUCERS creates an element of the set KEY APPLICATION in the KP. This element provides the connections that are needed to solve the subproblem (the set APPLICATION makes it possible to represent explicitly in the semantic network metarelations between the set of relations and the procedures that calculate them). A new element of the set TO PRODUCE is then created; this allows us to establish the connections needed to answer the initial question.

The operation of the PII can be outlined as follows: The PII analyzes all the unlinked lines in an SP, attempting to find corresponding lines in the KP. If such lines are in fact found, the initial and final vertices of the lines are also put into correspondence. This process is repeated until all the lines in the SP are linked. From the practical point of view, this process is extremely complex, so it has to be supervised by some controlling structure. The difficulties here are aggravated by the fact that at every step of the process there are several alternative ways of continuing it. First, any of the unlinked lines in an SP can be chosen for matching, and for each such line there are several lines in the KP that may possibly correspond to it. Second, some structures from an SP cannot be directly matched with the KP, because the facts in it are represented either inexplicitly or in the form of general statements. The deductive mechanism should be activated to elaborate an explicit representation that could be put into correspondence with structures of the KP. Third, during the work of the deductive mechanism a choice has to be made between alternative strategies leading to an inference, and between statements from the KP that may be used to create structures in the KP which could be put into correspondence with structures in the SP.

The controlling component of PII therefore creates a tree of alternative possibilities. Each vertex of this tree forms an "informational environment" which includes the set of choices of sentences and subproblems. The processes of retrieval and inferring always take place in some "environment" of this tree. Any choice made by the controlling component occurs in a certain environment (X^i). To represent the result of the choice a new environment (X_1^i) is created (this is a descendant of X^i). A typical example of a choice that produces the creation of a new environment is the establishment of a connection for an element of the SP. Such a choice may contradict other choices and limit possible connections. A particular choice of connecting an element of an SP with some element of the KP should be considered separately (i.e., in a different environment) from other possible choices of connecting this element. Another typical example of a choice that produces the creation of a new environment is the formation of a subproblem during the process of inferring. For instance, during the processing of an implication, a subproblem may be created for which the antecedent of the implication is assumed to be true; what is sought is a connection for the implication's conclusion. The descendant of an environment inherits all the knowledge that was connected with the parental environment. Thus, for instance, the environment X_1^i indicated above contains all connections that were present in X^i, as well as the new connection for, say, z.

The work of the controlling component begins at one vertex of the tree of environment. Three subtasks are then created: the searches for the answers YES, NO, and UNKNOWN. The alternatives are then investigated. Let us suppose that the search for the answer YES has been chosen. This starts with the procedure of choosing an element from the SP in question. Preference is given to those elements with the minimum number of candidates for connections (i.e., preference is given to elements that involve the most rigid limitations). Potential candidates from the KP are then selected for each element of the SP. The order in which these candidates are considered is one of the most important factors in determining the efficiency of the operation. Generally speaking, preference is given to candidates that do not require inferring while being processed. Of the other candidates (i.e., those that do require inferring), those from higher-level spaces are considered first. The choice of a particular line from the SP corresponds to several different strategies of choice. Each such strategy is a function that carries out connections, and indicates – if necessary – what additional strategies it may need. Every new function for connecting added to the system is added to the common list of strategies. The mechanism of calling a function of connecting by pattern provides a means of choosing a strategy. Let us consider the standard function of connecting (CONNECTION ST). This is called when no specialized procedures have been assigned to the chosen line. The standard (nonspecialized) function generates candidates for connections in the following way. Let us assume that the chosen element of the given SP is the vertex Q_1. Each line α ($Q_1 - R \rightarrow N_i$, where R is a relation) originating at Q_1 indicates a potential connection. In particular, if the vertex N_i is connected with some vertex from the KP, such as K_i, (or if N_i itself lies in the KP), then all initial vertices K_i^j of the lines (of type R) that enter K_i are potential candidates for connection with Q_1. The built-in mechanism of drawing conclusions (see below) will have to be used when the relation is of the type "e" ("se") or "s" ("ss").

Let us now suppose that the chosen element of the SP is a line α ($Q_1 - R \rightarrow N_i$), and that the vertex Q_1 is connected with a vertex K_1^1. Every line of the type R originating at K_1^1 is then a candidate for connection with the line α. This point holds true if R is "e" or "s".

Let us clarify what we have said above using the example of the SP and KP shown in Fig. 6.11. Let the chosen element of the SP be the vertex Y_1. The line "Y_1 – e → TO PRODUCE" originates at Y_1 and is connected with the vertex TO PRODUCE in the KP. All vertices (P_1 and P) which are connected with TO PRODUCE by the "e" line are candidates for connection with Y_1. Preference is given to the vertex P_1, as it lies in a higher-level space and a connection with it does not require the mechanism of deduction. Let us suppose now that the line α(Y_1 – theme → PREC. LATHE C) has been chosen, and that the vertex Y_1 is connected with the vertex P_1 from the KP. The line "P_1 – theme → PREC. LATHE C" is then a candidate for connection with α.

To limit the number of potential candidates, a special function is introduced – BRANCHING. This function's role resembles that of unification in theorem proving (see Popov and Firdman 1976, Sect. 5.2), i.e., BRANCHING determines the set of substitutions that must be made for matching to be carried out. The input of the function consists of an element (X) from an SP and an element (Y) from the KP that is a possible candidate for connection with X. The task of BRANCHING is to determine the set of connections which result from the fact that X is connected with Y. For instance, connecting lines entails connecting the corresponding initial and final vertices. If several semantic cases stem from one vertex, and the vertex is connected with another one by one of them, restrictions are thereby imposed upon connections involving the other lines. Let us now assume that the choice of a potential candidate (after the function BRANCHING has been applied) entails certain connections that contradict those already established. In this case, BRANCHING rejects the candidate in question. If a potential candidate has not been rejected by the function BRANCHING, the standard procedure CONNECTION ST is brought into operation. This determines whether inferring is needed for this particular connection. If inferring is not needed, the procedure creates a descendant of the environment (in the tree of environments) by copying the parental environment and establishing a link between the candidate involved from the SP and the potential candidate from the KP (referred to as the "target element" after the link has already been established). Thus, at every moment of time, every terminal environment in the tree is in fact a partially formulated answer to an input sentence. In the process of choosing potential candidates and carrying out the procedure CONNECTION ST (without inferring), the built-in functions draw certain conclusions, making it possible to find candidates that are connected by the lines "e" ("se") and "s" ("ss"). These built-in functions ensure the following:

1. For every vertex v, obtaining vertices w, such that $v - \mathrm{e} \rightarrow w$, $w - \mathrm{e} \rightarrow v$, $v - \mathrm{s} \rightarrow w$, and $w - \mathrm{e} \rightarrow v$
2. For every two vertices v and w, determining whether the following relations between v and w are true: $v - \mathrm{s} \rightarrow w$, $w - s \rightarrow v$, $v - e \rightarrow w$, $w - \mathrm{e} \rightarrow v$. The possible answers here are: YES, NO, UNKNOWN.

In addition, there is a recursive rule that is also built in: two sets are different if either of the vertices that represent them is connected with the same vertex (z) by an "ss" line, or if these sets are subsets ("s") of two different sets.

It should be stressed that the fact that such conclusions can be drawn solely by using built-in functions and procedures makes it possible to infer swiftly and automatically, without using the standard (general) mechanism of inferring. If inferring is needed, the CONNECTION calls the procedure EXTRACTION. This procedure may be employed – where necessary – for an SP as well as for a KP. The procedure EXTRACTION "extracts" – from a theorem that is a general statement – a concrete piece of information that may be matched with the processed element of an SP. The extraction is carried out by creating subtasks and suppositions to be inferred. Once the required information has been extracted, the procedure CONNECTION ST comes into operation and performs the connection. The entire process is then repeated with new elements from the SP until all the elements are exhausted. If an attempt to obtain the answer YES results in failure, an analogous attempt to obtain the answer NO is carried out. If this also ends in failure the answer will be UNKNOWN.

6.4.2 Checking Applicability and Matching Immersed Structures

When the procedure CONNECTION ST has already considered all concrete (i.e., explicit) candidates for connection, it moves on to an analysis of general and inexplicit statements (e.g., implications, disjunctions, negations). Such inexplicit statements (InS) form the basis for deriving the connection required. When an InS is found it is checked for applicability to determine whether this particular statement may be of use in inferring a connection for the particular element of the SP. The task of such checks is to unify (to match) a statement from the KP with the statement from the SP containing the given element. If matching is successful, it produces the set of substitutions for universally quantified variables. These substitutions "define" the InS involved with the help of the KP; in this way, the resulting statement may be matched with a statement from the SP.

Performing these checks is by no means a straightforward task, since the facts in both an SP and a KP are not stored in canonical form. This approach enables statements to be stored in the most convenient and effective form for the given subject matter; moreover, it makes it possible to avoid time-consuming transformations of input statements into their canonical form, and vice versa. However, the fact that the canonical form is not used leads to certain difficulties, particularly during the attempt to determine the logical sign of a relation or the quantifier governing a given variable. Thus, for instance, the statement

$$(\neg x \wedge y) \rightarrow (\neg u \vee v)$$

may also be written in the following forms:

$$(y \wedge u \wedge \neg v) \rightarrow x$$
$$(\neg x \wedge u \wedge \neg v) \rightarrow \neg y$$
$$(\neg x \wedge y \wedge \neg v) \rightarrow \neg u$$
$$(\neg x \wedge y \wedge u) \rightarrow v$$

and, consequently, may be employed to prove $x, \neg y, \neg u, v$. This statement may also be used to infer a connection for x, but not for $\neg x$. The logical sign of a relation contained in a given statement (X) that is to be used for inferring may be defined as the sign that this relation assumes when the statement X is reduced to its disjunctive normal form (see Mendelson 1964). For the statement mentioned above, for example, the disjunctive normal form is $x \vee \neg y \vee \neg u \vee v$. There are only two rules that produce a change of the sign of a relation while transforming a given statement into disjunctive normal form. These are:

$$\neg(\neg x) \equiv x,$$
$$(x \rightarrow y) \equiv (\neg x \vee y).$$

Consequently, the logical sign of a relation may be calculated by counting negative spaces and the spaces of the antecedents of implications that the given relation is included in. This allows us to compare logical signs of relations that are included in two statements which are to be matched.

Let us now suppose that the two statements being matched are not expressed in canonical form. It is then necessary to be able to determine what type of quantifier (the universal or the existential one) refers to each variable in a given statement. For example, the statement

$$[\neg(\forall x) P(x) \wedge (\forall y) Q(y)] \rightarrow (\exists z) R(z)$$

may also be written in the following forms:

$$[(\forall y) Q(y) \wedge \neg(\exists z) R(z)] \rightarrow (\forall x) P(x)$$
$$[\neg(\forall x) P(x) \wedge \neg(\exists z) R(z)] \rightarrow (\exists y) \neg Q(y)$$

and, consequently, may be used to prove $(\exists z) R(z)$, $(\exists y) \neg Q(y)$, and $(\forall x) P(x)$. The statement may also be used in inferring a connection with a vertex which is governed by the existential quantifier and participates in the R-relation. The type of quantification of variables entering relations contained in a given statement may be determined on the basis of the type of quantification of these variables when the statement is reduced to its preliminary normal form (see Mendelson 1964). Thus, the preliminary normal form of the statement indicated above reads:

$$(\forall x)(\exists y)(\exists z) \{[\neg P(X) \wedge Q(y)] \rightarrow R(z)\}.$$

There are only two rules that can change the type of quantification when a statement is being transformed to its preliminary normal form. These are:

1. $\neg(\forall x) P(x) \equiv (\exists x) \neg P(x)$ and
   $\neg(\exists x) P(x) \equiv (\forall x) \neg P(x)$.
2. $[(\forall x) P(x) \rightarrow y] \equiv (\exists x)[P(x) \rightarrow y]$ and
   $[(\exists x) P(x) \rightarrow y] \equiv (\forall x)[P(x) \rightarrow y]$.

Thus, as we noted, the type of variable in a statement may be determined by counting the negative spaces and the spaces of the antecedent of implications which this variable is included in. Let us note here that this rule for determining the type of quantification of variables (vertices) coincides with the one for determining the logical sign of relations (lines).

The process of matching, performed with the aid of the checks already described, is a generalization of the process of BRANCHING; logically, it is identical to the unification of the formulae of predicate calculus in theorem proving (on this subject, see Popov and Firdman 1976, Sect. 5.2). This process consists in attempting to find substitutions that allow two descriptive sets (SP and KP) to be matched with each other. An SP contains a description of elements that should be found in the KP or inferred from it. If matching is accomplished successfully, it determines the set of substitutions – for variables governed by the universal quantifier – that have to be carried out if certain elements of the KP (the description KP) are to answer the description SP. These substitutions make it possible to produce "examples" of statements from the KP, which may then serve as a basis for inferring. Let us suppose, for instance, that the chosen line from an SP is a constituent part of a relation $Q(a)$, and that the candidate for connection is the antecedent of the implication $(\forall x)(P(x) \rightarrow Q(x))$. The "example" created will then read $P(a) \rightarrow Q(a)$.

The following principal rules are applied in matching "immersed" structures (i.e., structures that are not at the outer level, and therefore require inferring to be matched). Variables from the KP that are governed by the existential quantifier (existential variables) may be placed in correspondence with existential variables from an SP, or with universal variables from the KP (i.e., variables governed by the universal quantifier). Universal variables from an SP may be put into correspondence with universal variables from the KP and existential variables from the SP. These rules are a direct consequence of the rules of unification. The central idea here is that rules of inferring correspond to those of unification in proving by negation when matching of the knowledge base is carried out by negating the input sentence.

Let us now clarify the notions of checking applicability and matching "immersed" structures by the example shown in Fig. 6.11 (space SP_2). In this case the system – with the help of standard means of connection – will establish that the line $\alpha(P - \text{e} \rightarrow \text{TO PRODUCE})$ indicates that the implication (I) is useful for connecting α with the line β ($Y_2 - \text{e} \rightarrow$ TO PRODUCE). Since both these lines (relations) have the same (positive) logical sign, the particular relation TO PRODUCE, inferred from the implication, will have the necessary (positive) logical sign. The process carries out connections for the vertices Y_2, X_2, and R, and for the lines "theme" and "agent". All members of the resulting pairs have positive signs, except for the vertex R. The negative sign of R (which is an element of the KP) indicates that R is a universal variable, and thus may be connected with a positive existential variable from the KP, i.e., with the vertex ROUGH. LATHES. The resulting substitution (R, ROUGH. LATHES) provides an example of an implication utilized to infer (FACTORY B – TO PROCUCE – ROUGH. LATHES).

6.4.3 Extraction from Immersed Structures

When the applicable inexplicit statements in the KP have been determined, inferring may be taken to be the process of extracting from these statements (using the procedure EXTRACTION) the required relations, which are such that they or their negation provide the sought-for connection at the outer level of the KP.

Inferring starts with the creation of a suitable example of a statement from the KP (indicated by checking applicability; see Sect. 6.4.2), and the application of the rules of extraction to it (these rules are given in Table 6.1). If the variables of an implication containing universal variables have been defined, they are included in a subproblem produced by extracting an antecedent (rule 3 in Table 6.1) or a conclusion (rule 4). They are then available for connection in the process of solving the subproblem. For instance, let an initial implication take the form

$$(\forall x)\,(\forall y)\,(P(x, y) \rightarrow Q(x, y)),$$

and after the process of defining has been accomplished, the form

$$(\forall x)\,(P(x, a) \rightarrow Q(x, a)).$$

If the conclusion is extracted from the defined implication, then the subproblem "Find such an x that $P(x, a)$" is created. If this subproblem is then solved, the statement is $Q(\langle\text{connecting } x\rangle, a)$.

A relation that is to be extracted may be immersed in another inexplicit statement. It is then necessary to apply the rules of extraction several times. The rules are applied "from the top downwards", i.e., from outer inexplicit statements to more internal ones. All rules of extraction are applied before the stage of solving subproblems that have arisen. Let us suppose, for instance, that what is required is to extract the relation $B(x)$ from the statement

$$A(x) \rightarrow (B(x) \vee \neg C(x)).$$

Applying the third rule from Table 6.1, we extract $B(x) \vee \neg C(x)$, with $A(x)$ thus remaining to be proven. Then, applying the first rule to $B(x) \vee \neg C(x)$, we extract the desired relation $B(x)$, and $C(x)$ remains to be proven. What is to be proven, i.e., $A(x) \wedge C(x)$, may now be considered to be a single subproblem, instead of two separate ones.

Table 6.1. Rules of extraction for inferring

No.	What is to be extracted?	Given	What is to be proved?
1	x_i	$x_1 \vee \ldots \vee x_n$	$\neg x_1 \wedge \ldots \wedge \neg x_{i-1} \wedge \neg x_{i+1} \wedge \ldots \wedge \neg x_n$
2	$\neg x_i$	$\neg(x_1 \wedge \ldots \wedge x_n)$	$x_1 \wedge \ldots \wedge x_{i-1} \wedge x_{i+1} \wedge \ldots \wedge x_n$
3	x	$y \rightarrow x$	y
4	$\neg x$	$x \rightarrow y$	$\neg y$

6.4.4 Spaces of Expansion

The procedures of extraction that perform inferring require certain means to create subproblems, to make suppositions, and to infer results. In the manner of representation we have adopted, these means are provided by the division of the semantic network into spaces. The problems just indicated may be solved by adding new spaces ("spaces of expansion") to the SP and KP. The spaces of expansion that are added to the KP are used to represent suppositions and inferred results, while those added to an SP represent subproblems. Let us use an example to clarify this process. Let us consider an environment E_1, and let KP_1 be the current space from the KP (i.e., the last of those introduced), for which the task of connecting the implication $x \rightarrow y$ from the SP initiates the following inference (rule 3): x is assumed, and y is considered to be a subproblem to be proven. Inferring begins by creating an environment E_2 (a descendant of environment E_1), adding to the KP a new space of expansion KP_2 (which contains a copy of x) from E_2, adding to the SP a new space of expansion SP_2 (which contains a copy of y) from E_2, and joining a certain "demon" to SP_2 from E_2 (see Bobrow et al. 1977). When all elements of y have been connected, this demon removes space KP_2 from KP and SP_2 from SP, establishes the statement $x \rightarrow y$ in space KP_1, and assigns the result achieved to the initial implication from the SP.

When the process of extraction is repeated, the results obtained in solving one subproblem may be utilized to formulate and resolve other subproblems. To make this possible, and to avoid using the results of a subproblem in resolving this particular subproblem itself, it is necessary to observe the order in which subproblems and their results occur. This can be done by arranging each subproblem in a separate space and adding these spaces (in the form of spaces of expansion) to the SP and KP in the order in which the rules of extraction were applied.

6.4.5 Nonstandard Functions of Connection

Besides the standard procedure CONNECTION ST, nonstandard functions of connection are also widely applicable. The most important of these nonstandard procedures are those involved in the strategy of inferring when input sentences contain inexplicit statements (conjunctions, implications, etc.). As an example of such a statement, let us take the sentence, "Have all roughing lathes with the trade name *A* been produced by factory *B*?" So far we have discussed inexplicit statements occurring in the KP (i.e., in the system's knowledge), not in an SP (i.e., in an input sentence). The peculiarity of such sentences is that there is a set of entities (not just one) that corresponds to them in the KP. Nonstandard functions of connection (NFC) employ the strategy of decomposing an inexplicit input statement into a number of simpler subproblems. This can be done using the rules shown in Table 6.2. Each NFC determines the order in which it creates its subproblems, simpler ones being created first. Each solution to each subproblem creates a set of connections corresponding to the initial statement that is to be proven. While being performed, an NFC creates a subproblem in the newly created descendant of the environment. The environment is then supplemented by: (a) the addition of a new space of expansion in the KP – this space contains

Table 6.2. Rules for decomposing an inexplicit input statement

No.	Initial statement being proven	Decomposition of the initial statement
1	$x_1 \vee \ldots \vee x_n$	Generate n subproblems of the form: ASSUME: $\neg x_{i+1} \wedge \ldots \wedge \neg x_n$ AND PROVE: x_i
2	$\neg (x_1 \wedge \ldots \wedge x_n)$	Generate n subproblems of the form: ASSUME: $x_{i+1} \wedge \ldots \wedge x_n$ AND PROVE: $\neg x_i$
3	$x \rightarrow y$	Generate subproblems: a) ASSUME: x, PROVE: y b) ASSUME: $\neg y$, PROVE: $\neg x$
4	$(\forall x \in X)(P(x) \rightarrow Q(x))$	Generate subproblems: a) CREATE: x', ASSUME: $x' \in X \wedge P(x)$, PROVE: $Q(x')$ b) CREATE: x', ASSUME: $\neg Q(x')$, PROVE: $\neg (x' \in X \wedge P(x'))$

the set of suppositions; (b) the addition of a new space of expansion in the SP – this space contains the expression that is to be proven and is the one the demon is connected with. The demon begins its work as soon as the subproblem has been resolved. It creates the task of linking the result obtained with the initial statement.

Let us now explain the first of the rules shown in Table 6.2 (the second can be processed analogously). During the process of proving the initial statement (disjunction), not just one, but two subproblems are created. One of these is to prove the truthfulness of, say, x_1, and the other is to demonstrate the falseness of the supposition ($\neg x_2 \wedge \ldots \wedge \neg x_n$). The solution to the second problem is equivalent to proving the truthfulness of the disjunction $x_2 \vee \ldots \vee x_n$, which in turn is split into two subproblems, and so on. The initial problem is thus split into n subproblems.

The rules corresponding to implications differ from those corresponding to disjunction in that subproblems created during the processing of implication may lead to the processing of universal variables (rule 4 in Table 6.2). During the processing of subproblems that contain universal variables, these variables are "assumed" to be included in an expanded space KP which has been created to solve the given subproblem. The variables constitute an entity contained in the KP, about which nothing is known except for the suppositions made by the given subproblem. If a statement being proven in a given subproblem demonstrates the truthfulness of this entity, this is sufficient for the subproblem to be resolved and, consequently, for the implication to be proven. For example, let us assume the system is attempting to prove the statement, "Only factory *B* produces roughing lathes" (represented in the form of the implication, "If $x \in$ ROUGH. LATHES, then TO PRODUCE(FACTORY *B*, x)"). To process the implication, the system creates a subproblem which assumes the truthfulness of the implication's antecedent and attempts to prove the conclusion. The supposition of this subproblem is a newly created vertex x'. This vertex represents an entity which is a "roughing lathe". It should be then proved that the entity represented by x' has been produced by factory B.

Let us note that it is impossible to determine whether or not a given question contains an inexplicit statement on the basis of external appearance alone. Let us consider, for instance, the question, "How much grain was produced in region A in 1976?" This may be explicit or inexplicit, depending on the knowledge base. If the information involved is stored explicitly in the system, then the question is explicit. However, it is possible that the system stores only information about the amount of grain produced by each individual kolkhoz in this region. The question is then inexplicit. To be answered, it has to be split into several subproblems (corresponding to the number of kolkhozes in the region). The system should resolve each of these subproblems separately, as it is possible that an explicit answer will again prove unobtainable (e.g., if the system stores information only about quarterly production figures, not about annual ones). After that, the system adds up the results obtained in each subtask.

To close this section, let us note that NFCs may also be used to obtain connections with "connected procedures". This happens when, for the sake of efficiency, the representation of connected procedures does not utilize an explicit description of the metarelations between relations and the procedures that produce them (see Sect. 6.4.1).

6.4.6 The Mechanism of Proving Based on Analysis of Particular Cases

There is an important class of tasks that cannot be performed using the deductive mechanism described above. This class includes tasks requiring analysis of particular cases (Loveland and Stickel 1973). Let us explain what is involved here using an example. Let us assume it is necessary to extract a relation R from the following statement contained in the KP:

$$(P \vee Q) \wedge (P \rightarrow R) \wedge (Q \rightarrow R).$$

When the mechanism of inferring is applied to this problem it will produce a closed loop. But when the method of particular-cases analysis is used, this mechanism will, for instance, attempt to prove R in the particular case where P is true, and then to prove R assuming that Q is true. If R is proven in both cases, and if the KP contains a statement indicating that either P or Q is true, then the initial problem can be considered solved. The main obstacle in developing a mechanism able to carry out proving using particular-cases analysis is the need to create procedures that would identify these particular cases. Every inexplicit statement in the KP identifies a set of potential particular cases (the implication $x \rightarrow y$, for instance, identifies the set $\{\neg x, y\}$). Consequently, the problem of identifying particular cases can be regarded as one of selecting suitable inexplicit statements from the KP. One possible approach to the problem of the mechanism of particular-cases analysis is described by Fikes and Hendrix (1977).

7 Synthesis of Statements in Natural Language

7.1 General Model of Synthesizing Texts

From the point of view of the process of conversation, the task of the component of synthesis is to express information that the user is interested in by means of a natural language, in terms comprehensible to him. Synthesis is divided into two subtasks: extralinguistic synthesis (ES) and linguistic synthesis (LS). The first of these tasks, as its name indicates, is not directly related to linguistics, and has yet to be fully developed. The second task has been studied in much more detail, particularly by specialists in automatic translation (AT). The role of semantics in contemporary works on AT is still rather minor; greater progress has been achieved in morphological and syntactic synthesis (see Kulagina 1973; Koz'mina and Korovina 1972; Mel'chuk 1974a; Apresyan et al. 1978). Nevertheless, there are a number of works which have dealt not only with morphology and syntax, but also with semantics (these works were geared toward systems of conversation rather than AT). This category includes such works as that dealing with the BABEL system, designed by Goldman (Schank 1975a, Chap. 6); that describing the system developed by Simmons and Slocum (1972); and those on the POET system (Popov 1978a; Popov and Rodionov 1978). However, even in the systems just mentioned, ES is not taken into account. This problem has not yet been resolved. Let us enumerate the chief tasks that have to be carried out in order to perform *extralinguistic synthesis* (this list is by no means exhaustive):

1. Identifying the information that should be communicated to the user (by a direct or indirect answer)
2. Determining the level of generality of the information being synthesized
3. Selecting those aspects that characterize an event to which a question refers which interest and are comprehensible to the user
4. Splitting the information to be communicated to the user into parts (semantic subgraphs) corresponding to future statements, and establishing the appropriate order of these parts in line with the order of statements in the output text
5. Determining which aspects of reality should be expressed obligatorily and which optionally in a given statement (i.e., formulating the semantic graph of the answer)
6. Identifying the lexemes that are the most compatible with the vertices of the semantic subgraph of the statement being synthesized

Linguistic synthesis includes the following problems:

1. Determining the syntactic structure of a statement
2. Carrying out anaphoric references
3. Assigning morphological information to the vertices of the syntactic structure of the statement
4. Determining the order of words in the sentence being synthesized
5. The morphological synthesis of word forms

We shall maintain the traditional division of the process of synthesizing an output text into semantic, syntactic, and morphological stages. The stage of semantic synthesis includes extralinguistic processing, while linguistic processing is divided into syntactic and morphological synthesis.

7.2 Semantic Synthesis of the Graph of an Answer

The entities distinguished at the stage of input text processing provide the basis for the extralinguistic synthesis of the output text. These entities, however, may be represented in an output text at different levels of detail, and with different aspects of them emphasized. In addition, a text may be divided into statements in several different manners, with regard to the number of statements and also to the composition of each one.

We would like to emphasize once more that the problem of extralinguistic synthesis has not yet been developed satisfactorily. Therefore, the description of it given below can in no way be considered complete. Let us note that solutions to most of the problems of extralinguistic synthesis depend on the objectives pursued by both the user and the system during a particular conversation.

7.2.1 Identifying the Information to Be Communicated to the User

The system's reaction to an input text is determined not only by the text itself, but to a great extent also by the knowledge and abilities it possesses. If an input text is incompatible with the system's knowledge and abilities, no answer will be formulated. However, if the user is to be able to understand the reasons for this incompatibility and paraphrase the input text so as to make it understandable to the system, the latter should be able to explain the reasons for the difficulties it has encountered (by means of an indirect answer). This substage of the system's work and its "consciousness of self" are probably the most important factors determining the given system's applicability for practical purposes. The task of "consciousness of self" is to provide the given substage with a sufficient amount of information comprehensible to the user. Since the problem of the system's "consciousness of self" (its ability to explain its own actions) has not been developed in sufficient detail yet, it is advisable to use – as a first approximation – the method of templates to overcome this problem. This method boils down to considering the forms of incompatibility that may arise in processing the input text, and in determining scripts that make it possible to process these incompatibilities. The scripts contain templates of statements in the natural language which explain the reasons for the given incompatibility and propose a method of removing it. Let us mention some of the main groups of incompatibilities. The largest of these are those incompatibilities which arise owing to the system's limited abilities, which produce failures at various stages of processing the input text: e.g., at the stage of morphological analysis, this might be described by the template "the word... is lacking in the dictionary"; at the stage of syntactic analysis, by "the syntactic structure of the sentence cannot be reconstructed, as the prerequisites for the sentence to be projective are missing"; at the stage of semantic analysis, by "there is no information in the system about any semantic relationship between the words *i* and *j*"; and at the stage of interpretation, by "information referring to this period is lacking, although the system does possess information referring to...".

The second group is composed of cases where a large number of facts have been put into correspondence with an input text during the stage of interpretation. There are two principal reasons for such a state of affairs. First, the user's question may be incorrect (see Sect. 8.1) because, for instance, he does not know the amount of information possessed by the system and therefore poses a question that is not concrete enough. In such cases, the system should ask the user whether he is aware of the volume of information he is asking for. For example, if the question is: "Which factories in the U.S.S.R. manufacture plastic products?", the answer should be given in an indirect form, e.g., "In the U.S.S.R. there are 1820 factories that manufacture plastic products. Do you want a full list of them?" Second, an answer may objectively contain a large number of facts which, however, are expressed in a generalized form. For example, let us assume the following question is posed: "Which schools in the city of Leningrad had no pupils repeating a year in 1978?", and let us also assume the system stores such information about each of the schools. If there are only a few such schools, the answer may be expressed by an enumeration, i.e., extensionally (e.g., "Schools no. 256, 317, and 152"). However, if it were necessary to mention all schools, the more reasonable form of answer would be the intensional one: "No schools in the city of Leningrad had pupils repeating a year in 1978".

In order to carry out the transformation of an answer into intensional form, a system should be able to locate identical descriptions that are included in the semantic graph and to unify them to form one generalized description (this may require use of the deductive mechanism). Some of the forms of these transformations can be anticipated in the scripts of incompatibilities. However, no general method of obtaining an intensional form from an extensional one is known (it is possible that such a method does not in fact exist at all). As a consequence, some systems are not able to distinguish such cases from cases where the question is incorrect.

To close this section, let us consider another group of incompatibilities, those that arise because the system lacks the explicit information the user is asking for. We shall include here only those incompatibilities that the system is able to remove by inferring based on certain assumptions. Strictly speaking, the user may consider these assumptions to be incorrect. It is therefore advisable for the system to inform the user as to what information the inferring is based on and what final inference has been arrived at. It may turn out to be sufficient to provide such information only when the given type of inferring occurs for the first time. In subsequent cases the system could then confine itself to providing the information that the answer has been obtained by using such-and-such a type of inferring. More complete information may be printed out by the system at the user's request.

7.2.2 Determining the Level of Generality of the Answer

We have already indicated (see Sect. 4.5.2) that to formulate an answer to an input text the system should determine the level of generality (abstraction/concretization) of the facts to be communicated to the user. This is necessary to ensure that the form taken by the answer corresponds to the user's needs and to guarantee that the answer is as compact as possible. The importance of this factor can be demonstrated by the following example: Let us suppose the question is, "What is Petrov doing?" Various answers can be obtained to this, according to the level of generality chosen: "He is moving his fingers", "He is writing", "He is working on a book", "He is fulfilling his responsibility to his publishers", "He is working to earn money to buy a motorcycle", etc. The user who poses the above question in a concrete situation is usually interested in only one of these answers, the rest being either obvious or irrelevant. A general solution to this problem has not yet been found. It is obvious that in order to formulate an answer at the correct level of generality the system should be aware of the user's objectives. However, work on methods of determining the user's objectives is still at the preparatory stage, and no reliable results have yet been obtained. The best that can be done is to provide the user with the means to raise or lower the level of generality on his own (this solution, of course, is rather inconvenient for the user). In order to provide the user with the opportunity to do this, the system should model actions (both its own and those taking place in the surrounding world) at various levels of generality simultaneously. If the level of generality chosen by the system is not found satisfactory by the user, he can then pose either the question HOW? (thus concretizing the answer), or the question WHY? (thus raising the level of generality – see Sect. 2.2.5). To return to our example, if the system's answer is: "He is working on a book", then, by posing the generalizing question WHY?, the user will obtain the answer "He is fulfilling his responsibility to his publishers", whereas by posing the concretizing question HOW?, he will obtain the answer "He is writing". Let us note two of the main shortcomings of this method. First, the system wastes time formulating answers which subsequently prove to have no practical use. Second, the system is forced to model phenomena at several levels of generality at once. Attempts to remove these shortcomings lead us once again to the need for the system to understand the user's objectives, either on the basis of context, or by referring to a priori knowledge of the model of the user. The latter may be illustrated by the following question: "Who has not fulfilled the plan?" The proper level of generality can be selected practically unambiguously here on the basis of a priori knowledge of the user's objectives (the selection being carried out at the stage of analysis, not of synthesis). For example, if the question has been posed by a foreman, the appropriate answer will be: "Worker N has not fulfilled the plan"; if it has been posed by the managing director of a factory, the answer will be: "Department no. 10 has not fulfilled the plan"; if the question was put by a government minister, a possible answer might be: "The Progress factory has not fulfilled the plan"; etc. Obviously, however, a priori knowledge of the user may in itself be insufficient to determine the level of generality.

7.2.3 Selecting Those Aspects of an Answer that Interest and Are Comprehensible to the User

The problem of the comprehensibility of a statement arises when several points of view on certain objects are present in the world being modeled. Let us suppose the system knows the following ways of identifying objects: indicating their coordinates; indicating their names; indicating their owners; indicating their properties. Let us now imagine that the system is to answer the following question: "What desk is the physics textbook on?" Various answers are possible here: "On the desk with coordinates x_1, y_1"; "On desk no. 205"; "On Alexeyevsky's desk"; "On the carved one"; etc. To give preference to one of these answers, the system should know which ways of identifying objects are most convenient to the user and which of them are applicable in the given situation. For instance, identifying objects by numbers or coordinates may be inconvenient, whereas identifying them by indicating their owner may be convenient, yet inapplicable in this situation, since the user does not know which desk belongs to Alexeyevsky.

Another problem associated with the one outlined above is that of the amount of information to be conveyed by an answer. Let us consider, for example, the following question: "Did John wash dishes in the snack bar?" Possible answers might be: 1. "Yes"; 2. "Yes, he washed dishes as payment for his meal"; 3. "Yes, he washed dishes because someone had stolen his money and he therefore could not pay for his meal".

The problem of determining the aspects of an event that interest the user can be illustrated by the following example: Let the system know the following sequence of facts: "On the way to the snack bar John had his money stolen, but did not notice it. When he had finished his meal and was about to pay for it, he realized that he had no money. The owner said that he should wash dishes as payment for his meal. John got back home very late". Let us now suppose the system is to answer the question, "Why did John wash dishes?" The following answers are then possible:

1. Because he could not pay for his meal.
2. Because he did not have enough money.
3. Because he had had his money stolen on the way to the snack bar.

What factors determine the choice of one of the above answers? A reasonable choice should be based on certain assumptions regarding the user's knowledge. Thus, from the very form in which the question is posed, it is obvious that the user knows that John washed dishes. Let us assume that the user also knows the following facts: (a) John washed dishes in the snack bar, and (b) "washing dishes" is considered a classic way of paying for a meal when someone lacks the necessary money. These facts allow the user to make the inference that "John could not pay for his meal". Thus, the first of the answers given above does not convey any information unknown to the user at the very beginning. But a reasonable ("good") answer ought to convey some new information. From this point of view, the first answer is "bad" (given the assumptions that have been made regarding the user's knowledge). Similarly, the second answer is "bad" too, since, knowing that "John could not pay for his meal", it is not difficult to draw the conclusion that "John did not have enough money". However, the facts that are known to the user are certainly not sufficient to infer that "John had had his money stolen on the way to the snack bar". Consequently, the third answer will be the "best" one (i.e., the most informative), taking into account the assumptions we have made. Let us note that other assumptions might alter the situation, thus leading to a different choice of the "best" answer. For example, if the user does not know that the event took place in a snack bar, the first answer might be more informative.

As we see, to determine which aspects of the event in question should be indicated in an answer, it is necessary for the system to possess (or assume) certain knowledge about the user. This problem is also connected with that of the perlocutionary acts which should be taken into account in the text being synthesized. In other words, in synthesizing a text, a system should take into consideration the influence that this text exerts on the user himself. Neither a solution, nor even a constructive approach to this problem, is known so far. Generally speaking, the idea is that the system should base its analysis of the statement being synthesized on the model of the user. If the analysis confirms the desired perlocutionary act, the synthesized statement is communicated to the user. It would be advisable to develop this approach, so that the system is able to generate statements conforming to the assumed perlocutionary act.

7.2.4 Splitting the Text Being Synthesized into Parts Corresponding to Future Statements

In order to resolve this problem, both the linguistic factor and that of sense should be taken into consideration. On the one hand (the sense factor), it is desirable for each statement to contain new information not given in the preceding part of the text; it is also desirable for each statement, if possible, to contain only one fresh piece of information (an analysis of statements that are confusing because several pieces of information are lumped together in them has been carried out by Paducheva 1963). In addition, we have to determine what information should be included in the "tacit knowledge", and what information should be expressed in the statement explicitly (see Sect. 1.1.6). For this to be possible, the system should know the user's interests, abilities, and requirements as to what information may be assumed "tacitly", and what must be – in order to avoid swamping the statement in an excess of detail.

On the other hand, a statement should conform to the syntactic and stylistic norms of the given language, i.e., it should be of acceptable length, should conform to the rules of communicative or logical/informational structure (its actual division), and should also be in line with the rules of psychological relief (emphasis). The division of an initial semantic representation into statements is determined by the interaction and possibly even "struggle" between the linguistic and sense factors indicated above. This problem, however, requires further study. We should bear in mind that the division into statements performed at this stage is solely preliminary in character. At subsequent stages, it may become necessary to split certain statements already constructed or unite two separate ones.

7.2.5 Distinguishing Obligatory and Optional Aspects

A statement being synthesized should not convey all the information concerning the event the original question referred to, but only that information in which the user is interested. The amount of information supplied might otherwise be far too great. Moreover, such an amount of information could not, in general, be incorporated into one sentence owing to the linguistic and grammatical limitations characteristic of any natural language. We shall assume that, in simpler cases, forming the semantic graph of an answer involves:

1. Determining the semantic cases of the event asked about which are to be indicated in the statement being synthesized, in order to identify the event unambiguously and convey its meaning
2. Determining which characteristics (corresponding to semantic cases) of each participant in the situation have to be communicated to the user in order to identify this participant unambiguously
3. Determining whether it is stylistically possible to convey information about all the participants and their characteristics in one sentence of the Russian language

The first of these tasks consists in identifying the obligatory semantic cases of an event, i.e., those which cannot be removed or replaced by others without altering the sense of the event as represented in the system. Let us suppose, for example, that all shipments of goods are classified according to the type of transport used. The semantic case INSTRUMENT is then obligatory for the event TRANSPORTING (and this case will have to be indicated in the representation of every event of this type). Obligatory semantic cases can be set out either explicitly or inexplicitly, i.e., by means of context (see Sect. 6.3). In addition to obligatory cases, the semantic graph of an answer has to contain cases corresponding to entities referred to in the question. As regards the stylistic rules that the semantic cases of an event should comply with, these are indicated in the form of proscriptions in the models of government (see Sect. 4.3.3) for each particular event.

The second of the tasks mentioned above involves finding for each notion which is a participant in an event the minimum number of characteristics known to the system that will allow us to define this notion unambiguously in the given context. In practice, this task can be achieved by adding successive explicit characteristics until an unambiguous definition of the notion is reached, simultaneously checking that each successive characteristic complies with the stylistic limitations. If it does not, it is rejected and another characteristic is chosen. In practice, it is normally sufficient to use only very simple stylistic rules expressing quantitative limitations on the ways of expressing characteristics. For example, in the POET system (see Chap. 8), the limitations imposed on the characteristics of a notion (a noun) are as follows: (a) the total number of characteristics defining any noun cannot exceed 6; (b) the number of adjectives and numerals qualifying it is less than 4; (c) the number of nouns is not more than one; (d) the number of proper names is not more than one; (e) the number of attributive adjuncts expressed by subordinate clauses is not more than one; and (f) the depth of "immersion" of subordinate clauses is not greater than 2.

To close this section, let us note the following: Each natural language possesses certain principles determining which aspects of reality must obligatorily be expressed. If, for example, a given language distinguishes between "definiteness" and "indefiniteness" (e.g., the articles "the" and "a" in English), or between genders (e.g., masculine, feminine, and neuter in Russian), then a speaker of the language is forced to make certain obligatory choices between different variants of expressing gender or definiteness/indefiniteness to ensure that his sentence is grammatically correct. The number of aspects that are mandatory may be small in one language and great in another. However, this number does not influence the communicative power of a language. If necessary, clarity may be achieved by using explanatory words. Thus, at the extralinguistic stage of statement synthesis, the system has to determine which aspects will be expressed by grammatical means and which by lexical ones.

7.2.6 Determining the Lexemes That Most Correspond to the Vertices in the Semantic Graph of an Answer

The greatest difficulties in assigning a concrete lexeme of an output statement to a vertex in the semantic graph arise when we deal with events (Popov 1978b). Let us clarify what these difficulties involve by citing an example. Let us assume the system is to synthesize a statement concerning the event constituted by Vladimir's handing a book to Mikhail. This event can be expressed by various words, depending on the previous situation. If the preceding context indicates that Vladimir has just arrived at Mikhail's birthday party, the lexeme "presents" may be the most appropriate. On the other hand, if it is known that Mikhail previously lent the book to Vladimir, the lexeme "returns" will probably be more suitable. Then again, if the book belongs to Vladimir, the lexeme "gives" may be used, etc. Thus, it can be said that a generalized event in the semantic representation of knowledge ("handing", in the above example) may correspond to various lexemes, differing in certain aspects of their meaning. The problem of selecting the right lexeme can be solved by the use of discriminative networks (Feigenbaum 1963) that correspond to generalized events of the semantic network. A discriminative network is a binary tree with predicates in its branching vertices and concrete lexemes in its terminal vertices. The predicates may be divided into three different groups:

1. Predicates classifying events according to the structure of the semantic graph of the answer
2. Predicates inquiring into the system's knowledge – with the use of the deductive mechanism, perhaps – in order to relate to the preceding context
3. Predicates comparing information about the event being processed with the meaning conveyed by concrete lexemes

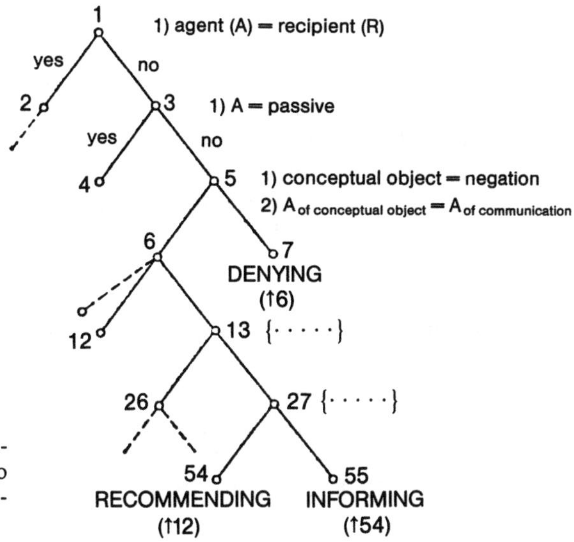

Fig. 7.1. Fragment of the discriminative network corresponding to the generalized event COMMUNICATING INFORMATION

Figure 7.1 shows a fragment of the discriminative network corresponding to the generalized event COMMUNICATING INFORMATION. This event can be expressed in various ways, depending on several factors, e.g.: (a) Does the event involve different agents or does it occur within one agent?; (b) What is the role performed by the agent(s) in the process of communicating information? (In other words, is it active, i.e., the agent is the sender of the information, or is it passive, i.e., he receives it?) On the basis of the first of these factors, the set of lexemes can be split into the class containing such lexemes as *reported, informed, received, denied,* etc. and the class containing such lexemes as *forgot, thought, recalled,* etc. On the basis of the second factor, the analogous classes are: *reported, informed, recommended,* etc. and *got, received, learned,* etc. The values that are assigned to predicates inquiring into the system's knowledge make it possible to choose the proper form of expressing the event COMMUNICATING INFORMATION. This may be *advising, insisting* (if the event is to someone's advantage), *threatening* (if it is to his disadvantage), etc. The analysis of the discriminative network culminates in determining a certain terminal vertex (i.e., a concrete lexeme) and a list of its features (the list being compiled as the analysis moves along the discriminative network). The lexeme thus chosen may prove inadequate at the next stage, i.e., during synthesis of a statement. However, it would obviously be very inconvenient to repeat the process from the very beginning in order to find a new and more appropriate lexeme. It is therefore useful for terminal vertices to be provided with references to those vertices that can provide the starting point for picking up the process of analyzing the discriminative network again. These references are marked in Fig. 7.1, at vertices 7 (reference to 6), 54 (to 12), and 55 (to 54).

To close this outline of semantic synthesis, we would like to call readers' attention to the following: Most of the problems indicated here have not yet been resolved. This, however, should not be taken to mean that systems capable of synthesis, sufficiently developed to be used in practice, cannot be designed at present. Indeed, assuming certain limitations are imposed on the system, these problems either do not occur or can easily be overcome. The problem of determining the level of generality, for instance, becomes completely irrelevant if the system recognizes only one such level. Similarly, if the system is designed to conduct dialogues solely in the form of isolated sentences (not in the form of texts), then the problem of dividing texts into sentences does not exist.

7.3 Syntactic Synthesis of an Output Sentence

In this section we shall briefly outline the process of syntactic synthesis, subject to several limitations imposed on the types of syntactic relations. Readers interested in this subject are referred to descriptions of the SENSE ↔ TEXT model (Apresyan et al. 1978; Mel'chuk 1974a, Chap. 2).

7.3.1 Constructing the Syntactic Structure of an Answer

This stage is the most important module of syntactic synthesis. It is here that the semantic graph of an answer is translated into a syntactic structure that corresponds unambiguously to a certain statement in a natural language. This can be done by using Δ-grammars (Gladky and Mel'chuk 1974). A Δ-grammar is an ordered 4-tuple (W, V, φ, P), where W denotes a dictionary of characterized, generalized lexemes, V – a dictionary of relations $\{a_1, \dots, a_k\}$, P – the set of rules, and φ – the set of conditions under which rules from P are applicable. The rules take the form of triples (d_1, d_2, f), where d_1 and d_2 denote trees of the rule, and f is a mapping of the set of vertices of d_1 onto the set of vertices d_2. The particular problem we are dealing with here, i.e., constructing the syntactic structure of a statement, is resolved by using a concrete form of Δ-grammar, namely $\Gamma_1 = (W_1, V_1, \varphi_1, P_1)$, where W_1 is the set of lexemes known to the system performing synthesis, V_1 – the set of semantic and syntactic relations, P_1 – the set of rules governing the transformation of semantic graphs of statements into syntactic structures, and φ_1 – the set of conditions under which rules from P_1 are applicable. The set P_1 can be split into three subsets: P_1^{comp} – rules for constructing, on the basis of models of government, completive syntactic relations (PRED, 1C–5C; see Sect. 4.3.3), P_1^{circ} – rules for constructing circumstantial relations, and P_1^{char} – rules for constructing attributive relations by utilizing the characteristics of notions.

At this stage of work the system applies successive rules from P_1 to the semantic graph of the answer. The rules are chosen according to the backtrack method (see Sect. 5.3), which offers the opportunity of modifying an incorrect syntactic structure instead of rejecting it. Let us consider each form of the rules from P_1. The left-hand side of a rule from P_1^{comp} is a list of the semantic cases that are indicated in a concrete MG (see Sect. 4.3.3). The set of subgraphs to which a given rule is applicable is determined by the list of semantic categories connected with each semantic case of the MG, and by the list of proscriptions occurring in

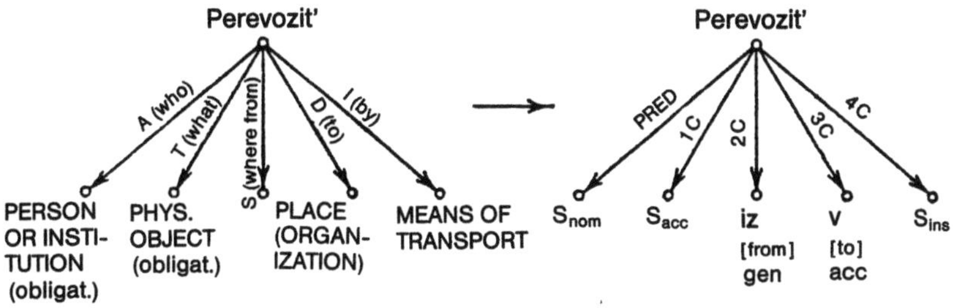

Fig. 7.2. Example of a rule from P_1^{comp} for the lexeme *perevozit'* [to transport]

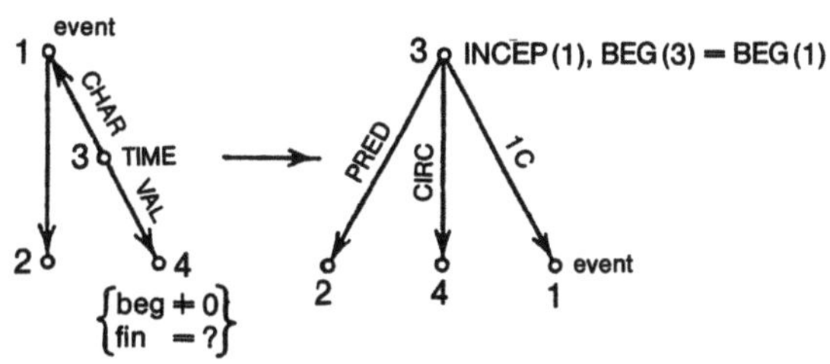

Fig. 7.3. Example of a rule from P_1^{circ} with an adverbial modifier of time

this MG. On the right-hand side of a rule from P_1^{comp} we have the syntactic relations PRED and completive relations 1C – 5C. Figure 7.2 shows the graphic representation of a concrete rule from P_1^{comp} connected with the lexeme *perevozit'* [to transport].

The left-hand side of a concrete rule from P_1^{circ} is a tree containing one or more characteristics assigned to a vertex-event. In practice, any event can be characterized by current time (pres), the time the event begins (beg), the time it finishes (fin), and the modality (m) or reality (r) of the event. In addition, depending on the type of event in question, it may be connected with characteristics specific to this particular event. Thus, for example, the event "transporting" may be characterized by "payload", "average speed", "distance", etc. The right-hand side of the rule is a tree containing one or more obligatory relations, the values assigned to a given vertex-event (aspect, mood, tense, person, voice), and new lexemes introduced by lexical functions (see Sect. 4.3.3). Figure 7.3 shows an example of a concrete rule from P_1^{circ}. On the right-hand side it is indicated that the event began at a certain moment of time "beg + 0", but has not been finished (fin = ?). The tree on the right-hand side of the rule contains the circumstantial relation and the additional vertex introduced by the lexical function Incep (1). This function expresses the meaning corresponding to the notion of "to begin" for lexeme no. 1, which is an event. The categories of aspect, tense, and voice that are connected with vertex 3 are assumed to be identical with those assigned to vertex 1. Let us note that there may be no lexeme in the output statement which corresponds to the vertex Incep (1). Thus, for instance, for the lexeme *perevozit'* [to transport], Incep (1) is expressed by the separate lexeme *nachal* [(he) began] (which expresses the meaning of the lexical function itself – see Apresyan 1974), but for the lexeme *letet'* [to fly], Incep (1) does not create any distinct word – it only changes the

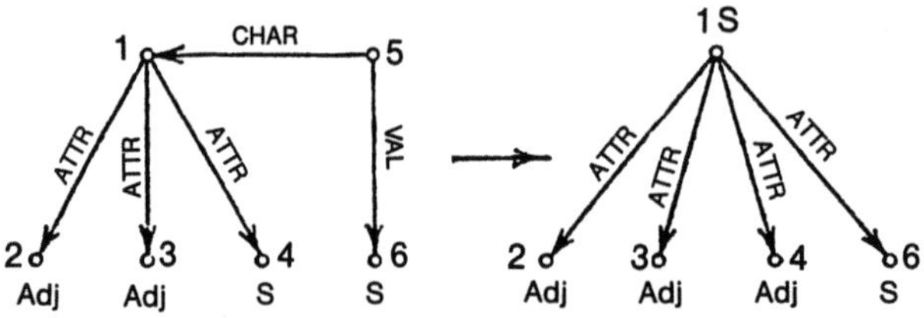

Fig. 7.4. Example of a rule from P_1^{char} with no change in the part of speech

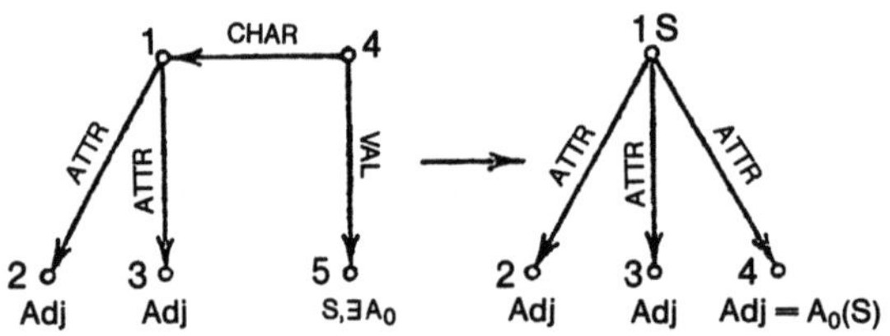

Fig. 7.5. Example of a rule from P_1^{char} with a change in the part of speech

initial form: *letet'* → *poletel* [fly → set off; the latter being formed from the Russian by adding the prefix *po-*; trans. note] (i.e., the meaning results from gluing together the meanings of the lexical function and of the argument).

The left-hand side of a rule from P_1^{char} is a notion accompanied by its semantic characteristics. In addition, this side of the rule also contains the semantic relations already established for this notion. These define the notion's context and are represented in the form of a minimal syntactic tree. By the term *minimal syntactic tree* we mean a tree where all vertices (except for the tree's root) are terminal ones, and all lines are labeled by syntactic relations. The right-hand side of a rule from P_1^{char} is a tree of dependencies, whose vertices may be labeled by either concrete lexemes or lexical functions. Figures 7.4 and 7.5 show two examples of rules from P_1^{char}. In the first example, a dual characteristic (vertices 1, 5, and 6) is translated into an attributive relation (vertices 1 and 6). The rule is applicable if the number of attributes corresponding to vertex 1 is no more than 3. In the second example, the characteristic is translated into an attributive relation, while the lexeme in vertex 5 is replaced by the value assumed by the lexical function A_0 (A_0 transforms a substantive into the corresponding adjective). For this operation to be possible, there has to be a value $A_0(S)$ of the lexical function for vertex 5.

7.3.2 Performing Anaphoric References

The most important types of anaphoric references – nominal and pronominal – have already been outlined in Sect. 4.1. The use of anaphoric references makes an output text clearer and more compact, thus facilitating comprehension on the part of the user. We shall distinguish the following ways of using anaphoric references during the synthesis of an output text: For nominal references – making use of generic notions (the lexical function Gener; see Sect. 4.3.3), replacing concrete participants in a situation by their generalized names (the lexical functions $S_1, S_2, \ldots, S_5$, where S_i is the typical name of the i-th participant in the situation), and synonymously replacing notions by more laconic ones (the lexical function Syn). The above-mentioned replacements are usually performed for the sake of compactness.

Pronominal references are used to ensure the compactness of a text as well; in addition, however, they perform an important role in precisely identifying the notions being used. The following example will make this clearer. Let us suppose that a given passage in the dialogue deals with four screws and holes. A statement indicating that precisely these four screws should be screwed into these four holes has to be synthesized. If the statement that is constructed does not contain a pronominal reference, it may turn out to be ambiguous [in English, the definite article – which does not exist in Russian – can substitute for a pronoun here; trans. note]. Indeed, the statements "Screw in four screws" or even "Screw four screws in four openings" are ambiguous, as it is possible that some other "four screws" exist. To ensure that the reference is absolutely clear we have to use certain pronouns: "Drive *these* four screws in", or "Drive *them* in".

There are certain semantic and syntactic criteria which can be employed to determine whether a given notion can be replaced by a pronoun without running the risk of confusion. The simplest of these is the criterion which involves using semantic categories to determine whether a pronoun could be understood to refer to a notion other than the one intended. Should ambiguity occur, the system verifies whether this can be eliminated by using syntactic criteria. Let us consider, for example, the following text: "These factories produce trucks with diesel engines. They have a maximum payload of 5 tons". If the system knows that neither factories nor engines have "payloads", but trucks do, then the pronominal replacement will be confirmed by the semantic criteria.

Syntactic criteria check whether the referent of a given pronominal reference can be established unambiguously by using morphological information that is connected with the pronoun and with notions used in the text. Let us consider, for example, the following text: "This ship carried the goods produced by factory *D*. They were delivered on time". The text will be understood unambiguously due to a syntactic criterion (not a semantic one), as "ship" and "goods" are of different number (i.e., singular and plural respectively). Let us note here that a pronoun can also refer to a whole fragment of a text – e.g., to a sequence of actions ("How did you do that?"). This type of pronominal reference requires mechanisms that are more precise than those considered.

7.3.3 Assigning Morphological Information to the Lexemes of the Syntactic Structure of a Statement

The task at hand here is to ensure the syntactic combinability of the lexemes in a sentence. This is achieved by using rules of Russian grammar in the form of a Δ-grammar, $\Gamma_2 = (W_2, V_2, \varphi_2, P_2)$, where W_2 is the set of generalized lexemes together with their characteristics, V_2 – the set of syntactic relations, P_2 – the set of grammatical rules, and φ_2 – the set of conditions under which rules from P_2 are applicable. All rules from the set P_2 can be divided into two types: rules for transforming syntactic structure (P_2^{trans}), and the actual rules for assigning morphological information (P_2^{assign}).

Fig. 7.6. Example of a rule from P_2^{trans} performing the transformation "active → passive"

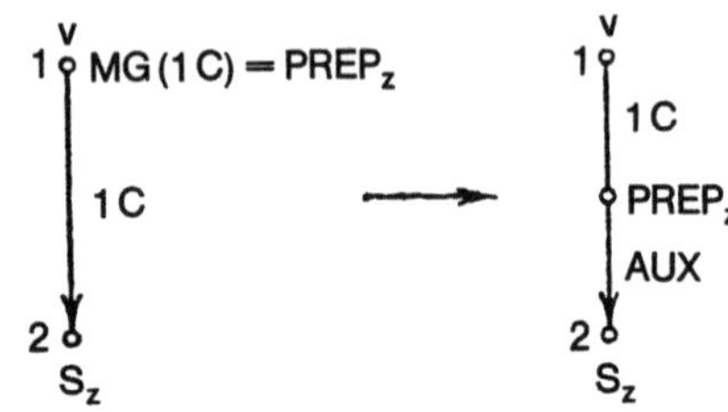

Fig. 7.7. Example of a rule from P_2^{assign} introducing a preposition into the syntactic structure

The algorithm of the system's work at this stage can be reduced to the successive application of rules from P_2^{trans} and those from P_2^{assign} to the syntactic structure of the answer. Let us now consider each type of rule from P_2.

The left-hand side of a rule from P_2^{trans} is a tree of dependencies, whose vertices correspond to partially characterized lexemes. The same tree, after the transformation has been performed, constitutes the right-hand side of the rule. The transformation consists in either renaming lines, or in introducing additional vertices, sometimes also in assigning morphological information to them.

Examples of rules from P_2^{trans} and P_2^{assign} are shown in Figs. 7.6 and 7.7. The first rule performs the transformation of an active verb into a passive one by replacing 1C by PRED, and a case z of substantive S (vertex 2) by the nominal case. The phrase *otpravili stanki* [they dispatched the lathes], for instance, will be transformed into *stanki otpravleny* [the lathes were dispatched]. The conditions of applicability that correspond to this rule are (a) the absence of any "slave" connected with the verb by the syntactic relation PRED, and (b) the existence of a passive form of the verb (vertex 1).

The second rule (7.7) introduces a preposition in a case z (prep_z). This preposition is the one envisaged by the i-th completive relation in the model of government corresponding to the verb v (vertex 1). For example, the MG of the verb *kolotit'* [to thump] according to its 3C syntactic relation, requires the preposition "*po* (dat)" to be used. The following fragment of the syntactic structure:

kolotit' $\xrightarrow{3C}$ *spina* (dat)

will be transformed into:

kolotit' $\xrightarrow{3C}$ *po* (dat) $\xrightarrow{\text{aux}}$ *spina* (dat)

[*spina* – back; *kolotit' po spine* – to thump sb. on the back; trans. note].

The left-hand side of a rule from P_2^{assign} is a tree of dependencies, whose vertices are partially characterized lexemes; the right-hand side is also a tree of dependencies, but with some new information assigned to the vertices. An example of such a rule is shown in Fig. 7.8. The rule establishes agreement as to number between a substantive with homogeneous parts (vertex 2) and a verb. This rule makes it possible to establish the number of the verb in the phrase: *Zavod i fabrika vypolnili plan* [The enterprise and the plant fulfilled the plan; *vypolnili* is the 3rd person plural, past tense, of the verb *vypolnit'*: to fulfill; trans. note].

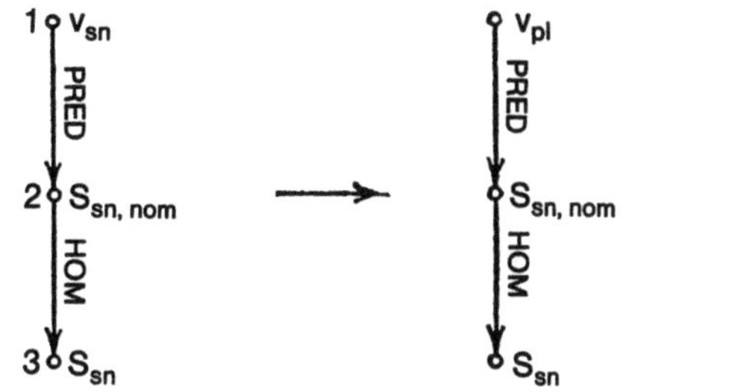

Fig. 7.8. Example of a rule from P_2^{assign} putting a verb and a noun into agreement as to number

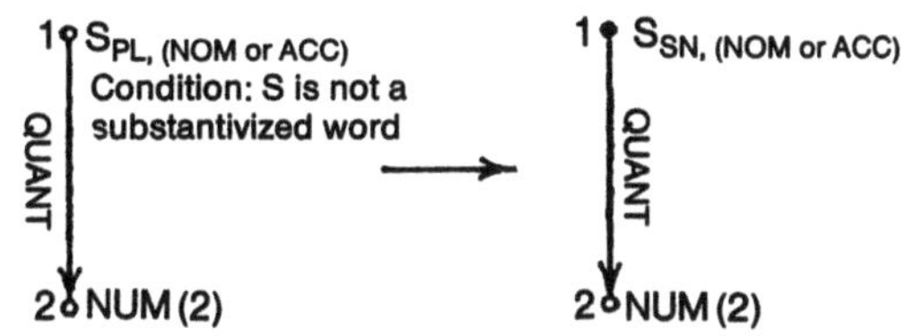

Fig. 7.9. Example of a rule from P_2^{assign} assigning a proper number to a noun governed by a numeral of the type "2"

Figure 7.9 shows another example of a rule from P_2^{assign}. This rule determines the morphological number of a substantive in the nominative or accusative case governed by numerals of the type "2" (see Sects. 4.2.6 and 4.3.2), e.g., "*52 zavoda*" (singular morphological number but plural semantic number). The condition of applicability here is that the substantive must not be a substantivized word, e.g., "*52 rabochikh*" (here the morphological and semantic numbers are both plural [see notes in Sect. 4.3.2; trans. note]).

7.3.4 Determining Word Order in the Sentence Being Synthesized

As we know, the word forms of a sentence in a natural language are always arranged linearly, while the vertices of a tree of dependencies are not. In performing synthesis, the system must therefore establish the order of word forms for every sentence being synthesized. This can be done in three stages (Mel'chuk 1974a):

1. Trees of dependencies are transformed into so-called *starting groups* (SG) – sequences of words connected with each other by "local" syntactic relations.
2. Starting groups are then unified to form so-called *reduced groups* (RG) – sequences of starting groups connected by "quasilocal" syntactic relations. Reduced groups roughly correspond to what are commonly called "the group of the main parts of a sentence" (the subject group, predicate group, object group, etc.).
3. The reduced groups are put in order using "global" syntactic relations.

Each stage of this process is carried out by special means. The first task can be performed with the help of automatic grammar (Gladky and Mel'chuk 1969). The composition and structure of starting groups can be defined by so-called *clamps*. Each clamp corresponds to one of four types of starting groups (SG). These are: substantival (nominal) starting groups (SG_S), adjectival starting

Table 7.1. Order of constituent parts in each type of starting group

Position in SG	Type of SG			
	SG_S	SG_A	SG_V	SG_{Adv}
	Copulative conjunction			
1	(*i*–and)	(*i*–and)	(*i*–and)	(*i*–and)
	Negation/Restrictive particle			
2	(*ne tol'ko*– not only)	(*yedva li ne*– probably)	(*tol'ko*–only)	(*otnud' ne*– anything but)
3	Preposition (*dla*–for)	Determinative adverb		
		(*ochen'*–very)	(*krayne*–extremely)	(*ochen'*–very)
4	Quantificational word (*vsekh*–all)	Adjective (*ustavshiy*–tired)	Verb (*volnuyetsa*– he is upset)	Adverb (*daleko*–far)
5	Demonstrative pronoun (*etikh*– of these)			
6	Cardinal numeral (*shesti*–of six)			
7	Possessive adjective (*nashikh*–of ours)			
8	Ordinal number (*tretikh*–of the third)			
9	Adjective (*vazhnikh*– of important)			
10	Substantive (*plat'ev*–of dresses)			
11	Name or attribute-uninflected word (*bezh*–beige)			

groups (SG_A), verbal starting groups (SG_V), and adverbial starting groups (SG_{ADV}). Prepositional SGs will be considered to be a variety of nominal group. Every starting group consists of a word (the nucleus of the group), together with all words linked to it by "local" syntactic relations. In the vast majority of cases, the components of an SG are subordinate to the nucleus of the group (i.e., they are "slaves"), with the exception of prepositions, conjunctions, etc. The clamp specifies the maximum composition of any SG of a given type. The internal order in a group remains constant during subsequent stages of determining word order. Table 7.1 shows the order of constituent parts in each of the above-mentioned types of SG. It should be borne in mind, however, that the order defined by a clamp can be considered only an approximation. To make provision for the nuances of the Russian language, certain additional rules have to be employed, taking the "fine structure" of an SG into account. As an example of the need to make provision for these additional correctional rules, we might mention a group of heterogeneous adjectives referring to one nucleus (e.g., "interesting French mathematical journals"). In a clamp, this corresponds to the ninth position. To establish the order of such adjectives it is necessary to develop certain special rules, which probably have to take into account semantic aspects.

All SGs that do not indirectly depend on a vertex of the dependency tree corresponding to a phrase are unified with the starting groups of their governing words ("masters"), thus forming a reduced group (RG). The simplest rule for establishing the order of SGs in an RG is to place subordinate SGs to the right of a governing SG (this is known as the "neutral" order). This rule very frequently proves successful. Exceptional cases arise when a governing SG (i.e., its nucleus) possesses a model of government. If this is the case, the neutral order is first established, then subjected to certain modifications according to special rules. For example, "SG slaves" and an "SG master" can be arranged either as follows: "SG master – SG agent – SG adverbial modifier – SG joined by 1C – SG joined by 2C – SG joined by 3C – SG adverbial modifier – SG adverbial modifier of manner", or thus: "SG master – SG adv. mod. – SG 1C – SG agent – SG adv. mod. – SG adv. mod. of manner" (provided that agent $\neq S_{\text{gen.case}}$ and both 2C and 3C do not occur in the statement). The arrangement of SGs within an RG may be altered as a result of many factors, of which the most important is the dependence of the order of SGs on the number of word forms contained in each starting group. If the other conditions remain unchanged, longer SGs tend to be located to the right of all shorter ones.

The stage of determining the order of word forms is terminated by arranging reduced groups. The arrangement of these groups in the Russian language is determined by several factors. Some of these are less important, others are more important – yet all are mutually interrelated in a very complex manner. The rules for arranging RGs can be divided into four groups: 1. arranging a verb, its actants, and parts of the compound predicate; 2. arranging adverbial modifiers; 3. forming logical emphasis (by taking into account the rheme and theme of the sentence being synthesized); 4. correcting the final order of words in a sentence should some inadmissible situation arise. Rules of the first and second type lead to the so-called neutral order of words, i.e., the order that would have been obtained by a speaker who constructed the sentence with no regard to context. Not going into details, the neutral order roughly corresponds to the following arangement of reduced groups: "RG adv. mod. – RG joined by the predicative SYR – RG of the verb – RG joined by 1C – RG joined by 2C – RG joined by 3C – RG joined by the circumstantial SYR".

Rules of the third type make provision for the influence the context may exert on the order of words. This influence is connected primarily with the notions of rheme and theme. Reduced groups which are constituents of the rheme (i.e., new information, expressed for the first time) are located to the right of the reduced groups constituting the theme (i.e., information already known from preceding sentences). The following rule may serve to illustrate rules of the fourth type: If there is no RG on one side of the verb and several on the other, then: (a) all RGs can be transferred from the right-hand side to the left-hand side, except for the RG referred to in the input question, and (b) all RGs can be transferred from the left-hand side to the right-hand side.

7.4 Morphological Synthesis of the Word Forms of the Sentence Being Synthesized

At this stage of synthesis, concrete word forms from the Russian language are constructed on the basis of their stem and the morphological information attributed to it. As in the case of morphological analysis (see Sect. 5.2), morphological synthesis (MS) may be carried out either in a declarative or procedural way. If the declarative method is adopted, all stems in the dictionary are accompanied by sets of morphological information (MI) and corresponding word forms. During declarative morphological synthesis, the system seeks the correct word form by reviewing information contained in the dictionary on the basis of the stem and the morphological information referring to it obtained at the stage of syntactic synthesis. If, in turn, the method of morphological synthesis adopted is the procedural one, the correct word form is assembled on the basis of tables of affixes that are classified into separate tables corresponding to different parts of speech. As far as synthesis is concerned, the most important parts of speech are nouns, adjectives, and verbs (verbal forms). Of these, it is the verbal forms that present the most difficulties.

Let us illustrate what forms the core of morphological synthesis by considering the example of a noun. All Russian nouns fall into one of seven categories, according to the manner in which the word forms are derived from the stem (Koz'mina and Korovina 1972). In other words, the type of stem determines the rule governing how endings are assigned to this stem. In order to provide for the way different types of stems are transformed while forming word forms, it is advisable – for certain types of words – to store two stems in the dictionary rather than just one. Thus, for instance, two stems, namely *rebr* and *reber*, will correspond to the lexeme *rebro* [rib]. Since nouns decline in different ways in the singular and plural, the corresponding tables of endings are stored separately for the two numbers (see Table 7.2). In addition, the case forms of nouns depend on the type of noun in question. In the Russian language we can distinguish just over

Table 7.2. Endings stored for singular and plural nouns of Russian

	Substantive													
	Singular							Plural						
Type of word	1	A	U	Y	YE	OY	YE	1	Y	Y	–	AM	AMI	AKH
	. . .													
	8	–	–	A	U	YEM	YE	10	A	A	–	AM	AMI	AKH
	. . .													
	23	–	–	A	U	OM	YE	21	Y	–	–	AM	AMI	AKH

Table 7.3. Fragments of tables for adjectival endings

Adjective													
Masculine singular							Feminine singular						
1	IY	IY	OVO	OMU	YM	OM	1	AYA	UYU	OY	OY	OY	OY
. . .	. . .						. . .	. . .					
7	IY	IY	OVO	OMU	IM	OM	3	AYA	UYU	YEY	YEY	YEY	YEY
. . .	. . .						. . .	. . .					
11	–	–	A	U	YM	OM	6	YA	YU	YEY	YEY	YEY	YEY

Adjective													
Neuter singular							Plural						
1	OYE	OYE	OVO	OMU	YM	OM	1	IYE	IYE	YKH	YM	YMI	YKH
. . .	. . .						. . .	. . .					
3	OYE	OYE	OVO	OMU	IM	OM	4	IYE	IYE	IKH	IM	IMI	IKH
. . .	. . .						. . .	. . .					
8	O	O	A	U	YM	OM	6	Y	Y	YKH	YM	YMI	YKH

20 types of declension in the singular and plural (see Table 7.2; see also Koz'mina and Korovina 1972).

Hence, the dictionary contains the following characteristics of a noun: type of stem (TS) and type of declension in the singular (TDS) and in the plural (TDP). The stem *trav* [from *trava* – grass] will thus be described by: TS = 1, TDS = 1, TDP = 1. Such information makes it possible to synthesize any word form which can be derived from a given stem. Let us assume, for instance, that we want to obtain the form "nn, sing, gen" of the stem *trav*. We refer to the left-hand side of Table 7.2 (as the number is singular), to the third column (as the case is genitive, i.e., the third case; 1 corresponds to the nominative, 2 to the accusative, 3 to the genitive, 4 to the dative, 5 to the instrumental, and 6 to the locative), and to the first row (as TS = 1). We thus find the ending *-y*. Since TS = 1, the word form is formed simply by adding the ending to the stem; we therefore obtain *trav-y*.

By way of example, fragments are presented in Table 7.3 of analogous tables corresponding to the part of speech "adjective". Readers interested in details of morphological synthesis are referred to Koz'mina and Korovina 1972, Korovina et al. 1977, and Belonogov and Novoselov 1979.

8 Work to Date on Designing Systems of Conversation

8.1 General Outline of the POET System

In this section we shall describe the POET system – its current state and the perspective for its further development. It is no accident that this particular system has been chosen. No other current system that might be regarded as an industrial SNL is known to this author. Obviously, this is not to say that POET offers solutions to all the problems involved in designing a system of conversation. But this particular system was designed in accordance with the principles we have outlined (see Sect. 2.1.1), which enable it to evolve, increasing its potential and capabilities. The first version of POET was designed in 1977 and has been in operation since November of that year. It took about 50 man-years to develop its mathematical software, and about 20 to prepare its information software. The following point should be noted here: the time consumed in developing the MS does not depend on the size of the dictionary possessed by the system, yet in the case of the IS this time is directly determined by both the volume of the dictionary and the amount of information stored in it. The following limitations were imposed on the first version of POET: (a) the language of conversation was restricted to business prose in Russian; (b) conversations were to be conducted in the form of separate and unconnected simple interrogative sentences, which did not contain nonstandard constructions, ellipses, anaphoric references, or nonprojective constructions (see Sect. 5.3); (c) the internal representation corresponded only to a static world, with no cause-and-effect relationships between events (dynamics, i.e., a varying data base, was the result of external factors); (d) the format of the data base was fixed, and this limited the subject matter the system dealt with; (e) the system was not equipped to guide the user in paraphrasing a question in case of incomprehension.

In this chapter we shall be examining the general principles on which the system was based and its most essential characteristics. A more detailed description of POET can be found in Popov 1976, 1977, 1978a, b, 1979; Baklanov and Popov 1977, 1978; and Popov and Rodionov 1978. The POET system comprises the following components: the language of conversation, a dictionary, an abstract network (A- network), a concrete network (C-network), a data base (DB), and the set of programs which carry out processing. The dictionary, semantic network, and data base are used to describe words, objects occurring in the outer world, and relationships that connect them. The above-mentioned set of programs consists of programs performing the following: morphological, syntactic, and semantic analysis; semantic interpretation; formation of answers; syntactic and morphological synthesis; and access to the dictionary, semantic network, and data base.

The system is designed to work with a dictionary containing up to 60 000 lexemes, an A-network consisting of up to 100 000 facts, and a C-network and DB of up to 500 000 facts. The speed of the system's work is virtually independent of the number of lexemes stored. The total number of commands is about 15 000. Of these, about 10 000 are written in the PL/1 language and about 5 000 in the assembly language. An answer to the question consisting of 15 words is obtained in about 15 s (using the EC-1060 computer). The system comprises twelve modules which are called sequentially; the capacity of the operating store is 200 K. When the whole system is translated from PL/1 into the assembly language, response time is reduced to about 10 s and the capacity of the operating store to about 60 K (there are then six modules).

The second version of POET is able to:

- Conduct a dialogue consisting of several interrelated sentences containing non-standard constructions, dependent clauses, ellipses, and anaphoric references
- Inform the user in comprehensible terms about the reason for failure to understand a question (the user's error, the ambiguity of the question, or the limited capabilities of the system), and to guide him in paraphrasing this question (using questions and statements)
- Store information in its internal representation concerning cause-and-effect relationships between events

The main difference between POET and other systems (see Sect. 2.3) is the fact that it is not an experimental system but an industrial one, designed to work with large-volume information software in a reasonable amount of time.

Let us give an example of a dialogue between a user and the first version of POET. [The English translation does not render the morphological complexity of the words; trans. note].

Q.1a: WHAT WAS THE TOTAL VOLUME OF SHIPMENTS BY RAIL IN 1970?

Q.1b: HOW MANY MILLIONS OF TONS OF FREIGHT WERE SHIPPED BY RAIL IN 1970?

Q.1c: HOW MUCH FREIGHT DID THE RAILWAYS SHIP IN 1970?

Q.1d: THE SHIPMENT OF WHAT AMOUNT OF GOODS WAS PERFORMED BY THE RAILWAYS IN 1970?

Q.1e: WHAT WAS THE TOTAL VOLUME OF SHIPMENTS BY RAIL IN 1970 EQUAL TO?

A.1: IN 1970 THE RAILWAYS CARRIED 1882 MILLION TONS OF GOODS.

Q.2: WHAT WAS THE SHARE OF SHIPMENTS BY RAIL IN THE TOTAL VOLUME OF SHIPMENTS BY ALL MEANS OF TRANSPORT IN 1975?

A.2: 18%.

Q.3: WHAT FIRMS DELIVERED ROUGHING LATHES TO THE MOSCOW REGION IN THE FIRST QUARTER OF 1970?

A.3: IN THE FIRST QUARTER OF 1970 ROUGHING LATHES WERE DELIVERED TO THE MOSCOW REGION BY THE FIRMS "ZARYA" AND "RUBIN."

Q.4: DID THE FIRM "ZARYA" CARRY OUT DELIVERIES OF ROUGHING LATHES TO THE MOSCOW REGION IN 1970?

A.4: YES.

In order to demonstrate the capabilities of the first version of POET as regards synonymous paraphrasing, the first question was given in five variants differing as to voice (active/passive), word order, and particular variants of synonymic expressions ("to ship" – "to perform shipment" [*perevozit' – osushchestvlat' perevozski*]). In addition, the POET system makes provision for synonymy resulting from: (a) the fact that different words correspond to a different relation to the situation on the part of its participants (*A* possesses *B* = *B* belongs to *A*), (b) the use of generic words, and (c) the occurrence of "tacit knowledge".

The potential of the second version of POET may be illustrated by the following connected dialogue (U – user, S – system):

U1: WHAT SHIPMENTS WERE PERFORMED BY WATER-BORNE TRANSPORT IN 1970?

S1: a) THE WORD "WATER-BORNE" DOES NOT OCCUR IN THE DICTIONARY.
b) "WATER-BORNE" IS UNDERSTOOD TO BE A CHARACTERISTIC OF TRANSPORT.

U2: WHAT IS KNOWN ABOUT FORMS OF TRANSPORT?

S2: THE FOLLOWING FORMS OF TRANSPORT ARE DISTINGUISHED: SEA, RIVER, ROAD, AND RAIL TRANSPORT.

U3: WHAT SHIPMENTS WERE PERFORMED BY SEA AND RIVER TRANSPORT IN 1970?

S3: IN 1970 SEA AND RIVER TRANSPORT PERFORMED 5716 SHIPMENTS. AM I TO LIST THEM ALL?

U4: NO. HOW DOES THE SYSTEM CLASSIFY SHIPMENTS?

S4: SHIPMENTS ARE CLASSIFIED ACCORDING TO: SENDER, RECEIVER, KIND OF FREIGHT, AMOUNT OF FREIGHT, AND TIME.

U5: WHAT SHIPMENTS OF LIGNITE TO LENINGRAD WERE PERFORMED BY SEA TRANSPORT IN THE FIRST QUARTER OF 1970?

S5: THE SYSTEM POSSESSES INFORMATION ON REGIONS ONLY.

U6: WHAT SHIPMENT OF LIGNITE TO THE LENINGRAD REGION WERE PERFORMED BY SEA TRANSPORT IN THE FIRST QUARTER OF 1970?

S6: LIGNITE WAS DELIVERED BY SEA FROM STRIP MINES TO LENINGRAD REGION ON FEBRUARY 10, 1970, AND MARCH 24, 1970.

U7: WHAT ABOUT HARD COAL?

S7: ...

8.2 Representation of Knowledge in the POET System

The knowledge possessed by the system is distributed among the dictionary, semantic network, and data base (DB). Of these, it is the semantic network – consisting of abstract and concrete networks (the A-network and the C-network) – which functions as the "intellectual" component of knowledge representation. This division of knowledge into parts stems from the fact that it is represented in different ways in each of the components, and also from the fact that different portions of knowledge are required at different stages of input question processing.

The dictionary stores knowledge about the natural language (Popov 1978a). It contains information about the stems of both words and word combinations. The information given in the dictionary entry consists of head, morphological, syntactic, and semantic zones (see Sect. 4.3). Table 8.1 gives an example of a fragment of the dictionary. The head zone contains the stem; if the stem can occur in several different forms, one of these is taken to be the "main" form, while the others are furnished with references to it. The morphological zone contains information about part of speech and the morphological type of the stem (cf. Table 4.2). Two types of syntactic-semantic zones are distinguished: one corresponds to events and the other to notions. The zone corresponding to an event contains the model of government (MG), the proscriptions specific to this model, and lexical functions (LF – cf. Sect. 4.3.3). A model of government takes the form of a table consisting of up to six columns (actants), depending on the number of semantic relations characteristic of the given word. Each semantic relation is provided with information about the typical lexical functions assigned to the word forms corre-

Table 8.1. Fragment of knowledge possessed by the system stored in the dictionary

Stem	Morphological zone								
	Part of speech	Numb.	Gen.	Anim.	Voice	Syntactic-semantic zone			
V [in]	PREP	–	–	–	–	–			
GOD [year]	NOUN	ANY	MASC	INAN		TIME			
ZHELEZNODO- [stem of rail (attr)]	ADJ	–	–	–	–	–			
KAMENN- [stem of hard]	ADJ	–	–	–		–			
PEREVEZ [stem of to ship, to carry]	VERB	–	–	–	ANY	NOUN NOM CAR-RIER	NOUN ACC PHYS. OBJ.	*NA* UNIT OF MEAS.	NOUN INS
SKOL'KO [how much/many]	CNUM	–	–	–					
TRANSPORT [transport]	NOUN	ANY	MASC	INAN	–	TRANSPORT			
UGOL' [coal]	NOUN	SING	MASC	INAN	–	PHYS. OBJECT			

sponding to the relation, about the way it influences the morphology of the given lexeme (the syntactic zone of the MG), and about the semantic categories corresponding to it. Each syntactic zone of an MG contains information about the possible morphological characteristics of all corresponding actants: the part of speech and case of a subordinate word, the concrete syntactic word form (preposition, conjunction), and the prepositional group. Each column of a group MG in the semantic zone of a dictionary entry is placed in correspondence with a group of semantic categories which "slaves" of this MG should comply with, and also with semantic cases which connect the "master" with its "slave". Forty semantic categories and 20 semantic cases are currently used in the system. These include AGENT (A) – the initiator of an event; THEME (T) – the object(s) of the event, i.e., what the event is directed towards; SOURCE (S) – what the "object" is obtained from; GOAL (G) – the result of the event; INSTRUMENT (I) – the physical object with the help of which the event is carried out; WAY (W) – the means or method of carrying out the event. In addition, vertices which characterize another vertex may be joined to lines such as VALUE (VAL), ELEMENT (E), etc. All word forms of an MG are of one of the following semantic types:action, state, empty, functional, phase, modal, connective, characteristic, or notion. As regards dictionary entries which do not possess an MG, these indicate the semantic categories that determine a given stem.

The proscriptions characteristic of an MG may be split into two types: syntactic proscriptions and semantic ones (see Sect. 4.3.3). The zone of lexical functions also contains two separate types: lexical replacements and lexical parameters. Lexical replacements are employed in paraphrasing a given expression.

The zone of notions consists of the prepositional area and the area of lexical functions. For each semantic case, the prepositional area contains prepositions which can occur before the given notion (Popov and Rodionov 1978). The zone of lexical functions for notions resembles that for events. All the zones we have mentioned are used to ensure the combinability of lexemes. The following types of combinability are distinguished in the POET system: semantic, syntactic, and lexical (see Sect. 4.3.3).

The semantic network, as we have said, comprises abstract and concrete networks (see Sect. 3.5). The abstract network (A-network) stores information concerning the "model of the world", i.e., the set of possible and permissible states of the subject area expressed in terms of general (generic) notions, events, and characteristics. The A-network is essential in processing linguistic information and understanding input questions. The C-network contains a concretization of the general situation expressed by the A-network. The C-network describes objects which are the concrete expression of notions occurring in the A-network. A mathematical model of the A-network is provided by a labeled, oriented graph, with the vertices corresponding to words and word phrases, and the lines to the semantic relations that exist between them. There are three main types of vertices: NOTIONS, EVENTS, and CHARACTERISTICS (Popov 1977). A line joining two vertices in the A-network indicates that the corresponding relation *may* occur in the world being modeled; an analogous line in the C-network signifies that this relation does in fact occur in the world being modeled. The vertices of the A-network correspond to notions from the real world, while those of the C-network correspond to concrete objects. It is therefore obvious that the number of vertices in the C-network substantially exceeds that of the vertices in the A- network. This, in turn, means that it is advisable to use a somewhat different form for representing information in the C-network. The C-network can also be viewed as an oriented graph, although its lines are not labeled and thus need not be represented explicitly.

Let us note here that the semantic zone of most dictionary entries contains references to vertices of the semantic network, and that reverse references (from the network to the dictionary) are equally frequent. In the part of the DB corresponding to the given vertex, the system stores quantitative information concerning characteristics that have been assigned to this vertex in the A-network. The format of such elements of the DB has already been fixed. This was possible due to the fact that the system has a narrow and strictly defined purpose. This fixed format ensures an effective form of representing data. The data base itself is not considered to be a part of the POET system; our view is that the structure of an efficient data base and the principles of designing it should vary according to the subject matter. A graphical representation of an A- network, C-network, and DB is shown in Fig. 8.1.

8.3 Practical Operations of the POET System

The POET system performs the following functions: (a) it analyzes input sentences in the NL, (b) it interprets these input sentences, and (c) it synthesizes answers in the NL. The first of these functions is performed in three stages: morphological analysis, syntactic analysis, and semantic analysis.

8.3.1 Morphological Analysis

Morphological analysis is performed using the "reverse method", i.e., endings and suffixes are discarded on the basis of the table of affixes. This leads to the identification of the hypothetical stems of the words being processed. A fragment of the table of affixes is shown in Table 8.2. By considering the affixes that have been discarded, the system assigns the appropriate morphological information (MI-line) to the stem. If a hypothetical stem located at the stage of MA occurs in the dictionary, and a corresponding part of speech indicated in the dictionary agrees with that indicated in the MI-line, then both the stem and the MI-line are transmitted to the stage of syntactic analysis (SYA). If not, the stem is rejected. Let us note that during MA there may be several MI-lines placed in correspondence with each word of an input sentence.

Morphological analysis ends with presyntax, where information needed at the SYA stage is prepared. During presyntax, the system marks both words which are likely to be included in word combinations and those conditioned by other words and uses syntactic filters to delete superfluous morphological information (see Sect. 5.2). Table 8.3 shows the result of the morphological analysis of the sentence "*Skol'ko kamiennovo ugla perevezeno zheleznodorozhnim transportom v 1975 godu?*" [How much (of) hard coal was shipped by rail (transport) in 1975 (year)?]

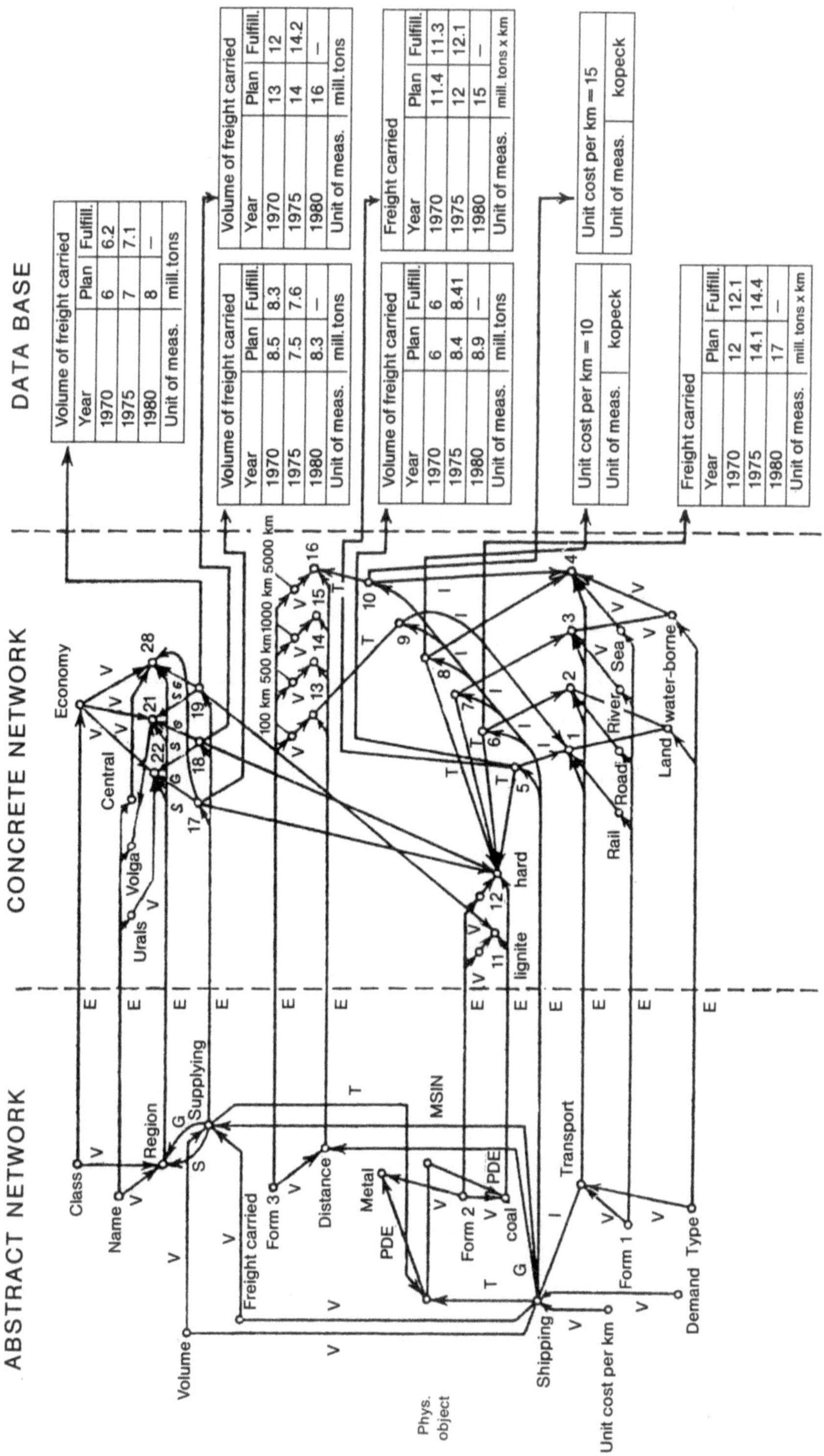

Fig. 8.1. Fragment of data representation in the POET system

Table 8.2. Fragment of table of affixes

No.	Endings								
	AFFIX	PART OF SP.	CASE		NUMB	GEN-DER	ANI-MAT.	TENSE	VOICE
17	OVO	ADJ	GEN	ACC	SN	M N	ANY		
...						M	ANIM		
21	YM	ADJ	INS	DAT	SN	N M PL	ANY		
...						ANY			
50	OM	NOUN	INS		SN	M N	ANY		
...									
82	U	NOUN	DAT	LOC	SN	M N	ANY		
...						M	INAN		
99	Y	NOUN	NOM	ACC	PL	ANY	ANY		
...							INAN		
103	YA	NOUN	GEN	ACC	SN	M	ANY		
...							INAN		
114	NO	VERB	–	–	SN	N	–	ANY	PASS
...									

No.	Suffixes				
	AFFIX	PART OF SPEECH		TENSE	VOICE
		STEM	ENDING		
1	NI	VERB	NOUN		
...					
5	YUSHCH	VERB	ADJ	PRES	ACTIVE
...					
17	YE	VERB	VERB		
...					
20	YA	VERB	VERB		
. 21	Y	VERB	VERB		
...					

8.3.2 Syntactic Analysis

The task of syntactic analysis is to construct oriented syntactic relations (SYR) linking word forms in the given input sentence. Let us note that – in the algorithm we have adopted – the syntactic structure need not take the form of a dependency tree (see Sect. 5.3). Our algorithm of SYA distinguishes the following syntactic relations: predicative (PRED), five completive (1C, 2C, 3C, 4C, 5C), circumstantial (CIRC), homogeneous (HOM), attributive (ATTR), negative (NEG), quantitative (QUANT), auxiliary (AUX), and appositive (APPOS). The general structure of the SYA stage as adopted in our system was outlined in Sect. 5.3.

Figure 8.2 shows the result obtained at the SYA stage for a particular sentence (the result obtained at the stage of morphological analysis of the same sentence is shown in Table 8.3). The upper part of the diagram illustrates standard transformations of the nuclear MG of the word *perevez* (see Table 8.1). These transfor-

Table 8.3. Morphological analysis of the sentence 'How much (of) hard coal was shipped by rail (transport) in 1975 (year)?'

SKOL'KO [How much case: – card. num.	KAMENNOVO (of) hard case: gen/acc number: sing gender: m/n anim.: any/anim adjective	UGLA coal case: gen number: sing gender: m anim.: inan noun
PEREVEZENO was shipped tense: any number: sing gender: n voice: passive verb	ZHELEZNODOROZHNIM by rail case: ins/dat number: sing/pl gender: m/n/any anim.: inan adjective	TRANSPORTOM transport case: ins number: sing gender: m anim.: inan noun
V in case: acc/loc number: any gender: any anim.: any preposition	1975 1975 case: loc number: sing gender: m/n anim.: inan/any ordinal numeral	GODU? year?] case: dat/loc number: sing gender: m anim.: inan noun

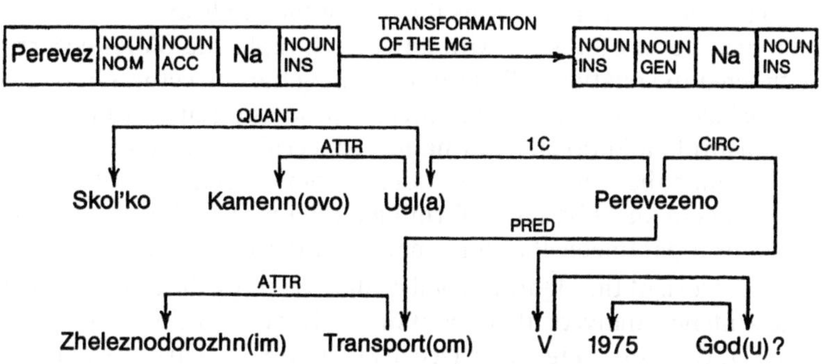

Fig. 8.2. Example of the syntactic structure of a question [cf. Tables 8.1 and 8.3; trans. note]

mations are needed to obtain the individual MG of the word form *perevezeno* (see Table 8.3). They result from the use of the passive voice and from the fact that the actant connected with *perevezeno* by the first completive relation is quantitatively conditioned. The syntactic structure of the sentence in question is shown in the lower part of the figure.

8.3.3 Semantic Analysis

Semantic analysis ends the phase of input sentence processing, producing the internal representation of the sentence (Baklanov and Popov 1977, 1978). This representation allows the system to seek the desired information in the concrete network and data base. We will call this internal representation the *semantic graph* (SG). The semantic graph can be viewed as an explicit formulation of the sense of an input question. It consists of a set of vertices/notions connected with vertices/predicates by lines which are labeled in the same way and have the same meaning as the lines occurring in the semantic network. Quantitative information and information concerning parameters is removed from the graph and arranged in an additional table, which also contains information – reduced to canonical form – about an event's location in time. In SEA an input question is received in the form of a list of pairs of words from the initial sentence. The words constituting a pair are linked by surface relations. The above-mentioned list is supplemented by another list, that of explicitly formulated predicates and nuclei of nominal groups (NG). The SEA stage comprises two substages: processing words which possess a model of government (MG), and processing words occurring in NGs (see Sect. 5.4). Not all words possessing an MG influence the sense of the sentence to the same degree. Three main groups of predicates can be distinguished in business prose: predicates of action, functional predicates, and empty predicates (see Sect. 5.4). It is assumed that every input sentence contains a predicate of action, which means that every circumstantial, completive, or predicative relation refers – in the final analysis – to this predicate. The semantic analysis of words possessing a model of government is carried out in seven steps: 1. classifying words according to the above-mentioned groups on the basis of dictionary information; 2. transferring predicative, completive, and circumstantial relations onto the word which performs the role of the predicate of action; 3. selecting the canonical form of a word with an MG; 4. replacing SYRs occurring in an MG with semantic relations (SER) and checking the correctness of these replacements on the basis of the semantic network; 5. processing circumstantial SYRs, as taken to constitute additional information concerning a given predicate of action; 6. determining the words – i.e., notions – from the sentence which perform the role of actants in an MG; and 7. forming a reference to the data base if the question contains a parameter that information in the DB describes.

The work of the algorithm will be illustrated by the example shown in Fig. 8.2. The sentence analyzed there contains only one word which possesses an MG – namely, the word *perevezeno* (see also Table 8.3). This word falls into the group of predicates of action. The dictionary entry corresponding to the word *perevezeno* contains a reference to the vertex of the abstract semantic network corresponding to the word *perevozit'* [to convey, to transport], which in this case is the canonical form of the word. The algorithm replaces the predicative and completive SYRs by the semantic relations "instrument" and "theme". The circumstantial SYR, which in this case links *perevezeno* with an adverbial clause of time, is reduced to an indicator of time and transferred to the supplementary table. The corresponding NG, i.e., the adverbial clause of time, is then erased (see Fig. 8.3). The information concerning the quantity of coal shipped is located in the data base, not in the network. Hence the question is extracted from the NG, and the parameter "volume" is formed.

When the processing of words with an MG has been completed, the syntactic structure of the input sentence is split into several subtrees constituting the NG.

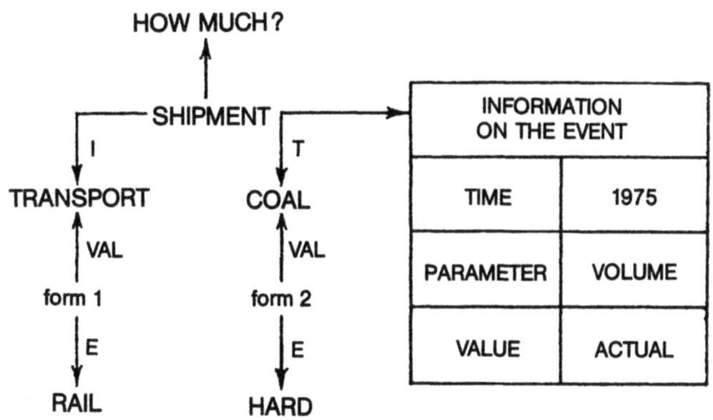

Fig. 8.3. Semantic graph of an input sentence. I, instrument; T, theme; VAL, value; E, element

The NG itself, therefore, does not include words with an MG. The factor that distinguishes processing an NG from processing words possessing an MG is the appearance of new vertices in the semantic graph (see Sect. 5.4). The POET system distinguishes the following groups of words without an MG: notions, characteristics without an MG (these are mainly absolute characteristics, such as weight, length, or the trade name of a product), the values of characteristics, prepositions, and numerals. As far as syntactic analysis is concerned, an NG can contain only attributive, auxiliary, quantitative, homogeneous, negative, and appositive SYRs. Processing an attributive SYR that links two individual words – which may be notions, characteristics, or values of characteristics – is particularly complex. During this process the abstract network must be used to specify the characteristic in question. To facilitate this, part of the information is entered in the dictionary (see Sect. 5.4). In addition to attributive SYRs, the system also examines appositive SYRs, which indicate the names of notions, and quantitative SYRs, which indicate the number of objects participating in a given event.

To go back to the sentence shown in Table 8.3, let us note that the words *ugol* and *transport* fall into the class of notions, while *kamienniy* and *zheleznodorozhniy* are taken to be values of characteristics. The characteristics "form 1" and "form 2" are inserted between *ugol'* and *kamienniy*, and *transport* and *zheleznodorozhniy* respectively (see Fig. 8.3). If the system fails to establish a characteristic between two word forms during NG processing, the NG and the syntactic relation between the given word forms are assumed to be incorrect.

The stage of semantic analysis is closed with the formation of the semantic graph. The interrogative word is identified and taken to be the root of the output tree. All other vertices are arranged in order according to the distance separating them from the root vertex. All vertices – except those corresponding to the values of characteristics – contain a reference to the abstract network. The values of non-numerical characteristics are formulated by referring to the dictionary. The final form of the semantic graph corresponding to the sentence in question is shown in Fig. 8.3.

8.3.4 Interpreting Input Sentences and Formulating Answers

At the stage of interpretation, the semantic graph is compared with the semantic network. As a result, the context of the question is established, the relevant information from the concrete network is obtained, references to quantitative information contained in the data base are formed, and how this information should be processed is determined (addition, comparison, determining of percentage, optimization, etc.). By specifying the context of a sentence, the stage of interpretation makes it possible to substitute real objects and the connections between them for abstract notions and predicates occurring in the input sentence. The components of the system's knowledge referred to in the question are also determined at this stage of the system's work.

The comparison of the semantic graph with the semantic network is performed by gradually contracting the graph, starting with the vertices furthest from the interrogative one, and ending with the interrogative vertex itself. In order to achieve this, special programs of contraction and projection are used. When the length of the path to the interrogative vertex becomes less than three lines, the program proceeds to process the interrogative situation.

A notion in the abstract network is expressed in the concrete network by a set of unique objects which constitute the essence of that notion in the world being modeled. Consequently, any vertex/notion is initially placed in correspondence with the set of all objects which can be interpreted as corresponding to that notion. This set is then contracted if the notion possesses any single-value characteristic or is involved in any event further from the interrogative vertex than it itself. Different predicates have different ways of influencing the set of objects which define a given notion (assuming that the program of projection has been applied only once.) There are predicates whose values identify the elements that are being sought more precisely than others. The corresponding contraction produces the minimum number of elements that conform to the question. For instance, the predicate "name" usually extracts the elements desired from the set "people" with sufficient precision. All such predicates are distinguished for each notion and together constitute the high-priority zone of a vertex of the concrete network. Once the contraction is completed, the system checks whether the number of elements remaining in the set is equal to zero. If it is, this indicates the presence of some contradictions between the predicates chosen as characterizing a given notion.

The main mechanism employed at this stage is that of projecting those predicates whose actants are all filled onto the network. The program of projection selects a predicate from the semantic graph and finds those events in the concrete network which conform to the input notions and the predicate. Since some predicates can be specified only when accompanied by quantitative information, the program of projection performs a comparison of the relevant numbers from the data base with the input quantitative information. This is done for each event chosen. If no event is found to correspond to an event from the concrete network, or if the input quantitative information does not agree with that stored in the data base, the given variant of the semantic graph is rejected and the program returns to the SEA stage to continue its investigations. Predicates are processed by the program of projection in three ways, depending on the number of arguments in the given predicate: one, two, or "more than two". This flows from the fact that predicates from these three classes differ as to how they are stored and interpreted. As a result of this work, the program produces the list of events from the concrete network which constitute the interpretation of an event from the semantic graph. The program of contraction then selects a set of elements which fit a given actant. This whole stage ends with the processing of the interrogative situation, which will fall into one of the following main categories: a question concerning the number of objects which constitute the interpretation of a notion, one concerning the values of characteristics which define a set of objects, or one concerning the numerical parameters of an event. Depending on the type of question involved, the program produces a numerical value, a list of the values of characteristics, or finally, a list of time indicators. When an answer has been found, the system begins to carry out the program that transforms this answer into a form convenient for the user.

The example shown in Fig. 8.1 will be of help in clarifying the essence of the system's work at the stage under review. The vertices "rail" and "hard" are the furthest away. They are connected with the notions "transport" and "coal" respectively. Let us consider the contraction of the notion "transport". Initially, the interpretation of the "transport" vertex of the abstract network is formulated by four vertices of the concrete network – namely, the vertices marked by the integers 1, 2, 3, and 4. By making use of the value of the characteristic "form 1" – "rail", the system rejects three of the four vertices, the only one remaining being vertex no. 1. Similarly, of the vertices corresponding to the vertex "coal", only no. 12 remains, i.e., the vertex "hard". After finding the concrete objects which provide the interpretation of the initial nominal groups, the system identifies the particular event that is being referred to in the input sentence. The latter is represented by vertex 5 in Fig. 8.1. Given this, the distance to the question becomes equal to unity. The system therefore proceeds to process the question itself. In the case at hand, the question concerns a parameter of the event. By making use of references indicated in the given event, the system finds the required information in the data base. The following procedure may be needed to obtain the final answer: procedures carrying out calculations such as +, −, ×, ÷, %, etc.; procedures performing transformations of units of measurement and of time intervals; specific procedures determined by the name of a predicate or of a notion; and universal procedures which search for the appropriate path in a graph, using the mathematical properties of relations.

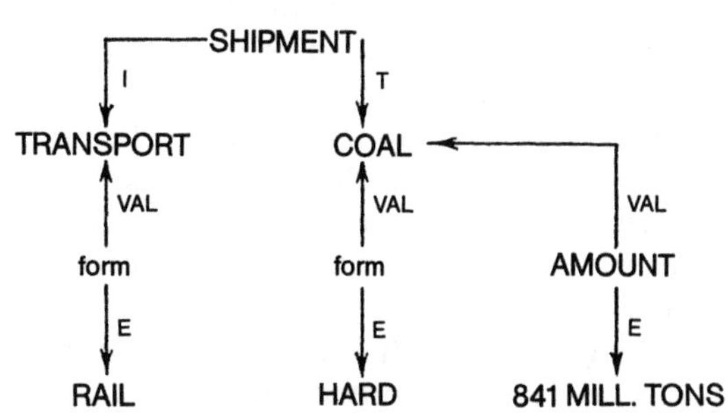

Fig. 8.4. Example of the semantic graph of an answer

In order to form the semantic structure of an answer, the POET system makes use of the graph of the question, which considerably simplifies synthesis of an output utterance. The graph of an answer is constructed on the basis of the graph of the question by providing the latter with the information obtained at the stage of semantic interpretation and with certain information essential at the stage of syntactic synthesis (vertices referring to the plural number, the vertex the question refers to, etc.). The graph of the answer corresponding to the example under consideration is shown in Fig. 8.4.

8.3.5 Synthesis of an Answer in the Form of a Sentence in the Russian Language

Synthesis fulfills the following functions in the POET system (Popov and Rodionov 1978):

1. It constructs a full sentence in Russian. This is usually connected with the presence of a certain amount of redundant information; nevertheless, this form enables the user to check whether the question has been correctly understood by the system. Let us suppose, for example, that the question posed is: "Do two firms called ZARYA exist in Moscow?" Let us now assume that the correct answers possible here are "Yes", and "Yes – there are in fact three firms called ZARYA in Moscow". The latter answer is undoubtedly more precise.
2. It constructs an unambiguous sentence, i.e., phrases such as "the department of the factory which fulfilled the plan" are excluded.
3. It yields concrete information the user is interested in.

As we have observed, the output language of the POET system is restricted to business Russian prose. In addition, the following main limitations are currently imposed on the grammar of the output language:

1. Anaphoric elements and anaphoric ellipsis cannot be used.
2. An answer must take the form of a simple sentence, or of a compound sentence containing at most one simple subordinate clause. For example, "Factory *A*, which is in Moscow, produces lathes *B*".
3. Participial and adverbial-participial constructions cannot occur in an output sentence.
4. Verbs in the first and second person do not occur in an output sentence.
5. All verbs must be used in the indicative mood.

The task facing the algorithm of synthesis is to translate the sense of an utterance into a sentence in the limited Russian language. We are convinced that this cannot be performed in only one step, for the time being, at least. This is due to the great wealth of synonymy in Russian. The POET system performs synthesis in four steps (see Chap. 7): 1. constructing the dependency tree corresponding to the given sentence; 2. determining the morphological information specific to the lexemes occurring in the vertices of the dependency tree; 3. determining the order of words in the sentence; 4. constructing the concrete word forms of the sentence.

The general structure of syntactic synthesis (SYS) used in the POET system conforms to the algorithm described in Chap. 7. We shall therefore confine

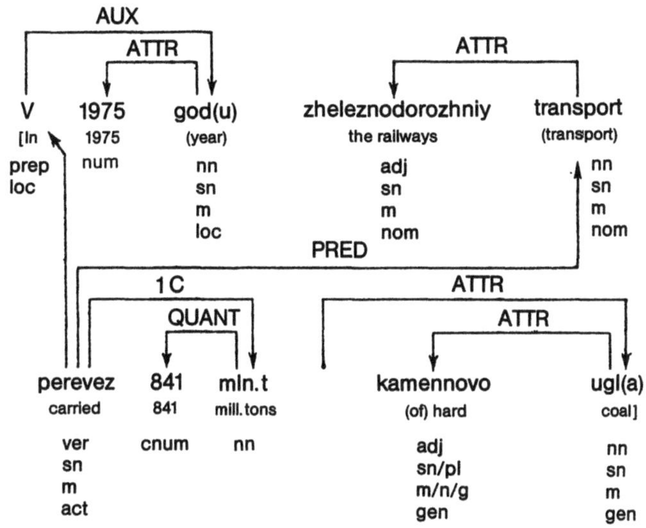

Fig. 8.5. Example of the syntactic structure of an answer

ourselves to illustrating the work done by SYS on the basis of a concrete example (see Fig. 8.5). The SYS stage starts its work with a given semantic graph of a sentence. All events occurring in the graph are expressed in terms of concrete lexemes. The following information is assigned to events in the graph: the time they came to an end, their modality, whether they represent an intention or a fact. Notions are accompanied by information concerning number, numerical information proper, and units of measurement. Dependency trees are constructed by substituting syntactic relations for semantic characteristics and semantic cases (see Sect. 7.3). In the example under consideration, the MG of the event *perevozit'* [to ship] allows the algorithm to establish the predicative and first completive syntactic relations for the notions "transport" and "coal" respectively (cf. Fig. 8.5). The characteristic "form", which connects the notion "coal" with the value of the characteristic "hard", is translated into an attributive syntactic relation, and appropriate numerical information, together with corresponding units of measurement, is then assigned to the notion "coal". The vertices "transport" and "rail" are processed in similar fashion. Then the system moves on to the construction of the nominal group which is to be connected with the verb by the circumstantial relation of time. Morphological information is assigned to the sentence being synthesized using two types of contextual rules: rules for transforming syntactic structure and the actual rules for assigning morphological information (see Sect. 7.3). The former transform MGs and introduce strong prepositions, conjunctions, and new auxiliary word forms such as "then" or "which". In the example we are examining, the nominative and accusative cases are assigned to the lexemes *transport* and *ugol'* respectively [transport, coal]. This is dictated by the MG. In turn, contextual rules assign masculine gender and singular number to the verb *perevozit'* [to ship]. It is also at this stage that the algorithm introduces the uninflected vertex "841 million tons" into the dependency tree. This vertex is connected with the verb by the first completive relation. The noun "coal", together with its subordinate words, is linked with this vertex by an attributive relation. The adjectives *zheleznodorozhniy* and *kamenniy* [rail, hard] are put into agreement with the nouns *transport* and *ugol'* respectively. The algorithm then determines the following order of fully characterized lexemes:

V 1975 god/u/ zheleznodorozhniy transport perevez 841 mln. tonn kamenn/ovo/ ugl/a/ – see Fig. 8.5.

The process of synthesis ends with morphological synthesis. In accordance with the algorithm adopted, the system constructs Russian word forms on the basis of information obtained during the preceding stages and extracted from tables of suffixes and endings (see Sect. 7.4; see also on this subject Koz'mina and Korovina 1972). To return to our example: the ultimate answer to the input question reads:

V 1975 godu zheleznodorozhniy transport perevez 841 mln. tonn kamennovo ugla.

8.4 The POET System as a Means of Automatically Describing Inquiries and Documents

All that has been said clearly shows that POET fulfills all the chief functions of a participant in a conversation in the limited Russian language. This allows us to consider the system a basic one, whose modules can generate various configurations suitable for concrete purposes. It should be emphasized here that using only part of the system's modules in a concrete configuration necessitates the introduction of certain additional limitations on the process of conversation, and particularly on the language the conversation is conducted in. The choice of a concrete configuration depends largely on the purpose the system is to serve and the tasks it is to perform. For example, the subject matter we are interested in may sometimes be too wide ranging to construct a corresponding semantic network that would be practically applicable within a reasonable amount of time. Even if this is the case, the system may still prove useful. It can then be utilized (and *is* in fact already utilized) in the following configurations: (a) automatic coding inquiries (ACI) in factographic information retrieval systems (IRS); (b) automatic description of inquiries (ADI) in factographic information retrieval systems; (c) automatic description of inquiries and documents (ADID) in documentational-factographic IRSs. The ACI variant makes use of the following POET modules: morphological analysis, presyntax, and the dictionary. The latter contains stems of words, word combinations, and the morphological information assigned to them. The ADI and ADID variants make use of the following modules: morphological analysis, presyntax, syntactic analysis, and possibly certain elements of semantic analysis. The information software then comprises a dictionary (containing stems, word combinations, morphological information, syntactic information, and possibly elements of semantics), a thesaurus, and a classifier (in the ADID variant).

Epilogue

The chief problems involved in the process of conversation can currently be considered to have been identified with sufficient preciseness. Moreover, assuming reasonable limitations on the language and subject matter, existing methods allow us to design conversation systems capable of performing tasks of real-life complexity. Obviously, we are not claiming that all major problems have already been definitely resolved. On the contrary, what has already been achieved is much less than what remains to be achieved. In this author's opinion, the most important directions for further research are (a) theoretical research, (b) developing various expressive means of conversation (text, voice, figures), and (c) designing systems for practical use.

As regards theoretical problems, these include further research into the model of conversation, the model of a participant in the conversation, and methods (above all, semantic and pragmatic ones) of describing the surrounding reality (the model of the language, of the user, of the surrounding environment, and of the system itself). Linguistic theory has to develop methods of describing semantically the structure of texts and sentences.

As regards the model of the surrounding environment, the most serious limitation is the lack of adequate means for representing the dynamically changing world. Closely related to this is the problem of how the system perceives statements (not questions) concerning the subject matter and concerning the rules of how it itself functions. This problem may be considered to be equivalent to the problem of learning, and in this author's opinion, no major progress has been made on this subject so far.

As regards the model of the system itself, research should focus on designing systems which would possess elements of a "consciousness of self", i.e., the capacity to explain their knowledge, potential, and states. The importance of a "consciousness of self" stems from the fact that designing systems capable of understanding and answering every question posed by the user seems altogether unattainable, at least in the foreseeable future (even in the case of limited subject matter). We are convinced that the task facing a conversation system is not to *understand* and to *know* everything, but to be able to *explain* to the user what it *knows*, what it does *not understand,* and *why*. We believe "consciousness of self" is the only way of resolving this problem. Let us note that the need for a "consciousness of self" does not flow from the language of conversation, but rather from the fact that in order to achieve the objective of the conversation the system should be able to express its knowledge and states, and the reasons for difficulties it encounters, in terms comprehensible to the user. In other words, the need for a "consciousness of self" is posed not so much by language as by the complexity of the surrounding world, which is the subject of the conversation.

The second direction of research concerns developing the "naturalness" of the language of conversation, i.e., developing a theory and systems capable of conversing by means of speech and images. Until fairly recently, research into this subject was conducted separately from work on systems of comprehension. In the vast majority of cases, the most intensive efforts were directed toward constructing an "artificial eye" or "artificial ear", i.e., toward the problem of the preliminary recognition of sounds and images, disregarding the fact that the full recognition of sounds, and in particular of images, requires extremely intensive work by the brain, by a mechanism that engages in inferring and semantic processing. We are drawing readers' attention to the question of "comprehension" because many specialists, such as those working on the problem of recognizing speech, seem to be convinced that the task of a conversation is to learn the sequence of words that has been inputted into the system. They completely ignore the problem of "comprehension" and of what the system's reaction to the input text should be.

The third direction of research is connected with designing practical systems of conversation. We would like to emphasize here that the difference between practical and experimental systems is not purely quantitative. In designing real-life systems of conversation, designers encounter fundamentally new problems, such as: (a) the enormous volume of information software, which makes debugging virtually impracticable; (b) difficulties in unambiguously describing limitations imposed on the language, since in practical applications these inevitably become confused with those concerning the system's abilities and those imposed on the subject matter; (c) the inability to foresee all the situations that may possibly arise in processing a text. We can therefore say that, in addition to its main objectives, work on industrial systems provides us with new theoretical ideas, demonstrates the weakness of certain existing theories, and defines the relative importance of various theoretical problems.

References

1 Amarel S (1968) On the representation of problems of reasons about actions. In: Machine intelligence 3. American Elsevier, New York, pp 131–170
2 Apresyan YD (1968) Ob experimental'nom tolkovom slovarie russkovo yazika. Voprosy yazikoznanya 5
3 Apresyan YD (1969) O yazikie dla opisanya znachenya slov. Izvestya AN SSSR, Ser. literaturi i yazika 5
4 Apresyan YD (1974) Lexicheskaya semantika. Nauka, Moscow
5 Apresyan YD, Boguslavsky IM, Yomdin LL, Krisin LP, Lazursky AV, Pertsov NV, Sannikov VZ (1978) Lingvisticheskoye obespechenye v sisteme avtomaticheskovo perevoda tretyevo pokolenya. Nauka, Moscow
6 Austin TL (1962) How to do things with words. Oxford University Press, New York
7 Baklanov VM, Popov EV (1977) Obshchenye pol'zovatela s EVM na osnove semanticheskoy obrabotki soobshchenya. Voprosy radioelektroniki, Ser. ASU 4: 70–75
8 Baklanov VM, Popov EV (1978) "Ponimanye" fraz ogranichennovo russkovo yazika. Tekhnicheskaya kibernetika 4: 66–73
9 Belonogov GG, Novoselov AP (1979) Avtomatizatsya protsessov nakoplenya, poiska i obobshchenya informatsii. Nauka, Moscow
10 Bledsoe WW (1971) Splitting and reduction heuristics in automatic theorem proving. Artificial Intelligence 2 (1): 55–77
11 Bledsoe WW, Boyer RS, Henneman WH (1972) Computer proofs of limit theorems. Artificial Intelligence 3: 27–60
12 Bobrow DG (1975) Dimensions of representation. In: Representation and understanding studies in cognitive science. Academic Press, New York, pp 1–34
13 Bobrow DG, Winograd T (1977a) An overview of KRL, a knowledge representation language. Cognitive Science 1 (1)
14 Bobrow DG, Winograd T and the KRL research group (1977b) Experience with KRL-O. One cycle of a knowledge representation language. In: Proc. 5th Intern Joint Conf on Artificial Intelligence, MIT, Cambridge, MA, pp 213–222
15 Bobrow DG, Norman DA (1975) Some principles of memory schemata. In: Representation and understanding. Academic Press, New York, pp 131–150
16 Bobrow DG, Raphael B (1974) New programming languages for artificial intelligence research. Computing Surveys 6 (3): 153–174
17 Bobrow DG, Kaplan RM, Kay M, Norman DA, Thompson H, Winograd T (1977) GUS, a frame-driven dialogue system. Artificial Intelligence 8 (2): 155–173
18 Bondarko AA (1971) Vid i vremia russkovo glagola. Nauka, Moscow
19 Bruce BC (1972) A model for temporal references and its application in a question answering program. Artificial Intelligence 3: 1–26
20 Brudny AA (1972) Kommunikatsii i semantika. Voprosy filosofii 4
21 Chafe VL (1972) Discourse structure and human knowledge. In: Freedle RO, Carroll SB (eds) Language comprehension and the acquisition of knowledge. Winston, Washington
22 Chang C, Lee R (1973) Symbolic logic and mechanical theorem proving. Academic Press, New York
23 Charniak E (1975) A partial taxonomy of knowledge about actions. In: Proc 4th Intern Joint Conf Artificial Intelligence, Tbilisi: 91–98

24 Chomsky N, Bush R, Galanter E (1963) Formal properties of grammars. In: Luce RD, Bush, Galanter (eds) Handbook of mathematical psychology, vol II. Wiley, New York

25 Chomsky N (1965) Aspects of the theory of syntax. MIT Press, Cambridge, MA

26 Church A (1956) Introduction to mathematical logic. Princeton University Press, New Jersey

27 Codd EF (1970) A relational model of data for large shared data banks. Communication of the ACM 13 (6):377–387

28 Collins A, Warnock E, Aiello N, Miller M (1975) On negative inferring. In: Proc 4th Intern Joint Conf on Artificial Intelligence, Tbilisi (This paper was presented at the Conference, but is not included in the proceedings.)

29 Davis R, Buchanan BG, Shortliffe EH (1977) Production rules as a representation for a knowledge-based consultation program. Artificial Intelligence 8:15–45

30 Davis R, King JJ (1977) An overview of production systems. In: Machine intelligence 8. Edinburgh University Press, Edinburgh

31 Feigenbaum EA (1963) The simulation of verbal learning behavior. In: Feigenbaum EA, Feldman J (eds) Computers and thought. McGraw-Hill, New York

32 Fennell RD, Lesser VR (1977) Parallelism in AI problem solving: A case study of Hearsay-II. IEEE Trans. on Computers C-26 2:98–111

33 Fikes R, Hendrix GG (1977) A network-based knowledge representation and its natural deduction system. In: Proc 5th Intern Joint Conf Artificial Intelligence, MIT, Cambridge, MA, pp 235–246.

34 Fillmore CJ (1968) The case for case. In: Bach E, Harms R (eds) Universals in linguistics theory. Holt, Rinehart & Winston, New York

35 Fillmore CJ (1970) Subjects, speakers, and roles. Synthese 21

36 Fillmore CJ (1971a) Some problems for case grammar. Georgetown University monograph series on languages and linguistics, vol 24, pp 35–56

37 Fillmore CJ (1971b) Types of lexical information. In: Steinberg D, Jakobovits L (eds) Studies in syntax and semantics. Dordrecht-Holland, Amsterdám

38 Floyd RW (1967) Nondeterministic algorithms. Journal of ACM 14(4):636–644

39 Gladky AV (1973) Formal'niye grammatiki i yaziki. Nauka, Moscow

40 Gladky AV, Mel'chuk IA (1969) Elementy matematicheskoy lingvistiki. Nauka, Moscow

41 Gladky AV, Mel'chuk IA (1974) Grammatika dieriev'yev I i II. K postroyeniyu Δ-grammatik russkovo yazika. Informatsyonniye voprosy semantiki, lingvistiki i avtomaticheskovo perevoda 4

42 Glushkov VM (1962) Sintez tsifrovikh avtomatov. Fizmatgiz, Moscow

43 Goldberg A, Kay A (eds) (1976) SMALLTALK-72 instruction manual. Xerox Palo Alto Research Center, SSL-76-6

44 Goldman NM (1974) Computer generation of natural language from a deep conceptual base. Report ISSC-2, Instituto per Gli Semantici e Cognitivi, Castagnola, Switzerland

45 Goldman NM, Riesbeck CK (1973) A conceptual-base sentence paraphraser. Stanford Artificial Intelligence Laboratory, Stanford University, Stanford, CA, Memo AIM-196

46 Goldstein IP, Roberts RB (1977) NUDGE, a knowledge-based scheduling program. In: Proc 5th Intern Joint Conf Artificial Intelligence, MIT, Cambridge, MA, pp 257–263

47 Golomb SW, Baumert LD (1965) Backtracking programming. Journal of ACM 12(4):512–524

48 Grosz BJ (1976) Discourse analysis. In: Walker DE (ed) Speech understanding research. Technical Report, Stanford Research Institute, Menlo Park, CA

49 Grosz BJ (1977a) The representation and use of focus in dialogue understanding. Technical Note 151, Stanford Research Institute, AI-Center, Menlo Park, CA

50 Grosz BJ (1977b) The representation and use of focus in a system for understanding dialogues. In: Proc 5th Intern Joint Conf Artificial Intelligence, MIT, Cambridge, MA, pp 67–76

51 Hendrix GG (1975a) Expanding the utility of semantic networks through partitioning. In: Proc 4th Intern Joint Conf Artificial Intelligence, Tbilisi, pp 115–125

52 Hendrix GG (1975b) Partitioned networks for the mathematical modeling of natural language semantics. Technical Report NL-28, Department of Computer Science, University of Texas at Austin

53 Hendrix GG (1977) Human engineering for applied natural language processing. In: Proc 5th Intern Joint Conf Artificial Intelligence, MIT, Cambridge, MA, p. 183–190
54 Herskovits A (1973) The generation of French from a semantic representation. Stanford Artificial Intelligence Laboratory, Memo AIM-212, SRI, Stanford
55 Hewitt C, Bishop P, Steiger R (1973) A universal modular ACTOR formalism for artificial intelligence. In: Proc 3rd Intern Joint Conf on Artificial Intelligence, Stanford University Press, Stanford, pp 235–245
56 Ingerman PZ (1966) A syntax-oriented translator. Academic Press, New York
57 Kaplan R (1975) On process models for sentence analysis. In: Norman DA, Rumelhart DE, LNR Group (eds) Explorations in cognition. Freeman, San Francisco
58 Katz J (1966) The semantic component of a linguistic description. In: Zeichen und System der Sprache. Berlin
59 Katz J (1967) Recent issues in semantic theory. Foundations of Language 3:124–194
60 Katz J, Fodor JT (1963) The structure of a semantic theory. Language 39 (2)
61 Kay M (1973) The MIND system. In: Rustin R (ed) Natural language processing. Algorithmics Press, New York
62 Korovina TI, Rumshinsky BL, Semenova VE, Tsinman LL (1977) Apparat dla opisanya morfologii flektivnikh yazikov. Predvaritel'niye publikatsii Instituta russkovo yazika, vol 91, Moscow
63 Koz'mina YL, Korovina TI (1972) Morfologicheskiy sintez v sisteme frantsuzsko-russkovo mashinnovo perevoda. Institut prikladnoy matematiki AN SSSR, Preprint No. 7, Moscow
64 Kubriakova YS (1974) Osnovi morfologicheskovo analiza. Nauka, Moscow
65 Kulagina OS (1973) O mashinnom perevode textov na yestestvennikh yazikakh. Problemy kibernetiki 27
66 Lehnert WG (1977) A conceptual theory of question answering. In: Proc 5th Intern Joint Conf Artificial Intelligence, MIT, Cambridge, MA, pp 158–164
67 Lesser VR, Erman LD (1977) A retrospective view of the Hearsay II architecture. In: Proc 5th Intern Joint Conf Artificial Intelligence, MIT, Cambridge, MA, pp 790–800
68 Levin JA, Moore JA (1977) Dialogue games. Meta-communication structures for natural language interaction. Cognitive Science 1 (4): 395–420
69 Litvintseva LV, Senin GV (1977) Dialogoviy lingvisticheskiy protsessor dla vzaimodeystvya s model'noy bazoy dannikh. NTI, ser. 2, No. 2
70 Loveland DW, Stickel ME (1973) A hole in goal trees. Some guidance from resolution theory. In: Proc 3rd Intern Joint Conf Artificial Intelligence. Stanford University Press, Stanford, CA, pp 153–161
71 Malhotra A (1975) Knowledge-based English-language systems for management support: an analysis of requirements. In: Proc 4th Intern Joint Conf Artificial Intelligence, Tbilisi, pp 842–847
72 Maltsev AI (1970) Algebraicheskiye sistemy. Nauka, Moscow
73 Mann WC, Moore JA, Levin JA (1977) A comprehension model for human dialogue. In: Proc 5th Intern Joint Conf Artificial Intelligence, MIT, Cambridge, MA, pp 77–87
74 Martemyanov YS (1964) O formie zapisi situatsiy. In: Mashinniy perevod i prikladnaya lingvistika, vol 8. Nauka, Moscow
75 Maslov YS (1975) Vvedenye v yazikoznanye. Visshaya Shkola, Moscow
76 Masterman MM, Wilks Y, Shillan D, Dobson J, Spark Jones K (1964) Semantic basis of communication. Cambridge Press, Cambridge
77 McCarthy J, Hayes P (1969) Some philosophical problems from the standpoint of artificial intelligence. In: Meltzer B, Michie D (eds) Machine intelligence 4. American Elsevier, New York, pp 463–502
78 McCarthy J (1962) LISP 1.5 programmer's manual. MIT, Cambridge
79 Mel'chuk IA (1974a) Opit teorii lingvisticheskikh modeley "Smysl-Text". Nauka, Moscow
80 Mel'chuk IA (1974b) Ob odnoy modeli ponimanya rechi. Nauchno-tekhnicheskaya informatsya 2 (6)
81 Mel'chuk IA (1976) Issledovanya po mashinnomu perevodu. In: Teoria veroyatnostey i matematicheskaya statistika. Statistika, Moscow

82 Mendelson E (1964) Introduction to mathematical logic. Van Nostrand, Princeton, NJ
83 Minsky M (1975) A framework for representation knowledge. In: Winston PH (ed) The psychology of computer vision. McGraw-Hill, New York
84 Minsky M, Papert S (1972) Progress report, A.I. Memo 252. Artificial Intelligence Laboratory, MIT, Cambridge, MA
85 Moore J, Newell A (1973) How can MERLIN understand? In: Gregg C (ed) Knowledge and cognition. Lawrence Erlbaum Associates, Hillsdale, NJ.
86 Mylopoulos J (1975a) TORUS – a natural language understanding system for data mangement. In: Proc 4th Intern Joint Conf Artificial Intelligence, Tbilisi, pp 414–421
87 Mylopoulos J, Cohen P, Borgida A, Sugar L (1975b) Semantic networks and the generation of context. In: Proc 4th Intern Joint Conf Artificial Intelligence, Tbilisi, pp 134–142
88 Newell A (1969) Heuristic programming: Ill-structured problems. In: Aronofsky J (ed) vol 3: Progress in operation research. Wiley, New York:363–415
89 Newell A (1973) Production systems: models of control structures. In: Chase WG (ed) Visual information processing. Academic Press, New York
90 Nilsson NJ (1971) Problem-solving methods in artificial intelligence. McGraw-Hill, New York
91 Norman DA, Rumelhart DE, LNR Group (1975) Explorations in cognition. Freeman, San Francisco
92 Paducheva YV (1963) Logicheskoye udarenye v textakh reklam i ob'yavleniy. NTI 5
93 Plesnevich GS (1974) Nerazreshimiye algoritmicheskiye problemy. In: Entsisklopedia kibernetiki, vol 2, Kiev
94 Popov EV (1976) Voprosno-otvietnaya sistema programmirovanya, vosprinimayushchaya ogranicheniy yestestvienniy yazik i obladayushchaya sposobnost'yu k deduktivnomu vivodu. Voprosy radioelektroniki, ser. ASU, vol 4
95 Popov EV (1977) Predstavlenye znaniy v sistemie dialoga "Cheloviek-EVM". Voprosy radioelektroniki, ser. ASU, vol 4
96 Popov EV (1978a) Sistema vzaimodieystvia s EVM na ogranichennom russkom yazike. Programmirovanye 4
97 Popov EV (1978b) Ideologia i printsipi postroyenya sistem osushchestvliayushchikh obshchenye s pol'zovatelem v yestestvennom yazike. In: Informatsyonno-programmnoye obespechenye sistem iskusstviennovo intelekta. Znanye, Moscow
98 Popov EV (1978c) Effektivniy algoritm sintaksicheskovo analiza fraz ogranichennovo russkovo yazika. Tekhnicheskaya kibernetika 5
99 Popov EV (1979) Sistemi obshchenya chelovieka s EVM na yestestviennom yazike. Voprosy filozofii 4
100 Popov EV (1981) Obshchenye s EVM na ogranichennom yestestviennom yazikie. In: Vichislitel'naya lingvistika. Nauka, Moscow
101 Popov EV, Rodionov YV (1978) Algoritm sinteza predlozheniy ogranichennovo russkovo yazika iz semanticheskoy seti. Tekhnicheskaya kibernetika 6
102 Popov EV, Firdman GR (1976) Algoritmicheckiye osnovi intellektual'nikh robotov i iskusstviennovo intellekta. Nauka, Moscow
103 Pospelov GS, Pospelov DA (1977) Problemi dialoga v chelovieko-mashinnikh sistemakh. Voprosy kibernetiki 8
104 Raphael B (1971) The frame problem in problem solving systems. In: Findler NV and Meltzer B (eds) Artificial intelligence and heuristic programming. Edinburgh University Press, Edinburgh
105 Rieger C (1976) An organization of knowledge for problem solving and language comprehension. Artificial Intelligence 7(2): 89–127
106 Sacerdoti ED (1974) Planning in a hierarchy of abstraction spaces. Artificial Intelligence 5:115–135
107 Sacerdoti ED (1975) The nonlinear nature of plans. In: Proc 4th Intern Joint Conf Artificial Intelligence, Tbilisi, pp 206–214
108 Sandewall E (1971) Representation natural language information in predicate calculus. In: Meltzer B, Michie D (eds) Machine intelligence 6. Edinburgh University Press, Edinburgh
109 de Saussure F (1959) Course in general linguistics. Philosophical library. McGraw-Hill, New York

110 Savvina YN (1976) Fragment modeli russkovo poverkhnosnovo sintaksisa. III. Sravnitel'niye konstruktsii. NTI, ser 2, no 1
111 Schank RC (1972) Conceptual dependency: a theory of natural language understanding. Cognitive Psychology 3 (4): 552–631
112 Schank RC (1975a) Conceptual information processing. North-Holland, Amsterdam
113 Schank RC, and the Yale AI Project (1975b) SAM – a story understander. Research Report No. 43. Yale University Press, Yale
114 Schank RC (1975c) The role of memory in language processing. In: Cofer C, Atkinson R (eds) The nature of human memory. Freeman, San Francisco
115 Schank RC, Tesler L, Weber S (1970) Spinoza II: conceptual case-based natural language analysis. Stanford Artificial Intelligence Project, Memo AIM-109
116 Schank RC, Abelson R (1975) Scripts, plans and knowledge. In: Proc 4th Intern Joint Conf Artificial Intelligence, Tbilisi, pp 151–157
117 Schank RC, Abelson R (1977) Scripts, plans, goals and understanding. Lawrence Erlbaum Associates, Hillsdale, New York
118 Schank RC, Charniak E, Wilks Y, Winograd T, Woods WA (1977) Natural language processing. In: Proc 5th Intern Joint Conf Artificial Intelligence. MIT Cambridge, MA, pp 1007–1013
119 Shapiro S (1971) A net structure for semantic information storage, deduction and retrieval. In: Proc 2nd Intern Joint Conf Artificial Intelligence. British Computer Society, London, pp 512–523
120 Schreider YA (1971) Ravienstvo, skhodstvo, poriadok. Nauka, Moscow
121 Schreider YA (1974) Logika znakovikh sistem: Elementy semiotiki. Znanye, Moscow
122 Schubert LK (1975) Extending the expressive power of semantic networks. In: Proc 4th Intern Joint Conf Artificial Intelligence, Tbilisi, pp 158–164
123 Scott AC, Clancey WJ, Davis R, Shortliffe EH (1977) Explanation capabilities of production-based consultation systems. Am J Computational Linguistics, Microfiche 62
124 Scragg GW (1975) Answering process questions. In: Proc 4th Intern Joint Conf Artificial Intelligence, Tbilisi, pp 435–442
125 Searle JR (1975) Indirect speech acts. In: Cole P, Morgan J (eds) Syntax semantics 3: Speech acts. Academic Press, New York
126 Siklossy L (1977) Question-asking question-answering systems. In: Proc Intern Seminar Intelligent Question-Answering and Data Base Systems, Bonas, France
127 Simmons RF, Slocum T (1972) Generating English discourse from semantic networks. Communications of the ACM 15 (10): 891–905
128 Simon H (1977) Artificial intelligence systems that understand. In: Proc 5th Intern Joint Conf Artificial Intelligence, MIT, Cambridge, MA, pp 1059–1071
129 Smith D (1970) MLISP.AI – Memo-135. Computer Science Department, Stanford University Press, Stanford
130 Sridharan NS, Hawrusik F (1977) Representation of actions that have side-effects. In: Proc 5th Intern Joint Conf Artificial Intelligence, MIT, Cambridge, MA, pp 265–266
131 Strawson PF (1952) Introduction to logical theory. Harlow, London
132 Sussman GJ, McDermott DV (1972) From PLANNER to CONNIVER: a genetic approach. In: Proc. Fall Joint Computer Conf, AFIPS Press, New York, pp 1171–1179
133 Valgina NS (1973) Sintaksis sovremiennovo russkovo yazika. Visshaya Shkola, Moscow
134 Walker DE (1976) Speech understanding research. Final technical report. Stanford Research Institute, Menlo Park
135 Wilensky R (1977) PAM – program that infers intentions. In: Proc 5th Intern Joint Conf Artificial Intelligence, MIT, Cambridge, MA, p 15
136 Wilks YA (1972) Grammar, meaning and the machine analysis of language. Routledge and Kegan Paul, London
137 Wilks YA (1973) Preference semantics. Stanford Artificial Intelligence Laboratory, Memo AIM-206, Stanford University, Stanford, CA
138 Wilks YA (1975) A preferential pattern matching, semantics for natural language understanding. Artificial Intelligence 6
139 Wilks YA (1976) De minimis: the archeology of frame. In: Proc AISB Conf, Edinburgh University Press, Edinburgh

140 Wilks YA (1977a) Frames, scripts, stories and fantasies. Pragmatics 2
141 Wilks YA (1977b) Knowledge structures and language boundaries. In: Proc. 5th Intern Joint Conf Artificial Intelligence, MIT, Cambridge, MA, pp 151–157
142 Winograd T (1972) Understanding natural language. Academic Press, New York
143 Winograd T (1975) Frame representation and the declarative/procedural controversy. In: Bobrow DG, Collins A (eds) Representation and understanding: Studies in cognitive science. Academic Press, New York, p 185
144 Winograd T (1976) Towards a procedural understanding of semantics. Revue de Philosophie 13 (3–4): 117–118, 260–303
145 Winston PH (1977) Artificial intelligence. Addison Wesley, Menlo Park
146 Woods WA (1970) Transition network grammars for natural language analysis. Communications of the ACM 13 (10): 591–606
147 Woods WA (1975) What's a link: foundations for semantic networks. In: Cognitive science. Academic Press, New York
148 Woods WA, Bates M, Brown G, Bruce B, Cook C et al. (1976) Speech understanding systems. Final technical progress report. Bolt, Beranek & Newman, Report No. 3438, vols 1–5. Cambridge, MA
149 Yezhkova IV, Pospelov DA (1977) Priniatye resheniy pri nechetkikh osnovanyakh. I. Universal'naya shkala. Tekhnicheskaya kibernetika 6
150 Yezhkova IV, Pospelov DA (1978) Priniatye resheniy pri nechetkikh osnovanyakh. II. Skhema vyvoda. Tekhnicheskaya kibernetika 2
151 Yomdin LL, Pertsov NV (1975) Fragment modeli russkovo poverkhnostnovo sintaksisa. II. Kompletivniye i prisviazochniye konstruktsii. NTI, ser 2, no 11
152 Yomdin LL, Mel'chuk IA, Pertsov NV (1975) Fragment modeli russkovo poverkhnostnovo sintaksisa. I. Predikativniye sintagmi. NTI, ser 2, no 7
153 Zholkovsky AK (1974) Model' "Smysl-Text". In: Entsiklopedia kibernetiki. Kiev
154 Zholkovsky AK, Leontyeva NN, Martemyanov YS (1961) O printsipal'nom ispol'zovanii smysla pri mashinnom perevode. Mashinniy perevod 2
155 Zvegintsev VA (1976) Predlozhenye i yevo otnoshenye k yaziku i rechi. Moskovskiy Universitet, Moscow

Subject Index

Abstracting 119
Access
  mechanism of 58, 68
  to data 67
  to knowledge 67
Accommodation 58, 65
Accretion 137
Accumulation of successes 58, 67
Act
  illocutionary 7
  locutionary 7
  of speech 4
  perlocutionary 7
Actant 162
Action 58, 63
  predicate of 208
  primitive 25
ADVB (adverbial syntactic relation), see Relation
Affix 149
  inflexional 150
Agent 135
Analysis
  component 17
  morphological (MA) 88, 190ff., 280
    declarative 190
    procedural 190
  semantic (SEA) 88, 283
  syntactic (SYA) 88, 196ff., 282–285
A-network (abstract network), see Network
AP (automatic process), see Process
Archive facility 61
Aspect 151, 152ff., 160, 219
Assimilation 58, 65
Associations (connotations)
  semantic 174
AT (automatic translating) 16
ATTR (attributive syntactic relation), see Relation
Attribute 103, 118
Autocontrol 58, 66
AUX (auxiliary syntactic relation), see Relation
Axiom 122

Backtrack method 200, 203
Ban, see Proscription
Basic notions 59

1C-5C (completive syntactic relation), see Relation
Case (role)
  semantic 18–20, 81
    obligatory 261
Categories 117, 134
CC (controlling component), see Component
CD (conceptual dependency model) 22ff., 78
Chain 105, 196
  length of 196
  point in 196
    governing 197
    subordinate 197
  segment of 196
Ch-rule, see Rule
Chunk 68
CIRC (circumstantial syntactic relation), see Relation
Classifier 21
Clause 146–148
Cluster 68
CMI (complex of morphological information), see Information

C-network (concrete network), see Network
Coefficient of specificity (CS) 178
Combinability 147
  lexical 147, 170
  morphosyntactic 147
  semantic 147
  syntactic 267
Compatibility
  semantic 20
Completeness of properties 59
Component
  analysis 17
  controlling (CC) 94, 189
  initiating (IC) 95
  main (prop) 197

Component (continued)
morphological (MC) 34
objective-creating (OCC) 94
point (trivial) 196
semantic (SEC) 18, 33
syntactic (SYC) 34
system 196
"hierarchized" 197
labeled 196
Concept 9, 37
Conceptualization 24
Concordance 63
anaphoric 141
aspectual-temporal 141
modal 141
stylistic 141
Connection 144
syntactic 147
Consciousness 75
of self 75
Construction
elliptic 142
nonstandard, see Turn
Context 109, 229
global 141, 229
isochronic (I-context) 108
local 141, 229
situational 141, 229
textual 229
Control 65
Conversation 1ff.
model of 40ff.
CR (conceptual representation), see Representation
C-rule, see Rule
CS (Coefficient of specificity), see Coefficient of specifity

Data base (DB) 17
DBOD (data base-oriented dialogue), see Dialogue
Denotation 9, 37
Dependency tree 197
labeled 197
projective 198
weakly projective 198
Designation 9
DFF (dictionary of final word forms), see Dictionary
Dialogue
data base-oriented (DBOD) 185
"helping" 43
macrostructure of 228
"purchasing" 43
structure of 226–228
task-oriented (TOD) 185
thematic structure of 227
Dictionary
morphological zone of 158–161
of final word forms (DFF) 191
of ready-to-use word forms 158
of stems (DS) 158, 191
pragmatic zone of 173–176
semantic zone of 170–173
syntactic zone of 162–170
Discourse 6, 141
Disjunction 131
DMR (deep morphological representation), see Representation
DR (declarative representation), see Representation
D-rule 79
DS (dictionary of stems), see Dictionary.
DS (dictionary stem), see Stem
DSR (deep syntactic representation), see Representation
DSS (deep syntactic structure), see Structure
D-table 127

EAP (extended automatic process), see Process
Effectiveness 74
of performance 75
Ellipsis 83, 142, 224–226
EM (elementary meaning), see Meaning
Ending 149
Entity 101
Error 62
ES (extralinguistic synthesis), see Synthesis
Event
canonical form of 210
Extension 10, 118
Extraction 247

Feasibility 57, 61
Filters 199, 225
FM (focal matching), see Matching
Focus 135, 229ff.
explicit 230–232
inexplicit 232
shift in 230, 236–239
Formula
semantic 21
FP (focal perspective), see Perspective
FR (frame representation), see Representation
Frame 68, 123
problem 58, 64
F-relation (formal relation), see Relation
FS (focal space), see Space
Function
BRANCHING 246
CONNECTION ST 246
lexical (LF) 33, 167

quantifying (Q-function) 216
YN 216

Generative power 75
Gluing 194
GMG (group model of government), see Model of government
Grammar 4, 143
Graph
semantic (SG) 31, 207, 262
structuralization of 214–216
unstructuralized 207
Group
nominal (NG) 199, 212
matrix of (MNG) 206
reduced (RG) 269
starting (SG) 269
GSS (generalized syntactic structure), see Structure

Hierarchy 75
Hierarchization 197
HOM (homogeneous syntactic relation), see Relation
Homograph 10
Homonym(y) 10, 89
lexical 192
of stems 201
semantic 162
syntactic 162, 197
HS (hypothetical stem), see Stem

IC (initiating component), see Component
I-context (isochronic context), see Context
Implication 131
Incompatibility 90
Indirect answers 1
Inference 14, 27, 79
classes of 29
Inferring 70, 240 ff.
Infinitive 148
Information
complex of morphological (CMI) 190
morphological (MI) 89, 159
InS (inexplicit statement), see Statement
Intension 10, 118
Interfix 149
Interrelatedness 68
I-relation intensional (informal) relation, see Relation
IS (information software), see Software
IScr (instantaneous script), see Script

Knowledge
about a participant 84–87
access to 67
active 176
declarative
morphological 155, 158–161
pragmatic 156
semantic 156, 170–173
syntactic 155, 156, 162–170
explicitness of 75
of the surroundings 109ff.
of the system itself 176ff.
of the user 184ff.
passive 176
pragmatic 173–176
simple 176
source (KS) 92, 189
activation of 95
tacit 13, 89, 187
unit of 68
KP (knowledge perspective), see Perspective
KS (knowledge source), see Knowledge

LAN (linearized A-network), see Network
Language 4
limited natural (LNL) VII
natural (NL) VII
norm of 5
predicate calculus 126
SENSE-TEXT model of (ST model) 16
tabular 126
vocabulary of 4
Level
of abstraction 66, 186
of generality 258
of screen 97
Lexeme 5, 262, 267
Lexical conversion, see LF-conversion
Lexical parameter, see LF-parameter
LF (lexical function), see Function
LF-conversion (lexical conversion) 167
LF-parameter (lexical parameter) 168
Line
"e" 129
IMMERSION 116
"s" 129
"se" 129
"ss" 129
Link
associative 68
external 68
internal 68
logical 68
LNL (limited natural language), see Language
LS (linguistic synthesis), see Synthesis

MA (morphological analysis), see Analysis
Macrostate 108
Macrostructure 41
Mapping 70, 73

"Master" 197
Matching 58, 68–70, 247–249
  compulsory 70
  focal (FM) 233–236
  parametric 70
  semantic 70
  syntactic 70
MC (morphological component), see Component
Meaning
  elementary (EM) 171
  grammatical 146
  lexical 19, 146, 171
  modal component of 174
Message form 20
Metainterpreter 95, 181
Metaknowledge 56, 57, 61, 176
  dynamic 176
  static 176
Metareasoning 72
Metarule (M-rule) 119, 180
MG (model of government), see Model of government
MGSE (semantic component of model of government), see Model of government
MGSY (syntactic component of model of government), see Model of government
MI (morphological information), see Information
MI-line 190
MNG (matrix of nominal group), see Group
Modality
  objective 144
  subjective 144
Model of a participant in the conversation (MPC) VIII, 40, 53ff.
Model of government (MG) 20, 162ff.
  group (GMG) 163, 165
  maximum 202
  nuclear (NMG) 165
  semantic component of (MGSE) 163, 170
  syntactic component of (MGSY) 163
Morpheme 149
MPC (model of a participant in the conversation), see Model of a participant
MR (matrix of relations), see Relations
M-rule (metarule), see Metarule
MS (mathematical software), see Software
MS (morphological synthesis), see Synthesis

NEG (negative syntactic relation), see Relation
Negation 131
Network 127ff.
  abstract (A-network) 127, 135
    linearized (LAN) 137
  concrete (C-network) 127
  discriminative 79, 262
  linearization of 137
  semantic 59, 126
  spaces 129
NG (nominal group), see Group
NL (natural language), see Language
NMG (nuclear model of government), see Model of government
NR (nominal reference), see Reference
N-rule, see rule
Ns-rule, see rule
Number
  category of 150
  morphological 150
  ordinal 159
  semantic 150

OCC (objective-creating component), see Component

Participle 148
  adverbial 148
Particular SENSE-TEXT model (PST) 20, 81
Pattern 109
Perspective 130, 231
  focal (FP) 235
  knowledge (KP) 234
  sentence (SP) 234
Planning 64
PLN-DEF, see Quantifier
PLN-NUMBER, see Quantifier
PLN-UNDEF, see Quantifier
POET system 275ff.
Point of discontinuity 57, 86
Polysemy 10
Postfix 149
  reflexive 149
Pragmatics 8
PR (PRED) (predicative syntactic relation), see Relation
PR (procedural representation), see Representation
PR (pronominal reference), see Reference
Predicate
  empty 209
  functional 209
  of action 208
Preference semantics model (PS) 20–22, 77
Prefix 149
Presupposition 11
  forms of 13
Presyntax 195, 280
Primitives 59, 179
Process 111ff.
  A-network representation of 135

automatic (AP) 114
extended automatic (EAP) 116
simplest 111
unification of 120
Processing 90
discourse 221ff.
nominal group 212–214
Production system (PrS) 96
Projection 58, 65
Property
categorical 144
individual 144
Proscription (ban) 166
PrS (production system), see Production system
PS (preference semantics model), see Preference semantics model
Pseudosense 45–48
PST (particular SENSE-TEXT model), see Particular SENSE-TEXT model

Q-function (quantifying function), see Function
QS (quantificational statement), see Statement
QUANT (quantitative syntactic relation), see Relation
Quantification 214ff.
Quantifier 132–134, 217
existential 109, 132
PLN-DEF 217
PLN-NUMBER 217
PLN-UNDEF 218
universal 109, 132
weighting of 217
WH 217
YN 217
Quasigraph 23

Reality 99
Reasoning 27, 58, 70–72
based on the system's knowledge of itself 72
by analogy 72
formal 71
inductive 72
negative 72
specialized 71
Reference 221–224
anaphoric 69, 488
indirect 108
nominal (NR) 141, 223, 266
pronominal (PR) 141, 223, 266
Referent 9, 222
Relation
"asterisk" 106
formal (F-relation) 101
informal (I-relation) 101
intensional (= informal) 102
matrix of (MR) 206
of dependency 197
syntactic (SYR) 162ff.
adverbial (ADVB) 162, 189
attributive (ATTR) 162
auxiliary (AUX) 162
circumstantial (CIRC) = adverbial (ADVB)
completive (1C-5C) 162, 189
homogeneous (HOM) 162
negative (NEG) 162
of dependency 197
predicative (PR, PRED) 162, 189
quantitative (QUANT) 162
surface (SSREL) 32
time 106
Representation
choice of 60
compatibility of 60
conceptual (CR) 78
declarative (DR) 64, 121, 125
deep morphological (DMR) 32
deep syntactic (DSR) 32
effectiveness of 75
form of 59
frame (FR) 122–124
method of 59
procedural (PR) 64, 121, 122
semantic (SEMR) 22, 31, 33
surface morphological (SMR) 33
surface syntactic (SSR) 32
transformation of 60
RG (reduced group), see Group
Rheme 31, 145, 271
R-rule, see Rule
Rule 117, 134
ch-rule 121
c-rule 120
M-rule, see Metarule
n-rule 118
ns-rule 118
of decomposition 120
of production 179
r-rule 119
s-rule 118
structure of 178–181

Screen 93
levels of 97
Script 68
instantaneous (IScr) 111
sustained (SScr) 111
SEA (semantic analysis), see Analysis
SEC (semantic component), see Component
Self-knowledge 2, 58, 66, 75

Self-recognition 2
Semantics 8
Semiotics 8
SEMR (semantic representation),
see Representation
Sense 45
atom of 18, 59
Sentence 6, 144–146
actual division of 145
affirmative 145
complex 146
division of 146
hortatory 145
interrogative 135, 145
narrative 145
negative 145
segmentation of (= division of)
simple 146
SES (semantic synthesis), see Synthesis
Set
beginning of 105
connecting 109
dense 105
end of 105
invariability of 101
ordered
linearly 105
partially 105
time 101
unbounded 105
universal 101
SG (semantic graph), see Graph
SG (starting group), see Group
Sign system 8
"Slave" 197
Slot 123
SMR (surface morphological representation), see Representation
SNL (system perceiving natural language) 16, 53, 76
Software
information (IS) 53, 100
mathematical (MS) 54, 100
SP (sentence perspective),
see Perspective
Space
focal (FS) 231
active 232
open 232
logical 231
network 129
of expansion 251
Speech 4
act of 4
parts of 148
S-rule, see Rule
SScr (sustained script), see Script
SSR (surface syntactic representation),
see Representation
SSREL (surface syntactic relation),
see Relation
Statement 104, 122, 141
"addition" 112
"deletion" 112
inexplicit (InS) 247
quantificational (QS) 109, 118, 131–134
Stem
dictionary (DS) 192
homonymic 192
hypothetical (HS) 192
ST model (SENSE-TEXT model of language), see Language
Structure
deep syntactic (DSS) 32
generalized syntactic (GSS) 199
immersed 249
Suffix 149
SYA (syntactic analysis), see Analysis
SYC (syntactic component),
see Component
Synonymy 10, 89
Syntactics 8
Synthesis
extralinguistic (ES) 255
linguistic (LS) 256
morphological (MS) 91, 272, 290
declarative 272
procedural 272
semantic (SES) 91, 256ff.
syntactic (SYS) 91, 264ff., 288
SYR (syntactic relation), see Relation
SYS (syntactic synthesis), see Synthesis

Taxonomy 117, 120, 129
Template 21, 108, 118, 179
Tense 219
category of 151
morphological 151
TEXT-SENSE-OBJECTIVE model 87
Theme 31, 135, 145, 271
Theorem 137
Time
changes 107
interval 105
orientation
absolute 104, 151
relative 105, 151
system 105
TOD (task-oriented dialogue),
see Dialogue
TSO (TEXT-SENSE-OBJECTIVE model),
see TEXT-SENSE-OBJECTIVE model
Turn (nonstandard construction) 190, 195

Understanding 50, 73, 79
  depth of 58, 72
  intensional 73

Valence 162
  collaterally subordinated 166
  separable (inseparable) 166
  semantic 162
  syntactic 162
  syntactically facultative 166
  syntactically obligatory 166
  quasiobligatory 166
Variable 118
  object 31
  predicative 31
Verb 148
  temporal forms of 151
Verboid 148

WH, see Quantifier
Word 148–150
  canonical 59
  composition of 149
  definition of 170
  full 148
  meaning (sense) of 170
  stem (root) of 149
  syntactic 148
Word combination 146–148, 195
  prop word of 195
Word form 150, 190
  dictionary of, see Dictionary

YN, see Quantifier
YN-function, see Function

MIX
Papier aus verantwortungsvollen Quellen
Paper from responsible sources
FSC® C105338

If you have any concerns about our products,
you can contact us on
ProductSafety@springernature.com

In case Publisher is established outside the EU,
the EU authorized representative is:
Springer Nature Customer Service Center GmbH
Europaplatz 3, 69115 Heidelberg, Germany

Printed by Libri Plureos GmbH
in Hamburg, Germany